THE AMERICAN BALLET

by the author of The Ballet Companion

WITH A FOREWORD BY TED SHAWN

illustrated with photographs

THE AMERICAN BALLET

by Olga Maynard

MACRAE SMITH COMPANY : PHILADELPHIA

The author and publisher wish to thank the following for permission to re-produce photographs in this book: AMERICAN BALLET THEATRE, *pp. 122, 179, 182, 185, 267; p. 114 (Alfredo Valente, photographer); p. 144 (Maurice Seymour, photographer); p. 168 (Walter E. Owen, photographer). The American School of Dance, Eugene Loring, Director, pp. 298, 302, 314. Ballet Russe de Monte Carlo, pp. 93, 95, 104, 318; pp. 91, 101, 107 (Maurice Seymour, photographer). William M. Como, p. 121.* Dance Magazine, *pp 51, 70, 273 (Walter E. Owen, photographer); p. 208 (George Platt-Lynes, photographer); p. 97 (Maurice Seymour, photographer). Agnes George de Mille, pp. 176, 243, 262; p. 192 (Louis Mélançon, photographer); p. 190 (Lido of Paris, photographer); p. 258 (Baron of London, photographer). Fred Fehl, photographer, p. 153. Jacob's Pillow Dance Festival, Inc., p. 128 (John van Lund, photographer). Studio Liseg, Paris, p. 155. Eugene Loring Collection, p. 171; pp. 234, 238 (Fritz Henle, photographer). Jack Mitchell, photographer, pp. 65, 141, 226. The New York City Ballet, p. 62 (Roger Wood, London, photographer); p. 73 (Martha Swope, photographer); pp. 64, 81 (Fred Fehl, photographer); p. 335 (George Platt-Lynes, photographer). Dance Collection, New York Public Library, pp. 34, 132, 133, 206. Walter E. Owen, p. 205. Ruth Page, p. 40 (Maurice Seymour, photographer). The School of American Ballet, p. 219; pp. 54, 291 (George Platt-Lynes, photographer); p. 293 (Martha Swope, photographer). The Walter Strate Studio, p. 152.*

The jacket is a composite of three photographs, two by courtesy of American Ballet Theatre, one by George Platt-Lynes. The photograph on the title page is used by courtesy of Dance Magazine *(Walter E. Owen, photographer).*

TO TED SHAWN, LUCIA CHASE AND LINCOLN KIRSTEIN.

For faith, hope, and charity in American Ballet

ACKNOWLEDGMENTS

It is true to say that *The American Ballet* could not have been written without the help of the people who make American ballet. I sought no reference source that was not interested and helpful, from patrons and founders of companies to the lowliest *corps de ballet* boy and girl. Wardrobe women alone are indispensable—they have the richest memories, and often the most succinct opinions.

There is no bibliography to list, unless I list all the people in and outside America who are the living sources of the book. The sixteen-year-old bibliography might then start with *Shawn, Ted: First American male dancer,* and terminate with the last dancer and choreographer with whom I talked before writing *Finis.*

I have used as reference, chiefly for the checking of dates and name spellings, George Amberg's *Ballet in America,* published in 1949; Anatole Chujoy's *DANCE ENCYCLOPEDIA,* published in 1949; and *25 Years of American Dance,* edited by Doris Hering, published in 1954. With the authors' permission, I quote comments on the scene into the mid-fifties, from George Balanchine's *Complete Stories of the Great Ballets,* published in 1954, and Agnes George de Mille's *Dance to the Piper,* published in 1951.

Prior to my personal records and research for the book I have relied on unimpeachably authoritative views, such as those of George Amberg, George Beiswanger and Edwin Denby, American poet and ballet critic. The passing scene has now and then been viewed through the reviewers of newspapers and periodicals in America, among them Ann Barzel, Doris Hering, Irving Kolodin, P. W. Manchester, John Martin and Walter Terry. For American ballet as viewed in the international theatre I have collected data from periodicals and private correspondence in Australia, Canada, and the other Americas; England, Europe and Japan. For these reports and firsthand observations I must thank H. L. and G. G. for the British and European; and S. F. M., in Tokyo, for those of Japan and the Near East.

Data impossible to acquire from print have come to me from large numbers of emigré Russians, and especially from Mme. Alexandra Danilova and Miss A. E. Twysden on the history of the Russian ballet; and from Ted Shawn on the early era of American ballet. Anecdotal accounts are derived from private collections—those of the European ballet from the Borde family; of the English ballet from the Edwardes family; and of ballet in America from the Elliott family. These represent programs, letters and journals, and are hitherto unpublished memorabilia.

The companies and schools have been most generous in making their records and theories available for study. I have to thank, in particular, Lucia Chase and Christopher Allan of American Ballet Theatre, and Doris Luhrs and Alan Howard of Ballet Russe de Monte Carlo; Mme. Eugenie Ouroussow, the executive director of the School of American Ballet, and Eugene Loring, the director of the American School of Dance. I am grateful to the faculties and students who

Acknowledgments Continued

accepted my observations with such good humor, and for the precise explanations and physical demonstrations they gave to all my questions.

The shape and content of the book are largely from the aid of William Como, of *Dance Magazine,* and my editor, Arnold Tovell, the first of whom helped me to select, and the second to catalogue and detail that enormous mass of data which exists on ballet itself from 1560, and on the ballet in America from 1767 to 1959.

Beyond all these, I must acknowledge my real debt to the mass audience in all the enclosed and *soi-disant* Greek theatres in the United States. I have for sixteen years eavesdropped shamelessly on it during intervals at the ballet, and picked bare the free opinions frankly offered by my seat-neighbors.

NEW YORK, 1943
CALIFORNIA, 1959

Having served American dance in many ways for many years, I am always deeply grateful to others whose work also serves to promote the growth and improvement of our burgeoning native dance art. When I read Olga Maynard's earlier book, *The Ballet Companion,* I was stimulated and excited as I had not been in years by any writing on the dance. I wrote Mrs. Maynard that to me this was the finest ballet book for children I had ever read, and one which was deeply satisfying to adult readers.

I have been privileged to read much of the present book in manuscript and in its various changing drafts, and with mounting admiration. While I do not agree with Mrs. Maynard on all of her evaluations of dancers, choreographers and dance companies, mine is a personal opinion, and a matter of minor importance. More important to the book is that she has written of what she knows, and how it has seemed to her. She has a trained and observant eye, a retentive mind, and scrupulous impartiality. To these she adds a gift for characterization which makes the pages alive. Her research has been tremendous and yet she writes with such a fluid, easy style that facts are never presented drily, in hard chunks, but evolve organically out of her central theme, in a beautiful and natural flowering.

Learning of Olga Maynard's personal history, I began to understand how she had been able to achieve such impartiality and detachment. Born and educated abroad and coming to America in the nineteen forties, she had made no alliances with any cliques or cults of American dance. Loving dance ardently, and backing this love with profound knowledge, she is more in accord with my own approach to dance than anyone else writing on the subject. Critic-journalists are so often so close to a tree that they "cannot see the forest," and also they are under the constant pressure of meeting deadlines. Mrs. Maynard has taken years to write and rewrite, and because she does not attach her critical view to one locality she sees the dance stage in America as a whole. Thus she gives us essence, the "kernel that nourishes."

Proud of her national theatre, and telling us what has been achieved so far, she is not blinded to what has not yet been attained and ultimately must be if we are to reach a maturity of American dance and American ballet. Not only does she give us the results of her unique insight into the artistic values of our dance theatre, but she goes into immensely important aspects which many writers neglect, such as the economic conditions which affect the artistic quality of performance, and the attitudes from the stage and street which affect theatre dancing. She shows why men of high caliber, and in great numbers, are vital to the fulfilment of our dance art. Much of what has lain, unformed in words, in the dance artists' consciousness is made explicit here—and a great deal of what the audience needs to know. The facts are told boldly and lucidly, and with great warmth and understanding for the artists and their audiences.

I am proud to have been asked to write the foreword for *The American Ballet,* for I am happy to hail the discovery of a major new talent in the constellation of writers about dance, and I believe that this book will have a strong and constructive influence on the future of dance in America. It is a book that I would urge every dancer and dance student to read, but it is not only written for them. As an ideal catalytic agent between stage and audience it should be read by the ever-growing dance audience, for it will produce a greater understanding, and thus greater enjoyment, of this oldest, noblest and most cogent of the arts.

Ted Shawn
R. af Dbg.

JABOB'S PILLOW, MASS.
SUMMER, 1959

Editor's Note: *R. af Dbg. is the abbreviation of "Ridder of Dannebrog." Ridder is the Danish word for knight. The Cross of the Knight of Dannebrog was conferred on Mr. Shawn in 1958 by Frederick IX, King of Denmark, in recognition of his world-renowned work as dancer, teacher, choreographer, writer and lecturer, and in appreciation of his attainments in the cultural field of the theatre.*

CONTENTS

A Foreword by Ted Shawn

A nation's character is typified by its dancers.

CONFUCIUS
551–479 B.C.

THE BEGINNING

On December 14, 1767, by command of His Excellency the Governor of New York, an entertainment called *Harlequin's Vagaries* was presented for ten Indian warriors newly arrived from South Carolina. There is no record of how these first Americans responded to this sample of Italian *commedia dell'arte,* but a form of theatre made fashionable by Catherine de' Medici at the court of the kings of France had crossed the ocean to the New World. Ballet had begun in the American colonies.

In that same month, December, 1767, the John Street Theatre opened in New York. Theatrical companies began to have seasons about a week long, in which drama, pantomime, opera and ballet were presented. The ballets were truthfully billed as "ballet-spectacles" and it was not until 1794, with *La Forêt Noire,* that serious art forms of dance were seen. Many of the English and European dancers imported as performers stayed to become dancing teachers and by 1787, after the passing of the American anti-theatre law, newspapers recorded that swarms of dancing masters were arriving from Europe with other undesirables. Unaffected by laws and press opinions, dance remained popular and was billed in the theatres as "lectures" until the law was repealed. In 1782 Baltimore had a dance academy.

About this time the first American dancer appeared. John Durang, born in 1768, was probably self-taught from watching the foreign dancers in the theatre, and soon perfected his natural talents in the companies. He had a long and successful career, rising to national eminence after the repeal of the anti-theatre law and at a time when politics made English dancers unpopular in the American theatre. He danced in the Placide company, which advertised "feats of activity" and ballets in the French style, and in 1794 appeared in *Tammany, or the Indian Chief,* one of the earliest American operas. Other members of his family, Charles, Ferdinand, Charlotte and Julia, were also dancers, the two first appearing in public when they were nine and seven years old. The Durang children were billed in *Cinderella* at the Park Theatre in 1808. The Durangs were the first American dynasty in dance, but made no such lasting effect on it as did the families Vestris, Taglioni and Karsavin.

Competition was lively between English and European dancers, and soloists and *pas de deux* partners—who were often husband and wife—collected audience claques no less enthusiastic, if far less informed, than those of the Paris Opéra and the other European theatres. There was no real center of theatrical art in the country, such as existed in the European opera houses, where ballet had become a fixture. Ballet in America fluctuated between New York and Philadelphia, and in the latter city there were three dancing schools by 1830, and three theatres. From Philadelphia came the first American *danseur noble,* the first lyric ballerina, and the only internationally acclaimed American dancer, all in one generation.

Harlequinades and pantomimes were frequent theatrical forms, and some operas included what the American printers sometimes spelled "Dancing Ballot." The Placides, who arrived in South Carolina in 1791, were so billed when presenting *The Bird Catcher* in New York. As "ballot" or "ballet," and always prefaced with the word "dancing" these entertainments were highly fashionable. One, *The Caledonian Frolic,* ran in revivals for several years in Philadelphia.

Among the best known dancers in the early years were James Byrne, who revolutionized the character of Harlequin in the contemporary theatre, and his family, and the families of the English Parker and Conway. The early dance tradition was in the English style, based on English and Scottish country dancing, and the minuet and gavotte. Conway published one of the first dance textbooks in America, on how to dance the cotillion.

In the eighteen twenties the French began to dominate ballet in America. The ballerina Francisque Hutin was an accomplished classical dancer, who showed an enchanted and wondering American audience the first *pointe* footwork it saw, in multiple *pirouettes* and other pyrotechnics of the *danse sur les pointes* which had evolved in European ballet. The fashion now was for "Parisian Ballet" and terminology like *pas de deux* and *corps de ballet* began to enter the language. The French dancers of note were Hutin and her husband Labasse, M and Mme Achille, Mlles Céleste, Héloise, Rosalie, Louise, Augusta and, above all, Charles and Ronzi Vestris, of the great French Vestris family, known as the "Dieux de la Danse." The Vestrises arrived in August, 1828, and stayed a year, elevating ballet to the most popular American phase since its importation. Nor was ballet restricted to metropolitan audiences, for, showing extraordinary courage and good humor, several of the companies toured the country. The best known troupe was that of the Ravels, a family of rope and ballet dancers and acrobats, who came to America in 1832. Besides acrobatics *à terre* and *en l'air,* they presented authentic dance, and employed Leon Espinosa, an excellent *danseur.*

Espinosa was the pupil of Coulon and Taglioni at the Paris Opéra, and after 1865 was taken into the Bolshoi Theatre for seven years. His later years were spent in England as dancer and teacher. Espinosa joined the Ravels in 1850—the Ravels toured extensively until 1866—and was captured on tour by Indians, who were charmed by his ability to leap into the air, and by his minute stature. He was so small that the Russians made a special position for him at the Bolshoi, with the rank *premier danseur de contraste.*

Many Americans, aboriginal and otherwise, were charmed by ballet. In the

East the two most admired ballerinas were Mlles Céleste and Augusta, who appeared simultaneously in the same ballet, *La Bayadère,* at the Park and National Theatres in New York. Augusta, a French dancer who was later known as the comtesse de Saint James, was the better technician but Céleste appears to have had the more persuasive personality. She danced in the United States in 1827 and 1834, married an American named Elliott, was presented to Congress, and in 1834 was congratulated by President Jackson on being made a free citizen of the United States of America. Possibly because so many of the dancers appeared *en famille* onstage, their offstage prestige was considerably higher than it later became. A ballerina was a theatrical divinity in the United States, and public adulation culminated in the "elsslermania" inspired by Fanny Elssler, which seized even the son of the President. Foreign ballet dancers were intriguing to the American audience, and that audience was no less strange to the foreigners. A letter written by a member of the company in which Mlle Céline Céleste danced records:

"The invitation being enclosed in a very well written letter, the language respectful and the hand [writing] very fine, and the gentlemen undertaking to be accompanied by their ladies Mlle [Céleste] consented to receive the company. [They] Arrived and were seated. Two ladies of middle years [in] purple silk with a small running design [and] grey shot with violet three young Daughters & Niece [in] white. A bouquet of flowers for Mlle which she graciously received. The conversation touched on the [Paris] Opéra where one gentlemen had visited for Sylphide. [Presumably, a performance by Taglioni or one of the other great Romantic ballerinas. Céleste danced the first *La Sylphide* in America.] The ladies expressed admiration for Mlle's lightness and quickness and examined the slippers. The gentlemen looked at them in turn and all expressed Wonder, Admiration and Joy."

There is a story of some physicians calling on Mlle Hutin with the request to examine her feet, to decide whether her toe-dancing was a freak of nature or "the cunning contrivance of [the] Shoe or Boot."

In Europe the Romantic Era was in its heyday, queened by five dazzling ballerinas, Taglioni, Elssler, Cerito, Grisi, and Grahn, who had become the belles of Europe, England and St. Petersburg. Ballet had been revolutionized by the *sur les pointes* technique, and dances of elevation or of speed, and light *pointe* work, *terre à terre,* were the vogue. Choreographers created long, involved plots, with principal and supporting characters, against wonderful scenic effects. The *danseuse en l'air* was an astonishment and a delight, with an ethereal air, *à la* Taglioni, or as a sparkling Ondine, *à la* Cerito.[1] Disporting about in one element or the other, they became as fashionable in America as they were all over the western world. American reconstructions of the Paris Opéra ballets were marvels of resourcefulness on the part of the foreign dancers, who had to work with makeshift theatre and a poorly trained *corps.* Céleste danced Taglioni's *pas seul* from *Robert le Diable,* and there were versions of *La Bayadère* and *La Sylphide* by Céleste and others. In 1839 Taglioni's brother Paul and his wife, Amalia Galster, danced *La Sylphide* at the Park, giving New York its most Classic dancing. This rather put the *Caliph of Bagdad,* a sensation in 1834, in the shade. And in 1840 Fanny Elssler came to America.

In Paris there then existed two balletomane factions, the Taglionists and the Elsslerites. Adherence to one or the other faction depended upon whether one's taste was for the dance "spirituelle" or the dance "pagan"—from Gautier's description of the dancers Taglioni and Elssler. No real opinion could be made as to which was the better dancer. Both were marvelous creatures, and each was celebrated for a special style. Taglionists and Elsslerites exist to this day.

The American audience never saw Marie Taglioni. Once they saw Elssler they were confirmed Elsslerites. Forgotten were Amalia and Paul Taglioni, and when Marie's cousin, Louise Taglioni, danced in New York in 1855 she occasioned not a ripple compared with Elssler's acclaim.

Elssler deserved to be fêted, first for her universally praised technique, but also for the courage she had shown in coming to America. She succeeded Taglioni at the Paris Opéra in 1938, came to America on a leave of absence to fill a two-month engagement, and stayed for two years. She came with some trepidation, having been warned against performing in this barbaric land, and called the engagement a mad freak which had seized her in a thoughtless moment. The journey was momentous; Elssler was attacked in her cabin by a sailor trying to rob her and repulsed the thief by kicking him so hard that he died a few days later.

In America she was an instant success. Champagne was drunk out of her slippers and red carpets were laid at her feet. Congress adjourned because so many of its members were absent, paying homage to the adorable Fanny. President Van Buren received her at the White House, and the government treated her like a visiting dignitary.[2] When she went out driving in her carriage infatuated young gentlemen took the horses from the shafts and harnessed themselves in their places. In the theatre, Elssler had only to appear to receive an ovation. She had arrived with a partner, James Sylvain, and added American dancers to her company, who appeared with her for the two years she stayed in America and Cuba. Her popularity never waned in that time, and American taste became rooted in the Elssler manner of dancing.

She was a magnificent *terre à terre* dancer, whose forte was the *danse caractère.* All her great roles introduced national dance into ballet—the Spanish *cachucha* in *Le Diable Boiteux,* the Italian *tarantella* in *La Tarentule,* and the Polish *cracovienne* in *La Gypsy.* She danced *La Sylphide.* The Paris Opéra balletomanes had hissed her for her performance of Taglioni's role but no one hissed her in America. She was a one-woman revolution in the theatre, onstage and in the audience. In 1827 Mlle Hutin at the Bowery had so offended the chaste ladies in the audience that they left the theatre in protest at the ballerina's brief costume, but returned at following performances when Mlle Hutin put on a pair of Turkish trousers under her ballet skirt. Elssler shortened her skirts to the knee, the better to dance *Esmeralda,* and in Paris the critics, to a man, went into rhapsodies over Fanny's legs, "beautiful, white as marble, in mesh stockings." Her sensational dancing, inspired by her own personality, made her one of the greatest dancers of all time. *La France Musicale* declared in 1839 that Mlle Elssler, sprightly and animated, in turn coquettish, passionate and witty, with wonderful intelligence, danced with that ardent character which is only found in Italy—or, as the case may be, in Spain, Poland or among the Romany folk, depending on what national dance Elssler had interpreted in the ballet. *La France Musicale's* description might have been written for Danilova, who was the adored ballerina of American ballet in the nineteen thirties.[3]

Elssler set the vogue for ballet in America, where the performer who is dynamic in both personality and technique still receives the loudest and most general acclaim. In the nineteen forties Tallchief, imported to Hollywood to dance Pavlova's Swan in *The Million Dollar Mermaid,* was told to liven up that venerable bird's decease by "some leaps and jumps." The movie director knew what kind of ballet the public wanted. From its earliest days, the American audience has enjoyed the spectacular and no amount of chastisement by huffy balletomanes has changed the taste. This undoubtedly accounts for the sweeping popularity of the Moiseyev Ballet in the United States in 1958 (called by the English "grinning boys and spinning girls") and the success of the Kiralfy brothers, Hungarians who specialized in ballet extravaganzas in the nineteenth century. Scarcely had Elssler departed when dance teachers were assuring their patrons they would teach one and all to dance just like Elssler.

When Elssler left America she left a memory of herself, not of ballet. Yet in Elssler's time America produced its first *prima ballerina,* Augusta Maywood, who danced in *Le Diable Boiteux* at the Paris Opéra in 1839. The history of ballet had begun in 1580, and the Opéra was still considered the cradle and throne of the art. Maywood was a child prodigy, trained in her native Philadelphia by Paul Hazard, a former member of the Paris Opéra, who went to Philadelphia in 1830. He taught Maywood, Mary Ann Lee and George Washington Smith, all of whom became nationally known.

Maywood and Lee made a joint debut in 1837, in a version of Taglioni's *La Bayadère,* called *The Maid of Cashmere.* (Taglioni and Elssler had made their debuts together in 1822 at the Vienna Hoftheater in Philippe Taglioni's *La Réception d'un Jeune Nymphe à la Cour de Terpsichore.*) Maywood was a virtuoso; Lee a lyric dancer. They were never national rivals, because after some appearances together as students of Hazard, their ways parted. Maywood married a European dancer, Charles Mabille, whom she later divorced, and had a brilliant career in Europe. She was especially successful in Portugal, and in Vienna where she was *prima ballerina* of the Hofburg. She organized her own company, an unprecedented thing for the ballerina of that time, who was usually forced to dance with whatever ensemble and *corps* the theatre gave her. Maywood, who was considered scandalous in America, never returned home, but shared the highest title in the theatre, *prima ballerina e prima mima assoluta* at La Scala, with her friend Elssler. Born in 1825, Maywood was well educated and came from a wealthy family, in contrast with Mary Ann Lee, who was two years older.

Lee's mother was a dancer, and her father, an acrobat, died while she was a child. To support herself and her mother Lee became a singer and dancer, touring with the P. T. Barnum circus and appearing in burlesque. In between, she studied Classic Dance with James Sylvain, an Irish dancer (his real name was Sylvester) who had partnered Elssler. He taught Lee many of Elssler's roles, including the *cachucha*. In 1844, Lee went to Paris to study at the *Académie* of the Opéra. Maywood had studied under Coralli, who created *Giselle*, and Mazilier, the choreographer of Elssler's *La Gypsy*. Lee studied under Coralli.

Lee did not dance at *l'Opéra*—no American did, between Maywood and Maria Tallchief, in 1947—but on her return home in 1846 Lee produced the first authentic *Giselle*, in a Boston première. It was a task that entailed knowing not only the title role but the whole ballet, in which she trained a company of dancers. She must have had a prodigious memory and considerable skill. Her Albrecht was George Washington Smith, the first American *danseur noble*. After so auspicious a beginning, Lee's career petered out because of her poor health, probably from the childhood of hard work and privation. She retired when she was twenty-four.

After Lee, an American ballerina, Julia Turnbull, was for a time the unchallenged *prima ballerina* of the theatre, partnered by Smith. He staged *Giselle* for her, which ranked her thereafter with Lee and Mlle Augusta, who danced the role in New York a month after Lee's Boston première. Turnbull's first major success was in *The Naiad Queen* in 1847. Mrs. Elliott, née Céleste,[4] wrote to a friend in New York that this was a bald theft of Perrot's *Ondine* choreographed for Fanny Cerito, in 1843, a smashing London success. With no Cerito to stand comparison, the American audience decreed Turnbull a sensation, which she remained until the Park, rival of her theatre, the Bowery, imported an Italian ballerina named Giovanna Ciocca. Smith danced with Ciocca for the gala opening of the redecorated Park (he was *premier danseur* and ballet master of the Bowery) and then the Bowery lured the Italian ballerina away from the other theatre. A backstage riot occurred when Smith refused to dance a polka with Turnbull, preferring to partner Ciocca. The Bowery ranked Ciocca as *prima ballerina*, demoting Turnbull, who retired in 1857, only a decade after her first great triumph, at the age of thirty-five.

Smith, like Maywood and Lee, was a Philadelphian and a pupil of Hazard. He toured with Elssler and studied under Sylvain, whose popularity he soon eclipsed. At the Bowery he staged ballets for Turnbull and partnered her until he defected to Ciocca. In 1848 he produced his major ballet, *The Magic Flute*. Smith might have become the Noverre, Petipa or Bournonville of America if he had been able to choreograph ballets for Maywood, one of the great ballerinas of her era. She was then being fêted at a Carnival at La Scala, in the Domenico Ronzani company, and thereafter ornamented Italian ballet, but when Ronzani brought his company (some two hundred members) to America in 1857, he had Louise Lamoureux, an American, as *prima ballerina*. In 1859, Smith joined the Ronzani company as dancer and choreographer, and it might seem, in retrospect, that this conjunction should have begun a tradition in American ballet. Had Ronzani been successful, would Maywood have returned, or Elssler? It is not too farfetched to believe that Elssler might have, after her tremendous triumphs in the New World, especially as she did not return to Paris for the rest of her life but remained in glamorous exile as the star of London, Vienna, Berlin, Brussels, Budapest, St. Petersburg, Moscow and Naples. The management of *l'Opéra* never forgave her for the message she sent in reply to a summons home from her extended two-month (into two years) engagement in America—that she was having much too good a time in America to come back to Paris.[5]

The Ronzani troupe came to America the year ballet waned in popularity and theatres were affected by a banking fiasco in Boston and New York, with its resulting financial panic. After 1861 and Fort Sumter, Americans were in no mood for Beauty and Art based on the light and the fantastic. Such dance as survived was of a distinctly robust, not to say coarse, genre. And yet, the European influence and the American response in ballet had been quite extraordinary, if we scan the record. It is surely of note that a male dancer like George Washington Smith had a long and successful career. He taught ballet and ballroom dancing in Philadelphia after 1881, and when he died in 1899 he was about eighty years old. He had been a stonecutter who learned clog-dancing just for fun, before he became the first of the American choreographers and its very first *premier danseur noble*. As such, Smith danced in the best of company. The Ronzani company included the Cecchetti family, and Smith was the partner of Lee, and, after his break with Turnbull, of ballerinas Giovanna Ciocca and Giuseppina Morlacchi; a famous Spaniard, Pepita Soto; and the infamous Lola Montez.[6] Of these, Morlacchi, with whom he was associated in Boston, was truly exquisite, according to contemporary accounts by informed observers. She was lost to the theatre when she married a friend of Buffalo Bill, an Indian scout named Texas Jack.

Smith, like Durang, might have started a dynasty of American dance. He had a son, Joseph, who was a *danseur* of merit, although he is remembered only for having invented the turkey trot. He introduced the Apache dance to his contemporary café society.

American ballet should have had a reliable crystal ball. An astute seer, peering into this uncommonly useful article, might have beheld the strong nucleus of an American ballet. The evidences of native talent were there. Maywood alone testified to a prodigious strength and quickness, the very same qualities on which Balanchine would base his development of the American classical technician in the next century. With an understanding and encouragement of the academic training a school of American ballet could have been formed. The opportunities were ample.

In 1839, the same year that the Paul Taglionis visited America, a family of dancers named Petipa arrived. Jean Antoine Petipa was a well-known *danseur* and teacher, who had two sons, Lucien and Marius. Marius accompanied his father to America. They were in the company of Mme Lecomte, who presented a version of *La Tarentule* and a ballet called *Jocko, the Brazilian Ape*. The Petipas were miserable failures and Marius caught the next boat back to Paris, where he danced with Grisi and Elssler. He was eighteen on his ill-fated visit to America. Before he died in 1910 he had exerted an influence on ballet that lasts into our time. He had created the Russian Imperial Ballet technician, who was to become the paragon of the Classic form.

Unknowingly, American audiences saw others almost as illustrious come and go. When the Cecchettis came to dance in the Ronzani company, father Cesare and mother Pia brought with them their son, Enrico, born in the dressing room of a theatre in Rome and destined to give his name to an academic style, the Cecchetti System, and to become one of the most famed of teachers. Seven-year-old Enrico made a debut at the opening of the Philadelphia Academy of Music in 1857, but his professional career as a *danseur* began at La Scala in 1870 and continued in London and St. Petersburg. Among his pupils were Preobrajenska, Kchessinskaya and Egorova, great ballerinas whose studios in Paris would later produce the great dancers of another generation. Cecchetti taught Fokine, who evolved Classic Ballet in its modern genre, and Nijinsky, whose name connotes a magical propensity for dancing in the air. He was the private teacher of Pavlova, with whom he toured, and he taught the dancers of the Diaghilev Ballets Russes in that company's greatest era. Albertieri, a pupil and protégé of Cecchetti, was for a brief tenure the ballet master of the Metropolitan Opera in New York, but little was derived from this transfusion, as we shall see.

The Johanssons, Cesare and Christian, also came to America—and left. Christian, with Cecchetti, was later instrumental in forming the Imperial Ballet technique under Petipa. When Madison Square Garden opened in 1890 the ballet master was the same Espinosa who had been captured by Indians on his tour with the ubiquitous Ravels. He presented two short-lived ballets, *War and Peace* and *Choosing the National Flower,* and then returned to England, where his son Edouard was later one of the founders of the Royal Academy of Dancing. The Espinosa family, of Spanish antecedents, is a ballet dynasty carried on in the English critic and teacher, Kelland-Espinosa. Edouard Espinosa taught Ninette de Valois, who taught Margot Fonteyn, the *prima ballerina assoluta* of English ballet.

There was no academic foundation for American ballet, and no theatre to speak of, between Elssler and the next acclaimed dancer, Anna Pavlova, in 1910. During the hiatus, American audiences went to the ballet theatre with a benevolent Persian attitude toward dancing girls. No *danseur* except Smith impressed the public and the male ballet artist was tolerated only when he could—as one or two are recorded to have done—soar like a rocket and twirl like a leaf. The intelligentsia scorned even these "feats of activity." In 1876 one Signor Mascagno pirouetted across the stage and jumped four feet into the air, drawing forth thunderous applause from the audience but a sarcastic review from the *New York Herald,* which declared that the play (it was Byron's *Sardanapalus*) had been hacked to pieces, and was nothing but spectacle and ballet from beginning to end.

There were, surprisingly, a number of gifted and accomplished dancers, many of them from the famed Blasis Academy in Italy. Ciocca, and the *danseurs* Gaetano Neri and Gaetano Morra came to America in the eighteen hundreds. The Monplaisir Ballet troupe, which toured as far as California and presented ballets like *Esmeralda,* included Hippolyte Monplaisir, who was later a choreographer at La Scala. Hermine Blangy, who appeared in Paris and Vienna, brought to America a large repertoire of the ballets danced by Elssler and Cerito. These two ballerinas danced with an air of abandon and cultivated a flexible, graceful style, two interesting points to note in the developing American audience's taste for ballet. And America continued to import ballet across a rough sea, in a journey of some peril (witness Elssler's) to survive some extraordinary adventures (observe Espinosa's). Often it was preserved in less than the classically pure and absolute but apparently with great verve and good humor. It may have survived in its American domicile only because it adapted itself rather adeptly from the *Place de l' Opéra* to places like the Melodeon Beer Hall in New York, where the Ronzanis appeared in 1861.

In 1866 a theatrical extravaganza called *The Black Crook* opened in Niblo's Gardens in New York, with the dancers Maria Bonfanti and Rita Sangalli. Bonfanti was a graduate of the Blasis Academy, and had danced at the Paris Opéra. Sangalli created Sylvia in Merante's ballet in 1876, at the Opéra.[7] Both were dancers of ballerina rank. *The Black Crook* was less than the most esthetic ballet, but it had a first run of nearly five hundred performances and was revived almost continually for the next forty-three years. It served as a huge training ground for American dancers. At its start, it employed thirty-nine American and twenty-three English girls. In mid-century, there were eight dancing masters in New York. In 1896 the New York Directory listed sixty-three teachers of dance, and seven of fencing.

The Black Crook exceeded all other attractions, but it had heavy competition. There were now, in New York alone, the Park and Bowery theatres, Tony Pastor's Opera House and Niblo's Gardens. In 1869 the Tammany auditorium was opened; in 1870 the Globe Theatre. Few impresarios equalled the Kiralfy troupe —Imre, Bolossy, and Haniola, the principals, and Emelie and Katie, the seconds, who arrived from Hungary in 1869. They danced with Sangalli in *Hiccory Diccory Dock* and *Humpty Dumpty*, which were advertized as "wondrous ballets." Ladies, fearful of being recognized, went veiled to see *The Black Crook,* whose costumes permanently affected the manners and mores of American theatre. The abbreviated costumes of ballet dancers, then called "fast" and "shocking," were forerunners of the semi-nudity of later burlesque soloists and chorines.

The management put the frankest emphasis on sex, and legs, according to a remark recorded by Amberg, became a permanently saleable commodity. The *New York Herald* advertized as follows: "The proprietor is well aware that visiters [*sic*] go to Concert Rooms to be amused and have a social chat, with a PRETTY GIRL [20 times repeated] and at the same time be gratified by seeing one of the BEST PERFORMANCES in the city." Gratification of this sort, based on "Handsome Ballet Girls" and "Pretty Water Nymphs" was to be found in *Bower of Beauty, The Belle of the Village, The Water Lily, The White Fawn, The Water Spirit, Nymphs of the Rainbow, The Sylphide Queen, The Twelve Temptations,* and *The Home of the Butterflies.* From this partial list the audience may be thought to have been composed of more undinists than balletomanes. For those pining for artistry it was of note that *The White Fawn* was danced to Beethoven's *Pastorale.* For others, there were the "gorgeous ballets . . . Parisian but proper" at the Parisian Varieties, a theatre on 16th Street and Broadway. The Parisian

Varieties outlasted many of the other extravaganzas, and in 1877 when the Kiralfys staged Jules Verne's *A Trip to the Moon* as a ballet with Offenbach music the show lasted for ten performances. Dancers *en travestie* were popular, although now and then a theatre advertized "nearly 100 males" in much the manner of flinging largesse among categories of "80 *coryphées,* 20 *solistes,* and other *premières* from Paris." *Coryphée,* in the Paris Opéra cadre, is masculine gender but we assume it indicated the popular *danseuse nymphae* here. The Kiralfys' *Ali Baba* at Niblo's Gardens had an uninterrupted run from September 18 to December 9 in 1876, with "50 lissome ballet ladies" in scenes like "Grotto of Emeralds," "Magic Ship," "Crumbling Palace," and "Field of Mushrooms." Immense sums, for that day, were spent on this purported ballet in America—more than enough to found an academy and a theatre of opera house status and dimension! The Kiralfys' *Excelsior,* a glorification of the electric light, cost $75,000 to stage. *Mathias Sandorf* and *Michael Strogoff* are reputed to have been richly mounted and graced with fine dancing. *Nero,* or *The Fall of Rome,* was a colossal production, with a cast of twenty-three hundred, staged at Staten Island. Scenes were three hundred feet long by eighty feet deep—"Interior of the Palace," "The Colosseum" and, naturally, "The Burning of Rome."

   In the midst of this, the dancers were poorly paid and socially ostracized. The American dancing girls of the period had the worst of reputations, especially as the management believed in advertising them as Parisians, and had them masquerade under Gallic names, with the supposed Gallic reputation for amorousness. They were required not only to dance but often to sing, act, and support comedians, trained animal acts, or starred singers, in variety shows. Mysteriously, singers were classified in higher, or purer leagues. Dance was believed to be aphrodisaic to the performers and the audience. How the performers endured the fatigue of their profession is a wonder. Many of them worked in factories by day and danced in the *corps de ballet* at night. Most of them were waitresses on the side. Often, their desire to dance involved them in other professions. In 1889 *The National Police Gazette* printed an exposé of a pair of gentlemen named Tuthill and Wayerhagen who, under the sign of "Dramatic Agency" outside a room at 48 Clark Street, in Chicago, signed contracts with singers and dancers for variety acts, always in "concert rooms" some distance away, and usually in the West. True, the girls were required to sing and dance but these were merest embellishments of the real job, which was to keep the customers thirsty. In 1862 New York had passed a law forbidding the sale of liquor by the girl entertainers in the various gardens, beer halls and "waiter-girl resorts," but outside New York the dancing girl had little police protection. There was, of course, no union like AGMA or AGVA.[8] Gentlemen of the old school, like Agnes de Mille's business manager of *Hooray for What,* flourished in the nineteenth century and endured well into the twentieth. The dancer was low on the scale in the American theatre and that theatre itself was so poorly considered that when the actor George Holland died a minister of a New York church refused to read the funeral service, directing the harassed pallbearers around the corner to a smaller place—thereafter changed from the Church of the Transfiguration to "The

Little Church Around The Corner." Mark Twain took up cudgels for the theatre and denounced the minister in a periodical, *Galaxy,* as "a self-righteous, sanctimonious snake."

American dancers began to be summarily separated from the more glamorized importations. The foreign style of dancing was deified as "Ballet," or toe-dancing and was to claim, for a considerable time, the total meaning of ballet for the general audience. Any *sur les pointes* movement on the part of the female dancer was ballet. At first it was always "Parisienne Ballet" but gradually this bland syllogism gave way to another and dancing that was "Russian Imperial" became the rage. This consisted of acrobatics that outdid the "feats of activity" of an earlier time. One type, called *à la Menzotti,* was described as follows: "The danseuse, perched on one hip of the danseur, lay on her back. The danseur, while supporting his ballerina, performed an arabesque adagio." After a glut of this, following the waning enchantment of "Parisienne Ballet," the *New York Sun* declared that the American public was fed up with Russian ballet.

Much of this was seen at the American Music Hall, on Eighth Avenue at Forty-second Street, in New York. No more Maywoods or Lees and Smiths appeared.

The American audience should not be too strongly vilified for its tastes in ballet during this era. Ballet everywhere, except in Russia, was hardly better as art. In England nothing national had emerged, despite close proximity to the greatest dancers from Europe from Noverre's time and before. Foreign ballerinas were admired, as were Legnani and Kyasht from the Imperial Russian theatre, and especially the Danish ballerinas Grahn and Genée. Genée was *prima ballerina* of the Empire Theatre in London for many years. A paragon of classicism, produced by the Danish school,[9] Genée was a great influence on the formation of the present English ballet. The titles of the ballets in which she so exquisitely danced were *The Press* (as the Spirit of Liberty), *Alaska, Around the Town Again, The Milliner Duchess,* and *High Jinks.* The management managed to insert *Cinderella* and *Coppelia,* in which Genée is fondly remembered, and she created a charming role as the Queen of the Butterflies in *Les Papillons.* London had two theatres given over to ballet, the Empire and Alhambra, where the dancing was uniformly fine but the ballets less than ideal works of art. They were extravaganzas of patriotic, historic and topical themes, and in them the dancers had only very little more prestige than their American cousins. Genée and the ballerinas were worshipped as deities of the dance but the *corps de ballet* had scarcely risen to higher esteem than those of the early nineteenth century, which *The Times* described as "a disgusting rabble." An English theatregoer of the mid-century wrote in a letter, "You will be disturbed to know that a great part of the Audience attends the Opera House only for the Pleasure of looking at The Ballet."

In England ballet reached such a low mark—of art, and of prestige for women —that Cecchetti was the only surviving *danseur* of note, Masculine roles were danced by women, *en travestie,* as Dorothy Craske's Prince to Genée's Cinderella in 1906. Nevertheless, the training went on, out of a blind fervor for dancing. French, Italian, Russian and Danish teachers were setting the feet of American and English children in the Turnout, in Positions One to Five. And studying the dance had become a respectable if childish occupation. About 1880, Americans grew so agreeably disposed to dance as a pastime that the dancing master was arbiter of social grace. This tolerance came largely out of the assimilation of Froebel's precepts in education. Learning to dance was also considered healthy, as well as sportive, for the correction of poor posture, knock-knees and flat feet. We shall never know how many small Markovas went to the first ballet classes for the reason Alicia Marks did—to correct her feet and legs. There was no intent toward academic and professional dance development. Any parent would have told an ambitious student that ballet was a haphazard and depraved career for a good woman.

THE EUROPEAN INFLUENCE

On October 22, 1883, the Metropolitan Opera House in New York opened with a performance of Gounod's *Faust*. Built by subscription at a cost of two million dollars, it had a seating capacity of thirty-five hundred, and could accommodate six hundred more standing. A new era of theatrical culture had begun in America, but it came too late to benefit ballet. What would have been the effect of Elssler at the Metropolitan? Would it have been like that of Taglioni at the Paris Opéra, or of Legnani and Kchessinskaya at the Maryinsky? However, inasmuch as many of the operas included ballet *divertissements,* the Metropolitan did have ballet, and its first ballerina was Malvina Cavallazzi. She danced *en travestie* at the London Empire and was a good mime and an excellent character dancer. Cavallazzi, who returned to England from her Metropolitan engagement, was followed by other foreign ballerinas, all imported to fill the position at the opera house.

The American Opera Company was formed by Theodore Thomas and lasted from 1885 to 1887, with Maria Giuri, a dancer of sufficient gifts to appear successfully in Russia later on. This company presented the two Delibes ballets *Coppelia* and *Sylvia,* and, from all accounts, offered consistently good ballet. After it disbanded, no ballet of worth was seen at the Metropolitan until Genée made a guest appearance in 1908. She had come to New York to dance in a musical called *The Soul Kiss*.

George Washington Smith had died in 1899 without leaving a successor to the male line in American dance. In that year a boy named Edwin Myers Shawn was happily scuffing his eight-year-old way along his native Missouri roads, unaware that by the nineteen fifties he would be internationally catalogued in encyclopedias as the Father of American Dance. For several years nothing of note occurred except the formation of the first ballet school, in 1909, by the Metropolitan Opera, under Cavallazzi, who was fetched back from England to direct it. This proudly holds first place as the oldest surviving ballet school in the United States.

In the spring of 1910, Anna Pavlova and Mikhail Mordkin appeared at the Metropolitan, supported by the Metropolitan's *corps de ballet,* in *Coppelia*. The response was sensational. Ballet had come back, in an elsslerite mania, to America.

However, it was not to be soundly based by tradition at the Metropolitan, or in any other theatre in the country. In France, ballet was entrenched at the Paris Opéra, which had had a continuous history from 1669, and was originally the Académie Royale de Musique. Its home, since 1875, has been an edifice called the Palais Garnier, which has a stage fifty-two feet wide and eighty-five feet deep —one hundred and twenty feet deep when it is thrown open to the Foyer de Danse. Here, in scenes immortalized by Degas, ballet ruled in Europe. In the Maryinsky Theatre in St. Petersburg, which had been the Imperial theatre since 1860, there was a stage ninety-seven feet wide and seventy-two feet deep, and in the Maryinsky's magnificence (curtains and coverings of blue velvet, glittering mirrors and chandeliers) the audience under the last of the czars rivaled in dress and decoration the sumptuousness of the ballet stage Petipa had created.

Ballet in America had to parade like a mountebank, hustled into theatres by adventurous impresarios, taking to the road with the same spirit as the insouciant Ravels—that spellbinding miscellany of trapezists, acrobats and rope dancers. Ballet in America was Pavlova. Wherever she appeared she was the corporeal form of the art.

Walter Terry has written that America and Danilova had the love affair of the century. America's love affair with ballet began with Pavlova. I can find nothing more eloquent to say of the ballerina's effect on American ballet than what de Mille has written of Pavlova's effect on her: *My life was wholly altered by her.* Genée had been thought deliciously sprightly (she returned with her own company, in 1912) but her impression was on a small audience in New York. Pavlova's was on America. Her impact was the same all over the world, wherever she danced, and she danced—literally—world-wide until she died in 1931 on tour at the age of fifty.

Anna Pavlova was born in January, 1881, of peasant parents. Her mother was a laundress in St. Petersburg, and the premature child was so frail that she was barely able to survive childhood illnesses. Pavlova was near death twice from scarlet fever and diphtheria. Her father died while she was very young and her mother worked to support them both. They existed in harshest penury. When Anna was about eight she was taken to a performance of the Petipa-Tchaikovsky ballet, *The Sleeping Beauty,* in which the principal character is Princess Aurora. Determined to study ballet in order to dance as Aurora, the weak and sickly little girl mysteriously persuaded the examiners at the Imperial Ballet School to admit her as a student when she was ten. She made her debut in 1899, danced Aurora in *The Sleeping Beauty* at the Maryinsky, was made a ballerina, and in 1906 became the *prima ballerina* of the theatre. The extraordinary child became the extraordinary dancer. Bred in the Petipa era, and following into the Imperial theatre the ballerinas Istomina, Preobrajenska and Kchessinskaya, Pavlova was an entirely different kind of dancer. The artistic descendant of Taglioni, she had an added fire and a magnetic personality that thrilled audiences, balletomane or no. She was the unqualified genius of interpretation in ballet, a lyric dancer in the Classic genre, with a technique wondrously light, graceful and strict. Regardless of the passing years and the paucity of her material (she was her own choreographer in much of her repertoire) she had an unquenchable artistry, and a radiant beauty such as no other ballet dancer has ever possessed. She danced less as a woman than as the Spirit of Classicism—and it was the formidable spirit of a poverty-stricken, sickly child, who had overcome the world she lived in and the perishable flesh that housed her to become the greatest dancer in the first part of the twentieth century.

Ballet had been defined by two leading styles, or schools, of Classic Dance: the French *danse d'école,* with emphasis on *adage* that displayed the "line," or idealized position of the body; and the Italian style developed under Carlo Blasis, which featured *allegro,* the virtuoso execution of dance *terre à terre* and *en l'air.* I think the clearest analogy to the contrast between the two schools is that the French danced the minuet with exquisite taste, and the Italians danced the exhilarating tarantella. The terminology alone describes the genres—the *balli,* or lively Italian dances, in contrast with *basse,* or low dancing. Out of the two styles—the elegance of *danse d'école* and its command of *adagio,* and the *allegro* technique—Marius Petipa formed the Russian ballet. The clearest analysis of the third style, Russian ballet as developed in the Imperial theatres, has been made by Nicholas Legat in *The Story of the Russian School.* He says, "The secret of the development of Russian dancing lay in the fact that we learnt from everybody and adapted what we learnt to ourselves." American ballet has followed the same pattern of growth. The only difference lay in national characteristics: physical, psychological, sociological and economic. For one thing, we did not build a theatre with a stage of the dimensions of the Maryinsky or the Palais Garnier. Also, ballet in America has struggled for its bare subsistence, and has grown, not out of royal and state endowments or the benevolence of a dilettante balletomane society, but out of faith, hope and charity.

Pavlova did not infect audiences with the frenzies of elsslermania but she made an impression far more serious and more lasting, chiefly on the feminine population. Here Pavlova exerted such a spell as followed the piping through Hamelin. Little girls went home bewitched from the theatre where Pavlova danced, and tried to summon from the depth of the household mirrors the same enchanted creations they had beheld onstage. These were myriad, for Pavlova could turn magically from *The Dying Swan* to the Dionysian *L'Automne Bacchanale,* and change from coquettish *Columbine* to *Papillon (The Butterfly).* It was pure magic that turned an aging woman in a fluffy costume and a white headdress into a bird as white and noble as an angel, but this is what, from all accounts, Pavlova became in *Le Cygne,* a *pas seul* created for her in Russia, in 1905, by a young choreographer named Michel Fokine. Pavlova's *Swan,* until her death in 1931, was the great white spirit of The Ballet, abroad in the awed and adoring world of the audience.

In America, little girls flocked to ballet schools. Their parents sent them there to save the towel racks in American bathrooms. And Americans, used to a brass foot-rail before the bar, grew to comprehend that other rail, spelled *barre,* which circled the walls of the ballet classroom. On this, like martyrs on the rack, hundreds of little Americans flung themselves with burning enthusiasm, taught by teachers, good and bad, in what were usually the precepts of the Imperial Russian ballet.

Pavlova appeared with various partners, and her own company was made up chiefly of English girls. She had exiled herself from Russia in 1913, and made her home in Ivy House, Hampstead. Indefatigably, she danced *The Indian Suite* —commissioned from the Indian dancer, Uday Shankar, who was then eighteen —*The Blue Danube Waltz,* and *California Poppy.* Although the ballerina and *danseur noble,* the top of the ballet heap, are seldom better than their material, it did not matter what Pavlova danced: it mattered only that she danced. It is of note that this inspired woman—a mistress of interpretation rather than technical virtuosity—affected American ballet in its second national burgeoning. She danced with simplicity, with a lambent sincerity, *la danse de toujours, dansée comme jamais*—the everyday dance, as it was never danced before. The Americans she so strongly impressed, like Agnes de Mille, later incorporated her simplicity and burning truth in their work, either classical or interpretive. Freedom might be exercised in style, but it was the kindling spirit of Pavlova that set alight half of American ballet.

In Pavlova's time, America's ballet theatre remained rather barren. From Paris percolated rumors of a new kind of ballet, headed by a Russian named Serge Diaghilev. Until the turn of the century, the leading genius in ballet was Marius Petipa—the same Petipa who had fled America after *Jocko, or The Brazilian Ape* was a failure in 1839. He went to Russia in 1847 as *premier danseur.* Between his appointment as *maître de ballet* in 1862 and his death in 1910, he produced fifty-four new ballets and seventeen revivals, and composed *divertissements* for more than thirty operas. He created a virtually new ballet technician, a blend of *adagio* and *allegro* techniques with idealized aplomb, whose thrilling abilities he demonstrated in magnificent Variations. These Variations have never been surpassed and remain, to the present time, the standard by which the classical dancer's technique is estimated. The "classics" in the international ballet repertoire are largely derived from Petipa and his assistant, the first Russian choreographer, Lev Ivanov—the three Tchaikovsky ballets, *Swan Lake, The Sleeping Beauty* and *The Nutcracker.*

Classic Dance, or traditional ballet, is based on a technique narrowly governed by the Turnout and the Five Positions, to which the *sur les pointes* elevation gave greater freedom and style. A basic rule of Classic Dance—as in architecture—is *aplomb,* the perfect balance of the performer in all movements, and in all poses. It has been defined since 1806 as the dancer's functional ability to hold head and small of back in a straight line over the supporting foot.[10]

Within the Classic form, strict as it is, lies the wide field of interpretation. The ideal thing to say about ballet is that technique and interpretation are one, but in fact technique is the dancer's craft, the bare supporting foundation of his profession, and interpretation is the spirit and the personal essence of the dancer. The Italian dancers, whose *allegro* skills Petipa imported into Russian ballet, were superlative technicians in spectacular *tours, pirouettes* and—the forte of the Italian Pierina Legnani, the first *prima ballerina assoluta* of the Imperial theatre—the *fouetté en tournant.* However, to Russian eyes the Italians sacrificed beauty and good taste in the attainment of spectacular acrobatics. Legat maintained that the difference in styles lay in principle and in taste, and arguments raged between the Imperial theatres at St. Petersburg and Moscow as to the respective merits of the lyric and the athletic. Balanchine records that the style of dancing at the Maryinsky in St. Petersburg was strict and precise, while in Moscow, six hundred kilometers distant, the dancing was closer to a circus performance. The Moscovites accused the St. Petersburg school of dance of being cold; St. Petersburg retorted that the Moscovites were in bad taste. Balletomane audiences took sides in the esthetic argument which still rages in international ballet. The Russian audience under the czarist court was not the hoi polloi. Ballet was performed almost exclusively for the aristocracy, and Balanchine recalls that among that audience "there were perhaps only a few gentlemen who were not primarily interested in what the ballerinas were doing after the performance." The ballerinas and all the other dancers were nevertheless compelled to achieve a fine technique in ballet. On a stage supported by the czarist Treasury Petipa produced ballets of an opulence undreamed of outside an imperialistic court. Tamara Karsavina has recreated the fabulous era in her biography, *Theatre Street,* and Balanchine describes the inventive and masterly stage effects, and the extraordinary richness and verisimilitude of the settings. This era continued until the revolution in 1917. Thereafter, there was a diffusion of Russian ballet into the international theatre.

This began in the early nineteen hundreds under the impresario Diaghilev, who presented a company of dancers from the Russian Imperial theatres in a season in Paris. Diaghilev had previously presented Russian music and painting with such success that he decided to introduce Russian ballet. It took the western world by storm and the French ideal of elegance in *adagio* gave way to the brilliant Russian technique. However, it was not Russian ballet in the Petipa style that Diaghilev brought to Europe, but a form that would come to be called modern, or the "New Ballet." It was evolved by Michel Fokine, born in St. Petersburg in 1880, trained in the Imperial School and a Maryinsky dancer. By 1902 he had become a *danseur* of first rank, and a teacher.

Fokine felt that ballet had become stultified and decadent in its stylized form, and wished to free it, in much the same way that Noverre had done earlier in ballet history. In 1904 Fokine submitted his ideas to the Imperial Theatre, writing, "Dancing should be interpretive. It should not degenerate into mere gymnastics."

In Russian ballet there had been dissension ever since the Italian influx, between the devotees of interpretation and the purists in technique. A director of the Imperial theatres, Prince Serge Wolkonsky, wrote in 1900 that he was shocked by the affectations and the stress on acrobatics. He here uttered the cry that was to echo for years, "Ballet dancing should have a meaning." He admired the Italian ballerina Zucchi, whose whole form, as she danced, seemed to speak—even her "lovely expressive back, when she turned it to the public." Wolkonsky was disgusted with a ballet Petipa created for *Tannhäuser,* in which he waited (in vain, he said) for ballerinas, who were "just tip-toe, tip-toe the whole time," to become the nymphs of Venus. Under Wolkonsky, by some accounts, began the new style of ballet, which still relied on the magnificent technique but adapted it to the profound Russian temperament demonstrated in music and literature. Wolkonsky, accused of trying to throw out the Classic technique in favor of Dalcroze's new eurythmics,[11] was dismissed.

Petipa's forty-third year at the Imperial Theatre was marked, in the 1899–1900 season, by a program that included *Esmeralda,* with the *prima ballerina assoluta* Kchessinskaya in the title role. With her in the ballet was her pet goat. Ballets followed a set formula and usually employed a romantic or fantastic theme. Long ballets of four to six acts consumed a full evening's performance and contained *pas de deux,* Variations for the partners, a coda, and *ballabile* for the corps. There were prologues and interpolated passages of mime, in which the characters related the involved plot, and *pas d'action* and *pas de caractère.* All was built about the starring ballerina, who had grand *entrées*—and sometimes even grand exits.

Fokine's rebellion was against the formula, not the technique of the ballet. He was more of a reformer than a revolutionist. Ballet was not only rigidly held onstage within its own academic bounds but was further hampered by the independence of the contributing artists, each of whom worked jealously in his own métier, except for poor hacks of composers like Pugni, who churned out reams of music on order for the dancing. The artists who designed scenery and costume were more concerned about their art creation than the suitability of the scene to the theme, or the costume to the dancer-character. With Fokine, ballet became more natural and more true to human motives and ordinary occurrences. He is considered the Father of Modern Ballet. His Five Principles[12] describe the ideas and ideals on which he framed his evolutionary ballets. Diaghilev's company, the Diaghilev Ballets Russes, employed Fokine as its first choreographer, and was an exciting avant-garde force in the theatre until Diaghilev's death in 1929. In its era of twenty years it affected ballet everywhere—even in Russia—and it presented to the western world the fabulous dancers of the Imperial Russian ballet, from Pavlova to Danilova.

Fokine's reforms were the most comprehensive since Noverre's. America beheld the New Ballet in 1911 in a pirated version by a Diaghilev dancer, Theodore Kosloff, who brought a company to the United States under the management of a vaudeville star, Gertrude Hoffman. Hoffman's La Saison Russe presented Fokine's *Cléopâtre, Les Sylphides* and *Schéhérazade* at the Winter Garden in New York. Two of the dancers with Kosloff were Lydia Lopokova and Alexandre Volinine—he had partnered Genée in 1908. The Diaghilev ballets were in marked contrast to what Americans recognized as Russian ballet in the style of Pavlova and her company. In the old classic ballets the ballerina wore a skirt like a giant powder-puff and, *sur les pointes,* dwarfed the rest of the company. The accent was on Beauty and Art, pure, pristine, and of an unearthly elegance. America did not know what to make of the New Ballet, which was more exuberant, and even shocking at times. When Diaghilev brought his Ballets Russes to America in 1916[13] Fokine had left the company and the choreographers Nijinsky and Massine had followed him in the artistic developments of the Ballets Russes, but the Fokine works were still in repertoire. The voluptuous *Schéhérazade* caused a commotion, and *Narcisse,* with Nijinsky, was banned from the Metropolitan as being a perversion. The scandalized Americans cared not a whit for the Ballets Russes' expostulations that *Narcisse* was from classical literature and represented the spirit of youth, and not of overt homosexuality. Nijinsky's *L'Après-midi d'un Faune* was a *succès de scandale.* When this startling sylvan male appeared on his summery hillside he was found to have usurped the prestige of the ballerina. The Faune was the central character, amorously inclined towards seven nymphs. There were heated debates as to whether all of this could be considered The Ballet, and at one performance the police arrived, called to protect the tender morals of the American audience, and carted the Diaghilev Ballets Russes off to jail, from which the dancers were released by the intervention of diplomats and impresarios. Nijinsky's feats of elevation in *Le Spectre de la Rose* made a better impression. His Faune had been danced by Leonide Massine (who later came to America and was of great influence on American ballet) at the Roxy Theatre and in the companies of Ballet Russe de Monte Carlo. The Diaghilev visit to America was marked by friction and strain within the company, and between the company and its host, the Metropolitan Opera. Before World War I Diaghilev had been the head of the most brilliant conglomeration of dancers, artists, and musical composers to exist since the Renaissance patronage of the arts.[14] In Europe and England the Ballets Russes was a revolutionary and admired company, but in America it pioneered among conservative audiences and under the halfhearted auspices of the Metropolitan. Amberg records that the Metropolitan's general manager was indifferent to ballet in general and Diaghilev in particular. Yet American audiences were deeply impressed by the New Ballet, and when the later Ballets Russes de Monte Carlo arrived, under de Basil, America became so converted to the new style of program and dancing that it adopted the company permanently. The Diaghilev programs featured two or three short ballets, instead of the full-length evening performance, which, incidentally, has never been a penchant of American ballet as it is of England's Royal Ballet and the Bolshoi Ballet.

From the Diaghilev visit American ballet acquired one of its great leaders, Adolph Bolm, who staged ballets at the Metropolitan and later formed a school and company. Fokine came to America on the invitation of the impresario Morris Gest, staged and designed dance for musicals, and in 1921 founded a school and a company in New York. The third great European influence, as teacher and choreographer, was Mikhail Mordkin, who had partnered Pavlova at the Paris Opéra and at the Metropolitan in New York. The impresario Otto Kahn brought Mordkin and Pavlova to America and in 1924, after serving as ballet master of the Bolshoi Theatre, Mordkin came again. Under Gest's management he toured the United States with a company he formed, and later taught ballet in New York and Philadelphia. In 1937 he organized the Mordkin Ballet, which was later assimilated into Ballet Theatre, now the American Ballet Theatre. Fokine spent his last years with this company.

Bolm did prodigious work in forming American ballet. He worked with the Chicago Civic Opera, helped to found Chicago Allied Arts, and worked in Hollywood and with the San Francisco Opera, where he helped to establish a school of ballet sponsored by the Opera Association. His company was Ballet Intime.

Between Pavlova's last American tour in 1925, and the advent of the Ballet Russe de Monte Carlo in 1933, ballet in America consisted of sporadic professional performances, like Diaghilev's not very successful visits. American dancers were desperate for a theatre to dance in, and they and the American audience believed that there was no American ballet as a national art. They were wrong. The theatre was gradually being made, not in grand opera houses as it had been developed in Europe and Russia, but wherever Americans would dance. The audience, enormous, scattered and somnolent, did not know of its own existence, but stood, in reality, waiting for the momentous year of 1933.

THE AMERICAN PIONEERS

We had begun to dance as Americans. Isadora Duncan, emerging like Minerva, carried the philosophy of Free Dance to Russia and Europe, preaching it as a religion that would free the race in mind and body. Rebelling against convention, she appeared in draperies, in movement expressive of music. Loring, in his Kinese, thinks of the impulse to dance as a spiral movement, up, down and out from the "plumb" line; Duncan declared dance to be the interpretation of inner impulse. Her ideas, although poetic, were not concisely expressed, and although she exerted an enormous world-wide influence which was said to have extended to Fokine's New Ballet, she left no science of dance such as had been founded in the Classic vocabulary. Her legacy to Modern Dance is her legend. She is romantically spoken of as the creator of Modern Dance but her influences, during her lifetime, were restricted to Russia and Germany and Americans had difficulty extricating her ideals of Free Love from her ideas on Free Dance. She left no standard vocabulary and the schools she founded perished when she died in a tragic accident in 1927. Duncan's dance-pantomime was a personal expression, an experience in self-revelation for the performer and the audience. Her genius was an intense and feminine one, and her whole intent was within the corporeal form of Woman and Beauty.

Twentieth-century dance moved far from the traditional concepts of form and order. Its tenet was freedom, and its prerogatives were the inventions of new styles, forms, motifs and costumes. Duncan rebelled from the classic tights and *pointes,* and in this set the precedent for the New Ballet of the twentieth century. Before Duncan, Sallé had freed the dancer in the realm of costume and interpretation. The rapport between Fokine's work and Duncan's may be likened to that between Noverre and Sallé.[15] But Fokine was inspired by even greater influences, those at work within the art and philosophy of his times.

The Nietzschean concept of music had ruled ballet: that there is Music in which the spirit dances, and Music in which the spirit swims; or that music is of two separate natures, one useful to the street and theatre, the other a purely transcendental thing.

In the twentieth century's recasting of philosophical and artistic values music produced revolutionary tenets, and side by side with music the dance be-

Ted Shawn, Ruth St. Denis and the Denishawn company in a 1916 production.

gan to exercise new freedoms and inventions. Some of them were in the Classic form, where gradually a diffusion of Modern Dance has granted a greater plasticity to the older style, and more feeling and stronger motives in interpretation. Fokine literally set ballet free of structure and style, and with works like *Les Sylphides* evolved the symphonic ballet that Massine, Nijinska and Balanchine developed. In the Balanchinean ideal the dance did not seek to interpret the music; it became the visual state of the aural creation, and the dancers were symphonic instruments rather than soloists and ensembles. As Modern Dance, the theatrical dance was developing another new spirit and form.

Modern Dance is based on metakinesis, dynamism, substance and form.[16] It comprises, generally, varieties of dance not based on the ethnological, nor on the traditional Classic text. Modern Dance originated in the United States, and its first stronghold was Denishawn, a school and company founded by the American dancers Ruth St. Denis and Ted Shawn. Denishawn was the first university of dance where all forms of dance were taught and performed. Its precepts are followed at Jacob's Pillow, the world-renowned summer dance festival which Shawn has directed since 1933. A development of Modern Dance in Europe has become known as Central European Dance. Its academic and spiritual life became largely centered in Germany, and its nominal head is Mary Wigman. Hanya Holm, her famed protégée, actively influences the American musical theatre.

In America, Modern Dance was developed less in a spirit of rebellion against the traditional than as the ingenuous use of natural resources and the passionate convictions of individuals. Both St. Denis and Shawn had classical training, and short histories of performance in the Classic genre, but they turned from traditional ballet out of personal inspiration into dance métiers which expressed them more eloquently. They were pioneers and independent geniuses, whose catholic use of music and all the related arts of dance established the freedom and expressiveness that connote Modern Dance. Shawn's "contrapuntal dances" to Bach's *Inventions and Fugues* began the Music Visualizations at Denishawn, and St. Denis's dance visualization of the *Sonata Pathètique,* with Doris Humphrey, was the interpretation of mood and emotion in music through a dance ensemble, the first of its form.

The disillusionment and suffering of World War I affected the development of Central European Dance. The American Modernists were not so much affected by outward pressure as they were inspired by a highly personal and versatile inventiveness. Among the American Modern Dance pioneers Woman and Beauty were symbolized by Duncan and St. Denis, and the virility of Dance by Shawn. They danced with a personal affinity for their material, and with an absorbed and almost innocent candor, far removed from the sadder profundities of the imprisoned and obsessed. Freedom, as the first principle of the American Modern Dance, was a radiant entity.

St. Denis, born in 1880 in New Jersey, was the daughter of an inventor and a mother who was a physician. She played at dancing from childhood but, unlike Duncan, was formally educated, and trained in Classic Dance. A few of her early lessons were from Bonfanti. She was an actress and a *pointe* dancer. On tour in 1904, she was inspired by a picture of the goddess Isis on a cigarette poster in Buffalo. Thereafter, she developed her famous repertoire of Oriental dances and danced as the visualization of music, devising special lighting effects as part of the performance. St. Denis became a great star in Europe, where her rippling arms so intrigued audiences that on occasion some learned men of science appeared backstage to beg permission to examine them, to find out if they were different from normal flesh and blood appendages. People had hardly changed since the time of Mlle Hutin, but now it was the European audience who marveled at American dancers.

St. Denis returned home after her foreign triumphs and six years later married Edwin Myers Shawn, another dancer. They managed Denishawn, as school and company, from 1914 to 1932. Thereafter St. Denis danced and taught in her own ensemble, and Shawn organized his Men Dancers and founded Jacob's Pillow.

Ted Shawn was born in Kansas City, Missouri, in 1891, the son of a newspaperman on the *Kansas City Star*. The senior Shawn was of German ancestry (the family name was von Schaun), and his forbears came to Indiana in the great anti-Bismarck exodus. His mother's family, the Booths, were Virginians from 1637, and held, as a grant of land, what is now Louisville, Kentucky. Norbourne Mordecai Booth built and operated the first telephone and telegraph system in Indiana and Kentucky, and later sold it to Western Union. One of his employees, a young telegraph operator named Shawn, married Booth's daughter and became a newspaperman. Their son, Edwin Myers Shawn, went with his parents from Missouri to Denver when he was fifteen, and his father became the chief editorial writer for the *Rocky Mountain News* and *Denver Times*.

Before he was sixteen, Ted Shawn graduated from the University of Denver Preparatory School and went on scholarship to the University of Denver. He was in his third year as a theology student when he contracted diphtheria. An overdose of antitoxin resulted in paralysis. The exercises he performed for therapy interested him in rhythmic movement and upon his recovery he determined to make dancing his vocation. His teacher was a student of Cavallazzi and Verhoeven of the Metropolitan Opera Ballet, and through them Shawn is connected with the old lineage of Classic ballet.

Since Shawn was over six feet in height and dwarfed the contemporary European *danseur* he believed himself unsuited to contemporary ballet repertoire. Nevertheless he did not then—or ever afterward—revolt against the tenets of the Classic Dance. Instead, he retained all the disciplinary elements of ballet and broadened its scope to include every way in which man has moved rhythmically to express himself. He danced in public performance for the first time in 1911 in a work he choreographed for himself, and then in some performances with his teacher, Hazel Wallack. In 1912 he went to Los Angeles, where, working in the daytime as a stenographer in the City Water Department, he experimented with dancing in the evenings. In Los Angeles he made one of the first dance movies, *Dance of the Ages,* with Norma Gould.

He had early been aware of the new movements in dance and was intrigued by what had been done by Duncan, St. Denis and the other Interpretative dancers. With Classic ballet as his foundation, not his prison, he began to create an American style, and one especially significant for the male dancer. He made use of American continental themes, and employed music far beyond the contemporary dance norm—and he brought to the dance in America a dignity, a masculine purpose and a spiritual awareness such as the theatre had not known until then. His size, looks and demeanor were such that he could dare to be serious and profound without appearing esoteric. With the advent of Ted Shawn on the stage American dance gained physical and moral stature.

Shawn's prodigious accomplishments as dancer, teacher and choreographer are too great to be catalogued briefly in this book. He is still an active influence in the American theatre, as a dancer as well as a teacher and impresario, having in 1958 created the role of the blind king in Myra Kinch's Modern work, *The Sound of Darkness*. Internationally, he is the most honored American dance figure, and is described encyclopedically as The Father of American Dance.

St. Denis' contributions, which have made her the First Lady of American Dance, were far greater than Duncan's, whose influence was not felt in America until long after her death—and then more in romantic concepts than in actual dance theatre.

From Denishawn came the hierarchy of American Modern Dance. Three of the giants are the famed Doris Humphrey, Charles Weidman, and Martha Graham, whose dances are motivated by, and expressive of, strong emotions.

Doris Humphrey was a prodigy who created a ballet, *Persephone and Demeter,* when she was a seventeen-year-old schoolgirl.[17] Her *Inquest* has been called the finest work of an American dance composer. Her concern was the broad human scene, rather than the individual, in such productions as *With My Red Fires.*[18] She joined forces with another Denishawn student, Charles Weidman, a master of characterization and mime developed under Shawn. They have been likened, in dance, to Molière and Racine. Weidman commented satirically on his times in such dances as *This Passion,* based on the Snyder-Grey murder, and *Flickers,* which ridiculed the silent screen. In *Daddy Was A Fireman* a pioneer civilization perished in Lincoln, Nebraska.

Martha Graham was preoccupied by Woman and human anguish. She was greatly influenced by the German Modern Dance ideals (described by St. Denis as "sadly earthbound") which developed out of the disillusionment and bitterness of World War I, but she formed her original methods of expression and became the best known of the Modern dancers.

There were many people besides Fokine who were dissatisfied with traditional ballet. Wolkonsky had innumerable confrères saying that ballet dancing should have a meaning. Thus, an infiltration of strong human motives and a complimentary kindling of expressiveness began to influence the Classic Dance.

Some of the choreographers in the traditional ballet genre would continue to follow the Five Principles set by Fokine, especially in costume and in the use of music as a contributary, not an arbitrary, force in ballet. Others would introduce boldly—as the American choreographers do—some of the actual forms of Modern Dance. And there would remain a group dedicated to the Classic technique, restricting themselves, with artistic deliberation, to its vocabulary.

The Classic Dance is not a natural, free and exuberant form of dance. It is the artistic exploitation of a difficult anatomical feat, whereby the dancer's leg is turned in the ballet angle, and his movements made to originate, in Turnout, from Five Positions.[19] It has a vocabulary and a terminology based on *danse d'école,* and it has constantly evolved, but it has never altered its concepts in nearly four hundred years. It is not intended to express emotion graphically, but is the idealized movement of the human body, with its ideas based on architecture and its ideals founded on nobility and good form.

Classic Dance is the foundation of the ballet theatre, in America as everywhere else, and that foundation is recognized as The Ballet. Costume changes have made possible new feats of technique, and the contributing arts of music and design and the literary worth of libretti have effected nuances of style in performance—but basically ballet is the same art conceived by master technicians and choreographers hundreds of years ago. Although Duncan's protesting bare feet and her state of undress inspired the costume and the freedom of twentieth-century dance, it did not affect the spirit and the Classic form of traditional ballet. The American ballet choreographers Loring and Tudor follow the Fokine ideal. De Mille and Robbins have been influenced by Modern Dance forms. De Mille declares herself to be strongly inspired by Graham; Robbins, like Michael Kidd and others, has symbolized American syncopation. The brilliant choreography in American musicals follows the precedent of de Mille, Loring, Robbins, and of Hanya Holm, a disciple of Mary Wigman. All these influences are part and parcel of American ballet—and still another of the American dance theatre is the Classic Dance, whose chief contemporary exponent is Balanchine.

As the decade of the 'thirties neared, the battle had only just begun, between the die-hards in the audience, and the profession, over the relative merits in American ballet of the Classic and the Modern. Classic Dance was suspiciously viewed as foreign and effete, a form of communication so complex and difficult as to be the special province of the *prêcheurs précieux*. Modern Dance was for some time stigmatized for being angry, miserable and ugly. It was preoccupied with such dismal themes and characterizations that one alarmed member of the general theatre audience declared that Graham should be restricted to church and chapel, and that Danilova's Sugarplum Fairy was the only thing of worth the Russians had given the American theatre. Of course there were intelligent and earnest audiences for the *danse d'école* and the Modern Interpretive genre, but these were not large enough to support either one métier or the other. The pioneers from Denishawn struggled alone to found a theatre with a stage and an audience; and the classicists, in order to survive as dancers, joined one little company after the other, or were absorbed into foreign companies. Among the latter—the pioneer classical dancers of American ballet—were the Christensen brothers and two remarkable women, Catherine Littlefield and Ruth Page.

The Christensens and Littlefield had incentive for their profession: they came from families with a history of ballet. Littlefield, whose mother had a school in Philadelphia, studied under her mother and then under Albertieri at the Metropolitan. She went to Paris and became the pupil of Egorova, and on return became a ballerina of the musical stage and in the Philadelphia Opera Company. In 1935 she formed the Littlefield Ballet, afterward named The Philadelphia Ballet, the first such to be organized and entirely composed of Americans. The company toured the United States and in 1937 had a season in Europe, where it was well received. It was the first American ballet company to appear in Europe. By poetic coincidence, this first American company emerged from Philadelphia, which had produced for the United States the first lyric ballerina, the first *danseur noble* and the first ballerina internationally acknowledged to be of *prima ballerina* rank.

Littlefield created several ballets, among them *Barn Dance, Terminal, Café Society,* and *H.P.* (for horse power). A number of dancers who were later to become well known in American ballet started under Littlefield's aegis, among them Paul Haakon, who came to America from Denmark as a child and began dancing in 1927 when he was thirteen. He was a protégé of Fokine and appeared in the Fokine company. Littlefield's company disbanded in 1942, when many of the male dancers went into military service. She died in 1951. Save for the loss of Littlefield and Humphrey, the roster of the American Ballet pioneers stands complete. The American national dance theatre has been formed as such for only a quarter of a century, and in that brief span the pioneers have developed an aura of sanctity which their continuing activity does not altogether dispel.

Among these immortals few have been as active as Ruth Page, now the head of the Chicago Opera-Ballet—a company of such worth that it regularly employs, on annual tours, the *premier danseur* and the *première danseuse* of the Paris Opéra, the Americans George Skibine and Marjorie Tallchief. Page was born in Indiana, and studied under Ivan Clustine, the ballet master of Pavlova's company, with which Page went on tour. In 1925 she was the *première danseuse* of the Teatro Colon in Buenos Aires, and was briefly a dancer with the Diaghilev Ballets Russes. She had lessons from Cecchetti. In New York, she studied and danced in the Bolm school and Ballet Intime, and in 1934 was ranked as *première danseuse* with the Chicago Grand Opera. In 1938 she began her association with Bentley Stone and the Page-Stone company, which was a large influence in Chicago from 1938 to 1941.

Page has the distinction of having been the first American *prima ballerina* of the Metropolitan—a distinction all the greater for the Metropolitan's studied ignoring of anything like an American ballet. She made several world tours, dancing at the coronation of the Japanese Emperor Hirohito, and in Moscow at the invitation of the U.S.S.R. The Page-Stone company was the first ensemble of American dancers to appear in South America. In 1950 Page presented *Ballets Americains* in Paris, and in 1957 choreographed a French musical, *Minnie Moustache*. She has choreographed for Dolin's Festival Ballet, the Lyon Festival, and Les Ballets des Champs Élysées. Among her best known works are *Frankie and Johnnie, The Bells,* and *Billy Sunday,* all of American genre. She is the leading choreographer of opera-ballet, and has converted into ballet form *Carmen* (with a Civil War locale), *Salome, The Barber of Seville* (as *Susannah and the Barber*), *The Merry Widow* and *Camille* from *La Traviata.*

Littlefield and Page also reconstructed classical ballets. Littlefield restaged *The Fairy Doll* (1895) and *Daphnis and Chloe* (1912). Page choreographed a version of *The Sleeping Beauty*. These two women, with the eldest Christensen, William, were the first American classical dancer-choreographers.

Meanwhile, in Europe there was another American labeled "the American dancer," whose name was Agnes de Mille. But no European or English audience recognized the existence of anything like an American ballet. Duncan, Shawn, St. Denis and Lois Fuller,[20] and in a later generation, Agnes de Mille, were phenomena in the American dancing tradition. In 1930, English ballet was founded in the Camargo Society, the parent of the Royal Ballet, by two Diaghilev dancers, the modernist-*cum*-classicist Marie Rambert, and the classicist Ninette de Valois. Ballet was blossoming richly on the international branches of the huge family tree.

When Diaghilev suddenly died in 1929, there was a transfusion of ballet into

Ruth Page as Susanna in Susanna and the Barber.

the western world. Each member of Diaghilev's company epitomized the centuries-old tradition of the ballet, and as these exiles scattered about the free world, cut off from Russia by their own determination not to return to Soviet government, they unwittingly became a dozen or more nuclei of national ballets. Their influence as choreographers and teachers was to form the tradition of twentieth-century ballet for the western nations. With Diaghilev dead, the Ballets Russes dynasty was a disputed kingdom. Laying claim to it in a dramatic gesture worthy of the most flamboyant theatre, Serge Lifar cast himself into Diaghilev's grave at the impresario's funeral. He was resurrected, however, and bequeathed his considerable talents, for some thirty years, to the Paris Opéra. Other Diaghilev choreographers and dancers went their several ways more sedately, and their variously diverted influence is to be seen in their adopted countries in the West.

Bolm, Fokine and Mordkin had come to America before Massine arrived at the Roxy in New York for a three-year tenure. In England Markova, in order to subsist, was dancing a four-a-day bill at an Odéon cinema for money, and with the parent companies of the Royal Ballet for love. With a weekly change of bill, Massine was partnered by a *prima ballerina* of indefatigable stamina and unusual gifts. The sublime work-horse was Patricia Bowman, born in Washington, D.C., a pupil of Fokine and Mordkin, who also studied with Legat and Egorova, and under Margarete Wallman, the celebrated German whom Shawn introduced to America. Bowman's partners at various times were Massine, Mordkin, Dolin, Eglevsky, Haakon, and Zoritch. She was Fokine's favorite American pupil, and one of only three dancers taught by Fokine, and authorized by him, to interpret his *Dying Swan*. The others were Pavlova, on whom he created the *pas seul,* and his wife, Vera Fokina. Bowman was one of the many American classicists, almost all of feminine gender, to emerge with startling precocity when the Kirstein-Balanchine companies were formed and Ballet Russe and Ballet Theatre looked for recruits.

There were also American *danseurs,* like the Christensens, and like Dollar and Loring, who would rise above all obstacles to become ranking dancers in ballet. In 1927 Ted Shawn wrote *The American Ballet* which was described by Havelock Ellis, in a foreword, as prophetic. Shawn reissued this book in 1959 under the title *Thirty-Three Years of American Dance (1926–1959) and The American Ballet* as the second part of his survey of American dance—a book that is of great importance to all students of American theatre.

As the 'thirties dawned, ballet began to attain artistic significance. When Massine, in 1930, created a ballet to the controversial *Rite of Spring,* it was performed at the Metropolitan and the orchestra was conducted by Leopold Stokowski. The sacrificial victim of Stravinsky's score was a Shawn protégée, Martha Graham.

However, between Pavlova's appearance and the advent of de Basil's Ballets Russes de Monte Carlo in 1933–1934, there seemed to be no evolutionary developments. Diaghilev's company caused a passing furore, and no more. Denishawn did estimable pioneer work as a school and company, but how many in

the audience realized that we now had a national dance theatre? It is only in retrospect that the contributions from foreign influences and native creative dance
can now be assessed. One of the most momentous changes was in the status of
male dancers. In 1933, Ted Shawn organized his Men Dancers, an all-male troupe
which toured for seven years. It danced over three hundred and fifty thousand
miles of the United States, in a total of twelve hundred and fifty performances.
The Men Dancers was the first organization to generate an American enthusiasm
for the Dancer, Male. In 1959, when the American dancer Gene Kelly was receiving awards and kudos for an "Omnibus" program, "Dancing is a Man's
Game," he divulged that seeing Shawn's Men Dancers as a high school student
had been one of the great inspirations of his life.

Suddenly, a momentous series of events precipitated the birth of American
ballet. In the season 1933–1934 America was host to two distinguished visitors,
giants in the métiers of the Classic and Modern Dance. The first was that of Col.
de Basil's Ballets Russes de Monte Carlo. The second, of Kurt Jooss' company,
the Jooss Ballet.

Ballets Russes had the first, the largest and the most permanent effect in
America. Danilova and her contemporaries were the catalyst needed to transfigure The Ballet, foreign, effete and incomprehensible, into popular entertainment for the general American audience. There were spellbound audiences in SRO
theatres and a concerted rush—greater even than the one following Pavlova's
inspiration—to the schools of dance. Enraptured Americans began to enjoy
dancing on tiptoe with as much *élan* as they had done in Mlle Hutin's day, and
the management kindly translated the foreign tongue for the theatregoers, altering Massine's *Gaîté Parisienne* into *The Gay Parisian*. Billboards did not matter
when inside the theatre, eyes sparkling, peerless legs flashing in a frothing petticoat, *prima ballerina* Danilova was dancing into the huge and ardent heart of the
American audience.

But this was the stage, a transient thing, on which bright stars wax and wane.
Something more was needed: a foundation for the production of a native instrument, and the development of a national craft. The art of dancing in the Classic
style had not changed in nearly four hundred years, and the academic discipline
remained that of Pierre Beauchamp (1639–1705) and Carlo Blasis (1797–1878).
In 1933 Lincoln Kirstein organized the School of American Ballet and brought
George Balanchine to America.

THE AMERICAN BALLET

Its history lies in the past, in that half-limbo of ballet in America, when Hutin
on tiptoe, and Céleste, filling the audience with Wonder, Admiration and Joy,
contributed a share of what Elssler, Pavlova and Danilova later gave the national
theatre. Its history lies also, in part, in the "Lissome Ballet Ladies" and "Pretty
Water Nymphs" of the "wondrous ballets." The famed and defamed, the famous
and notorious, have helped the theatre to build both its physical stage and its
audience, neither of which could have existed without the other.

How ballet in America became the American ballet is told here in the histories of *The Companies, The Ballets, The Choreographers,* and *The Schools.* The Schools, which come last in this record, are, in actuality, the foundation. On them are built the companies, the perches of those wondrous birdlike creatures, the dancers, and the workshops of those master craftsmen, the choreographers. The ballets themselves are the product and the prize of the teaching, the craft, and the companies.

In the season 1958–1959 the Kirstein-Balanchine association, described in *The Companies* and *The Teaching,* was twenty-five years old. The progeny of their parent companies is the New York City Ballet which, though modestly celebrating ten years under that name, is in reality a child of the whole first quarter of a century of American ballet. The Kirstein-Balanchine collaboration has been the mainstream in the emergence of the national ballet (q.v. *A Dictionary of Ballet,* 1957). Ballet Russe de Monte Carlo, which adventured into the American theatre in 1933, celebrated its twentieth year as an American company in 1958–1959. So did the American Ballet Theatre, born out of the old Mordkin Ballet.

In the files of the companies' offices, and the lives and works of the company founders and members lie the true record, and the exciting history of American ballet. The epochal season of 1958–1959 marked the American Ballet Jubilee: a twenty-fifth anniversary, a time of rejoicing, a day of joy.

The first clear vision of an American ballet began with Shawn. It is directly owing to his tolerance of all forms of dance and his energy as a dancer-choreographer and impresario that American ballet has its present panoramic stage and its comprehensive nature. In its history the works of the choreographers are of equal worth—in quality, if not in style—and there is no prejudice against a theatre which houses Balanchine and Tudor, and is also graced with modern masterpieces like *The Moor's Pavanne* and *The Lament for Ignacio Sanchez.* The lusty, democratic American ballet speaks eloquently of the artists and the audiences who developed it, yet its artistic basis and its chief sustenance is drawn from Classic Dance, and for this foundation it is forever indebted to Lincoln Kirstein and Lucia Chase.

American ballet had no endowment other than wit and energy, and no support except the charity of its patrons. It had a past bankrupted by a frivolous attitude toward dance, and no possibility of a future, unless it could establish itself in the theatre. It was without an academic standard of teaching and performance, and it had no company as a base of operations. There was no such patron of princely estate as had lavished dowries on ballet elsewhere. And the United States government proffered no state subsidy.

Every great western nation had national ballet theatres, of which the finest were those of France, Russia and Denmark. Ballet artists in Europe were salaried, pensioned and, occasionally, honored for their services exactly as though they were civil servants. Dancing was a profession and a vocation.

The last country to found a national ballet was England. In 1930 the Camargo Society, formed on Diaghilev dancers, kept ballet alive in England post-Diaghilev. In 1928 Ninette de Valois had a school and company resident at London's

Old Vic Theatre, and an English company on tour narrowly missed being captured when Holland was seized by Germany in World War II. The Sadler's Wells Ballet got its name from its home theatre, the oldest in London, which was built in 1683 for performances by singers, acrobats and rope dancers. When the Covent Garden Royal Opera House reopened after the war, in April, 1946, it was a performance by the Sadler's Wells Ballet that marked the Opera House's post-war rebirth. Since 1956, when it became the Royal Ballet, the company has held a Royal Charter, under Queen Elizabeth II. Previously, it was government-subsidized through the British Council of Arts.

Even before there was a national company in England, there was a school and an academic standard for ballet. The Royal Academy of Dancing was founded in 1920, with P. J. S. Richardson and Edouard Espinosa as co-founders. Its first president was Adeline Genée, who in 1950 was created a Dame of the British Empire, and holds, besides, decorations from the Danish government for her contribution to ballet. Britain's oldest continuous dance company is Ballet Rambert, a company which emerged from the London school founded by Marie Rambert in 1920.

The growth of American ballet is most easily traced in the companies developed after 1933, when the School of American Ballet was organized as an academic foundation. As we have noted (see page 29), ballet in its traditional, classical form is based on very old techniques of stylized performance which have not altered in their strictness. The training in Classic technique involves teacher and student in the same sort of authority and disciplines that are to be found in military and naval academies. In other words, there is a definable international standard of art and theatrical performance known as the ballet. It was this art, already in its fourth century, that Americans now set out to master and to produce with their own positive style and kindling spirit as American ballet.

Twenty-five years after the momentous season of 1933–1934, we have three major resident companies: the New York City Ballet, the American Ballet Theatre, and the Ballet Russe de Monte Carlo. A fourth company, resident in Europe, but American nonetheless, is that of the Marquis de Cuevas. De Cuevas is an American national, the company is supported by his wife's inheritance from her family, the Rockefellers, and de Cuevas Ballet originated in the United States, formed on American dancers and choreographers. It is now, in its European residence, composed of both European and American members. The choreographers and ballet masters of note who have helped to form the de Cuevas Ballet are Dollar and Taras, and in the company three great American dancers have developed—Rosella Hightower, ranked as its *prima ballerina assoluta,* Marjorie Tallchief, and the dancer-choreographer George Skibine.

Besides the four major American companies there are the San Francisco Ballet, Ruth Page's Chicago Opera-Ballet, and the Metropolitan Opera House company. Other than these are the grouped affiliations of civic companies, called regional ballet here, which have already produced new roots for the national ballet theatre. Two such (Southeastern and Northeastern) are nationally recognized at this writing and were first established in 1956. There are, besides, concert ensembles of American dancers in classical and modern repertoire, the *pas de deux* concert artists, and the concert soloists.

We have no one company and school established as our National Ballet, and no universal academic standard for all American dancers, and yet American ballet is internationally recognized, to its honor, and ranked with the national ballets of France, Russia, Denmark and England. In the international hierarchy, where the national *prima ballerina* is the symbol of the national theatre, the ranking four are Yvette Chauviré in France, Galina Ulanova in Russia, Margot Fonteyn in England, Maria Tallchief in America. Danish ballet has no category to correspond with this, but its lineage is the same; its origin, the international ballet. The Royal Danish Ballet's policy of *solodancer* rank for its ballerinas does not quite obscure the *première* position of Margrethe Schanne, but the company's unique character and repertoire embellish each star with special prerogatives. Schanne is the great Danish Romantic ballerina of her era, in style the peer of Markova. Inge Sand is an incomparable ballerina, versatile in character and style, unclassifiable in temperament, ranging as she does from the nobly classic to *soubrette* roles. The national ballet companies are joined together, like branches, on a tree rooted in the room of the Louvre where in 1661 Louis XIV founded the Académie de Danse. In 1669, Louis founded the theatre that is now called the Paris Opéra.

In 1726 the Court of Denmark employed a French ballet master and started a school, and the Royal Danish Ballet is the second oldest national ballet.

In 1735 the Empress Anna Ivanovna founded the Imperial Dancing Academy in St. Petersburg, and hired a French and an Italian director and dancing master.

In 1748 the Royal Theatre, the home of the Royal Danish Ballet, was opened in Copenhagen, ten years after the establishment of the St. Petersburg Theatrical Academy in Russia. Teatro alla Scala opened in Milan in 1778 and for a time usurped the Paris Opéra as the throne of international ballet. The Bolshoi Theatre in Moscow was opened in 1825, and the Maryinsky in St. Petersburg in 1860. London's present Royal Opera House was built in 1858.

America's great opera house, the New York Metropolitan, was built in 1883. The School of American Ballet opened its doors to students on January 2, 1934, and when the first company from the first American classical academy emerged that year, the first native *prima ballerina* of American ballet was nine years old. She had already begun to dance, taught by an itinerant teacher who traveled twice a week from Tulsa, Oklahoma, to the Indian reservation in Fairfax, where little Maria Tallchief had blithely whirled on tiptoe to "The Stars and Stripes" at the age of four. In 1947, the product of the teachers Nijinska and Balanchine, Tallchief danced at the Paris Opéra. It was one hundred and eight years after Augusta Maywood.

GEORGE BALANCHINE

As Georgi Melitonovitch Balanchivadze, the son of a famous Georgian composer, Balanchine was born in 1904 at St. Petersburg, and entered the Imperial

Ballet School when he was ten. His principal teachers were Andrianoff, Chekry-guine, and Victor Semenoff, and he had lessons from Gerdt. He was miserable in his trial year and loathed dancing. He preferred music, and had been study-ing piano from a very early age.

In his second year at the school everything changed, for the permanent students became a part of the Maryinsky Theatre. Balanchine first set foot on its splendid stage in the garland dance of *The Sleeping Beauty,* and was a cupid on one of the carriages in the last act. That evening changed his life. The magic of the Maryin-sky's stage, where fires blazed, fountains cascaded, swans glided about a lake in a lifelike manner, and waves rolled onto shore, was the wondrous reality of fairy-land. Under the spell of theatre Balanchine began to work as hard at his dancing as he had learned to work at the piano—from which he used to be sent supper-less to bed when he did not practice. At ten, when a child is fully prepared to make a life and death choice, Balanchine became a dancer.

His training was the long and authoritative one, never surpassed, seldom equaled, which turns out the unique Russian ballet technician. So absorbed were the students in the training that they were hardly conscious of the outer world. When the first World War broke out it left them largely unaffected and during the Russian Revolution Balanchine and some fellow students went to hear a man haranguing a crowd from the balcony of the Imperial Theatre's *prima ballerina assoluta,* Kchessinskaya. The boys thought the man was a lunatic; he was Lenin. By the time Balanchine graduated, an honor student, his academy had changed from an imperial to a state school.

As a graduate student, Balanchine received the education of a dancer in a government-supported theatre. The school curriculum was that of a good Euro-pean boy's school and in addition the students studied ballet and character dance, and learned to play at least one instrument. In 1921 Balanchine entered the Con-servatory of Music in St. Petersburg, then under Glazunov, and for three years studied theory, composition and piano, while continuing to work as a graduate of the State Academy of Opera and Ballet. Besides dancing at the Maryinsky he appeared at the Alexandrinsky, the Imperial dramatic theatre, and at the Mikhailovsky, the Imperial theatre of *opéra comique.*

In 1920, to Rubinstein's *La Nuit,* Balanchine produced his first ballet. He was tremendously stimulated by what little he knew of the New Ballet under Diaghi-lev (some Fokine ballets had been taken into State repertoire) and attempted to choreograph in the new quality of movement. His dancers were his fellow students, who hugely enjoyed the experience, but their teachers disapproved. Nevertheless, Balanchine produced a full program in 1923, *Evenings of the Young Ballet,* with the designer Vladimir Dimitriev, showing the evolution of Ballet in Russia from Petipa's era through Fokine's reforms to his (Balanchine's) own ideas of move-ment. It is noteworthy that the nineteen-year-old Balanchine had formed his own ideas of movement, but the theatre authorities were unimpressed, and so dis-approved that they forbade the dancers, on threat of being barred from the state company, from taking part in Balanchine's ballets. Unable to secure a theatre for his *Evenings of the Young Ballet,* Balanchine presented it in an amphitheatre formerly occupied by the *Duma,* the czar's parliament.

Narrowly restricted in his native theatre, Balanchine went on working, beginning on his version of *Pulcinella,* which had previously been produced by Diaghilev. On the suggestion of his friend Dimitriev, then a singer at the State Opera, Balanchine formed a little company, the Soviet State Dancers, with a *soliste* from the State Ballet named Alexandra Danilova, and a *corps de ballet* girl named Tamara Geva. What befell this little troupe is part of the history of American ballet.

After a jaunt about Europe, during which they overstayed their leave of absence from the U.S.S.R., Balanchine's company reached Paris and was presented to Diaghilev. The historic audition took place in the home of a patron of the arts, Mme Sert, and there the little Danilova, who was twenty—Geva was only sixteen—took off her street shoes and danced a part of a Variation from *The Firebird.* Diaghilev rescued the troupe and in time Danilova became the last of the Diaghilev ballerinas. The impresario changed Balanchivadze to Balanchine and the young choreographer inherited the mantle that first Fokine and then Nijinsky and Massine had worn in the Ballets Russes.

Balanchine choreographed ten ballets for Diaghilev, and in one of them, *Le Rossignol* (1925), Diaghilev presented a young dancer he had discovered in London, at the studio of the teacher Asafieva. The infant prodigy was an English girl, fourteen years old, and her name was Alicia Markova. *Le Rossignol's* score was by Igor Stravinsky, who created some of his avant-garde music for Diaghilev's ballets. In 1928, Balanchine choreographed Stravinsky's *Apollon Musagète,* of which he wrote: "I look back upon that ballet as the turning point in my life." This was the commencement of collaboration between composer and choreographer which was to culminate in a repertoire which, by 1959, ranged from the exaltation of *Orpheus* to the metronome complexities of *Agon.*

After Diaghilev's death Balanchine and Danilova were at loose ends. Both worked in musical revues, one as choreographer, the other as dancer, and both joined the de Basil-Blum Ballets Russes de Monte Carlo. Here Balanchine discovered two more young ballerinas, Tamara Toumanova and Irina Baronova, reputedly aged thirteen and eleven, from the Preobrajenska school in Paris. A third student of emigré Russians joined the others. She was Tatiana Riabouchinska, then aged fourteen. This trio was to become know internationally as the "baby ballerinas." They, with Markova, and Danilova and Balanchine, eventually emigrated to American ballet.[21]

Unable to agree with the artistic policies of the de Basil-Blum company, Balanchine left after one season and formed his own company, Les Ballets 1933. It was founded by an Englishman, Edward James, whose wife, Tilly Losch, was the *première.* Toumanova went with Balanchine, and an exquisite English ballerina, Pearl Argyle, joined them. Les Ballets 1933 had a Paris and a London season, caused an artistic furore, and had no great financial success, but it was seen by a young American, Lincoln Kirstein, who at once resolved to bring

Balanchine to America. After Diaghilev's death Balanchine was *maître de ballet* of the Danish ballet, and no doubt could have returned there. He was asked to direct the Paris Opéra but fell ill, and Serge Lifar substituted for him. By the conspiracy of events, and through Kirstein's insistence, Balanchine came to the United States to head the School of American Ballet.

He did more than head a school, or direct its teaching. More precisely, he established an unimpeachable standard for ballet in the United States, in academic calibre and in performance.

Despite the talent and artistic conscience of ballet artists in the United States, the popular audience, into the 'thirties, detected little difference between traditional ballet—i.e. the Classic Dance—and "ballets" that were theatrical presentations in which dancing had a primary character. This literary delusion continued to confuse the mass audience, especially as "ballets" became increasingly popular and were performed not only by humans but by animated cartoon figures and trained animals. Balanchine's ballets had an immaculate decorum, and such unity with the music that it never became mere accompaniment; indeed, the dancing often was sublimated into visual music. Balanchine seldom occupied himself with plot and characterization, and his work moved steadily away from operatic dancing to a form that has come to be called Neoclassicism. The Classic Dance, in principle, continued as the basis of his ballets, but the style and substance of the dancing were individual to George Balanchine.

The precepts of teaching which he transported to American ballet were those inculcated in the St. Petersburg School, and the visit of the Bolshoi and Moiseyev companies pointed up the sharp contrast between his style and that created for the dance theatre in Moscow.

The Balanchine technique, in the first quarter of a century of his influence on the American dance theatre, is more noticeable in the *danseuse* than the *danseur*. It is doubtful if he could have fashioned this exact product in any country other than the United States. Here he found numbers of healthy, athletic young girls with limber, long legs. They did not resist Balanchine's Neoclassic theories with ethnic pride or prejudice. On such emotionally innocent, ethnically ignorant, young American females Balanchine imposed his ideal ballerina shape and technique. Almost universally Balanchine's *danseuses* had small, light bones, long, high extensions, and a deceptively fragile look. Their extraordinary physical mobility was emphasized by the conspicuous lack of emotion in the Balanchine ballets, whose beauty depended on the perfection with which they were executed, rather than on a seductive confluence of arts in ballet, such as costume, scenic design and mime.

In an astoundingly short time ballerinas were formed who were peculiar to Balanchine's repertoire. They were too young to have been influenced by the first dazzling stars of the century, and Balanchine impressed on them principles of control and balance in *adagio*, tremendous thrusting force and speed, and an awesome precision and ease. They were not the ballerinas of the effervescent *demi-caractère* style, nor did they have the warmth, languor and sweetness characteristic of romanticism. Instead, they were like superb engines, seemingly able to check themselves in mid-movement, and to demonstrate control and balance at a command; or to leap prodigiously and turn swiftly in intricate designs. As dance prodigies, they appeared superhuman.

The fame attached to his ballets and ballerinas caused Balanchine to be accused of neglecting the *danseur* in favor of the *danseuse*. Balanchine is still believed to choreograph primarily for women, but to this repeated criticism he has a reply: "I create roles which best suit the qualities of my best dancers. Most often, the best dancers have been women and so I have created for them. If I had had more outstanding male dancers I should have featured them as much as the women. When I have outstanding male dancers I shall feature them in outstanding roles in ballets created for them."

Balanchine had been called Diaghilev's boy-wonder, and his reputation was already made when he came to the United States. The ballerina Markova had made a debut with his choreography, and he had considerably aided the careers of Danilova and Toumanova. However, it was in America that his greatest gifts became manifest, as a teacher and choreographer, and as such Balanchine's creative force made him one aspect, and one great contributary part, of American ballet. Between 1933 and 1960 he compiled a repertoire more prolific and individual than any other in contemporary theatre. He did it almost exclusively with American dancers, in ballet of a style different from the popular concept of Classic Dance. Ballet in America now advanced from European and Russian domination to American Neoclassicism.

BALANCHINE'S AMERICAN BALLET AND KIRSTEIN'S BALLET CARAVAN

Out of the School of American Ballet came, in December 1934, The American Ballet Company, a performing group made up of the students of the first year's classes. The company made its debut at the estate of Felix M. Warburg in White Plains, New York, and afterwards appeared at the Avery Memorial Theatre in Hartford, Connecticut, and at the Adelphi Theatre in New York. The repertoire was Balanchine's *Dreams, Mozartiana,* and *Errante,* from Les Ballets 1933, and —newly created for The American Ballet—*Alma Mater,* a spoof on Joe Collegiate. Among the dancers were Ruthanna Boris, Gisella Caccialanza, Annabelle Lyon, Elise Reiman, and two boys: William Dollar and Eugene Loring. There were also the guest artists Tamara Geva and Paul Haakon, and the *danseuse* Leda Anchutina who married André Eglevsky.

In 1935, The American Ballet became the resident ballet company of the Metropolitan. Out of the stipend paid by the opera house Balanchine employed the *premier danseur* Anatole Vilzak, and added to the company Ruby Asquith, Kyra Blanc, Lillian Moore, Harold and Lew Christensen, and Erick Hawkins.

The management and the audience of the Metropolitan were no less conservative than they had been when Diaghilev's company performed in 1916. Balanchine's radical changes in what the Metropolitan believed to be The Ballet exasperated rather than aroused interest, especially when he committed the lese majesty of staging Gluck's *Orpheus* as a ballet onstage, with singers in the orchestra pit. But Kirstein believed in his protégé, and, apparently, Stravinsky, who conducted both performances of the historic Stravinsky Festival Balanchine produced for a two-day season in 1937. The ballets were *Apollon Musagète,* now called *Apollo; Jeu de Cartes,* sometimes called *The Card Party,* or *Card Game;* and *Le Baiser de la Fée, The Fairy's Kiss.* Possibly not a dozen people, including the press reviewers, of the audiences on April 27 and 28, 1937, knew that a new era was being born in American ballet. Balanchine and Kirstein would live to hear such undiluted praise of these works as would for all time settle the debate as to whether Balanchine was bad or, simply, mad. The only argument to survive was whether *Apollo* is better ballet than *Le Baiser de la Fée,* or vice versa. *Jeu de Cartes* was the first Stravinsky ballet Balanchine choreographed in America. It employs twenty-six dancers as portions of four suits, and a Joker. It is nothing so simple as a card party, but is the allegorical statement that important people (kings and queens) may be ousted by the common people—the faceless cards. Dollar created the Joker. The ballet has been danced by Ballet Russe de Monte Carlo and the New York City Ballet—notably with Bolender, Maule, Moncion, Reed, Tallchief and Wilde.

In spring, 1938, Balanchine and the Metropolitan parted with a great press furore and Kirstein published his *Blast at Ballet,* which contained a vindication of Balanchine's works. The American Ballet was not seen publicly for the next three years.

Meanwhile, in spring, 1936, Kirstein founded another company, Ballet Caravan, also emergent from the School of American Ballet, as an outlet for American choreographers, composers and designers. The company had a summer season for two years and for the rest of the time were members of Balanchine's American Ballet. In autumn, 1938 (when The American Ballet had resigned from residence at the Metropolitan and its dancers were unattached), Ballet Caravan altered its name to American Ballet Caravan and went on tour. In 1940 it was employed by the Ford company (the first time American industry had hired ballet) to dance at the Ford Pavilion at the New York World's Fair. The company was divided into two units and danced ten times a day for a six-month season.

Ballet Caravan produced the works of the American choreographers Lew Christensen, Eugene Loring, and (at the New York World's Fair) William Dollar's *A Thousand Times Neigh.* Its most ambitious ballet was *Billy the Kid,* presented on October 16, 1938. According to Amberg, *Billy* marks the start of American Ballet. Loring created for Ballet Caravan the ballets *Harlequin for President, Yankee Clipper* and *Billy the Kid.* Next in importance to *Billy* was *Filling Station,* by Lew Christensen, who also created *Pocahontas* and *Encounter.* Hawkins, later a member of the Graham company, created a ballet called *Show Piece.*

In 1941 the two companies, Balanchine's American Ballet, and Kirstein's American Ballet Caravan, merged under the latter name to go on a Latin-American tour. The trip was sponsored by a committee headed by Nelson Rockefeller as director of the United States commission to propagate cultural and commercial relations between the American republics. On the good-will tour were the dancers Helen Kramer, Mary Jane Shea, Beatrice Tompkins, Todd Bolender, William

André Eglevsky and Maria Tallchief in the Stravinsky-Balanchine ballet Jeu de Cartes (Card Game).

Dollar, John Kriza, Nicholas Magallanes, Zachary Solov and John Taras. One ballerina was Caccialanza, a student of Cecchetti and of the American School of Ballet. She married Lew Christensen and was *prima ballerina* of the San Francisco Ballet, and a member of the faculty of the School of American Ballet. The other ballerina was the first produced from the School, Marie-Jeanne (Pelus de Quesada) who entered the School on full scholarship. She was later guest artist with Ballet Russe, Original Ballet Russe, and at opera houses in Chicago, St. Louis, and Minneapolis, and at Palacio de Bellas Artes in Mexico. The *premiers danseurs* were Christensen and Dollar.[22] Loring did not go to South America, but his *Billy the Kid* stayed in the repertoire. Balanchine's ballets for the South American tour were *Apollo* and *Errante,* and he composed *Ballet Imperial* and *Concerto Barocco,* which later became treasures in the repertoire.

Ballet Imperial, intended by Balanchine as a tribute to Petipa, illustrated its choreographer's statement that dancing today is more difficult, more complex, more intricate, more demanding, than in Petipa's era—although some people think that the great dancers of the past are incomparable. If Balanchine had meant *Ballet Imperial* to be a means of educating his critics he could not have more effectively proved that he could make an American technician comparable with the best. *Ballet Imperial* is seldom danced successfully outside the American companies.

On its return to the United States in October, 1941, the American Ballet Caravan dissolved, its finances depleted. Its members went their several ways, but Balanchine remained (as he has continuously done) as director of the School of American Ballet. Shortly after this, Kirstein entered the Army.

THE DANCERS AND CHOREOGRAPHERS

The period from 1933–1934—when Kirstein, with Warburg, founded the School of American Ballet under Balanchine—to 1941, when the Balanchine-Kirstein companies temporarily dissolved, was one of tremendous accomplishment for American ballet. The two companies provided a base for the development of American dancers and choreographers, and these came to the fore with such rapidity and brilliance that Balanchine and Kirstein appear like magicians, pulling dancers and choreographers out of a pair of top hats. Two of the most outstanding *premières danseuses* developed in those fruitful years were Boris and Lyon, former students of the Metropolitan Opera's ballet school, who had studied with Fokine. There was also Caccialanza, a ballerina with a remarkably fine "line." Ruby Asquith had danced in vaudeville with the Christensens. Elise Reiman had been a Bolm pupil. Jane Deering had been with the Littlefield Ballet. The student body has illustrious graduates in the persons of Lillian Moore, Beatrice Tompkins and John Taras, who are now, respectively, writer, dancer, and choreographer of note.

I write by hearsay of The American Ballet and Ballet Caravan, but discover that there is an overwhelming degree of admiration for Mary Ellen Moylan. Joining the School of American Ballet, she was a protégée of Balanchine and went with him to Ballet Russe for his tenure with that company. Balanchine choreographed a *première* role for Moylan in *Rosalinda,* and she danced in his *Song of Norway* and *The Chocolate Soldier.* She was a ballerina with Ballet Russe from 1943, and with American Ballet Theatre in 1951, and a *prima ballerina* of the Metropolitan. She is known to a large audience of the musical comedy theatre. Born in 1926, in Cincinnati, Ohio, Moylan studied all forms of dance, as well as voice and drama. She was a beauty and a fine dancer, and retired from American ballet (as Mrs. Robert S. Balies) after the birth of a son in 1958.

The boys were especially interesting. Three of them became extraordinary dancers and choreographers: Lew Christensen, William Dollar, and Eugene Loring.

Christensen came from a professional dance family and had been a dancer before joining Balanchine. Loring was an amateur actor in Wisconsin who came to New York to enter the School of American Ballet without previous dance training. And Dollar, who was born in St. Louis, Missouri, to a family without theatrical connections or aspirations, taught himself to dance.

Dollar worked, as a boy, in his father's modest business, without incentive or opportunity to dance. Once, casually leafing through a magazine, he found pictures and an article on dancing that aroused such a deep and lasting interest that he devoured every book he could find on the subject. With no help other than books, Dollar learned to dance well enough to win a scholarship to a local school, then went to New York and was accepted as a student by Mordkin. He was later the pupil of Fokine, and of Balanchine and Vladimiroff at the School of American Ballet. In Paris, Dollar studied under Volinine, famed for his teaching of the Classic *danseur* Variations. Dollar became a *danseur* of exceptional technical command and fine presence, until a leg injury restricted his career to that of a choreographer. He and Lew Christensen are considered the first *danseurs nobles* of American ballet.

Loring was the confrère of these *danseurs nobles,* but a character dancer. As a choreographer he eclipsed the classicists Christensen and Dollar, whose works have been influenced by Balanchine. Dollar's best known works are *Le Combat,* sometimes called *The Duel* (which he created for Janine Charrat), *Constantia,* and *Five Gifts.* He has been connected with American Ballet Theatre for several years and, on leaves of absence, directs a school in Teheran. Dollar has been especially notable as a *maître de ballet,* with American Concert Ballet, Ballet Society, and the de Cuevas Ballet. He was a member of Ballet International, the first company formed by de Cuevas in the United States in 1944, from which subsequent de Cuevas companies were drawn.

The factual accounts of Dollar's and Loring's early careers have the fascination of romantic fiction. They were not, as was Duncan, "free dancers" but the advocates of the cruelly disciplined Classic Dance, and although they came to it still young, they were past the early 'teens, which is usually the matured age for the male student in ballet. The marvel of their work lay as much in natural gifts as in perseverance and the will to dance. All over the United States the same will, the same longing, was transforming Americans into dancers. It seized on Henry George's granddaughter, as well as on the Pennsylvanian, Martha Gra-

William Dollar and Marie-Jeanne in Ballet Imperial *for The American Ballet Company, in 1941.*

ham. Loring had been an excellent gymnast at school, with no thought of being a *danseur,* until ballet was shown to him as an integration of theatre arts. He took from the Classic genre all he required: discipline, muscular command, a sense of form and spatial design. Dollar became a splendid Classic instrument. He danced in Balanchine's *Ballet Imperial, Errante, Concerto Barocco,* and others, and was the Angel in Balanchine's memorable *Orpheus and Eurydice* at the Metropolitan, with Christensen as Orpheus.

In retrospect, Christensen and Loring as dancers appear dwarfed by their works as choreographers. In a short time, these two, and Dollar, were the backbone of

Ballet Caravan. And their youthful inspirations have lasted uncommonly well. Nothing has surpassed *Billy the Kid* in its genre, and *Filling Station* is still lively and apt, in style and characterization.

The real and amazing extent of the developments in American ballet may be measured only against past accomplishments in ballet. Although it began in 1580 in France, the first great choreographer was not produced until Noverre (1727–1810). Russia had French choreographers until Ivanov (1834–1901) and even in his time he was dominated by Petipa, a Frenchman. The American dancer-choreographers developed under the Balanchine-Kirstein aegis were left singularly free and independent. They drew from the source, but developed their own strong personal inclinations.

In assessing the accomplishments of so short a span in American ballet, we are bound to hold in high esteem Kirstein's contribution. Without Kirstein, Balanchine would not have come to America; Christensen might have stayed in cheerful but ill-rewarded work in vaudeville and the theatre circuits; Dollar might have achieved eminence, but would probably have done so under a Russianized name, as one more American absorbed into the foreign métier. And Loring might have remained in the hardware business, with Little Theatre acting as his hobby, instead of becoming the first American choreographer.

Lincoln Kirstein has been called many things, among them brilliant, erratic, and quixotic. He has been described by the Balanchinephobe as an angry balletomane, or hailed by Balanchine's admirers with pious blessings. He was, in fact, a courageous man and a visionary, who gambled a fortune on his personal convictions. He brought to America a foreigner from the Ballets Russes genre—which had not had extraordinary respect in America. Balanchine was persuaded to come to America by Kirstein before Ballet Russe de Monte Carlo, under de Basil, made its electric appearance. Balanchine in America was immediately repulsive to the American opera house. The Balanchine ballet was not, in those days, dignified with the term "avant-garde"; it was considered a crime against The Ballet, judging by the tone of the vituperative press reviews of early Balanchine productions. The arch-criminal against the holy ideal of The Ballet (meaning the pre-Diaghilev ballet) brought a storm of criticism upon Kirstein. When Ballet Society was formed Kirstein came in for further, and even more indignant, criticism. The kindest attitude towards Kirstein in the early 'forties was one of sage head-wagging and solemn pronouncements of hopes doomed.

That he was quixotic is beyond doubt. When a government, state or monarchist, founds a ballet company, it does so on a firm basis of a school and one or more proven choreographers. Kirstein's School of American Ballet turned out a crop of dancers, but the company that Kirstein formed in 1936 as Ballet Caravan was founded for three unknown and inexperienced young Americans who wanted to choreograph. Few had heard of Loring, Dollar, and Christensen, who were as yet mere ciphers in the profession, known only as dancers of sorts.

And Kirstein had a catholic tolerance for imported influence and native creative force. Except for a none-too-successful essay into the Ballet Americana genre in *Alma Mater,* Balanchine made no pretence of acclimatizing his talents to suit the nationality of his patron. He went about his business much as though he were still with Diaghilev, and this is what Balanchine has said of Diaghilev: "He was not just the director or manager of a ballet company who guessed what the public would accept and what it would reject. He did not follow the public; the public followed him. He did not really care very much whether people agreed with him or not. What mattered to him was the work done by the best and most suitable choreographer, musician, designer and dancers. If they succeeded, their work was a success."

When Kirstein had the inspiration for a ballet about the American outlaw Billy the Kid he did not order it, delivered on commission, from the world-recognized Russian choreographer he had brought to America; he gave the idea to an American, Eugene Loring, who was allowed to work on his own. Such separation in Kirstein's stable of choreographers is particularly eloquent of Kirstein's honest purpose: he wanted to establish a school and a theatre for American ballet. A lesser man might have been pardonably anxious or conniving, and might have tried to persuade the world-recognized choreographer to collaborate with the unknown American experimentalist in choreography. *Billy the Kid* might have emerged, but not as the first American ballet. Nor would Eugene Loring have been able to become the first American choreographer.

Like Diaghilev, Kirstein was neither a choreographer nor a dancer. His contributions have been literary, in libretti like *Filling Station,* and in books, monographs and articles. His genius has been in recognizing, with something like precognizance, the future of the ballet. What he saw of Balanchine's Les Ballets 1933 in Europe, convinced him that Balanchine's ideals and work were the modern foundation of the Classic Dance. He has identified the New Ballet in its three stages: Fokine's dance of exoticism and picturesque nationalism; Massine's period of theatricalized character-dance and pantomime; Balanchine's style, the absolute form of the Classic Dance, the basis of ballet. In bringing Balanchine to America Kirstein in fact brought the tradition begun under Pierre Beauchamp (1636–1705), the first teacher of the French *Académie,* in 1671.

Dedicated as Kirstein was to the concept of ballet as the pure Classic Dance, he supported Ballet Caravan, whose important productions were *Filling Station* and *Billy the Kid.* Ballet had been set, traditionally, in scenes regal, romantic or fantastic. Under Kirstein's aegis it emerged in an American gas station and in the American West. Kirstein was the patron not only of the traditional and the pedagogic but also of the truthful and inventive.

Safe in the eye of the storm raging about him, Balanchine calmly went about creating his Neoclassic ballet. Kirstein tackled all phases of the storm, in print and out of it. Not even Kirstein knew what Balanchine was about. But Balanchine was quite sure. He had been sure since 1928, when he choreographed *Apollon Musagète.*[23]

In 1943, when I had begun to collect impressions and literary records for a book about American ballet, I was told that a millionaire named Kirstein had tried to found a theatre and had failed. True, there was an excellent school, also founded by Kirstein, that was still flourishing—with the best classical training anywhere. But Kirstein had organized three companies and placed one in the Metropolitan, and all had failed. Balanchine had gone on teaching at the School of American Ballet. Presently he seemed to have become absorbed as choreographer and ballet master in his old association with Ballet Russe de Monte Carlo.

But before the decade had turned into the next, lo and behold! Balanchine was the savant of American ballet and Kirstein was its savior!—or so ran the comments orally, and literally in press reviews. Kirstein was a Daniel and a Solomon, and he was later awarded the annual Capezio Award for his services to dance in America. He had founded the dance archives in the Museum of Modern Art in New York, with George Amberg as the first curator, and he had organized a company with Balanchine, Ballet Society. Ballet Society became resident at City Center as the New York City Ballet in 1948 and thereafter quickly rose to the front among internationally ranked companies.

In the years since that time Kirstein and Balanchine have been placed in a position of authority and prestige oddly founded on failure. The "failures"—of Balanchine at the Metropolitan, and of the defunct companies of the American Ballet and Ballet Caravan—have, in retrospect, become splendid accomplishments. The attainments of the School of American Ballet are without parallel in ballet history. No other national ballet in a comparably short time has been accorded such world-wide recognition in the Classic genre. No other patron of ballet has done more, in fact and spirit, than Kirstein.

BALLET SOCIETY

In 1946, after his period of Army service, Kirstein joined with Balanchine to form a new company, Ballet Society. It was non-profit, supported by subscribers, and the audience was therefore strictly a dilettante one. The company proposed to stage ballets and operas, and also to have lectures and dance films. Along with theatre tickets, members got books on ballet and the magazine *Dance Index* edited by Kirstein. John Taras created *The Minotaur* for the organization and Balanchine contributed *Four Temperaments, Symphonie Concertante, Divertimento* and the now famous *Orpheus.* Operas included *The Telephone* and *The Medium* by Menotti. The musical director was Leon Barzin and the ballet master Lew Christensen, and Jean Rosenthal, an artist with stage lighting, joined the company as Technical Supervisor. Ballet Society had its première on November 20, 1946, at the Central High School of Needle Trades, New York.

In pleasing its avant-garde audience, the company was immediately recognized as revolutionary in both artistic policies and repertoire. The *succès d'estime* did not support its costs, however, and although it spread a feast in dance, opera, music and literature there were not sufficient balletomanes, with enough dowries, to patronize it in royal fashion.

There were admirable developments in Ballet Society. Moylan became of ballerina stature and has never been surpassed in *Ballet Imperial,* and a *soliste* named Tanaquil LeClercq graduated out of full scholarship in the School into a fellowship in the company. LeClercq was a rarity—a *soliste* who never experienced the foot-soldiery of the *corps de ballet.* No epochal work like *Billy the Kid* was created but Christensen choreographed *Blackface,* in the same American Negro genre as Ruthanna Boris' later *Cakewalk* for the New York City Ballet.

The capricious public which had failed to support Balanchine's avant-garde ideas at the Metropolitan now took umbrage at being excluded from an elite balletomane society and Kirstein was called undemocratic. Balanchinephiles retorted that ballet in other theatres had been cultivated by aristocrats, not the hoi polloi. Outsiders clamored to be admitted to the closed Ballet Society when the news leaked out that *Symphony in C* and others were wonderful to behold. Maddened by rumors and hints, the public was determined to see what was going on in Balanchine ballet, and especially in the ballet called *Orpheus.*

Orpheus, a gem in the repertoire to this day, marked the turning point in the history of the Kirstein-Balanchine companies. It was not the Gluck *Orfeo* which Balanchine had staged at the Metropolitan as *Orpheus and Eurydice,* but the same theme treated differently, to a score by Stravinsky. The Leader of the Bacchantes was LeClercq, and of the Furies, Beatrice Tompkins; Francisco Moncion was the Dark Angel and Herbert Bliss was Apollo. The lovers were Maria Tallchief and Nicholas Magallanes. *Orpheus* followed Tallchief's debut at the Paris Opéra in 1947, where she had danced while Balanchine was directing the Opéra, while on a leave of absence during the summer recess of Ballet Society. The Parisian furore over Tallchief had centered on her extraordinary technique, and on the doubt that she was an American. "Tallchief" was said to be a blatantly symbolic pseudonym to indicate an American dancer, and she was suspected of being another one of Balanchine's Franco-Russe discoveries who had gone to the United States during the war. This was not improbable, as Fonteyn was here as a child and the present ballerina of the Royal Ballet, Svetlana Beriosova, was trained in New York by Anatole Vilzak, although she never danced in American ballet. Some of the audience went to see *Orpheus* because it was Balanchine ballet, and a large number went to see the American dancer who was called "Tahl Sheff" by the Parisians and had raised much the same sort of balletomanic fever as had the first American to appear at *l'Opéra,* Augusta Maywood.

Orpheus had a première for the Society on April 28, 1948, at the New York City Center, and the next evening was repeated for general admission. The public came, saw, and was conquered—with such suddenness that I must be pardoned for the irresistible cliché. It is interesting to note that *Orpheus* is a strong "story" ballet, as well as having a remarkable and lovely design in choreography and décor. Orpheus and Eurydice are mortal and passionate. The Dark Angel represents compassion, and Apollo represents the imperishable nature of music. Orpheus in death lies buried, but from his grave the God of Music invokes Orpheus's lyre, indicating that beyond death music shall endure and live as the soul of Orpheus. With sets by Isamu Noguchi and lighting by Rosenthal, Earth and Hades are pictorial contrasts of blue and scarlet as Orpheus passes through them in quest of his dead wife, Eurydice. The movement and the music are splendid and compelling, and the plot and emotion are of the most romantic and exalted kind. Ballet's best seems to be its most tragic, on the evidence of the classics. A great many believe that *Orpheus* is Balanchine's masterpiece.

Shortly after the public admission to Ballet Society programs, which continued as premières for subscribers and were then offered to the public at the box office, Kirstein was invited to place his company in permanent residence at the City Center theatre, where it would command a civic title. Kirstein accepted and Ballet Society made its première on October 11, 1948, as the New York City Ballet. The première program included *Concerto Barocco, Orpheus,* and *Symphony in C.* Opened to the mass audience, the New York City Ballet was at once a huge success with both critics and general public. It attracted and retained a faithful and earnest public, more dilettante in its attitude to ballet than is the average theatregoer in America. The audience, in its fringes, is rather precious in attitude toward other ballet companies, and toward other forms of dance in America. It remains, into the second decade of City Center's resident company, a special sort of audience—one more balletomane than made up of fans.[24]

With the emergence of the New York City Ballet from Balanchine's classical academy, Kirstein and Balanchine had founded a school and a company, and now they had found a theatre. In doing so they seemed to have almost matched the magic with which Apollo plucked the lyre from Orpheus's grave. In 1952 the company was invited to represent the United States at the Paris Exposition, "Masterpieces of the Twentieth Century," and there it was acclaimed. It has since appeared in every major cultural center in Europe and the Near East, and its popularity with balletomane audiences and authoritative critics has established it as the foremost classical company on the American continents. There is a major opinion that the New York City Ballet is technically the best of contemporary companies in the international ballet theatre.

THE COMPANIES

IT is only since the establishment of major companies that we have been able to claim an American ballet. From the time of Maywood, America has produced individual dancers of excellence, and from Duncan's era Americans have been recognized as a creative force in twentieth-century dance. But these individual dancers were inevitably absorbed by their adopted countries, just as American ballet has absorbed the choreographers Balanchine and Tudor, the *prima ballerina* Danilova, and the *danseurs* Eglevsky, Franklin, and Youskevitch. Today American ballet is recognized for a distinctive style and is established in companies large, stable and important enough to occupy a "company" category in international ballet. Now we are judged by our repertoire, not by individual dancers.

The companies represent, in their histories, the "present" of American ballet. They would seem to wholly contain its future, also, because American ballet is autonomous, and has no patrons other than its audiences. If the companies perish, American ballet as it exists now will cease to be. A company is, traditionally, nursemaid and despot to its members and in the legitimate ballet theatre the choreographer and the dancer depend on the company not only for economic livelihood, but also for creative life. The audience sees only the brilliantly lighted space behind the curtain; the rest of the company, from its founders and patrons to its stage mechanics and wardrobe women, has little identity. Even the orchestra in the pit is apt to be overlooked in the footlights' glare, unless it makes more execrable sounds, or plays with considerably more artistry, than are the norms for music at the ballet. But all these entities, a reservoir of many arts and crafts, sustain the company; each is a little world in itself and yet a part of the larger world of ballet.

In America, the companies depend entirely on the support of the audience, and their future lies in the artists and the teachers and students in the ballet schools.

THE NEW YORK CITY BALLET

When the School of American Ballet began in 1934 the classes were irregularly attended, by seventeen, or nine, or only three girls. Balanchine began to choreograph a ballet, designing it on each day's class, as they varied. One day a girl came late to class; at another time a girl fell while she was rehearsing. Balanchine left these real-life incidents in the ballet. When boys joined the class he invented steps and movements for them, linking these with his choreography for the girls. As the ballet got more and more complicated and difficult in performance Balanchine left out the dancers who could not keep up with the difficult passages, and put them into simpler ones. Obedient only to the music, and based on the perfect execution of movements designed by the choreographer, the ballet *Serenade* was thus created.

The invention was practical: Balanchine placed his dancers in diagonal lines because they were an odd number, and the ballet began not with movements of the leg, but of the arm, so that the girls could practice hand movements. But the choreographer was a master craftsman and *Serenade* became an extraordinary ballet. First performed by The American Ballet at the Adelphi in 1935, it was borrowed by Ballet Russe in 1940 and costumed by Lurçat, and the principal roles were danced by The American Ballet's ballerina Marie-Jeanne, and Youskevitch and Franklin of the Ballet Russe. In 1941 Balanchine mounted a new production of *Serenade,* with costumes by Alvin Colt, for a South American tour. In 1947 *Serenade* was taken into the permanent repertoire of the New York City Ballet, costumed by Karinska, and in 1950 was given its foreign première at the Royal Opera House at Covent Garden. Among the dancers associated with *Serenade* are Diana Adams, Ruthanna Boris, Alexandra Danilova, Melissa Hayden, Marie-Jeanne, Tanaquil LeClercq, Yvonne Mounsey, Mary Ellen Moylan, Janet Reed, Maria Tallchief and Patricia Wilde. Other than Franklin and Youskevitch some of the *danseurs* in the various productions of *Serenade* have been Herbert Bliss, Leon Danielian, Frank Hobi and Nicholas Magallanes.

The ballet is one of the signature works of the New York City Ballet, and is seen every season. In its present staging, it has a blue background, and the twenty-six dancers are costumed in the same color. The music is Tchaikovsky's *Serenade in C major for String Orchestra.*

When Balanchine's American Ballet merged with Kirstein's Ballet Caravan to become American Ballet Caravan for the South American tour, Balanchine mounted *Concerto Barocco,* set to Bach's *Concerto in D minor for Two Violins.* Two principal roles were danced by Mary Jane Shea and Francisco Moncion. Moncion, a native of the Dominican Republic, came relatively late to ballet, at the age of nineteen. He was a student at the School of American Ballet, dancing in that school's performing company and later with the New Opera Company. His career was interrupted by army service from 1942 to 1945, but he joined Ballet Society when it was formed in 1946.

Concerto Barocco was danced by the American Concert Ballet in 1943, and by Ballet Russe in 1945. For the première appearance of the New York City Ballet

Concerto Barocco—*a Balanchine work of pure dance.*

Marie-Jeanne appeared in a principal role. Sometimes with Berman décor, and at others with a bare backdrop and the dancers in practice clothes, this ballet has often been repeated. It is one of the hallmarks of Balanchine's Neoclassicism, extraordinary for linear beauty and, equally, for the perfection of execution by the New York City Ballet. Ballets of pure dance cascaded from the Company like the fountains of the Maryinsky, marvelous, glittering, and in gushing degree. They made a chronological table by which to mark the growth of the dancers. In 1953, critic Doris Hering assessed this development. She noted that *Serenade,* with its gentle simplicity, gave way to *Four Temperaments,* which displayed a steely and capricious command of masterly movement design. There was a new elegance, with more complex counterpoints, in *Concerto Barocco,* and in *Symphonie Concertante* Hering discerned a new richness in texture, a velvety quality of gesture, a courtliness of behavior. These developments spanned thirteen years, and were the fruit of the School of American Ballet. Balanchine's most distinguishing attitude was his preoccupation with music. The *Symphonie Concertante,* to Mozart's *Sinfonia Concertante in E-flat Major,* was clearly an extension of the music, with the ballerinas interpreting Violin and Viola.

Balanchine's ballets instantly pleased the audience's eye. They presented beautiful shapes, moving about with serene confidence and no apparent effort, as though both earth and air were their natural elements. But for many in the audience there was a sterility in so much physical beauty. Such people longed to have Balanchine turn back to works like his *Orpheus* and *Le Baiser de la Fée*, or to the poignant love of *Night Shadow,* which he choreographed for Ballet Russe in the 'forties. Looking for stories or meanings in the ballets, the audience could find no plot or characters, and no circumstance or expressive idea. Disappointed, it now and then invented episodic but *meaningful* expression for itself, but Balanchine reiterated what his ballets had stated: they were, in *Serenade,* for example, simply dancers in motion to music. There was no concealed story, and if the audience sought one, there was the music's—a serenade. "A dance, if you like, in the light of the moon."

Balanchine seemed to have no intent toward realism, and he contrasted strongly with other choreographers in America who were spending every effort to teach dancers how to appear natural onstage, and how to move like real people in ballets set in themes and places true to life. Balanchine's dancers did not interpret emotion, as we commonly think of emotion, and there were no plots which required them to walk, or run, or converse with each other in ordinary ways. The several identities of his dancers almost vanished in the uniform perfection of dancing. No personality was exploited and some were so integrated in the Balanchine ballets as to assume, in artistic spirit, the selfsame aloof and beauteous quality of the dancing. Maria Tallchief had shown dramatic gifts in the Ballet Russe, and on guest appearances with her alma mater and Ballet Theatre continued to produce kindling, responsive interpretations of ballerina roles, but in the Balanchine ballets she became a scintillation of dance, less a woman of feeling and more and more the gifted instrument of the choreographer. She had a physique and aplomb perfectly adapted to Balanchine's Neoclassicism, and under Balanchine's training she became a brilliant dancer, able to execute virtuoso feats that were labeled incredible by the critics, doing so with such impeccable Classic technique that her virtuosity ranked second to her classicism.

Tallchief had been an exciting Gypsy in Balanchine's revival of *Le Baiser de la Fée* for Ballet Russe. She became, in *Orpheus* for New York City Ballet, a wonderfully tender and loving Eurydice. Yet her fame began to rest almost solely on her glittering technical forte, and Balanchine created some imperial roles for her: *Symphonie Concertante,* the *Sylvia pas de deux,* and the role with which she is indelibly stamped, The Firebird. A classicist by taste and training, Balanchine was also an accomplished mime, but related dance-play did not appear in his ballets, although in 1958 he revised the theatre piece *Seven Deadly Sins,* to a Kurt Weill score sung by Lottie Lenya, which he himself had created twenty-five years earlier, before he came to America.

In 1947, commissioned by Ballet Theatre, Balanchine choreographed *Theme and Variations,* one of his most radiant dance designs, and the grandest for the *danseur.* Created on Youskevitch it was, for many years, danced only by Youskevitch, but has recently been danced by Erik Bruhn and Royes Fernandez at American Ballet Theatre. Having no *danseurs* with the qualifications of these,

Maria Tallchief and André Eglevsky in the Sylvia pas de deux.

Balanchine concentrated on choreographing his most difficult and intricate works for the *danseuse*. He often created two or more ballerina roles in a single ballet, and used the *corps* with as much purpose and flexibility as other choreographers usually gave to soloists. In many of his abstract ballets the visual marvel was not only in the complexity of dance design, but the contrasting forces in it, as when he held a *corps* motionless, in a pose that sustained the movement, and meanwhile his ballerinas—one, two, or more—were held by the *danseurs* at the other end of the stage, and turned and lifted, in the extension of the movement. In Balanchine's musical apotheosis of ballet, tension opposed to relaxation created the effect of dance pouring from one end of the stage to the other, with no set places where it began or ended.

Nicholas Magallanes and Tanaquil LeClercq in La Valse, *Balanchine's Neo-Romantic ballet that in mood and style differs from the choreographer's characteristic classicism.*

Balanchine's ballerinas were too young to have been influenced by the stars of the early twentieth century. Although Tallchief had the gift of a dramatic dancer, and the exquisite Tanaquil LeClercq a mobile one suited for characterization, they were developed in Balanchine's Classic principles and never in the mold of an Elssler or a Pavlova. Balanchine often choreographed ballets that were grand dancing, but not grandiose ballet. By intent, and perhaps by expediency, he defined ballet as akin to Schopenhauer's Music—"expression of the world, a universal language." He created no *demi-caractères,* and employed no regional and colloquial subjects, and did not adventure into the operatic. Likened to Petipa, he resembled Petipa chiefly in that he developed a prodigious technician ideally suited to his choreography. Like Petipa, he was a prolific choreographer. Petipa's Variations remain the standard by which the classical dancer's perfection is tested, and there may be little doubt that Balanchine set awesome standards, especially for the ballerina.

Balanchine maintained that the lyric is often close to the lethargic, and he shunned lethargy. His use of *adagio,* coupled with the tensility of the Balanchine dancer, produced an ineluctable calm full of power. His ballerinas in *adage* did not have the soft, warm, feminine charm of the old classic style. They were radiant, with a sharp, glittering starriness. Tallchief was said to sparkle like a diamond, and no great lyric ballerina emerged to shed a pearly glow on the New York City Ballet.

The unquestioned authority of Classic Dance rested in Balanchine and the Company, and for the comparatively small and serious audience at City Center there was an educational process, a development of taste, for the avant-garde principles of his ballets. Balanchine was a subject of controversy abroad, where his detractors said he was fighting a war of attrition with beauty in The Ballet, but some of the foreign disapproval of his ballets resulted from their being altered when danced by foreign dancers whose physiques and training were not typical of the Balanchine American *danseuse.* Also, Balanchine's works were best seen in a theatre like City Center, for he had naturally arranged them for the small American stage. *Palais de Cristal* at the Paris Opéra was subtly different from *Symphony in C* in the United States. *Le Baiser de la Fée* was seen in impoverished surroundings in America, compared with its setting at the Opéra. But even in such circumstances, Edwin Denby pronounced *Le Baiser* to be ballet at its grandest, and poetic theatre at its truest. Many of Balanchine's abstract ballets required the ballerinas to dance Variations as lengthy and difficult as those in a Petipa ballet, and for a great many of his fans Balanchine's ballets began to have the noble, evocative and timeless character of ballets usually referred to as "classics." But if the truth were told, the most loyal Balanchine audiences contained members eager to see him represented in the full-scale magnificence of ballet theatre, and anxious to have him create again in the genre of story ballet. The taste for grand ballet, as proved again and again at the box office, was rooted in America. It caused a great deal of the early esthetic quarrel over George Balanchine and the New York City Ballet.

If we look back as far as the ballets of the Scots and the nymphae we see that ballet in America had been a transposition of life to the stage, either in fact or disguised as dreams and fancies. The Scottish James in *La Sylphide* was embroiled with an airy nymph, but he himself remained singularly human—in fact, that is the basis for the tragedy of *La Sylphide*.[1] All the elaborate ballets, whether they were the "wondrous ballets" of the Kiralfys, or artistic reconstructions like Lee's *Giselle,* had something resembling a story that was communicated in dance, often with pantomime, and a narrator in a stage aside. Into the twentieth century, the audience had a strong predilection for "story" ballet, and was never offended or bored by the most fantastic plots. Pavlova enchanted in *Coppelia,* and second in popularity was another Imperial Russian ballerina, Ekaterina Geltzer, who appeared with Mordkin's All-Star Imperial Russian Ballet in a repertoire of excerpts from the most "ocular" ballets: *Coppelia, The Legend of Azyade, The Seasons,* and *Swan Lake.* With the assistance of program notes—never the most explicit guide to the ballet, but as serviceable as a score card for identifying the players—the audience grasped the essentials of Girl, Boy, and Villain. Their trials and triumphs unreeled in antique form, but to the present day, the audience never tires of agonizing with Odette and becoming infuriated with fickle Prince Siegfried. On tour through the more robust provinces the sorcerer Von Rotbart was soundly hissed. The Pavlova-Mordkin tours, together and separately, were the only authentic Imperial Russian Ballet performances ever seen in the United States, and those ballets had a power impossible of communication by succeeding dancers. Converted to ballet by these most fanciful and lovely roles, the audience believed that such "ocular" works were the ideal form and implicit métier for classical dancing.

Fokine was the next influence, and he kindled, especially in American choreographers, the passionate intent voiced by Prince Wolkonsky: *ballet dancing should have a meaning.* Fokine worked in *ballet d'action—Cléopâtre, Schéhérazade, The Firebird, Petrouchka, Le Coq d'Or, Cinderella, Bluebeard*—in which characterization and plot were especially telling, and his so-called "storyless" ballets plainly conveyed a character or a locale. *Le Cygne* is not a dancer performing *bourrées* but a beautiful white bird in death-throes; the Poet in *Les Sylphides* is the music's composer, with his Muse; the magnificent male in *Prince Igor* is that revolutionary character, the Polovtsian Chief, by which Adolph Bolm restored the *danseur* in twentieth-century ballet to the virility he had possessed before the Romantic Era. (After *Prince Igor,* the most accomplished character *danseuse* would be hard put to match the male *en travestie.*)

Next came Massine's influence, a permanent one for the American audience. Massine composed the first contemporary symphonic ballets but he impressed America more with ballets of strong action, developed characterization, and relevance between action, character and plot, or story-line. For example, his *Le Beau Danube* and *Gaîté Parisienne,* although episodic, perfectly represent certain places and certain people. Massine himself states that, while his style of composition is closely connected with the musical theme, when the music did not give him what he required for light and shade he contrived opportunities on his own for contrasts. Since Massine himself danced in his best ballets, his delicate sense of style and atmosphere and his sinuous elegance are impressed forever on roles like the Hussar in *Le Beau Danube* and the Peruvian in *Gaîté Parisienne. The Three Cornered Hat,* to Manuel de Falla's *Tricorne,* actually begins with cries of *"Olé! Olé! Olé! Olé!"* from behind the curtain, and the sounds of castanets and hand clapping. Once the curtain rises and the music and the dancing begins, the audience is enraptured by one of the most enchanting "ocular" ballets ever created.[2] Nothing, in its métier, could possibly be finer!

In his American era, Massine was not simply the greatest choreographer in America. He was, as de Mille records, the biggest box office draw in the business. He deserved his professional reputation as a dancer and choreographer, and also as the single force that reorganized Russian ballet in the western world. When he left America it was to exert his tremendous influence on the Sadler's Wells Ballet, where its first *prima ballerina,* Fonteyn, was being developed.

With such influences as forerunners, Balanchine began to be discovered in America. He had already discovered what he needed to know about American dancers. He knew that they were well fed, and therefore had stamina and strength, more so than European and Franco-Russe students, who were precariously reared in the aftermath of the Russian Revolution and World War I. The Americans had bounce and verve and instinctive syncopation. The Franco-Russe contingent had been carefully indoctrinated in Imperial Russian ballet, and a part of this indoctrination was a complete indifference and contempt for any other form of ballet. Americans had no tradition, either of the French, Italian or Russian schools, as an academic standard, but they had learned to jump for a basketball, to run in track sprints, to tumble in high school gyms and to swim in the nearest municipal pool or rural swimming hole. They never argued when Balanchine directed them to turn, twist or leap in certain ways, because they had no basis on which to contradict him, or to despise what he was doing as not being the absolute form and style of The Ballet. But they could do anything Balanchine set them to do. And they did!

The audience now split into -phile and -phobe, with a *brouhaha* reminiscent of older, foreign controversies, such as the debate on the brilliance of Petipa's classicism, versus the "interpretative" dance of Fokine. Paradoxically, Balanchine was labeled both as an anarchist and an anachronism. The first accusation stemmed from the dynamic propulsion of his dance design, in contrast with the old, flowing line. He was rebuked, at the same time, for regressing from the ideals of the New Ballet to the strict and narrow pedantry of the Classic Dance, whose great forte was an elegance of deportment. No one understood, for some time, that Balanchine's ideas of movement were not classifiable as Nineteenth or Twentieth Century, or as Russian, or Franco-Russe. The ideas were characteristic only of George Balanchine.

He turned out a covey of glittering *danseuses,* whose aplomb and strength so dominated the ballets that all artistry seemed obscured by prodigous physical achievement and the Balanchine ballerina, especially Tallchief, was condemned as cold and expressionless. Treating his ballerinas without protocol, Balanchine put two or three together in a ballet, in roles of equal importance but keyed to various styles and fortes. Sometimes he advanced the soloists, and even the *corps,* to paramount positions, eclipsing the ballerina temporarily. He was intent on a uniform perfection, not on stars. Here it is useful to remember that when Balanchine began to work in Russia Fokine had already left and Pavlova, consummate artist and intensely individual performer, had been replaced at the Maryinsky by Tamara Karsavina, a fine technician who was wholly the instrument of the choreographer. Later, when Balanchine joined Diaghilev, Fokine had left the company. So Balanchine, alone of his confreres, did not come under Fokine's "interpretative" influence. Balanchine developed alone, following Blasis' precepts of the academic ballet as developed by Petipa, and his work as a choreographer was strongly influenced by the avant-garde theories of modern music.

Using music never designed by composers for dancing, Balanchine has filled with dance the time measured by the music, and has set his dancers to moving in tempo different from that of the ballet score. A choreographic genius, he is, first and always, a musician, and in both aspects of his art he is inventive and fearless. His original use of movements and sequences of steps in the Classic métier has invested the *danse d'école* vocabulary with spirited contemporary life. Familiar leaps and turns, *glissés* and *arabesques,* have been made pristine and beautiful. He is unrivaled in the complexity and the intricacy of his dance movement, and his dancers regularly execute neck-breaking feats.

The Balanchine-Stravinsky collaboration is one of the most significant in music and dance, and has marked off signposts in the fortunes of Kirstein and Balanchine. *Orpheus* is said to be responsible for the Company's enviable residence at City Center. It is the only American company of its rank with a home theatre. *Firebird* established Tallchief in the international hierarchy of ballerinas. In 1958 Stravinsky's new *Agon* was made into ballets in America, Europe and England, and the American version by Balanchine was hailed as a revolution in dance theatre. A ballet difficult for its dancers to perform and its audiences to understand, it is eulogized by some as a turning point in ballet, with the influence on ballet exerted on art by Giotto and Picasso. An opposite opinion relegates it to mere Balanchine pyrotechnics in dance, calling it arid and engineered, and a denial of everything conceived by Noverre and Fokine. A third, and innocently happy, stratum of the American audience simply accepts *Agon* as "American ballet," considering its athletics to be sublimely descriptive, the ballet itself to be classically witty. The naïve view is furthered by the costuming of the ballet—black practice clothes, with the *danseurs* in white cotton T-shirts.

The New York City Ballet furnishes George Balanchine with the most generous and exclusive stage for his choreography, and the School of American Ballet furthers his inflexible authority in the Classic Dance. From these founts Balanchine draws an endless stream of noble, witty and handsome inventions, which form the Company's unique repertoire.

THE REPERTOIRE

It is large and ephemeral and, on Balanchine's word, more than half of it is comprised of absolute novelties. The active repertoire includes five of Robbins' ballets, and three by two choreographers developed in the company, Todd Bolender and Francisco Moncion. These are Robbins' *Afternoon of a Faun, The*

Melissa Hayden and Francisco Moncion in William Dollar's Le Combat (The Duel).

Cage, Fanfare, Interplay and *Pied Piper;* Bolender's *Souvenirs* and *The Still Point;* and Moncion's *Pastorale.* Others are Ashton's *Illuminations;* Dollar's *The Duel;* and *The Unicorn, The Gorgon and The Manticore,* an opera-madrigal with music and lyrics by Gian Carlo Menotti and choreography by John Butler. *Con Amore,* which Christensen created for the San Francisco Ballet, is included. It was first danced in the New York City Ballet by the principal dancers of the San Francisco Ballet. Balanchine's ballets dominate the repertoire, and he does not recognize a national style for ballet, only Ballet Americana in subject matter. His excursions into the genre have been playful, with the exception of the fine *Ivesiana* to a score by the American Charles Ives. His American subjects have ranged from Joe Collegiate to the race horse Native Dancer.

Balanchine has composed more than one hundred ballets. The few failures include *Roma* (1955) and *Jeux d'Enfants* (1956)—the latter with Moncion and Barbara Milberg. Almost forgotten are *Balustrade* (1941) for Original Ballet Russe, and *Trumpet Concerto* (1950) for Sadler's Wells Ballet. The choreographer has a greater sense of humor than many of his more devout admirers and continues to mystify and surprise the City Center audience—the best-behaved balletomanes in the United States. Outside that theatre, although Balanchine's stature is unquestioned, there is controversy between the avant-garde and the ordinary audience as to Balanchine's pre-eminence in American ballet. The Neoclassic balletomanes authoritatively define Balanchine as separate from all contemporary choreographers, and therefore exempt from critical assessment. The less authoritative faction, adherents of "dancing with a meaning," find a Balanchine-dominated repertoire too astringent and repetitive.

It is of note that a new and more flexible choreographic policy has begun to operate in the Company with the adjunct of choreographers drawn from outside. Some rather adventurous introductions of ballets and dancers have made recent seasons exciting and precedent-breaking, while well-known works have continued to be staged, like harmonious signatures to the long years of work and hope with which the Company was created.

The New York City Ballet's repertoire is characterized by Balanchine's cerebral ballets which appeal more to the intellect than the senses. Two on the active repertory list are examples of his inventive and intricate dance design, the characteristically close relationship between his dance and music, and the storyless ballet and the ballerina forte of his repertoire. They are both marked by Balanchine's sense of form in space with which he makes mobile architecture.

Divertimento No. 15 is a recent revision of the *Caracole* of 1952, to Mozart's *Divertimento No. 15 in B-flat major* (*K. 287*). Balanchine describes it as designed for "a constellation of five ballerinas (of which the one who dances after the fifth movement is the *prima*), three *danseurs,* and a *corps de ballet* of eight girls." The ballet exactly follows the music: *Allegro, Andante Grazioso, Minuet, Andante—Fourth Movement,* and *Allegro Molto—Andante.*[3]

The Four Temperaments, a première ballet for Ballet Society, survives not as a period piece but as a translation in dance and music of the Greek interpretation of the four humors: Melancholic, Sanguinic, Phlegmatic and Choleric. The music is by Paul Hindemith, and a somber violin solo introduces *Melancholic;* a waltz with a gay tempo and dancing with open movements characterize *Sanguinic;* a moody *danseur* is diverted by four girls and a gay melody in *Phlegmatic;* and a ballerina dances a Variation for *Choleric.* The four humors are preceded by *Theme,* with three *pas de deux.* Principal roles were first danced by Tallchief, LeClercq, Herbert Bliss and Todd Bolender, in costumes of abstract patterns, later replaced by plain ballet practice clothes.

Agon and *Gounod Symphony,* in the gala Tenth Anniversary of the Company, set new challenges for the dancers and audience of the New York City Ballet, and augured another decade, in the nineteen sixties, of Balanchine's surprises. In that season he also revived a work first produced in his "Les Ballets 1933," *Seven Deadly Sins,* which is not a ballet but a theatre piece combining song and dance. Its plot is an ironic modern Restoration-type drama. Hugely acclaimed, *Seven Deadly Sins* made a sort of musical comedy star of Allegra Kent, and capsized the Classic ivory tower in which the Balanchinephiles had immured the New York City Ballet. This claque had been severely jolted before, with *Stars and Stripes,* danced to Sousa's marches. The debate has not yet been settled as to whether Balanchine intends that as a compliment to the United States or a joke on its natives who love a brass band and a parade. When Balanchine deliberately invokes the genre *americana* he does so in a formal ballet like *Western Symphony,* to a score by Hershy Kay. The rondo is an American mood in the frame of the *danse d'école.*

Robbins' ballets on the active repertory list are indicative of his range and impulse, from the serious *The Cage* to the playful *Afternoon of a Faun;* from the noble *Fanfare* to the contemporary *Pied Piper.* Moncion's *Pastorale,* a title Balanchine used in 1926 for a ballet about a film star's elopement with a telegraph messenger, is a gentle, romantic story of a blind man and a compassionate girl. Bolender's *Souvenirs* satirizes the pre-jazz era, and *The Still Point* is the classical dancing of a modern work he created for Mark Ryder and Emily Frankel, about loneliness. The Butler-Menotti madrigal-fable of the *Unicorn* is a theatre piece that fuses massive effects of opera and ballet. The Unicorn, Gorgon and Manticore of a medieval bestiary are combined with a human Poet in a modern allegory.

Few other choreographers have created for the Company. Tudor mounted his *Lilac Garden* and composed *Camille* and *La Gloire,* of less consequence than his other works. Ashton more successfully created *Illuminations* on LeClercq, Hayden and Magallanes, and *Picnic at Tintagel,* based on the Arthurian characters Tristram and Isolde, in which Diana Adams had a poetic role.

In 1959, in the gala Tenth Anniversary season, two ballets were added by the choreographers Lew Christensen (*Octet*) and Swedish Birgit Cullberg (*Medea*). *Octet* was created for the occasion; *Medea* had its American première, having been originally created for the Royal Swedish Ballet. Christensen has long been associated with the Company, but Cullberg's association was new. A pupil of Kurt Jooss and another Laban pupil, Sigurd Leeder, she has been the choreographer of the Royal Swedish Opera since 1951.

Patricia Wilde and Jacques d'Amboise in Native Dancer, *one of Balanchine's* Ballet Americana *works.*

In the third part of its Tenth Anniversary year the New York City Ballet presented some distinguished visitors, the Japanese Imperial Household's Gagaku, an ancient orchestra of musicians and dancers. The most provocative foil to the ritual Orientals, and to Classic Dance itself, was the unprecedented collaboration of Balanchine and Modern dancer Martha Graham in a work called *Episodes*. An hour-long work, it was set to miscellaneous music by Anton Weburn, a modern Austrian twelve-tone composer (1883–1946). Graham choreographed and danced the première role of what may be called the First Episode, and her work related a definite occurrence, based on historical fact: the tragedy of love and power between Mary, Queen of Scots, Bothwell, and Elizabeth I. The Graham ballet was lavishly costumed, and appeared with a décor by David Hayes, as did Balanchine's work. His "episodes" were plotless and danced in practice dress, and represent cerebral dance of such intellectualized caliber and unemotional statement that its interpretation may not be made by any one observer. We shall have to wait for Balanchine's own description of its choreography and intent, for until he chooses to reduce it to the written word *Episodes* remains a challenging enigma. John Martin, who exactly records the seasonal triumphs of the New York City Ballet, has written his own and most erudite explanation of *Episodes,* in which he declares Balanchine a "preacher" who has demonstrated the peril in which modern man has placed the race—ultimately, a fateful and undimensional conclusion—and adds that Balanchine makes a noble restatement of humanity at the ballet's close, restoring "something of a declaration of faith."

The Weburn opus, if only in the collaboration of the outstanding Modern dancer and the avant-garde Neoclassicist, has established a boundless precedent for the New York City Ballet. *Episodes* was the first work choreographed by Graham for a company independent of her own, and the first work in which Balanchine shared honors with a representative modernist. In this conjunction, Classic and Modern Dance bridge a gulf once believed impassable by the loyal and dissenting fans of Graham and Balanchine.

The top-heavy repertoire of Balanchine's cerebral ballet would become more splendid in juxtaposition with others, especially in dramatic themes. The company has now grown far beyond being a merely adequate technical tool of choreography, and its roster includes dancers of strong and varied dramatic styles. Adams, Hayden and Tallchief have found and matured distinctive abilities. Their artistic growth must inevitably proceed out of their technique into the subtle development of force and form that the term "artistry" connotes; otherwise they shall become immured, like static flies in amber. Kent shows a mobile gift of interpretation, and her expressiveness does not one whit impair her Classic technique. Wilde dances with an exhilaration unmatched in her theatre, but she is too honest and fine a dancer to be fated forever to leap and jump for the notion of jubilant movement alone. The best, the most matured of Balanchine's dancers hold true to the purity of the Classic form, and in the galaxy he has framed for them they glow with an elegant luster, or glitter with brilliance. When he has given them roles of depth in characterization the Classic style has been kindled with a sweetened fire.

And perhaps no eye better perceives this than the *maître's*. He has, after all, an eye that retains the memory of the Maryinsky's stage, and if he has not set one of such lavish design for American ballet it may be because he does not command the economy of an imperial treasury. There was once a faction so loyal to Balanchine that it resolutely blinded itself to the charm of a more ample style for the New York City Ballet, preferring to speak loftily of intellectual classicism as the sole forte. There were others who perfectly recalled another type of Balanchine ballet, in which the action of the dance, along with music, libretto and scene, conveyed clear meanings and evocative feelings to the audience. After hearing Balanchine discussed so arbitrarily by the avant-garde who lay exclusive claim to him, it is a decided pleasure to encounter in the Company's ballet book for its tenth anniversary the statement that with *The Nutcracker* in 1954 "Balanchine proclaimed once more that ballet is not only dance, but a synthesis of dance, pantomime, music, poetry, and painting."

In the Company's beginnings, a rough and ready disposal of dancers thrust the best technicians into the most technically difficult roles without much scruple as to whether the dancer was suited to the role by style or temperament. Now, in its twenty-fifth year, the Company under Kirstein and Balanchine begins to exert a more judicious choice in casting, especially among its several ballerinas. These, under the *prima ballerina* Maria Tallchief (in 1958–1959 on maternity leave from the Company) are alphabetically listed under a new management policy, which incongruously places the young Allegra Kent before Violette Verdy. American Ballet Theatre, when known as Ballet Theatre, experimented with this democratic arrangement of its principal dancers and then reverted, under audience pressure and box office demand, to the protocol of ranking stars. The only company of importance which has ever succeeded in maintaining anything like a non-starring roster is the Royal Danish Ballet, using the euphemism "solodancer," which in no way alters the theatrical prestige, or the artistic recognition of the *Who's Who* in Danish ballet, either on the stage of the Royal Theatre or in the audience. The New York City Ballet plays largely to a small dilettante audience in New York, and is the arbiter of Neoclassicism in international ballet, but its brisk box office business depends on the annual production of *The Nutcracker,* which grosses princely sums in every city where it has a regular season—usually, New York and Chicago. The initial success of *Seven Deadly Sins* in 1959, and its box office returns, point to it as a possible source of revenue equal to *The Nutcracker.*

Although both these money-makers are Balanchine compositions there is nothing in past history to indicate that Balanchine is adapting himself to an admiring general audience. He has always inhabited the world made for him by Kirstein with peculiar serenity, diffusing a powerful influence on the ballet scene, and appearing uncaring and unaware of his effect on it.

His pride of the moment is the advance of the male technician in the New York City Ballet, as shown by the fact that he is working less for his beloved *corps de ballet,* and composing works like *Agon,* which the Company could not have performed ten years ago. With this alteration in the old balance between its *danseuses* and *danseurs* the New York City Ballet enters a new technical phase. Balanchine, and other choreographers, now have in the Company both masculine prowess and feminine flexibility. It remains, most excitingly for American ballet, to be seen how this physical power will influence the artistic maturity of the New York City Ballet.

The Company chooses to ignore the well-known classics—and its adherents incline to disparage the productions of these by every other company, from the Royal Ballet to the Ballet Russe de Monte Carlo. Balanchine has reconstructed *The Nutcracker* from *Casse Noisette,* and has produced his own untraditional versions of *Swan Lake* and *The Firebird.* They have caused endless arguments at home and abroad, but remain in the repertoire and are used to debate the respective merits of succeeding ballerinas in the roles of Balanchine's Swan Queen and Firebird. The first was said to have lost her original regal position to the Little Swans and the corps, and the second is sometimes referred to as "Balanchine's poor, emaciated Firebird" by balletomanes loyal to Fokine's or the carefully revived *Firebird* of the Royal Ballet. Balanchine has scrupulously identified these works in the Company repertoire, as *Firebird, 1949* and *Swan Lake, 1951.* The birds he has created are of a totally different feather from those of Fokine and Petipa-Ivanov.

The Company's significance is larger in ballet as an international art than it is to ballet in America. It does not tour the United States in one-night stands, as do the Ballet Russe de Monte Carlo and the American Ballet Theatre, but has European seasons of short duration in the large continental cities and in dance festival centers, from Edinburgh to Florence. The refusal to tour the United States, in the one-night-stand circumstances that govern ambulant American ballet, is a company policy to protect the quality of its performance from the threats of fatigue, illness and accident to the touring dancers. As a result, the New York City Ballet is better known abroad than at home although the Company has had short seasons in Chicago, Washington, D.C., Los Angeles and San Francisco.

Critics in England, Europe and the Near East rank the Company as the best of the Classic contemporary theatre. In Japan, it was authoritatively ranked, in performance and choreographic design, as superior to the Bolshoi Ballet. In Italy, Denmark and Austria critiques are universally complimentary. Oriental audiences are puzzled by its lack of mimetic tradition, and find the Balanchine-Robbins tempos (neoclassical and American) too sharp, abrupt and fast. They complain of the machinelike velocity and mechanical nature of the dancers in the ballets. In France, Balanchine is considered a renegade to the classic French ideals of beauty, in which flowing grace and elegance are essential. The French consider a Balanchine dancer as the *"danseuse mécanique,"* in *"le style Frigidaire."* The lack of opulence in décor, and sometimes in costume (although many of the ballets are costumed by Barbara Karinska, whose work is a spectacular adjunct to design in American ballet), offend the French notion of the ballet. The English greatly admire the technique of the dancers and Balanchine's command of the Classic vocabulary, but regard the ballets as beautiful elaborations of classroom exercises, devoid of heart or matter, and so prolific in the

Balanchine-dominated repertoire as to make for dull theatre, in the evening's unvaried performance. These performances, in the Diaghilev métier, are usually of two or three ballets, and until Balanchine's reconstruction of *The Nutcracker* the Company offered no full-length ballet that consumed an entire program.

Despite Balanchine's profound themes, such as *Orpheus,* his European detractors persistently categorize his works as "abstract" and dismiss the major part of his repertoire as *rigaudon*—showy, frivolous dancing, without heart or substance. For the Balanchinephile—the most intense balletomane in the United States—the Company's forte lies in its "cerebral" ballets and its accomplished dancers.

THE DANCERS

As the only major American ballet company with a home theatre, the dancers have more permanence and security than many of their contemporaries. Kirstein remains the Company's general director, and goes on tour with it. He is, actually, still as much a part of the Company as is Balanchine.

Backstage at City Center the Company behaves quite like one with an ancient tradition. There is an atmosphere settled and almost sedate, compared with the frenzy of many a backstage melee. Instead of excitement, there is a huge dynamo of ordered energy. The stars have dressing rooms to themselves, in which they receive visitors with a far more lordly air than the hasty chat in the wings that is the rule for dancers in less favored companies. And the dancers who have established themselves with the Kirstein-Balanchine company are notably literate and fluent in discussing their profession. To a man, the veteran dancers are pro-Balanchine in the enduring controversy about the degree of feeling (or "interpretation") in Balanchine ballet. The dancers who have been developed in the brilliant Balanchine choreography resist the implication that they are of the mechanical variety. They speak, learnedly, of technical perfection as the acme of traditional ballet, and declare that "interpretation" or "emoting" in ballet is merely a way of disguising imperfect or mediocre technique. There are those, in and out of the Company, professionals and balletomanes, who dispute the separation of "technique" and "interpretation," and insist that one contains the other; this is generally the opinion of the Balanchine dancer. The veteran dancers at the New York City Ballet are not so much a troupe of performers, with the usual United States meaning, as they are artists in ballet. This comes not wholly from their formidable technique as dancers but from their deliberate, almost dedicated attitude toward ballet. Forced in dancing to subjugate all personality traits that might endow them with the quality of a "star," they have much the same attitude when they discuss their profession and their company. One or two are inclined to grow unctuous about the superiority of the Company's repertoire over that of all other American ballet—sometimes, over all other contemporary ballet! One lovely creature, with perhaps three years of a *soliste's* career behind her, made the sweeping statement that all the old classical ballets should be junked, and that American ballet is only to be distinctively recognized in the New York City Ballet's repertory. These convictions come, in large part, from the dancers' having to defend themselves against the calumnies of *"danseuse mécanique"* and *"le style Frigidaire."* In fact, the Company has been, as a unit, on the defensive for its whole career, but has staunchly lived up to its convictions. It is avant-garde in repertoire, nonconformist to older mores in ballet, and impervious to the proximity of modern ballet in the American genre.

During its first decade, the Company had a character far less stable than that of the Bolshoi Ballet, with which it has been too fondly compared by some of its admirers. It has just entered a period of violent change whose effects can scarcely be more surprising than their abrupt introduction. The rank of its *premiers* has been reduced by the democratic alphabetical roster, and the change in musical direction means a wide difference in temperaments of conductors. The Balanchine ballets relate more than others to music, so that the music for the Balanchine ballets is a paramount part of the Company. Leon Barzin, long the musical director, resigned in 1958 and was succeeded by an English conductor, Robert Irving, who comes from the Romantic atmosphere of the Royal Ballet.

The most serious flaw in the character of the Company is its absolute dependence on Balanchine; serious because Balanchine is human and mortal. A great ballet company requires an imperishable force on which to base its tradition. By comparison, there is no similar threat of dissolution for the Bolshoi, the Paris Opéra, or the Royal Danish Ballet.[4] There is little risk for the company closest in age to the New York City Ballet, the Royal Ballet. Even if the New York City Ballet became state-supported, and was established in a proper opera house of its own, it would still lean wholly on Balanchine. There is the evidence that without Balanchine it might shatter like an edifice of glass. Remarkable for its stability, and the singleness of direction in its artistic policy, the Company is a Balanchine creation, but it must find its own strength, and enough to stand independent of influences and contributing artists, before it can be called a great ballet company. When Balanchine's personal direction is withheld, the caliber of performance and the Company's esprit de corps deteriorate alarmingly, as in one New York season when Balanchine worked in Copenhagen, and in the 1958 Pacific tour when he did not accompany the reduced troupe to Australia and Japan.

The Company is affected, not in its performance standards but in its particular identity, by the absence of the *prima ballerina* Maria Tallchief. It is easy to understand this. The *prima ballerina* of a ballet company is not made by program billing, nor is she a pretty fancy. Her title stands for the mystical force with which a ballerina sustains her company. In the United States the title "ballerina" is so misused as to make it useless except for an informed member of the audience. The average theatregoer thinks of a ballerina as a toe-dancer, and believes that a *prima* of the species is a ballerina who collects the largest number of leading roles in the repertoire. In fact, a ballerina is formed as mysteriously as a butterfly from the pupa. In any fair-sized company there are always a dozen talented dancers, and seldom a dancer with the mark of a "ballerina." This is the inflexible rule of the ballet. It is only long after an impeccable technique is acquired, and the truly gifted dancer goes beyond the mastery of her craft into a realm of artistic accomplishment, that she emerges as a ballerina. All that is coarse and showy is gone and ballerina attains a quality that I, like many others, must describe as "mystic." In this glow the ballerina and her company work and grow. No great ballet company exists without an aspect of this mystic climate which breeds the *prima ballerina.* Every company's tradition has ample proof of it. Often the proof lies more clearly in the loss than in the possession of the ballerina, as when Danilova left the Ballet Russe de Monte Carlo.

In the New York City Ballet much of the repertoire has been created on its first *prima ballerina,* who has been a protégée of Balanchine since 1943. In at least one role (the Siren in *Prodigal Son*) she has been more suitably replaced, but in most of her roles she is irreplaceable. The competent ballerinas who follow her either interpret the roles too literally or do not possess Tallchief's individual effulgence. The difference is noted not to disparage technique, but to point out the total impossibility of making one skin fit another body. Balanchine's Variations for Tallchief, as in *Pas de Six,* are as closely fitted to Tallchief as a skin and she shines in them with crystalline power, bright and sharp as a diamond. The other ballerinas of the New York City Ballet have several other, and precious, attributes. Adams has a silky quality that makes her revered as the first lyric American ballerina, especially in the English view; Hayden has opalescent tints that she shows wonderfully in her character tones; Wilde is all nerve and sinew, with a free and joyous power of elevation; Verdy has the ability to gleam from whatever setting she adorns with a pearly lambency, or a twinkling brilliance. Any one of these—Adams, Hayden, Kent, Verdy, Wilde—might grace an inferior company in *première* rank. Their uniform excellence makes them an enormous cachet, but their close juxtaposition creates tremendous artistic responsibilities for the New York City Ballet. In Tallchief's absence, through no fault of the five ballerinas, they appear to be more in contest with each other than in harmony in a company. Rejoining the Company at the end of the 1959 season Tallchief took her alphabetical place on the new roster, following a dancer named Dorothy Scott, who joined the New York City Ballet in 1957. Her place, however, was qualified by Tallchief herself, and her *prima* position, established in *The Nutcracker* in 1953, remained unquestioned. In Tallchief's serene radiance every other of the Company's notable ballerinas took on a brighter glow and a deeper lustre. The first native *prima ballerina* of American Ballet, entering her eighteenth year of dancing, had the mysterious quality which Edwin Denby described in 1949: a tragic beauty and a distinction that set her apart.

Principals and *corps de ballet* alike have strong techniques. The only flaw that the most carping Balanchinephobe may find is the general restraint of feeling in dance, which—when seen in a full evening's program of cerebral ballets— causes audience complaints of aridity. In the main, the dancers are the products of the School of American Ballet, but many of the Company's best were recruited from other schools and other companies.

The senior *premier,* André Eglevsky, is a contemporary of Youskevitch, and a veteran of European and American ballet companies. He came to the United States as one of de Basil's prodigious young performers, and has for years sustained the masculine roles of New York City Ballet. Famed for his elevation, he is a tall, strong *danseur,* with spectacular virtuosity, and able characterization.

Among the *solistes,* Diane Consoer came from the Joffry Theatre Ballet, and Sonja Tyven from Ballet Russe, where her sister is a ballerina. Francia Russell is a London student of the Russian teacher Vera Volkova, now the *maîtresse de ballet* of the Royal Danish Ballet. Adams and Hayden came to the Company from Ballet Theatre, as did Verdy. Adams and Allegra Kent, like Tallchief, are Americans. Hayden and Wilde are Canadians. Verdy is a French ballerina created in Europe, and assimilated, in that precise rank, into American ballet.

The usual "remote and cold" appellation given the Company's ballerinas does not apply to Hayden or to Verdy, who entered the Company with their dramatic personalities already developed in other companies. Both are beautiful and dynamic performers and, like Adams, have exceptionally flexible bodies.

Hayden was a member of Ballet Theatre and Ballet Alonso, and the ballerina of the Chaplin film "Limelight." She was guest *première* with the Company in 1950, joining it in 1955. She has precision in the Balanchine choreography, but her strong personality has not been subdued. Like Nora Kaye, Hayden does not easily take over a created role, and does not happily alternate with another ballerina in it. She dances with passion and dedication, and is dramatic by temperament. Her admirers find a likeness to Elssler in her style, and Hayden is said to be not at all adverse to attempting the great classic ballerina roles, in full-scale productions. She created in the United States Clorinda in *Le Combat,* and strong roles appear to be her forte. In Tallchief's absence, although not so ranked, she is obviously of *première* importance. Hayden is a very intelligent dancer, and possibly the most energetic American ballerina of her era—and this character, with a combination of fine Classic technique and histrionic gifts, endows all her performances with fire and feeling. She has successfully ignited, with her own warmth, some cool Balanchine ballets, giving to them a new and interesting dimension onstage. Most suited to a dramatic role, and happiest when she creates it in première, Hayden is wonderful to see in *Medea,* in the title role. She has taught in her own school, and danced with various companies in concert work including a stint as *prima ballerina* of the Metropolitan Opera—all of which give her an energy and theatrical sense which augment her ballerina stature. Fine as she is in "cerebral" repertoire, she moved back into her forte with happy alacrity in *Medea,* and in 1960 appears with Ruth Page's Opera-Ballet on annual tour. In 1959, with Eglevsky, she toured in Ballet Quintette.

Diana Adams was developed under Agnes de Mille, for whom she danced in musicals on Broadway. She was later with Ballet Theatre, and married (and later divorced) the English character *danseur* Hugh Laing. Adams is suited to romantic roles but she has adapted herself in exquisite performances of Balanchine's Neoclassic works, among them *Agon* and the *Gounod Symphony.* A very tall bal-

Violette Verdy, Jacques d'Amboise and Melissa Hayden in Birgit Cullberg's Medea.

lerina, she might be lost in a more traditionally classical company, but here she is well cast and sensitively directed by Balanchine. She has the high Balanchine extension, but more pliancy in the upper back and arms than is the norm for a Balanchine ballerina. Like Tallchief, Adams is blessed with the dancer's rare gift of musicality, and is endowed with a lyric line. By temperament she has a sweet and gracious demeanor. There have been glimpses in her of unearthly and melancholy beauty, such as is associated with the great Romantic ballerinas, but as yet no role has been created for the full exploitation of her style.

Patricia Wilde is the first-rate *allegro* technician of the Company. She is a strong, bold technician and very fine in roles Balanchine has specially tailored to her gifts such as the *Native Dancer* and *Waltz Scherzo* of the 1958–1959 season. She was a soloist with Ballet Russe from 1945, and the memorable creator of one ballerina role in Balanchine's *Pas de Trois* from *Raymonda*. She also created the Hoop Dance in *Night Shadow*. She studied ballet in Canada, and was a pupil; in the United States, of Dorothie Littlefield and the School of American Ballet. Although overshadowed by Hayden, Wilde's *allegro* technique has won her a claque all her own, especially in New York and on the West Coast.

Allegra Kent is a visually and technically exciting dancer, whose early development marks her with the rare appellation of the "born ballerina." She was the pupil of Nijinska, as was Tallchief, and also studied under Maracci. At fifteen she went on full scholarship into the School of American Ballet and was there developed, in the tradition of the ballerinas Marie-Jeanne and Tanaquil LeClercq. Before she was twenty, she was a principal dancer in the New York City Ballet. She has danced some of the roles created by LeClercq, whom she somewhat resembles in mobility and interpretative instinct. Able to dance lyrically in *The Still Point* and brilliantly in *Divertimento No. 15,* she was promoted to Balanchine's Swan Queen in 1958, and received enormous acclaim as the dancing Annie in *Seven Deadly Sins.* In this arresting role, by the happy coincidence of her perfect suitability in dance and characterization, and the popularity of the theatre piece, young Kent eclipsed all her sister ballerinas in the second half of the Company's 1958–1959 gala anniversary.

Violette Verdy is a product not of the Paris Opéra, as is Yvette Chauviré, but of the modern French ballet. She was born Nelly Guillerm in 1931, and was first the pupil of her mother, and later of the teachers Gsovsky and Rausanne. She appeared in the French film *Ballerina,* in 1949, for which her name was changed to Violette Verdy. A member of Les Ballets de Champs Élysées, she came from the group of *enfants prodigieux* organized under Roland Petit and Janine Charrat in 1944. In 1950 she joined Petit's Ballets de Paris and was the *première danseuse* by 1953, creating the ballerina roles in *La Perle* and *Le Loup*—the second a ballet about a werewolf. She was an actress at Theatre Marigny, with the mime Jean Louis Barrault, from which experience her dancing derived added scope. In 1945 she was the ballerina of Festival Ballet, then came to America and appeared in two movies with Leslie Caron. In 1955, still the *première* of Petit's company, she was a ballerina at La Scala. In the late 'fifties she joined American Ballet Theatre until the end of the 1958 season, when she accepted an engagement with the New York City Ballet—the first given a European ballerina, which caused conjectures as to the future artistic policies of the Company.

Verdy has very pretty feet and legs, and the flowery wrists of the French style, with characteristic elegance of the arms and head. She is soft or brilliant, at will, and despite a very petite figure has exceptional dramatic force. Verdy is so far removed in physique, style and temperament from the typical Balanchine ballerina that one wonders whether Verdy will conform to the New York City Ballet or the New York City Ballet will acclimatize itself to Verdy. Her last significant role with American Ballet Theatre was *Miss Julie,* Cullberg's modern ballet about an aristocratic lady who seduces her butler and commits suicide. It is a Scandinavian work of somber theme and Tudoresque implication.

In the blinding light of its constellation of ballerinas the New York City Ballet *danseurs* are barely discerned. Coming quickly to the fore is Jacques d'Ambroise, an American born about the time Balanchine came to America. D'Amboise has creditably danced Balanchine's Apollo, and in Cullberg's *Medea*. He looks, and dances well, as partner to the dramatic Hayden, but hardly suits a *danseur noble* role in style or looks. At present, he causes the most excitement for his prodigious jumps, and his élan and Puckish looks remind some older balletomanes of the curious Arcadian quality of Vaslav Nijinsky. As a modern Pan, he has danced in Robbins' *Afternoon of a Faun*. His widest renown comes not as a *danseur* but in the movie *Seven Brides for Seven Brothers,* with choreography by Michael Kidd. He is wholly the product of the School of American Ballet, which he attended from childhood, and is one of the few original members of the Company. While d'Amboise is of front rank, and a dancer of elevation, he may not be said to parallel Eglevsky, whose European finesse and romanticism are not qualities of d'Amboise's style. What is more interesting to note is that d'Amboise is taller, stronger, with more *brio* than Moncion and other veterans, and he may already be seen as another new facet of the New York City Ballet.

Of high standing in the Company are the *danseurs* Herbert Bliss, Todd Bolender, Nicholas Magallanes, Francisco Moncion, Roy Tobias, and Jonathan Watts. These veterans have given the Company estimable service, and they are skilled and intelligent dancers. Another outstanding *danseur* is Robert Barnett, who year after year brings to dancing a thoughtfulness so conspicuous and consistent that he is notable in American ballet.

The new generation, of which d'Amboise is the star, has other men of exciting promise like Arthur Mitchell, Conrad Ludlow, and Edward Villella. Mitchell is one of the few Negro classical *danseurs,* and a former student of the New York High School of Performing Arts, who entered the School and Company on scholarship. His forte is jazz, which he also teaches at the School. He has had an important role in *Agon,* in première performance, and has also danced in other roles, including one in a revival of *Filling Station.* Ludlow is a protégé of the San Francisco Ballet, school and company, whose American looks and athleticism are pronounced attributes in his classic dancing. Villella, who has been trained from childhood by Balanchine, already has shown a fine *bravura* style, and a range which includes roles in *Western Symphony* and *Symphony in C.* In mien, he adapts easily to both classic and contemporary styles, and at his age, twenty-one in 1959, his possibilities as a *danseur* seem endless. He was seen as demonstrator in the Classic Dance in the television show *Dancing is a Man's Game,* presented by Gene Kelly for "Omnibus."

Deni Lamont, formerly a principal dancer with Ballet Russe de Monte Carlo, joined the New York City Ballet in 1958, and was seen as the Chinaman in the Christmas-televised *Nutcracker,* a role he danced with great success for Ballet Russe. Lamont's twin fortes are characterization and elevation, and his roles with Ballet Russe, those of the Peruvian in *Gaîté Parisienne* and Ko-Ko in *The Mikado,* were especially suited to his style—so much so that his advent into the New York City Ballet is yet another surprising development of the Company's new decade. A foreign importation is Bengt Anderson, a young *danseur* trained in the Royal Swedish Ballet, and holding soloist rank there. His teacher is Mary Skeaping, *maîtresse de ballet* of the Swedish ballet, and formerly of England's Sadler's Wells Ballet.

The new and striking developments of the New York City Ballet are immediately visible in the confluence of its members. To those mentioned, Erik Bruhn was added in his 1959 contract to appear in 1960 with the New York City Ballet. Bruhn brings to the *danseur* ranks a virtuosity equal to Eglevsky's and a graciousness of demeanor as notable as his technical skill.

No other single new addition augers more change in the Company's style than the advent of its new ballet mistress, Janet Reed, who replaced Vida Brown, long the assistant to Balanchine in mounting such ballets as *Symphony in C* for the Royal Danish Ballet. Reed is a veteran of American ballet, trained by William Christensen, who danced with the early Kirstein-Balanchine groups, and was a star of Loring's Dance Players. She is peerless in interpretation as a character dancer and a superb comedienne. The marvel of Janet Reed is that despite technical weaknesses and faults she has the most endearing qualities of any *danseuse* of her generation. In retirement she has frequently danced character roles with the New York City Ballet, as the Countess in *The Unicorn, the Gorgon and the Manticore.* In her ability to project onstage and develop the full scope of a role, Reed is the feminine counterpart of William Christensen. As a strong personality, if not as a strong technician, Reed as ballet mistress from the 1958–1959 season will undoubtedly affect the dancing of the New York City Ballet.

The Company, passing from its first decade to its second, was never more exciting and never so acclaimed. No other company, certainly none in America, exceeds it in quality. The first decades of advancement must be directly attributed to the American Kirstein and the self-exiled Russian Balanchine, and the visible fruits of their endeavor are the dancers in their company. The best of these dancers have a marvelous *aplomb, terre à terre* and *en l'air,* which marks a distinguished lineage. They move and stand and dance like aristocrats—a word that their creator, Balanchine, has precisely defined as "the rule of the best."

Of *Serenade,* his first American ballet, Balanchine said: "The class contained, the first night, seventeen girls and no boys. The problem was, how to arrange this odd number of girls so that they would look interesting. . . . Boys began to attend the class and they were worked into the pattern."

Well within the next twenty-five years George Balanchine would solve his problem. In his matchless style, with American boys and girls, he designed some of the most dazzling patterns ever beheld in ballet.

BALLET RUSSE DE MONTE CARLO

This is the company that the American audience knows best and calls the premier company of American ballet. Founded in Europe in 1932, it has been American since 1938. Cut off from Europe by World War II, Ballet Russe became wholly American in character and almost entirely American in membership, and has subsisted for twenty years as an ambulant ballet company in continental America. Its dancers are the greatest troupers in ballet, and their audience holds them in greater affection than any other company. Their audience is by no means ignorant of ballet, because it has had the chance to see, in the Ballet Russe, the great stars of the international theatre from Danilova, the last of the Imperial Russian ballerinas, to Chauviré, the present *prima ballerina assoluta* of French ballet.

Ballet Russe does not occupy one theatre, but dances all over the Americas. It appears in full panoply of décor and orchestra where no other major company goes, and as a result has formed much of the American audience's taste in ballet. Although retaining the glamorous title Ballet Russe de Monte Carlo, the Company's American characteristics are especially marked, not only by its large percentage of American personnel but also by its liberal artistic policy, which permits the leading dancers to develop their individual styles rather than subjugate them to a company métier. As a result, the leading dancers have included some of the most prodigious "stars" in American ballet—personalities with vivid identities for the audience. While the New York City Ballet and American Ballet Theatre are distinguished in repertoire, the Ballet Russe's distinction lies in its dancers. It has filled theatres for twenty years without materially altering its repertoire, but the dancing is *con amore,* the forte is characterization, and the technique virtuoso, excelling in speed and elevation. To the balletomane *prêcheur* the dancing is altogether too emphatic, and the dancers are reproved in New York for being too showy, in the manner of "musical" stars. To the audience outside New York, especially to the cities whose annual visits from the Ballet Russe are the sole link with "live" ballet, the requirement and demand is for exhilaration and energy—and it is this *audience en masse* that supports the extremely healthy life of the Ballet Russe. Its director is a former Russian banker, Sergei J. Denham, who has been an executive of the American Ballet Russe from its inception. The Company is his life's work, and he goes on tour with it, supervises every performance, and determines its artistic policies. A living legend in American ballet, Denham is a master executive, and the first man to steer a big ballet company successfully through twenty years of the rough seas of American ballet. The Company disbanded once for financial reasons but formed again after a lapse of two seasons, and now seems about to enter a new phase of its veteran existence, with the vital introduction of Polish ballet influences, and some styles of Soviet ballet.

With its former *prima ballerina* Alonso and *premier danseur* Youskevitch as guest artists, its 1958–1959 roster listed Nina Novak as *prima ballerina,* Borowska and Tyven as second ballerinas, Zoritch and Howard as *premiers danseurs;* Grantzeva, D'Antuono, Kowalska, and Tennyson as *solistes;* and Slavin, Gillespie, Edmund Novak, Harsh and Collins as the principal *danseurs.* They are the present generation of ballet troupers who have made the Ballet Russe de Monte Carlo the best known and the best loved of the American Ballet companies.

THE HISTORY

From the turn of the century, *ballet russe* has been symbolic of glamour in the international theatre, and *de Monte Carlo* has been its usual cognomen. Diaghilev's defunct Ballets Russes had an amoeba life in René Blum's Ballets de l'Opéra de Monte Carlo, and de Basil's l'Opéra Russe à Paris. Blum's survived until the Germans invaded France and Monaco.

In January, 1932, a merger between Blum and de Basil produced the first Ballets Russes de Monte Carlo of the contemporary swarm; this is the company that Hurok brought to America in 1933. Its choreographer was Leonide Massine. After an engagement at the St. James Theatre in New York it went on tour; and although in that first season Hurok lost money, it was a great artistic success. He continued to bring the company back annually, and in so doing fostered a taste for ballet in the American theatre. Next to the Americans who were the actual founders of companies and schools, like St. Denis, Shawn, Kirstein and Chase, no one did more for American ballet than the impresarios Morris Gest and Sol Hurok.

Blum parted from de Basil in 1934 and in the autumn of 1935 Hurok moved the Ballet Russe de Monte Carlo (shorn of the plural endings in *Ballets Russes*) into the Metropolitan Opera House. This was nothing short of an artistic coup —ballet suddenly acquired the significance of opera. Led by the astute Hurok, New York theatregoers made the season a great success; Massine became the fount of Ballet and Danilova the ornament. Until then, a goodly number of the audience might have hesitated in the pronunciation of "ballet"—some were inclined to give it full phonetic value as late as the nineteen forties.

Internecine warfare spiced and eventually split de Basil's company, and in 1937 Massine terminated his contract after a performance in Oakland, California. Massine went back to Monte Carlo and Blum, who again entered into an artistic partnership with Massine. This time Massine was backed by American money, and the company was called World Art, Inc., and later renamed Universal Art, Inc. Two of the founders were Julius Fleischmann and Sergei Denham.

In the 1938–1939 season Hurok relinquished his management of de Basil's Ballet Russe de Monte Carlo and became the impresario for Massine's company. As both these companies clung to the title *Ballet Russe de Monte Carlo,* they propagated the confusion that still exists among American balletomanes and will probably plague the readers of this book.

De Basil's company lost to Massine's the *prima ballerina* Danilova, the ballerina Toumanova, a European soloist named George Zoritch, and the American dancers Eleanora Marra, Roland Guerard, and Marc Platoff. In addition, Massine brought in the English *prima ballerina* Markova, *danseurs* Serge Lifar, Igor Youskevitch, and Frederic Franklin, and *solistes* Nathalie Krassovska and Nina Theilade.

In 1938, de Basil's company, called Ballet Russe du Col. de Basil, appeared in England as the Covent Garden Russian Ballet, supported by a company, Educational Ballets Ltd., which was founded by Victor Dandré, Pavlova's husband,

and Germain Sevastianov, who married the "baby ballerina" Baronova. For this company Fokine arranged *Cendrillon* and *Paganini,* and Lichine revised his *Le Fils Prodigue,* and composed a new ballet, *Protée.* In 1939, with de Basil as chairman of Educational Ballets Ltd., this many-titled company became the Original Ballet Russe.

London balletomanes were caught up in the great ballet "war" of 1938, between Massine and the Colonel (de Basil clung to his military title through his career as impresario). De Basil's company was at Covent Garden while Massine's was dancing around the corner in Drury Lane. A law suit was fought between de Basil and the American backers of Massine (Universal Art, Inc.) over the exclusive rights to produce the Diaghilev repertoire. De Basil won the suit, but it was believed that Universal Art had triumphed—they had Massine and the two reigning *prima ballerinas,* Danilova and Markova.

The company that is now Ballet Russe de Monte Carlo has been American since 1938, supported by American money. At first it was Russian in spirit, in the *ballets russes* genre. Its repertoire and backstage lingo were Franco-Russe. American dancers who joined the Company learned to read the rehearsal board, and changed their names to sound properly foreign in that coterie. The audience that sat down in the theatre and waited for the *zanovess,* the Russian for curtain, to rise onstage, expected to see Russian ballet.

Until de Mille's *Rodeo* the language of the Ballet Russe remained foreign, although by then the Company had taken other American ballets into the repertoire. De Mille recalls that she thought it an advantage that the Russians spoke a language she could not understand: in this way she was spared their objections when she was teaching them to dance the characters of *Rodeo.*

Massine resigned from the Ballet Russe in 1942 and the direction of it passed wholly into Denham's hands, where it still lies. During his tenure with the Ballet Russe Massine and Danilova filled theatres to overflowing, including places as large as the Hollywood Bowl. A legend of "champagne ballet" was to remain after Massine's symphonic ballets (the first of the genre) had been forgotten by the public. In Danilova, partnered by Massine, Franklin, and later by Leon Danielian, the personification of the "champagne ballet" legend was to survive into the nineteen fifties.

Meanwhile, de Basil brought his company to America in 1940 under Hurok's management (Hurok was, at the same time, presenting Massine's Ballet Russe) and the companies followed each other into the 51st Street Theatre while the Metropolitan Opera was closed for repairs. New York balletomanes saw Danilova, Markova, Eglevsky, Youskevitch and Franklin in Massine's company. In de Basil's they saw the three "baby ballerinas," Baronova, Riabouchinska and Toumanova.

Original Ballet Russe, with Hurok as impresario, began a tour of Central and South America, but in Havana eighteen of the dancers went on strike, alleging breach of contract. The tour was canceled, and the troupe stranded. Marina Svetlova reminisces that the dancers used to faint regularly, in the daily class they gave themselves, because they were living on little else but oranges and tangerines, the cheapest food they could buy in Havana. The company eventually returned, bankrupt, to the United States, and de Basil put his company under the management of Fortuno Gallo of the San Carlo Opera Company. This impresario lasted two months in a Washington season, after which the management was terminated. In December, 1941, de Basil took his company to South America, and stayed for four years. He returned under Hurok's management to the United States in 1946 and 1947 for seasons at the Metropolitan, and toured in the 1946–1947 season. In autumn, 1947, the de Basil company went to Europe. In 1951 de Basil died in Paris, and his company disbanded.

Col. Wassily de Basil was an able administrator, if a controversial artistic director. It has become the fashion to sneer at him but it must be remembered that his peregrinations about the American continent and in Australia are largely responsible for the interest in ballet there. He was a star-maker, especially of baby ballerinas and boy wonders, whom he recruited from the studios of the emigrée Imperial Russian Ballet teachers. He created a company for Danilova and her contemporaries after Diaghilev died, and he provided a stage for Balanchine and Massine. The latter created, for de Basil, *Jeux d'Enfants, Le Beau Danube* and his first symphonic ballets, *Les Présages* and *Choreartium*.

In his first company, l'Opéra Russe à Paris, de Basil revived a number of the Diaghilev ballets, under Romanoff. In the second company, the first of the Ballets Russes de Monte Carlo, he maintained the Diaghilev style through Serge Grigoriev, later the guide for the English ballet's reconstruction of the Russian classics. In 1940, de Basil commissioned *Graduation Ball* from Lichine, which remains among the best-loved works in Ballet Russe repertoire. In Covent Garden in 1947, de Basil had a brilliant company, including the dancers Jeanmaire, Riabouchinska, Lichine, Dokoudovsky, Jasinsky, and his (de Basil's) wife, Olga Morosova.

After de Basil's death the Grigorievs briefly revived the company for a 1951–1952 season in London, and a tour.

The American company, Denham's Ballet Russe de Monte Carlo, had a flexible artistic policy, governed chiefly by the effort to please the audience—and that audience was set in its ideas of ballet. It wanted Russian ballet and this was construed as pyrotechnics in dancing and sumptuous décor. Ballet Russe, however threadbare the décor grew in lean times, satisfied the taste for spectacular dancing. And Ballet Russe survived. Without anything like the government subsidies and royal patronages of the English ballet, which was growing in England at the same time that Ballet Russe was becoming Americanized, the Company held together and had a sweeping influence on the popular taste.

The glib statement that would eventually persecute it in critiques ("not a first-rate company") harmed its popularity not at all, and to summarily dismiss the Ballet Russe as no consequence to American Ballet would be tantamount to dismissing the mass audience from America.

It was this audience that supported Ballet Russe—if not with as much security as the state and royal ballets, then certainly with as much, and more, affection. Costumes and scenery might grow seedy—and did—as the years went by, but the Ballet Russe still generated excitement when it came to town, over the largest part of America.

The war years did more to Americanize its character than anything else. Russian dancers, *sans* passport, could not go on tour to Canada and places outside the United States, and Denham hired American girls as replacements. In recording the war years we should note that Ballet Russe's male dancers became personally involved. Among these, as a Second Class Seaman, was the *danseur noble* Youskevitch. When he was on shore leave he could be seen partnering Danilova as a Cavalier in *The Nutcracker* or a fickle lover in *Coppelia.*

The star roster of Ballet Russe remained of glittering significance under Danilova as *prima ballerina.* The second ballerinas were Mia Slavenska and Nathalie Krassovska, and the *danseurs* Youskevitch, Franklin, Zoritch and Guerard. Slavenska, born Mia Corak in Yugoslavia, was a pupil of Egorova, Kchessinskaya and Preobrajenska in Paris, and of Celli in New York. She danced in Nijinska's company and came to America with ballerina status. A woman of remarkable physical beauty, she is reputedly the most reliable ballerina in her theatre and her contemporaries say that she has never given a poor performance in her career. Slavenska was among the first dancers to form a touring company—her Ballets Variant.

Krassovska, the daughter of a Diaghilev dancer, Lydia Krassovska, was born in Leningrad and studied in Russia and then was a student of Preobrajenska. She, too, was a member of Nijinska's company and also of Balanchine's Les Ballets 1933. Until 1952–1953 she danced as Krassovska, but is now known by her father's name, Leslie, in English ballet.

Under Youskevitch and Franklin the Company had nobility and character— both dancers, at various times, were artistic directors—and began to develop some of the most outstanding dancers of the native theatre. One, who joined Ballet Russe in 1943, was Leon Danielian, who had danced with the Mordkin Ballet and Ballet Theatre. He has remained with Ballet Russe, to its great profit, and is one of its choreographers, represented on the repertoire by *Sombreros* and other works. He is also on the faculty of the Ballet Russe de Monte Carlo School.

Some of the girls who were part of the *corps de ballet* in the war years are among the best-known names in American ballet—Tallchief, Chouteau and the Ballet Russe's ballerina, Tyven, who at first danced as Gertrude Swoboda.

The Company pioneered a development of national ballet with *Ghost Town* (1939) by Platoff, now better known as Marc Platt, and *Lola Montez* (1947) by Caton. *Rodeo,* in 1942, was the Ballet Russe's great American ballet, but before *Rodeo,* Massine adventured jauntily into ballet Americana with *The New Yorker, Saratoga* and *Union Pacific.* However, these did little more than place American characters onstage. In 1779 Maximilian Gardel had done this in the third act of *Mirza,* and there was another European ballet, called *Les Mohicans,* which identified an American as a dancer costumed in an Indian roach of feathers. In 1920 Bolm composed *Krazy Kat* from an American comic strip that is said to have been the forerunner of Mickey Mouse cartoons. No American ballet like that of Ruth Page, Lew Christensen and Eugene Loring was created by the European ballet.

Prima ballerina assoluta *Alexandra Danilova as* Lola Montez.

When *Billy the Kid* was produced in 1938 it was not at once considered revolutionary. It had its widest effect in the revival by Ballet Theatre. When Ballet Russe commissioned *Rodeo* from de Mille it courageously introduced realism into a repertoire thronged with fanciful creatures of myth and allegory—bird-women, fauns, dolls, and various poetic emanations from Massine's and Nijinska's symphonies, nocturnes and études. *Rodeo* later passed out of the repertoire but its diffusion of flesh-and-blood energy remained in the Company, and all the sylphides became more corporeal after it. Within a stubbornly Franco-Russe tradition, in which the dancers belonged either by birth or adoption (the Americans changed their names, in many instances, to conform, as when Betty Low became Ludmilla Lvova) an American spirit began to manifest itself. The most precious of balletomanes would deplore it, but to succeeding generations it merely gave a heartier flavor to the soupçons of Massine. It is notable that the symphonic ballets melted from the repertoire but Massine's "people" continued to be reincarnated, in a series of Hussars and Street Dancers, and Peruvians and Glove Sellers. Even the best of Ballet Russe's Giselles, Alonso, retains a human element, and is less Markova's ethereal *wili* and more a woman in love.

In retrospect, it is plain that if Ballet Russe de Monte Carlo had not been able to acclimatize itself to America it would have dissolved entirely. In surviving, it subtly changed, and for that the balletomanes despised it and the critics began to persecute it. Into the present, some percentage of the criticism is motivated by malice. It has become a metropolitan habit to sneer at Ballet Russe in a few news reviews. When these criticisms are repeated over a period of years some of them seem as worn and trifling as the repertoire they disparage. They have not, in any year, affected the box office grosses, and Ballet Russe continues a lively existence. Although it has come under the dictates of various ballet masters its chief concern has always been to entertain the audience.

The first Diaghilev ballets (chiefly, by Fokine) gave way to a regime absolutely Massine. The Massine ballets were brilliantly danced, even after he left the Company, by Danilova and Franklin in *demi-caractère* roles. During the war, while Youskevitch was in the Navy, Franklin—disqualified from active service—was the mainspring of Ballet Russe. A *danseur caractère,* he now danced anything and everything with such gusto and bonhomie that the Ballet Russe, and the American audience, must be forever in his debt. His influence on his old company is now more positive than Massine's, especially on the *danseurs,* and there he is still spoken of with love and awe. If there is less accent on awe it is because there is so much on love. Franklin was de Mille's partner in *Rodeo* and she has given a lively portrait of Freddy Franklin the dancer in *Dance to the Piper.* He is now associated with the Washington (D.C.) Ballet.

With the disbanding of the Balanchine-Kirstein companies Balanchine went to Ballet Russe, whose policy then underwent a classical reconstruction. Balanchine created *Danses Concertantes* and *Night Shadow* for the Company, discovered and married the Ballet Russe's *soliste* Tallchief, and then formed Ballet Society with Kirstein.

The Americanization of the Company, begun under Massine, continued under Balanchine, whose American ballet dancers, and students from the School of American Ballet, have a history involved with the Ballet Russe. The fine dancers Ruthanna Boris and Mary Ellen Moylan were *solistes* with the Company, as was Dorothy Etheridge. And it was in Ballet Russe that Boris began to choreograph.

A pupil of the Metropolitan's ballet school and of Fokine, Boris joined Ballet Russe in 1943 and danced in everything from *Serenade* to *Frankie and Johnnie.* She is well remembered for her Variation as Florisse in the *Bluebird pas de deux.*

In 1947 Boris choreographed her delightful little circus ballet, *Cirque de Deux,* and in 1948 her *Quelque Fleurs.* The première of *Cirque de Deux,* which is still in repertoire, was danced by Boris and Danielian, by Boris' husband, Frank Hobi, and the *danseuse* Patricia Wilde. The two latter are now in the New York City Ballet—Hobi as stage manager, Wilde as ballerina.

Rodeo's success moved the management to encourage American choreographers. Besides Boris' early works Ballet Russe produced a notable trio by Ruth Page, none of which reached the permanent repertoire as did *Cirque de Deux,* or had the overwhelming success of *Rodeo.* Page's ballets were *Frankie and Johnnie* (1945), *The Bells* (1946), and *Billy Sunday* (1948). The most popular was *Frankie and Johnnie,* based on the ballad. *The Bells* was after Poe's poem and excited less notice than *Billy Sunday,* which was banned in some United States theatres as being sacreligious. Franklin nevertheless made a memorable Billy Sunday and Danilova a delightful Mrs. Potiphar, in which roles they have appeared in countless photographic memoirs.

Ballet Russe's unprecedented contribution to American dance was in the production of a work by a Modern, Valerie Bettis. Her *Virginia Sampler* was the first ballet by a Modern dancer to be presented by a traditional ballet company. Produced in 1947, and danced by Bettis and Franklin in principal parts, it was later danced in the Company with Tallchief and other classicists in the Bettis role. It was not an unqualified success, but a healthy and vigorous controversy furthered the rapprochement between the classic and modern in American ballet.

From 1938 to 1951, Danilova was *prima ballerina* of Ballet Russe de Monte Carlo. Her influence in the tradition of spun-sugar romanticism and Gallic wittiness is ineradicable. Her most successful protégées were Yvonne Chouteau and Moscelyne Larkin, who entered the Company as children—Chouteau at fourteen—and rose from the *corps de ballet* to ranking status. Larkin (who has danced as Moussia Larkina) founded a ballet school in Tulsa, Oklahoma, with her husband, Roman Jasinsky. She was remarkable for her tiny physique, sparkling personality and tremendous jump—the greatest, for her size, in the contemporary theatre. Chouteau, on leave of absence after the birth of a child, is the wife of a former *maître de ballet* of the Ballet Russe, Miguel Terekhov, and is, with the two Tallchief sisters, Rosella Hightower and Larkin, one of the Oklahoma ballerinas. She has danced in North and South America, and, of all the Americans, has most closely approached Danilova's spontaneous charm in the roles Danilova immortalized in the Ballet Russe.

Alexandra Danilova, the best loved of all ballerinas in America, is the last of

Leon Danielian and Ruthanna Boris in Boris's first ballet: Cirque de Deux.

the Imperial Russian ballerinas, and the last of the Diaghilev Ballets Russes' ballerinas. She is the link with the Maryinsky in St. Petersburg and the theatre
Diaghilev created early in the twentieth century. Danilova personifies all the history stored in books and static ballet pictures. She makes alive and vital the old
memoirs and the fading prints. The marvel of Danilova is that she is not a ghost,
but a warm, sparkling, laughing woman, who still sometimes dances and still
teaches—most recently at the Metropolitan Opera Ballet School. There, in the
1958–1959 season she added a new breadth to her career by turning choreographer for the ballet, *La Gioconda*. Danilova is the peerless ballerina of *demi-
caractère*, and a *prima ballerina assoluta* of American ballet—the first dancer to
earn that title, which she holds by esteem and seniority in her adopted theatre.
Her mere appearance on a stage causes a sensation in the audience, and although she has officially retired, American ballet will never yield her up while
she lives, and will compose the same sort of legend about her after she dies that
makes Pavlova survive in hearts and history. Danilova makes it easy for even
the most casual theatregoer to understand the incorruptible nature of ballet and
the passion of the balletomane.

Following in the great tradition set for Ballet Russe by Danilova and her partners, came Alonso and Youskevitch. A *pas de deux* of international fame, they
are unquestionably the greatest in their genre in American ballet. Alonso was a
ballerina of Ballet Theatre but it is within the Ballet Russe that she became *prima
ballerina* and developed as a great dancer and a hugely popular star. No other
ballerina of the Romantic métier approaches her artistry or her charm. Added to
these is the awe with which American ballet has regarded her since she capti-
vated the Russian audience and critics in her Soviet tour of 1958.

Alicia Alonso is a Cuban-born ballerina, who studied in New York with Vilzak
and Fedorova. Although not of ideal physique (having a short neck and body)
she dances beautifully, transmitting her own warmth and sweetness in an excellent technique. In her *pas de deux* with the celebrated Youskevitch her dancing
is distinguished by femininity and feeling, qualities she has been encouraged to
develop in her tenures with Ballet Theatre and Ballet Russe. She does not possess the musicality of Tallchief and Adams, or Tallchief's unerring accent,[5] but
she has an immediate response to mood and theme, and her dancing is the most
richly interpretative in American ballet. Alonso is the once-in-a-blue-moon ballerina, as was Tamara Karsavina, who can dance any classic role, from Coppelia
to Giselle.

By invitation, she appeared in the opera houses in the U.S.S.R. in full-length
productions of *Le Lac des Cygnes* and *Giselle,* and was extravagantly praised.
Her laurels from the throne of the Romantic classics have crowned her queen
of American ballet. She may have influenced the Bolshoi itself! This company's
European and London appearances in the 'fifties won them ovations for spectacular dancing but rebukes for an archaic style, and a less-than-meticulous
Classic form. Alonso's technique struck the Russians as extremely sharp and exceedingly meticulous. The dancers were especially intrigued by her unsupported
pirouettes, which have become known as the "American pirouette." The bal-

Alexandra Danilova and Frederic Franklin in Ruth Page's Billy Sunday.

lerina's husband, Fernando Alonso, gave lessons in its exercise and, so I am informed, a rigorous classroom technique was thereafter imposed on the dancers, to sharpen up their form while retaining their pyrotechnical abilities. In return, the Russian ballet has subtly affected Alonso's dancing, which now shows more mimetic sense, a more intense characterization, and a velvety smoothness of movement. When she danced with Youskevitch on the Ballet Russe's 1958–1959 tour she was received by theatre audiences with a reverence such as I have not observed before in America. Yet she is performing, at a peak of artistry, in the "feeling" manner that we had been led to suppose was contrary to American classicism. Alonso's impressive attainments, and her international renown, may make her a paragon of Classic style for her adopted theatre in the United States. In Cuba, she is an honored citizen, a *Dama,* and head of the state-supported Cuban ballet.

The New York City Ballet's spirit is in its repertoire; Ballet Russe de Monte Carlo's is in its dancers. The greatest of these have been the classical *demi-caractère* stylists Danilova, Massine and Franklin, and the Romantic classical dancers Alonso and Youskevitch. Of their styles, these are the best in the world. In respect to Danilova's unique magnetism, the reputations of her partners Massine and Franklin, and the world-wide acclaim given to Alonso and Youskevitch, it is no exaggeration to state that these five, in their respective genres, are unrivaled in international ballet.

American ballet drew on the Ballet Russe for this monopoly of talent and it is in the Ballet Russe that Americans have been able to see these great stars at the peak of their artistry, in the full panoply of classic ballet. This gave the Ballet Russe a truly imperial power, which it still retains.

With the frankest use of a tried and true attraction, the Company's repertoire is based on "classics" of universal popularity, including *Giselle,* with which the Ballet Russe made its debut in 1938. This arouses a great deal of derision from the New York critics and a stratum of the audience *précieux,* a large number of whom believe that *Giselle* should be danced only by Markova and possibly by Alonso. Many comment that *Giselle* is best left to the Bolshoi although they may be persuaded to accept it from the Paris Opéra, where it was first produced.

The fallacy in the critical survey of the Ballet Russe lies in the comparison of the American Ballet Russe with its European antecedent. Ballet Russe makes no claim to European and Russian interpretations of the classics. The splendid old war-horses are being danced by American dancers, or by foreign dancers amalgamated in an American company. Its sylphides in *Les Sylphides* appear less like supernatural females than exceedingly lithe and agile young women in pretty white dresses. This establishes a hearty rapport with the audiences in America, where athletic boys and girls are better understood than legendary nymphae. There is a remarkably interesting *Schéhérazade,* in which the voluptuous scene has been metamorphosed into a nimble contest of dancing between houris and the Shah's young men. These protagonists, if less in keeping with the roccoco plot, are much more easily recognized by the audience whose empathy is at once aroused by Robbins' three sailors and the girls who pass by. To the contention

Alicia Alonso and Igor Youskevitch in The Nutcracker.

that such a company should cease dancing the "classics" of the romantic and *demi-caractère* style there is the sweeping reply that the American audience wishes to see the "classics." The proof is in the box-office figures. Undeterred by the weighty critiques from one or two large cities in the United States, Ballet Russe's ambulant success continues in continental America. It presents, for its harshest critics, dance-spectacle and not ballet—but this is the opinion of people who classify ballet as a codified language of motion, a technique whose perfection in performance establishes its formality as art. Ballet means several other things to the audience, and the largest portion of the American audience believes it to be a theatrical combination of dance, music and scenic design, preferably with libretto.

Preferably, for ordinary audiences, ballet should say something, or at least mean something. The stronger the characterization, the livelier the plot—however episodic—the more the audience enjoys the ballet. Such is the audience whose purchase of theatre tickets ensures the existence of the Ballet Russe.

In baroque settings, some of the most spectacular American dancers command the Company's stage. The Company makes full use of dynamic personalities. Its *corps* is not notable for discipline but it very often dances with a Byronic joy, in contrast with many a major *corps* that dances for the weekly pay-check. If the arms of the *corps de ballet* are less admirable in *port de bras* than the studied and discreet beauty of other *corps,* the feet of the dancers make up in *élan.* No other American *corps* performs czardas and mazurkas with the fine frenzy of the Ballet Russe on its best nights. And this verve is all the more noted for being sustained on gruelling tours. It is perhaps just as well that the Ballet Russe dancers rely on frank athleticism, because it might be even more difficult to reconstruct their "classics" on the spirit alone. No real estimate of the Company is possible from its annual appearance in any one great city. Its true life is lived on the road, and that is where it must be observed.

Traveling by the truckload like any other American commodity, the Ballet Russe has a caravan of dancers, costumes, décor, musicians, plus the latter's bulky instruments and all the paraphernalia of ballet behind stage. Every autumn it sets out on its journey, and there is nothing to rival it in its general effulgence of Art and Beauty amid the commonplace. Eagerly awaiting it, and in no mood to disparage what it brings, are a multitude of cities and towns. In some of the large cities, the Company has a short season of a week or so. It often gives ten evening performances and two matinées in such places, and then moves on to fill the next engagement. Arriving in the town where they will dance that night the dancers have a class and then repair to their lodgings. Never sumptuous, these are often seedy. From firsthand knowledge, I know the little hotels where dancers are usually billeted. In their dim foyers there are sometimes furtive gentlemen who address you in a foreign tongue or make an incomprehensible remark in English, but who, discovering you to be a dancer, or someone waiting for a dancer, abruptly vanish. The dance has its own marvelous insulation in America.

Happily for the dancers, they need only fall asleep, or wash their hair and do little laundries, in these lodgings. The American Ballet Russe, in its free hours, behaves like a visiting basketball team. The members are likely to go out and look at the view and pose each other for photographs against the changing scene. They have, in short, the indefatigable energy and imperturbable good humor of Americans, and these qualities are important cargo in the touring season. Temperamental fits are early jettisoned.

Dining as lightly as discretion enjoins them, they arrive at the theatre two hours or so before performance—later, if they are inexperienced or disorganized. The wise and the responsible, of which there are a large number, arrive early and make up (a lengthy process) and get partially dressed. *Corps de ballet* girls try to get first dibs at the smartest pieces of their regalia—feathers and furbelows which are handed out by the wardrobe people and have to be collected after the ballet. There are always one or more groups of early backstage visitors. A surprising number of former Company members, now retired, faithfully convene throughout the tour, and there are also old friends from generations of audiences. The soloists are generally in self-isolation onstage, rehearsing bits and pieces from their roles of the night's bill. The *danseurs,* doing a *barre,* appear cool and collected, although already breaking into the first fine sweat of the evening. Looking amiably out of exotic masks of ballet make-up are Alan Howard of Chicago and Kenneth Gillespie of Tasmania, who will presently appear onstage as Prince Siegfried and his friend Benno, in the famous chase of the swans. The Queen of these fabled birds was created by a ballerina named Pierina Legnani in St. Petersburg in 1895, and tonight, on a stage altogether unlike the Maryinsky's, she will be re-created by Gertrude Tyven, who was born in Brooklyn in the nineteen twenties. An especially sinister sorcerer, Von Rotbart, is a young man from Los Angeles named Howard Sayette.

In mid-tour, the girls look a little haggard before curtain rise (they remark that they get less sleep than the boys, from having to wash and dry their hair) but if they are more distraught it is not that they are less talented: the distaff side takes ballet more seriously, and becomes high-strung more easily. The debonair *premier* Zoritch hardly needs his warm-up at the barre because he has been captured that afternoon by a local ballet school and pressed into giving a "guest lesson." Some of the anxious *solistes* approach the *danseurs* to confer about last-minute changes and replacements, and to demand that they be given another quick practice. Obligingly, they are lifted, turned, or flung about, as the case may be. It is impossible for the layman to appreciate the extent of the training that must include a repertoire of roles, and all the supporting roles, in the Company's ballets. These troupers are used to alternating on an hour's notice, and to quick changes in costume, character and style. Before the ballet begins they are all merely stripped dolls to the *directrice* of wardrobe, Sophie Pourmel, who, with her myrmidons, every night toils up the steep stairs to the stars' dressing rooms and then precipitously down to the inevitable cellar of the *corps de ballet.* In Pourmel's hands, boys and girls become *danseurs* and *danseuses* and at the sound of the overture they are the gallant Ballet Russe, feathered and in full flight. They assume the characters that choreographers, dead and alive, have invented, and with such verve and skill that time and again the same ballets evoke enthusiastic applause in the theatre.

The Company is a giant family and Denham is the father-figure, benign or stern. Some of the dancers are married—Chouteau and Terekhov, Larkin and Jasinski, Tyven and Slavin. Ballet dancers are often likened to birds. This connotation is only partly because dancing is as close as we come to natural flight. It is also because of the restless flutter of the ballet professionals from company to company, like birds from perch to perch, seeking the best and happiest roost. In the Ballet Russe the peripatetic breed has a remarkable permanence. Zoritch and Grantzeva are dancing with their home company in America, and when Youskevitch is guest artist he is in the company where he made his American debut in the nineteen thirties. A long, long time has gone by, not so much in years as in the audience's taste for ballet. There used to be nights when the *danseur,* in his tights, would be greeted with ribald shrieks and catcalls, instead of applause and bravos. Youskevitch and Zoritch and Eglevsky have survived those times, and in their footsteps have risen the young American *danseurs*— few of these yet commanding the aplomb and charm of the seasoned veterans who are still dancing on the stage they helped to create.

Even among the young generation in Ballet Russe there is the same sense of permanency as Howard has, who traces his whole career in this company, from a huntsman in the train of Prince Siegfried to the Prince himself, ardently wooing the Swan Queen. Eleanor D'Antuono, the pet of the 1958–1959 tour, was created *soliste* in 1957–1958 and shares a leading role with Borowska, who came into the Company as a ballerina while D'Antuono was still in the *corps.*

This rise from the lowest ranks to the heights among the principals not only is of intense interest to the Company but also intrigues and delights its massive audience. This feature of the Ballet Russe has a tremendous influence on its existence. No other American ballet company is endowed with it.

Largely because of its tradition the Company presents a close-knit front, in which the usual jealousies and hates are digested along with the liaisons and marriages. The principals have remarkable cohesion behind the curtain, where they are more than dancers. *Premier* Howard doubles as the stage manager, *première soliste* Grantzeva is also ballet mistress, and *prima ballerina* Novak teaches classes and is closely associated with the Company's artistic policy. The dancers of the Ballet Russe never free themselves completely from the Company, and after the evening's performance, when they have wiped off the make-up and changed to street clothes, they remain a part of Ballet Russe. The close involvement comes partly out of continuous touring, partly out of the Company spirit, which is not a cool, calm and intellectual one, but an extremely volatile and emotional one. And in this *esprit de corps* the audience is also involved because there has been a Ballet Russe company dancing in America since 1933 and this present one, under Denham, has been an American company since 1938. Some of its members were not even born then, but their parents saw, in the Ballet Russe, the first ballets they had ever known.

Through the years, Ballet Russe has collected not only fans, but whole fami-

Leonide Massine's Gaîté Parisienne *in 1959 production, with Gertrude Tyven and George Zoritch.*

lies of fans. These arrive, in two, three or more generations, at a theatre when the Ballet Russe appears much as though they were calling on an aged relative who had come to town. The evening's program is not judiciously discussed, but is the subject of heated controversy, because of the arguments that rage over past exponents of the roles in comparison with the present dancers. The arguments have been about Massine and Franklin versus Danielian and Terekhov, and now, fattened with the years, they are in full spate about these four, versus Howard and Slavin. Other disputes animatedly involve Danilova and Alonso, Chouteau and Tallchief, Novak and Borowska. Ballet Russe is the alma mater of the American *prima ballerina,* Maria Tallchief, who returned as guest artist to the Company in the nineteen forties, for a season, at the highest salary ever paid a ballerina—two thousand dollars a week, reputedly.

In the animated discussion about the dancers the Ballet Russe's audience does not share the metropolitan critic's view of the time-worn repertoire. Far from staling *Gaîté Parisienne* and *Le Beau Danube,* time has enhanced them. And the dancing, as has been remarked, reaches the audience with a curiously heart-warming effect, because no Ballet Russe dancer ever saves himself, or worries about the critical assessment of the evening's bill. The dancers are all caught up in the ballet and dance their hearts out, while they are dancing their feet off. The Company's vitality on the stage is a quality that no metropolitan critic assesses, but its worth is indicated in the SRO signs, often a month and more ahead of Ballet Russe's arrival in the theatres.

The major problem for the critics is the divergence in the Company's dancers. These are so individual, and are allowed such frank freedom in style, that they develop independently rather than within a strict artistic policy. This is not a fault that the audience finds, because most of the audience does not go to the ballet looking for a formal esthetic appreciation; it goes seeking entertainment. Abstract and avant-garde ballets would mystify, and the remote and classically schooled mode would disappoint. Ballet without décor would be unthinkable. This is an audience not so much *aficionado* as one comprised of enthusiastic fans, and the dynamic personality onstage is the audience's physical attachment to the ballet. Yet who is to say that this is not an audience of balletomanes? In the western states it often travels hundreds of miles to the theatre, or a reasonable facsimile thereof in high school auditoriums and Masonic halls. Into these, as well as into formal edifices more properly called theatres, the Ballet Russe de Monte Carlo adventures. No other company, either American or foreign, will hazard the trip.

Ballet Russe, as a result, has the nature of an institution and the pomp and glamour of an old-time circus. Wheeling ponderously through the Americas for twenty years, it has brought The Ballet to town.

THE REPERTOIRE

It is ocular ballet of strong characterization and thin plot, all well known in the western nations. Every so often a new ballet makes a debut, and sometimes it is added to the permanent repertoire. Under the economic stress from which the Company suffers severely—despite large grosses, since traveling costs eat up the box office take—the Company now and then lops scenes from the classics, for example, the "snow scene" in *The Nutcracker*.

The Company seldom numbers fifty and its small *corps* impoverishes the grand theatre tradition of *Swan Lake* and *Giselle*. It has a breezy attitude towards the sacred classics and presents them whether or not its principals are temperamentally suited to the roles. To its credit, the dancers meet the technical demands of the roles, and the audience apparently wishes to see *Giselle* in 1959—although it has seen *Giselle* continuously since October, 1938—on the Company's première bill. The role has been danced by Chauviré and Alonso, and although it is not suited to the *prima ballerina* Novak she has matured in its demanding title, and gives a creditable performance of the tragic *wili*, and a very good one of the peasant in the first act. The Company's classic forte lies in *Coppelia* and, except for shabby settings, *The Nutcracker*. The latter is of exceptional interest, since it has influenced United States audiences' attachment to the ballet.

In 1940 the Ballet Russe's version was staged by Alexandra Fedorova, who was a 1902 graduate of the Imperial Russian Ballet School, and therefore a student when *Casse Noisette* was first performed at the Maryinsky in 1892. According to Fedorova, her *Nutcracker* remained true to the original but was adapted to contemporary ballet, and she felt that the Maryinsky would have adapted it in the same vein in the 'forties. The ballet choreographer was Ivanov but the *grand pas de deux* for the Sugarplum Fairy and her Cavalier is obviously in the Petipa métier. For the past generation Danilova was an enchanting and romantic Sugarplum. Novak's is a coruscating performance, in which she is more royal than delectable. With the abrupt removal, in 1958, of the *pas de deux* he choreographed for the Sugarplum and the Cavalier, Balanchine's version of *The Nutcracker* becomes less *Casse Noisette* and more a new ballet that could easily be titled *The Nutcracker and the Mice*. It is now wholly a children's Christmas play-ballet, of the English pantomime variety, whereas the original Balanchine *Nutcracker* had a *pas de deux* first performed by Tallchief, with the alternate Cavaliers of Eglevsky and Magallanes. In contrast with the New York City Ballet's revised version, Ballet Russe's Fedorova-version of *Nutcracker* is staged to emphasize theatrical glamour. As danced in the 1958–1959 season in Ballet Russe it had two alternating *pas de deux* executions. The one by Alonso and Youskevitch, especially in the "snow scene," was glowing and radiant; the other by Novak and Howard, who excel in the virtuoso *pas de deux* of Sugarplum and Cavalier, is brilliant and regal. Thousands of people in hundreds of cities, every year since 1940, have seen *The Nutcracker* performed by Ballet Russe, or derivations from its production. At least twenty regional companies perform excerpts from it and many of these are not only copied from Ballet Russe but have been directed, staged and taught by Ballet Russe dancers. The Houston Youth Symphony's version is directed by Nathalie Krassovska; the Louisville Ballet's by Danilova and Slavenska—who have also performed as guest artists in the ballet;

The Ballet Russe de Monte Carlo production of Fokine's Les Sylphides.

the Philadelphia Ballet Guild's by Alfredo Corvino; the Tulsa Civic Ballet's by Larkin-Jasinsky; and the Washington Ballet's under Franklin. Innumerable small companies give performances of *The Nutcracker* in recitals and in Christmas performances, and the Dayton Civic Ballet's annual production alone reaches an audience of more than seven thousand primary school children.

The Ballet Russe's permanent repertoire lists Balanchine's *Ballet Imperial, Danses Concertantes, Pas de Trois Classique* from *Paquita,* and (with Danilova) the *Raymonda Divertissements;* Massine's *Le Beau Danube, Gaîté Parisienne* and the symphonic *Harold in Italy;* Fokine's *Schéhérazade;* Lichine's *Graduation Ball;* and Nijinska's *Snow Maiden. Ballet blanc* is faithfully resurrected in *Le Pas de Quatre* and *Les Sylphides.* The excerpts are spectacular classics—the Blue Bird *pas de deux* from *Sleeping Beauty* and the Black Swan *pas de deux* from *Le Lac des Cygnes.*

Of newer vintage are three ballets by the American choreographer Antonia Cobos: *Madronos, The Mikado,* and *The Mute Wife;* and a ballet on *commedia dell'arte* by Boris Romanoff, *Harlequinade.* From within the Company three choreographers have added works to the repertoire—Leon Danielian with *Sombreros,* Nina Novak with *Variations Classiques,* and Edmund Novak with *Springtime* and *Slavonic Dances. La Dame à la Licorn* has a Jean Cocteau libretto.

In 1958 Edmund Novak, brother of the ballerina, immigrated from Poland to the Company, and with him his wife, a Polish ballerina, Irina Kovalska. The advent of Novak into the Ballet Russe has caused a minor evolution in the dancing, whose ultimate effects depend largely on the audience.

In the 1958–1959 season, following the impact of the Russian male dancing in the Bolshoi Ballet, and the appearance in the United States of two Russian folk companies, the Moiseyev and the Beryozka, Novak's style is a notable asset to Ballet Russe. He is a *danseur caractère,* whose forte is the comic—he dances the Peruvian in *Gaîté,* and Dr. Coppelius in *Coppelia*—but he is something more important: a technician in the Russian school, whose skill and training lie in the spectacular theatre advocated by Soviet ballet. Its bases are masculine power and the indigenous influence of folk dance and music, and on these primal forces Novak has developed a facile gift for teaching.

In current seasons Novak's influence is most obvious in the dancing of the male technicians in the *corps de ballet,* not only in his two small ballets but in all the dancing. He is a passionate believer in *feeling,* and has already infused the Ballet Russe's happy-go-lucky air with fervency. In his suite of *Slavonic Dances,* which only a few critics found too obviously in the mold and form of the Moiseyev's, most United States audiences derive a great satisfaction from seeing American boys jumping and leaping and twirling about in a manner as energetic, if not quite as inspired, as the Russian dancers. This public mood, made patent in the theatre, corresponds exactly with the feeling of rivalry about putting men into space or graduating classes of crack mathematicans. Whether or not Novak's overwhelming success is due to the mood of the moment, the theatres in the 1958–1959 season echoed with the same roar that fills the sports arena. Seldom have I seen such jubilant audiences at the ballet in America, and the occasional critical statement that these ballets are *borsch* have done nothing to alter the taste for them. *Springtime,* a long *pas de deux* with the elevation and pliancy of the Soviet style, instantly reminded audiences of the Bolshoi Ballet's *Spring Water,* another *pas de deux.* Danced by Nina Novak and an American danseur, Eugene Collins, it thoroughly satisfied the audience, who thought it beautiful and extraordinary.

Choreographically, neither the Slavonic suite nor *Springtime* will make history for the American ballet, but their impression on the audience may be far-reaching. The trend is obviously toward folk dancing, and dancing with fervor, judging by the immense successes that the Moiseyev and other such companies have achieved. By contrast, the critically praised and European-lauded American jazz style of Ballets U.S.A. failed so dismally to attract the home audience that its seventeen-week tour was abruptly canceled after four weeks.

The Ballet Russe may be inaugurating a new phase in which ballets of characterization, based on national music and dance, will become strong fortes. Outside the greater metropolitan areas, the critics have been more than cordial, and several have enthusiastically commended the Company for the vitality of the new additions. Beside Novak's influence, the return of Tatiana Grantzeva, who was an original member of Ballet Russe, has meant that already the ragged arms of the *corps* have melted into better *ports de bras.* Also, and in keeping with the Company's vital nature, under the influence of the Polish Novaks the older curvilinear design has been replaced by a dynamic lift and thrust, all of it up and out, with large and open movements.

More sharply disciplined than in past years in daily classes and rehearsal under the Novaks and Grantzeva, the Ballet Russe has been energized and vitalized for its brave, bold advent into its third decade in American ballet. From it, declares one metropolitan critic, may come a native American development of ballet inspired by indigenous dance out of which music and libretto will naturally emerge, as in the ballet history of other nations.

THE DANCERS

The three ballerinas are all young, and form vivid contrasts in looks and temperament. Novak and Borowska are of Polish antecedents, and brunette; Tyven is blonde and American. They have strong techniques—Novak's and Borowska's *virtuoso*, Tyven's *adagio*. All are called on to dance character roles in the predominating *danse caractère* repertoire.

Novak is the outstanding classical character dancer in her theatre. Her Swanilda in *Coppelia* is authoritatively classed with the best of contemporary interpretations, although her company is small compared with the Royal Danish Ballet and the Royal Ballet. She has the apparent fragility of a porcelain figurine, but her *pointes* are steel-strong and her technique sharp and hard. Her multiple *sauts de basque* and her unsupported *attitudes* are phenomenal in balance and ease, and she is at her best in roles where attack and grand *pointe* work embellish strong characterization. Her *épaulement* is so positive an attribute of her dancing that it appears to puzzle some critics, who now and then comment adversely on the unfamiliar style.[6] Novak arouses definite claque opinions, according to tastes accustomed to American classicism or the more effusive eastern style. Like other dancers of her school, she relates *feeling* to the technique of dancing, and as she is very strong as both a technician and a personality she sometimes overpowers her partners. Developing in stature, the *premier* Howard, whose virtuoso technique is not overawed easily, has begun to match Novak, and they achieve a *pas de deux* rapport that is visually exciting. While the Novak-Howard rapport is not a conventionally Romantic one, nor of the caliber of Alonso-Youskevitch, it must be noted as being extremely interesting in its modern concept: its dependence is not on sweetness, warmth and romance, but on sharp, crisp, strong design and a special quality of fearlessness. Since it appears in a major American company it may be said to be an American development. Its nature, while not at all asexual, is totally different from the proscribed European "romanticism."

Sometimes criticized for being brittle in style and literal, rather than evocative, in interpretation, Novak's direct, intense approach to dance is out of the ordinary. She was ranked *prima ballerina* at a younger age than her American contemporaries and her personal sense of responsibility, as well as her strength, has developed her stature. She dances the major roles in repertoire and now, supported by a *corps* disciplined by Grantzeva, she is beginning to emerge more beneficently. Her dancing of the lead in the 1958 revision of *Ballet Imperial* was performed with as much brilliance as ease, and her *Giselle* has appreciably matured—and in her own interpretation. Seen in her former setting in ballet—on

Prima ballerina *Nina Novak in* Don Quixote.

an opera house stage, and with a traditionally large *corps de ballet*—Novak's authority is an asset rather than a deterrent to her technique. In the reawakened American vogue for spectacular ballet dance she and Borowska and some other Ballet Russe soloists have advanced the Company's general popularity.

Irina Borowska, an Argentine of Polish parentage, is one of those fabulous creatures in ballet who are adored as much for their personalities as their dancing. Critics regularly wax hysterical in print over Borowska on tour, and audiences become addicted, with feverish balletomanic symptoms. She is a beauty, and a strong virtuoso, who was the *prima ballerina* of Teatro Colon at twenty-one. Her characteristic style is warm and free, and she gives the rare impression of performing difficult feats spontaneously. She has been a great favorite in ornate ballets, beguiling in the lead of *Sombreros* and ballets of *danse caractère,* and in 1958–1959 developed into a powerful young Odette. Borowska's Swan Queen is mysterious and very feminine, with rich and rounded movements, and shows a new side of the versatile ballerina.

Gertrude Tyven is the pupil of a famed teacher, Vecheslav Swoboda, under whose name she first danced. Her line is clean and sumptuous—possibly the most beautiful in her theatre. Tyven has been in the Company since 1942, when she joined the *corps,* and has danced roles in every ballet from *Rodeo* to *Swan Lake.* She is always competent, and often grand in *adagio,* but with her potential as a lyric dancer she seems to require a great première role in which to develop her attributes. These are a gift for delicate characterization, a calm that could become radiant, and a magnificent line and poise. In a company of virtuosos Tyven is overlooked by audiences of the more boisterous element but she has diffused her own sure glow in American ballet for more than a decade.

The Ballet Russe's *danseurs* are an asset, and are ranked more conspicuously than in many companies. George Zoritch studied under Preobrajenska, Vilzak, Oboukoff and Nijinska, and has been a soloist with the Ballet Russe since 1935. In the 'fifties he danced with the de Cuevas company and in the season 1957–1958 rejoined Ballet Russe. He has also had a career in musicals and has a very large and enthusiastic following in the United States. One of the most accomplished virtuosos of the Franco-Russe school, the Russian-born Zoritch has been absorbed by American ballet, in which he holds a very important place, as a veteran *premier danseur.* He can appear romantic in a debonair manner, or properly aristocratic as the ballet princelings, and with Borowska handsomely decorates the baroque ballets with character and fire, as in the *divertissement* from the Crusader ballet *Raymonda.*

The American *premier* in the Company is Alan Howard, born and trained in the United States, and one of the youngest *premiers danseurs.* He rose from the Ballet Russe *corps* and with such rapidity that critics have been apt to compare him unfairly with Youskevitch, overlooking the fact that Howard danced his first Albrecht in 1958, and Youskevitch has been dancing since 1932. The critical survey, however, makes a point of justly remarking that while Howard lacks Youskevitch's graciousness Howard has not once been seen to falter in a lift, wobble in a turn, or ruffle the skirt of his partner. The comparison with Youskevitch comes partly because of Howard's partnering demeanor, which is of the courteous deportment in the great *danseur noble* style, and partly because Howard has given herculean support to his company from an early stage of his career. In a recent season, when the *danseur* ranks were decimated by illness and accident, Howard danced seven male roles in one day, between matinée and evening performance. A brilliant technician, he has creditably disciplined his virtuoso flair for characterization. He studies drama as well as dance for more scope in ballet. His elevation and aerial form are likened to those of the Royal Ballet's David Blair and Brian Shaw, and he has an elegance of physique and the serious mien suited to classic roles. In the *danse caractère* he served the finest apprenticeship a *danseur* could have in the contemporary theatre, and his King of the Dandies in *Le Beau Danube* is now a tradition on tour. His potential is boundless, given the right direction. A student of the great Fedorova, he has a fine sense of theatre and is intent on perfection of form and clarity of communication.

Eugene Slavin, an Argentine of Russian parentage, was a dancer at Teatro Colon and a soloist with the Igor Schwezoff Concert Ballet in South America, becoming a soloist of the Metropolitan Opera Ballet in the early 'fifties. He joined Ballet Russe in 1954, and has become a first rate *danseur caractère* in the Massine ballets; his Hussar in *Le Beau Danube* is actually preferred by some American balletomanes who know Massine's. Slavin has been able to inject more credible character into *Schéhérazade* than audiences have seen since the earliest times of Ballet Russe. He is not a strong technician, and does not have the sinewy knees and neat, well-placed feet of American dancers, but his sincerity and conviction more than compensate. His Hilarian in *Giselle* is as good as any—and better than all in English-speaking ballet—in the contemporary scene. About to interrupt his career, at the end of the 1959 season, to begin his United States military service, Slavin was dancing better than ever, and in the formidable company of the *danseurs* Youskevitch, Zoritch, Howard, Gillespie and Collins. He acquitted himself nobly in the male lead of *Ballet Imperial,* as Novak's partner. Early in the season a leg injury prevented his dancing a première role created for him in the *Springtime pas de deux,* by Edmund Novak.

Kenneth Gillespie is a foreign importation, from Australia by way of English ballet. He was a leading dancer of the Borovansky Ballet in Australia, and went to the Sadler's Wells Ballet School on scholarship. He later danced with the Royal Ballet, and Dolin's Festival Ballet, with which he toured America as a soloist. He joined Ballet Russe in the 1956–1957 season as a principal dancer, and is the chief performer of lyric *danseur* roles in *Les Sylphides,* for example. Gillespie is the fine product of a sound and serious school, and he is consistently excellent as a dancer. Not as bold and hearty as American virtuosos, he is most interesting to see in the *danseur* role in the *Bluebird pas de deux.* Gillespie is an example to young *danseurs* in his adopted theatre when he is seen as Benno. A model of attentiveness to the ballerina and the *premier danseur,* he does not stint the nobility of the second male role with the lackadaisical attitude some assume in the role of *Swan Lake's* faithful *danseur seconde.* Gillespie has partnered Nina Novak in concert engagements and in *The Song of Norway* in summer recess from the Company and in 1959 danced with Borowska in a European tour.

Besides the principals, the most outstanding present soloists of the Ballet Russe are Edmund Novak and his wife, Irina Kowalska; two lovely young *solistes,* developed in the Company, named Eleanor D'Antuono and Paula Tennyson; a new discovery of 1958–1959, Eugene Collins; and Tatiana Grantzeva. Two *danseurs* about to move up in the Company echelons are Roy Harsh and James Capp.

The *corps* has exciting possibilities. The girls are young, pretty and very talented, and the boys—even younger (some of them only fifteen years old)—are full of bounce and energy, and equally nimble. They are dancing in a company where it is a tradition for "stars" to rise up out of the *corps* and this seems to give the youngest dancers sparkle and enthusiasm. Given a ballet like *Giselle,* they manage to transform it, with the dingiest sets, to effervescent scenes of frolicking peasants in the first act, and supernatural *wilis* in the second. The cancan is flourishing again, with an American agility as great as Gallic vivacity, and in *Gaîté* the little *danseuses* whirl merrily in the *fouettés* that bring such cheers—according to an acidulous New York critic—as might be heard in Yankee Stadium. The boys are leaping blithely and as high as they can in the Soviet style, and grinning so happily when they do that no audience has the heart to carp at the fact that American syncopation has not quite mastered the Eastern tempos of Russian and Polish music. This mastery will, with persistence in training, be acquired, but nothing can substitute for the *joie de vivre* that is this *corps'* best and most graphic feature.

Little D'Antuono is a supple, graceful dancer, with such a warm, rich softness that she makes one think of a young Alonso. Collins has been most marked, in his first season with the Company, for his strength and virility, especially as the partner of Nina Novak in the non-classic *pas de deux, Springtime,* where the *danseur's* lifts of the aerial *danseuse,* and support of her in her breathtaking dives, require great strength and rhythmic sense. Collins is the pupil and protégé of Vladimir Dokoudovsky, at the Ballet Arts, Carnegie Hall. He is American-born and trained, and has burst on the audience with rave notices such as we customarily give foreign celebrities. Collins' bold masculine approach to the dance is excitingly used in Novak's choreography of *Springtime,* in which the *pas de deux* is not traditionally romantic. Instead, the *danseuse's* aerial, fluid movement is contrasted with a strong, almost coarse *danseur* temperament. The result is spectacular, with lovely airborne moments, in which the sex of each dancer is subtly emphasized as a complimentary force. Seldom are the sexes so clearly identified in *divertissement,* and Collins plays his part with nicely balanced properties of man and of dancer. He was seen by smaller audiences, before his Ballet Russe tour, at Jacob's Pillow with the Stroganova-Dokoudovsky ensemble, and has danced in concerts in Canada and the United States, and partnered Grantzeva in supper club appearances.

Tatiana Grantzeva is a veteran dancer in American ballet, who in 1958 returned to her home company from a successful career as a dancer and teacher in South America. She had a school in Venezuela, with which the American Ballet Theatre's Michael Lland was affiliated, and influenced the ballet through the South American countries in her many tours. Her advent into Ballet Russe as *première soliste* and *maîtresse de ballet* has immediately brought discipline and sinew into the Company, especially in the conduct of the *corps*. She has good background on which to base her authority.

Grantzeva is the student of Preobrajenska and Kchessinskaya, and has been dancing all her life. She appeared in a command performance before the King of Bulgaria when she was four. From 1938 to 1945 she was a featured *soliste* with Ballet Russe, and in 1946 was the ballerina of a company called Ballet for America, which she founded with Yurek Shabelevski and Yurek Lazowski. Both Shabelevski and Lazowski are among the first-rate character dancers of the twentieth century, and the latter's Petrouchka interpretation is a landmark in ballet. Also dancing for Ballet for America were Nana Gollner and Paul Petroff. The company lasted for only one season, but toured extensively north and south in the United States. The repertoire included Caton's *Lola Montez,* works of Massine and of Ruth Page. Grantzeva went on the musical stage in *Song of Norway, The Great Waltz,* and others, and was in the movie *The Gay Parisian* which Hollywood made from Massine's *Gaîté.* In the early 'fifties she was ballerina and actress in the Metropolitan's *Fledermaus,* and danced with Nicolai Polajenko, an American classicist of Les Ballets Champs Élysées and Ballets de Paris, who is remembered in the United States as dancing the male lead in Petit's famous *Carmen.* Grantzeva and Polajenko appeared at Jacob's Pillow, and Grantzeva toured in England with the Markova-Dolin Company, and founded Ballet Quartet. With Ballet Russe in 1958–1959, she made many in the audience shed a tear of nostalgic joy as Street Dancer in *Le Beau Danube.* She appeared in this, partnered by Massine himself, at a gala for British royalty in the 'fifties. The tear is partly for Grantzeva herself, well remembered for her dancing, and partly because of her great personal resemblance as a dancer to the adored Danilova. In the same coiffure that Danilova used in the role, Grantzeva's Street Dancer is uncannily like Danilova's and press reviewers erroneously reported that the great *prima ballerina* had returned to tour with Ballet Russe.

There can be no better evidence of American balletomania than the tear so tenderly shed to welcome Grantzeva home, and the enthusiasm that sent parties trekking hundreds of miles from surrounding cities, some out-of-state, to Phoenix in 1958, to see young Howard dance his first Albrecht in *Giselle.*

Thus it is that the Ballet Russe peregrinated into its twenty-first year. Contrary to the best artistic policies, its dancers have not danced only once in a while, at stated intervals, with great thought and preparation, nor have they appeared only in roles to which they were perfectly suited. Instead, Ballet Russe has danced every night and several matinées a week, and has tried to give its best at every performance. The décors wilt, the dancers tire, fall sick, and suffer accidents that disable them, but the miles unroll between "Kennewick, Wash.," and "Mobile, Ala.," and through all the cities and towns among which the Company's caravan zigzags. Drawing its dancers and its audiences from American places whose names the Ballets Russes dancers of 1933 had never heard, Ballet Russe de Monte Carlo has moved imperially along the route it blazed for ballet in America. Its audiences have done well to cherish it. America had not known its like before 1938, and, were it dissolved, America might not know its like again.

AMERICAN BALLET THEATRE

This company has, in the course of its twenty year history, been called "Ballet Theatre" at home and "American National Ballet Theatre" on foreign tours. In 1957 it formally took the name American Ballet Theatre, at home and abroad.

It is our best known company internationally, having traveled in England and Europe, and in Africa and the Orient. It is accepted, generally, as the most representative of American ballet companies, and a great many of the foreign and home audience consider its *prima ballerina,* Nora Kaye, the unrivaled dance-actress of her time. The Company's style is pliant, and has contained the widely divergent techniques of Erik Bruhn, the *danseur noble par excellence* of the generation, and of Gemze de Lappe, an American freestyle dancer. In a repertoire of vital American ballet it has included the works of a French modernist, Jean Babilée, and it also reconstructs many of the classics, among them *La Fille Mal Gardée.* It is the designated inheritor of *Les Sylphides,* yet it also has danced *The Harvest According,* which de Mille says no other company could create, involving as it does several different dance techniques and a high degree of acting.

In the American Ballet Theatre there is the best and most striking confluence of the classic and the modern ballet genres, and there is also a national pride and responsibility that causes the Company to maintain in active repertoire more American ballets than any other company. These include *Billy the Kid, Rodeo, Fancy Free, Fall River Legend* and *A Streetcar Named Desire.*

THE HISTORY

That young man Richard Pleasant, who used to lounge about Agnes de Mille's classroom at the Perry Studio, confiding in her his dreams of founding a company, realized his ambition in 1939 with the formation of Ballet Theatre. It grew out of the Mordkin Ballet, which had its first basis in Russian dance, and its stars were Vera Nemtchinova and Xenia Makletzova. The latter made the *fouetté* popular long before de Basil brought his infant prodigies to America. This incredible creature, who in Russia was the favorite dancer of the Imperial family, went on the Publix Theatre circuit and danced four times a day, every day, thirty-two *fouettés* at each performance.

After his Metropolitan debut with Pavlova, Mordkin formed his own company (Pavlova had a number of partners, among them Bolm, Mordkin, Vladimiroff and Volinine), and toured America and Europe. He returned to Russia in 1911 and became ballet master of the Bolshoi Theatre, until his artistic principles proved incompatible with the new regime. He returned to America and in 1924 formed a company for an extended tour with Nemtchinova, a Diaghilev ballerina, and Makletzova. The following year, after the company dissolved, Mordkin opened a school in New York and commuted between there and Philadelphia, holding classes in both cities. He seemed well on his way to forming the American technician in the Classic mold of the Imperial Russian Ballet, and the recital programs of the day take note of this fact! Mordkin also staged ballet productions for clubs and social groups and at a Junior League ball production he met a young American woman, Lucia Chase.

Lucia Chase was widowed, and an heiress twice over; her husband was Thomas Ewing. She was one of five sisters, who had been well educated and had traveled in Europe, and Chase had studied dance, voice, drama and languages as part of her general education. After meeting Mordkin she became his pupil and found herself drawn so strongly to ballet that she made it her profession. She has since given it her time and money, as Kirstein has done, and all her abilities as a dancer and an executive, both of which are considerable. She and Kirstein are the most active founders of the national ballet theatre. Kirstein's work has been in literary comment and record, aside from his influence in the New York City Ballet. Chase's personal contribution has been in her development as an outstanding character dancer, of which there are very few in American ballet. In their generation, no character *danseuses* surpassed Lucia Chase and Janet Reed and a third alumnus of Ballet Theatre, Muriel Bentley.

The last Mordkin Ballet was founded in 1937 with Chase's assistance, and she was Mordkin's ballerina in his reconstructions of *The Sleeping Beauty* and *Giselle,* partnered by Leon Varkas, an American who received his dance training in Russia. There was also Viola Essen, of whom Genée had commented that she had the perfect ballerina physique. Essen later went to Hollywood and was starred as the girl in *Specter of the Rose,* a movie version of Fokine's *Le Spectre de la Rose.*

When Patricia Bowman, from the Roxy, joined the Company, Chase stepped down voluntarily from *première* rank to second Bowman. Chase's modesty and practicality have been of great value to Ballet Theatre, a point of note in the history of ladies who have loved to dance and have had enough worldly goods to acquire stages. By this time Chase had added to her enthusiasm for ballet a determination to found a company for American dancers—one that would endure, and become a national pride. To this end, she has been consistently self-effacing, devoted, and hard-working.

Chase had first to convince the profession that she was not a rich dilettante. Her inheritances from the Chase banking profession and the manufacture of Axministers have been the bane of her existence as the executive head of her

company, which actually subsists, as do all American ballet companies, on the charity of its patrons and the gross receipts of the box office. How well Chase succeeded in overcoming the sardonic and suspicious comment and winning universal respect her collection of honors proves. In 1946 she was elected to England's Grand Council of the Royal Academy of Dancing, the first foreigner to be so honored. Her company, Ballet Theatre, was the first American one to be invited to the Royal Opera House at Covent Garden.

Her most notable roles have been The Girl in *Great American Goof,* Minerva in *Judgment of Paris,* The Greedy One in *Three Virgins and a Devil,* and the Queen in *Bluebeard.* Her role in Tudor's *Dark Elegies* was a minor classic, and she is forever associated with her two masterpieces, the roles of The Older Sister in Tudor's *Pillar of Fire,* and of The Stepmother in de Mille's *Fall River Legend.* In 1937 no one, and least of all Chase herself, imagined all her potentialities as a dancer and as one of the founders of the national ballet theatre.

Other Americans joined the Mordkin Ballet: Karen Conrad, trained by Catherine Littlefield in Philadelphia; Leon Danielian, a student of Mordkin—he was a lowly *corps* boy—and Edward Caton, born in Russia of American parentage, who had been in the last of Pavlova's companies. Mordkin recruited some of the Franco-Russe dancers: Vladimir Dokoudovsky, a great-nephew and pupil of the great Olga Preobrajenska, whose Studio Wacker in Paris is one of the most famous schools in the world; and another Preobrajenska pupil, Kari Karnakoski.

Soon the little Mordkin Ballet company was of such a standard that it lured the *prima ballerina* Nina Stroganova from the Paris Opéra-Comique. She joined the Mordkin Ballet, married Dokoudovsky, and later danced with Ballet Theatre, Ballet Russe de Monte Carlo and Original Ballet Russe, and in concerts with her husband. Stroganova was Danish—born Nina Rigmor Strom—and a product of teachers of the Royal Danish Ballet, Preobrajenska, Egorova, Vilzak and Shollar, Nijinska, Mordkin and Lubov Tchernicheva—a formidable roll-call of "greats" in ballet.

The Mordkin Ballet acquired foreign properties of no common value and their influence on the American dancers was a valuable contribution to American ballet. To the audience, the Russian dancers seemed beautiful and grand, and they were no less so to those who stood in the wings of the theatre, gazing entranced at the superb creatures. Leon Danielian, born of Armenian parents in New York, was studying ballet for fun and physical exercise, but one night he stood in the wings at the Metropolitan and watched Danilova onstage. That night he decided to make ballet his career, and not very many years passed before he was Danilova's partner.

In 1958 he and she danced again, with their old, incomparable *joie de vivre,* in a mediocre musical on Broadway called *Oh, Captain.* People came to the theatre night after night just to see them dance, and then left; but this audience response to Danilova and Danielian prolonged the Broadway run of the musical and testified to the lasting brightness of the star to which Danielian had pinned his hopes on that long-ago night in the wings of the Metropolitan's stage.

Lucia Chase in Michel Fokine's Bluebeard.

In 1938 the Mordkin Ballet, as a performing outlet for the teacher's advanced students, was too small to accommodate its growing roster of dancers. A new company was formed, on the Mordkin nucleus, with Richard Pleasant as director. The company was named Ballet Theatre and represented at that time the most ambitious project of Americans in ballet. The Kirstein-Balanchine companies were home-grown in the School of American Ballet, and had precarious beginnings in one form and another. The accouchement of Ballet Theatre was attended with pomp and circumstance.

No expense was spared, and choreographers and dancers were accumulated from the scattered Diaghilev dynasty, while the best of the Americans were added. The intent was to encourage American choreographers and develop American dancers, and the brave ideal was to compose an American repertoire. To begin with, the only ballet of this repertoire was *Billy the Kid,* which Ballet Theatre acquired from Kirstein's defunct Ballet Caravan. The Company hired Loring, the choreographer of *Billy,* and another dancer-choreographer who had been identified in Europe and England as "an American dancer," Agnes de Mille. These two alone comprised the American Wing of Ballet Theatre. There was also a Russian Wing, and an English Wing.

The Russian contingent at the start of Ballet Theatre consisted of Michel Fokine, Mikhail Mordkin, Adolph Bolm, and Bronislava Nijinska—all the important Russian choreographers in the western world, with the exception of Massine, Balanchine, Lichine and Lifar. Lifar remained with the Paris Opéra but in time Massine, Balanchine and Lichine were represented with ballets in the Ballet Theatre repertoire. With the addition of the English Dolin, Tudor and Howard, the Company lacked only Ashton and de Valois of English ballet to complete its impressive list of choreographers.

Chief of the Russian Wing was Fokine, who came to America to choreograph a ballet for a musical called *Aphrodite,* and stayed to work in musicals, including the Ziegfeld Follies. Some of his works starred Gilda Gray, and the same Gertrude Hoffman who had brought Le Saison Russe to New York.

From 1924 until his death in 1942 Fokine was the undisputed head of academic ballet—indeed, I catch more than one American dancer deftly easing the years of study back so as to win a cachet from Fokine's teaching, by repute. Actually, there are comparatively few of the current dancers from that glorified coterie of Fokine's American students, and few dancers who danced in the Fokine companies at the Metropolitan, the Capitol Theatre, the Lewisohn Stadium and the Hollywood Bowl.

Fokine was providentially placed in the United States in the middle 'twenties, when the trend moved so strongly towards ballet schools, but Fokine did not especially care to teach. He preferred to create choreography. School and company dissolved in 1930, and Fokine's friends bitterly blame the filmdom magnate who allegedly arranged with Gest for Fokine to come to Hollywood to film the entire repertoire of his Diaghilev era—what was to be, under the choreographer's direction, the American recreation of the birth of the New Ballet. Fokine was supposed to establish a school in Hollywood, from which he would draw his dancers for the film series. Arriving in Hollywood, that reservoir of American talent and arbiter of popular taste, Fokine was informed that plans were altered, because the film magnate had decided ballet was too serious to be entertaining.

Fokine returned to New York, possibly a shade bitterer than when he left it, and continued to choreograph until his death, of pneumonia contracted on a Mexican tour with Ballet Theatre. He never deviated from his principles which he had practised under Diaghilev: "Above all, dancing should be interpretative. It should not degenerate into mere gymnastics. It should in fact be the plastic word. The dance should explain the spirit of the actors in the spectacle. More than that, it should express the whole epoch to which the subject of the ballet belongs. . . ."

Fokine was not alone in his ideal of theatre. In Milwaukee the actor Glagolin was framing these same precepts for the young Loring—who later heard them from Fokine himself. Agnes de Mille was struggling alone to become articulate, in an original vocabulary, in the plastic words of dance. In London, Tudor, a clerk in a meat market, saw his first ballet and was seized with the desire to dance as self-expression. He found that in his free time he could swap his services as secretary and errand boy in return for lessons from Marie Rambert.

These were the disparate—one might say the "desperate"—young forces that helped to forge the life of the company now called American Ballet Theatre. The Company rests still in part on their influences, although not one of the choreographers Loring, de Mille or Tudor continues to be attached to it—but the nature of the repertoire, rare in American ballet, consists of dramatic theatre and strong interpretation in the genre of Fokine.

In 1939, when the Company was still functioning under Pleasant, Fokine's influence was paramount among the Russians, and the two last Fokine ballets, *Bluebeard* and *Russian Soldier,* were created for Ballet Theatre. Fokine was at work on *Helen of Troy* when he died. This was afterwards made into a ballet by David Lichine, who with his wife, Riabouchinska, joined the Company in 1942 and created his ballet romp, *Fair at Sorochinsk.* A year or two later, when Lichine revived *Graduation Ball* for Ballet Theatre, one of the danseuses merrily twirling in it was a Lichine and Nijinska protégée, the younger Tallchief sister, Marjorie. Massine, who had been with the Ballet Russe, was with Ballet Theatre from 1942 to 1945, creating *Aleko, Don Domingo* and *Mlle Angot*—not among his masterpieces, it is true, but serving to diffuse the Massine effervescence in Ballet Theatre. The Russian influence of Nijinska's reconstruction of *La Fille Mal Gardée* has long since been converted into an American athleticism close to Robbins' *Interplay* in Tyrolean costume, and Mordkin, whose company was the cradle of Ballet Theatre, is no longer represented with *Voices of Spring.* Bolm's *Peter and the Wolf* survived beautifully, and charmed succeeding generations of young balletomanes from its first performance, January 13, 1940, with Loring as Peter, Dollar as the Wolf, and Essen, Conrad and Stroganova enchanting as Bird, Duck and Cat. Under Pleasant and Fokine the Company's artistic policy was clear and strong, but Fokine died, and Pleasant resigned to go into the Army.

The first seasons were wonderful milestones for American ballet. Fokine's productions of *Les Sylphides, Carnaval, Le Spectre de la Rose* and *Petrouchka* were created on the new American company whose dancers were the last to have worked with the Father of Modern Ballet. De Mille, who was part of Ballet Theatre from its inception, records that on opening night the sylphides seemed not to touch the earth, and that Conrad clove the air like a swallow "in the highest jump of any living woman, again and again and again, on tireless young legs."

Some felt this to be nearer acrobatics than poetry, but others viewed it with awe. Native American qualities of stamina, strength and speed were beginning to emerge under the fine Russian hand.

Dolin, technically in charge of the English Wing, worked in the *ballets russes* métier, staging *Giselle* and *Swan Lake*. In 1941 he revived his *Le Pas de Quatre* and designed a suite from *The Sleeping Beauty,* as *Princess Aurora.* The other English choreographers were Antony Tudor who scored an instant success with *Jardin aux Lilas,* retitled *Lilac Garden;* and Andrée Howard, who with Tudor and the dancer Harold Laing had been de Mille's contemporaries at the Rambert school in London. Howard contributed *Lady into Fox* and *Death and the Maiden,* and then returned to England, where she was associated with the Sadler's Wells companies and became a noted choreographer and designer.

The American Wing, made up of Loring and de Mille, were not immediately dazzling with their ill-fated *Obeah* and *Great American Goof.*

Ballet Theatre's avowed American character did not derive as much from its repertoire, which was more foreign than native, as from its dancers. Besides the nucleus drawn from the Mordkin Ballet, there were Loring, de Mille, Dollar, and Annabelle Lyon, a pupil of Fokine and the School of American Ballet. Lyon was an American of Russian parentage. She danced in musicals, in the Kirstein-Balanchine companies, and with Ballet Theatre from its founding until 1943. She was later a principal dancer in *Carousel,* on Broadway, from 1945 to 1947.

In retrospect, the greatest glory of Ballet Theatre appears to have been its *corps de ballet,* in which, it was critically assessed, there were dancers the equal—and sometimes the superior—of some Diaghilev soloists. In the first and second year, the *corps* included the "unknowns" Nora Kaye and Maria Karnilov, besides Muriel Bentley, Jerome Robbins, John Kriza and a Cuban dancer named Alicia Alonso. Karnilov, born of Americanized Russian parents in Connecticut, was a pupil of the Metropolitan Opera Ballet School, as were Kaye and Bentley. Bentley had a catholic education in dance, from Russians like Vecheslav Swoboda, and interpretive moderns like Ruth St. Denis. Robbins had studied several forms of theatre, and Kriza was trying to build his physique to entrance standards of the Sokol in Chicago. A basic Classic technique, a wide range in the modern interpretative dance, and a professional degree of athleticism all contributed to the formation of American ballet. This was the basic mixture of Ballet Theatre, with which Tudor made his short, brilliant and unique contribution to the American ballet tradition.

In its company policy Ballet Theatre was as revolutionary as in its artistic ideals. It established no star system, no division in rank between the echelons of dancers, who were called "principals" and "company" instead of *ballerinas, premiers danseurs,* and *solistes.* And there was no *regisseur general*—no single and sole person responsible for mounting and rehearsing the repertoire. This authority for his own works was given to each resident choreographer. Alas for such democratic and creative precepts—they did not work, and very soon Ballet Theatre was compelled to form a company in the old established formula, with ranking stars whose names on the programs and advertisements would bring the audience into the theatre. Ballet Theatre, labeled "an American company," found itself hard put to survive in its own country, in competition with the Ballet Russe de Monte Carlo. American ballet's foundation had been the Russian Imperial school, and for a very long time its productions were in the *ballet russe* métier, which delighted audiences and impressed impresarios.

After some debate, and a lull in activities—during which the disbanded Ballet Theatre dancers repaired to Jacob's Pillow and danced under Markova and Dolin —impresario Sol Hurok began to present the Company in the winter season of 1941. Richard Pleasant resigned as director, and his position was occupied by Germain Sevastianov, who held it until 1943, when he left to join the United States Army. He was succeeded by J. Alden Talbot until the end of 1945, when the Company began to be managed by Chase herself in conjunction with the artist Oliver Smith. At this time Tudor was made Artistic Administrator and the Company reverted to its original precepts. It became independent of a top-heavy "guest star" roster, and concentrated on the development of a company essentially American in style, repertoire and character. Impresario Hurok ceased to present it.

Into its twentieth year, this large company—it began with more than a hundred dancers and in 1959 numbered fifty—has remained the only typical American ballet company for international audiences. Authoritative views in the foreign theatre consider its classicism strict and fine, yet vitally influenced by "American" characteristics of speed, mobility of form and an urge toward self-expression. Its American thematic ballets are considered the most representative of American ballet repertoire. The New York City Ballet, from the international viewpoint, is an impeccable American copy of the Imperial Russian school, as well as the workshop of Balanchine's Neoclassic theories. American Ballet Theatre in style and repertoire is taken to be characteristic of our national classical ballet.

The Company's classical nature, after Fokine and the other Russians, came largely from the English ballet, with its contemporary Russian-trained dancers Alicia Markova and Anton Dolin.[7] Certainly the *ballet d'action* forte of Ballet Theatre owed more to Dolin than Fokine, and the audience response was intense to Markova and Dolin in *pas de deux*. Dolin cheerfully sidestepped the avant-garde. He said, in an interview in the 'forties, that the first thing he and Markova looked for when they planned a *divertissement* was a ballet *with* a *story*, either sentimental or tragic. A good story, said Dolin astutely, means a good *divertissement*. Now the head of his own company, Festival Ballet, Dolin's career stems from the Diaghilev era. He was a seventeen-year-old boy of Irish-English antecedents when he changed his sonorous British name for the properly "foreign" Anton Dolin. In style, he became an incomparable European classicist, bringing to the art of partnering a theatrical dash and romance. He had a long and justly famed association in *pas de deux* with Markova, and they were acclaimed all over the world. These two gave classic dance in America its romantic character, and they did it with intelligent techniques and a consummate gift for communication.

Dolin admitted that *Giselle* was pure "corn" but he and Markova between them convinced the world that the story of the unfortunate little peasant girl who fell in love with an ardent but irresponsible nobleman was real, heartbreaking tragedy. Markova, like Danilova, with whom she shares the distinction of having been a Diaghilev ballerina, is a living legend. In the 1958–1959 season she was still dancing Giselle, with Bruhn as Albrecht, for American Ballet Theatre. She was then forty-eight years old and had been dancing for thirty-four years. All that the years have brought are a deepening of the substance, and a greater gloss to the patina of Markova's art. She is the epitome of classic romanticism.

Critic Irving Kolodin remarks that Markova's Giselle is the despair, not the useless envy, of her contemporary Giselles. She combines lightness of body and interpretation of character; gaiety and despair; the earthly Giselle and the unearthly *wili,* with muscular control and spiritual poise. Never a virtuoso technician, and incredibly retaining her own special buoyancy, Markova seems to defy the years. Her art is a constantly maturing force, and she regards Dance with a spiritual fervor. In contemporary ballet, which still subscribes to the ancient superstitions, Markova is said to believe that she is possessed by the spirit of Pavlova.

It was this fervor that helped to create American ballet, and Markova's place in the hierarchy is as estimable as Danilova's. These two hold the internationally acknowledged title of *prima ballerina assoluta* in the English and American theatres. Danilova is greatly beloved in her profession—Markova is held in something like superstitious awe. For me, the most cherished eulogy came from a wardrobe woman with whom I stood in the wings of a theatre, watching Markova: "She never went onstage as the ballerina Markova." Going there as *the dancer,* trained, gifted, inspired, she becomes onstage the living person of the ballet.

Because of her special quality, Markova in person or Markova absent still impresses American ballet. Her influence on all other American Giselles and on her counterparts in the Romantic genre is incalculable. Into the third decade of American ballet Markova is still the standard by which the *taglioniste danseuse* —the pure classicist, in conventional romantic roles—is judged. The fine facets of the woman and the artist are sharpened by the intensity Markova brings to *Giselle* and the gentle irony with which she dances the Taglioni role in *Le Pas de Quatre.*

After 1945, Markova and Dolin were not regular members of Ballet Theatre; Massine left the Company at the same time. The "stars" in the public view began to change from the foreign ones, among them Irina Baronova and Vera Zorina, to American, and few shone so brightly as Nana Gollner, Rosella Hightower, and Sono Osato.

Alicia Markova and Michael Maule in Orfeo, *at the Metropolitan Opera House.*

Nana Gollner.

Gollner was born in Texas in the nineteen twenties and began to study ballet as therapy after an attack of poliomyelitis. She developed such a strong *pointe* that she could stand on it without supporting shoes. She made a debut in the Max Reinhardt production of *A Midsummer Night's Dream,* after studying with Kosloff in Hollywood, and danced with Balanchine's American Ballet in 1935. She is the first American ballerina to have held a *prima* title with a Russian company, as she did in de Basil's Original Ballet Russe.

What a charm she exerted in her native theatre in the 'forties! She was the spirit of Ariel, young as an angel, with the leap of a gazelle. To many of us in the audience she seemed to personify American ballet itself!

Gollner married the Danish *danseur* Paul Petroff, formed a company as the Gollner-Petroff Ballet Russe, and toured widely on the American continent. Gollner was a leading member of the English International Ballet in 1947. Hightower and Osato are her contemporaries.

Hightower was born in Ardmore, Oklahoma, of Amerindian parentage, and was trained at the Dorothy Perkins School of Dance in Kansas City, Missouri. She joined Ballet Russe in 1938 and in 1941 went to Ballet Theatre as *soliste,* rising to ballerina rank, to which she has peripatetically returned from her position as *prima ballerina* of the de Cuevas company. In Paris she studied with Preobrajenska but it is notable that her prodigious technique derives from American training by an American teacher. When Hightower appeared in Paris in the late 'forties, she was an overnight sensation and she remains the superb example of American ballet in Europe. A strong technician, she has the grand manner and authority that Europeans associate with the *prima ballerina.* In her return engagements in the United States in the nineteen fifties Hightower has appeared altogether too forceful to the critics. She has, however, a virtuoso ability and particularly fine *port de bras,* the latter not the uniform forte of the American classicist. Her Odile in the *Black Swan pas de deux,* and her Myrtha in *Giselle* are unrivaled in the contemporary theatre.

Sono Osato, whose dancing career has been brightest in musicals, is a Japanese-American from Omaha, Nebraska. She is an actress-dancer, and has been featured frequently in Agnes de Mille's ballets. She was a pupil of Caton and Berenice Holmes, and later of Egorova and Oboukhoff. Her style is flexible, and derives as much from her personal feeling as from her training (Holmes had a catholic education in dance, under Classic and Modern influences from Bolm, Nijinska, the School of American Ballet, and Kreutzberg).

Gollner, Hightower and Osato shared a theatre with Danilova and Markova, and in their wake appeared others from nowhere—meaning, to the Russians, Brooklyn and Fairfax, Oklahoma, the birthplaces of Ruthanna Boris and Maria Tallchief.

There were now the established companies of Ballet Russe, a visitor from 1933 and a resident from 1938, and the big and beautiful American company, Ballet Theatre. In one manifestation or another, either in the Kirstein-Balanchine companies or in companies formed by their protégés, ballet's roots were taking hold in America. And people who had never gone into a theatre to see a ballet before went now, out of wartime restlessness, and the easy economy of the times. I often shared standing room with "bobby soxers" who had never before set foot inside the Metropolitan. Now and again this enthralled audience demanded of its neighbors what was going on in something like *Waltz Academy*.[8]

Under Hurok's management, the Ballet Theatre's direction moved irresistibly towards a *russe* métier—Hurok was also managing Ballet Russe de Monte Carlo —and Ballet Theatre seemed about to assume a Euro-American character. Loring left it, and de Mille choreographed, other than *Obeah,* only *Tally-Ho* and *Three Virgins and a Devil.* Ballet Theatre's greatest impression was made in the Freudian ballets of Antony Tudor. Tudor was hailed as a genius and a revolutionist in ballet, but some regretted the passing of Ballet Theatre's vigorous American element from the Company. The ballets were fine, new and reconstructed, and the dancing was excellent, but where was the repertoire that signified American ballet? A large part of the audience had hoped, and expected, that Ballet Theatre would develop compositions to rank with other national ballets, in which the Classic Dance would join with American choreography, libretto, music and design to form a native ballet like that in England. *Billy the Kid* and *Filling Station* had been created out of the Kirstein Ballet Caravan, and when Ballet Theatre's American choreographer, de Mille, produced *Rodeo* in 1942 it was for the Ballet Russe company! As had been done in *Billy,* *Rodeo* combined American theme, music, and style of dancing, and was created by an American (not Americanized) choreographer, composer and artist. It began to seem as though only under the Franco-Russe aegis would American ballet emerge.

Then in 1944 *Fancy Free* rocketed into the august Metropolitan Opera House and thenceforth merrily around the world. The English described it as a ballet about American manners, and called it the most delightful dance work to cross the Atlantic. Not even Ballet Theatre knew what it was producing before *Fancy Free* made its debut. The little minnow of a ballet, one act, and with a cast of five dancers in one scene, made as big a splash as though it had been a whale. Using contemporary American dance-hall dance and music within the Classic tradition, the choreographer Jerome Robbins and the composer Leonard Bernstein made their lively statement on American ballet.

Ballet Theatre began to be a more American company and in 1946, when its direction passed to Chase and Smith, its stated aim was to consolidate its artistic principles and to define, in repertoire, the national American ballet. The statement seems not to have excited America but when the Company—the first to do so—was invited to appear at the Royal Opera House at Covent Garden it was hailed as a remarkable and revolutionary force in ballet. On regular tours of the European continent, and farther east, it is still the most admired and affectionately regarded of American dance groups.

THE REPERTOIRE

Fancy Free and *Fall River Legend* were created in the Company. It acquired *Billy the Kid,* which Loring revised in the 'forties for it, and *Rodeo* from de Mille and Ballet Russe, which no longer has performing rights to the work. In its permanent repertoire is *Interplay,* very American in style, created by Robbins, who also created *Facsimile* in the Company. *Facsimile* is intended to be a general comment on restlessness and spiritual poverty but is generally taken to be an indictment of contemporary life in the United States. Ballet Theatre performs *A Streetcar Named Desire,* which was choreographed by Valerie Bettis for the touring Slavenska-Franklin company in 1952. It has produced de Mille's *The Harvest According* and Loring's *Capital of the World,* which were considered, in each instance, the most notable ballet productions of the seasons.

Two important American choreographers, William Dollar and John Taras, are represented in the permanent repertoire. Dollar's *Le Combat,* sometimes called *The Duel,* is based on the tragic love of the Crusader Tancred for the pagan Clorinda, whom he kills, in ignorance of her identity, in a duel. It was first danced by Ballets de Paris in 1949, with Janine Charrat in the Clorinda role afterward taken by Melissa Hayden and Lupe Serrano in Ballet Theatre. Taras' *Design for Strings,* known as *Dessins pour les Six* in France, was created for the Metropolitan Ballet in 1948, and exists in several classic repertoires, including the Royal Danish Ballet's.

The Company also presents reconstructions of the "white" and "black" scenes from *Swan Lake*—which were features of its seasons in Bruhn's tenure as *premier danseur—Giselle,* and *La Fille Mal Gardée,* the oldest ballet in contemporary repertoire arranged by Nijinska. Mordkin also arranged a version for the parent company, his Mordkin Ballet. Fokine's abstract ballet *Les Sylphides* is said to be the best extant in Ballet Theatre, which also preserves Bolm's *Peter and the Wolf.* Contemporary choreographers are represented: Ashton with *Les Patineurs,* Balanchine with *Theme and Variations*—commissioned from him by the Company in 1947; and Lichine with *Graduation Ball* and *Helen of Troy.* The Company produced *Winter's Eve,* the first ballet in America of the English choreographer Kenneth MacMillan, which (like the New York City Ballet's *Pastorale*) has a theme of blindness.

The Company did not return, in its second decade, to the avant-garde nature of its beginnings when it produced Loring's *Great American Goof* and de Mille's *Obeah.* Having anticipated, by nearly twenty years, a ballet style that would mature in the now popular ballet-play, the Company abandoned theatre pieces of the *Goof's* genre. And having been so revolutionary as to hire sixteen Negro dancers for de Mille's Caribbean ballet it never again advanced a Negro dancer, although the Metropolitan Opera, a most unlikely ark, adopted Janet Collins as *prima ballerina,* and the New York City Ballet made a place for Arthur Mitchell. In 1944 the Company produced Catherine Littlefield's *Barn Dance,* which she revised for the occasion, with her sister Dorothie in a lead role. And in 1945 Michael Kidd, a dancer-choreographer from Loring's Dance Players who was also associated with Ballet Theatre, created *On Stage!* a charming little ballet about a stage hand as altruistic, and as American, as Lew Christensen's Mac in *Filling Station.* But Littlefield did nothing more, and Ruth Page was not represented, and Kidd went into the musical theatre, where he occupies a place comparable to that of Robbins and their predecessors Loring and de Mille. Robbins left to join the New York City Ballet.

Then in 1951 Ballet Theatre presented the modern French dancers Jean Babilée and Nathalie Philippart as guest artists. It was an education for the American balletomane, and an avant-garde introduction for an American company to make. It brought to a large audience an understanding of the European modern ballet (not to be confused with Central European or Modern Dance) in which natural gesture is one aspect, but more important is the reflection of a state of mind. The Babilées danced *l'Amour et Son Amour, Til Eulenspiegel,* and *Le Jeune Homme et la Morte,* which is considered, in Europe, one of the most important works of the century—as epochal as *Spectre de la Rose.*

Ballet Theatre's repertorial pride lay in Tudor's ballets—a pride it still retains, buttressed by the momentous ballets of de Mille and Robbins, in the permanent repertoire. Ballet Theatre toured from coast to coast in the United States and in the Americas and Europe. It had its third season's première in Mexico City and its first coastal tour in 1943, went to England in 1946, and celebrated its fifteenth anniversary with a Metropolitan Opera season, when it boasted a repertoire of thirty-one ballets. Twenty-four of these had been created in the years 1940–1945. In 1956–1957 it toured Europe and the Middle East, and on its return home had a brief United States tour. In that summer it held its Workshop at the off-Broadway Phoenix Theatre in New York, with a Festival that won it critical esteem. Immediately after, American Ballet Theatre went on a transcontinental tour, visiting ninety American and Canadian cities. In 1958, on its eighth foreign tour, it represented the United States at the Brussels World's Fair during the "United States National Days" in July. Few tours have been so publicized as its advent behind the Iron Curtain. The tour was sponsored in 1958 by the President's International Exchange Program, administered by ANTA, and newspaper reports and firsthand observers have recorded a triumphal march for the American company, who were everywhere hailed as the true evidence of a national American ballet.

Like Ballet Russe, American Ballet Theatre has never had a permanent base, for which it has a crucial need. Its artistic development has been baffling, because its seasons are punctuated by semicolons, rather than marked out as periods of growth. Bad luck has sometimes dogged it. In 1958 the settings and costumes for several ballets were burned on the European tour. These had to be replaced for the 1958 Metropolitan season, at a cost disproportionate to the insurance on the old equipment.

Lucia Chase has managed to hold the Company together. She and her co-director Oliver Smith have coped with the industrial revolution in the theatre, which has brought strictures like curtain falls on curtain calls, dictated by the bugaboo of "Overtime." Intent on remaining true to its artistic principles, the Company's great fear and protest have been against adapting to the rough-and-ready character of a traveling road show. Yet, until it can find a home theatre, it must lead an itinerant life or cease to exist altogether.

Its principles have been three: to recognize and support the American cho-

reographer and dancer, to preserve the Classic technique while remaining tolerant of modern forms, and to hold the national theatre democratically open to
the talents and influences of foreign dance artists. The Company has been singularly faithful to these precepts, and among its most commendable achievements
is the Workshop, established in 1954. This provides a stage for young choreographers, a performing outlet for dancers from the Ballet Theatre schools, and
an opportunity for established choreographers to experiment with new ideas.
Out of the Workshop has emerged Herbert Ross, whose ballets *Caprichos* and
Paean are in the Company's repertoire, and the Company has produced his
controversial works, *The Maids* and *Tristan.*

Seen in its gala seasons at the Metropolitan, the American Ballet Theatre appears as much at home there as its *prima ballerina,* Nora Kaye, whose childhood was spent at the opera house as a ballet student and a minor operatic
character. For a time, brief in duration and of passing consequence, Ballet
Theatre was the resident dance company at the Metropolitan and when its tenure ceased its artistic director, Tudor, remained to head the Metropolitan's
dance school and company.

ANTONY TUDOR

Although Antony Tudor now has no direct influence on American Ballet
Theatre, it is impossible to separate him from the company in which his revolutionary ballets marked an epoch in the theatre. His works, from the English-
created *Jardin aux Lilas, Dark Elegies* and others, to his masterpiece, *Pillar of
Fire,* were produced by Ballet Theatre in America. Tudor has been the subject
of articles, monographs and debates, and only his comparative inactivity as a
choreographer relegates him to a less notable position than Balanchine. Besides
Balanchine he is the most important foreign influence on American ballet, but
whereas Balanchine has worked in the traditional form in developing the female
American technician and his own Neoclassicism, Tudor is the ballet phenome-
non of his time—a choreographer free of other influences, who has incalculably
influenced modern ballet. Amberg declared Tudor the most momentous and
significant reformer in ballet after Fokine, stating that twentieth-century ballet's
esthetic concepts were wholly evolved between the realism of *Schéhérazade* in
1910 and that of *Pillar of Fire* in 1942. Fokine ended one era, and Tudor began
the one in which modern ballet has grown. Fokine wished dance and mime to
serve more expressively in communicating the drama of life. Tudor advanced
this ideal further, examining the nature of the expression and following it to its
psychological motivation.

Much is made of Tudor's rise from a London slum to the immortal position
he occupies in the theatre. He was born in 1909 to hard-working Cockney parents in Clerkenwell, a lower class district in London, and went to work at sixteen as errand boy in the Smithfield Meat Market. In 1928 he went, out of curi-
osity, to see a ballet and was sufficiently intrigued by it to go regularly to see

Anna Truscott as the Russian Ballerina in the Ballet Rambert production of Balanchine's Gala Performance *at Jacob's Pillow, in 1959.*

the Pavlova company and the Diaghilev Ballets Russes, then playing in London. The impressions these dancers made on Tudor changed his whole life. He gave up a chance of advancement in business and, despite his parents' disapproval, joined Marie Rambert and the young pioneers in English ballet—Frederick Ashton among them. Tudor's early teaching was from Pearl Argyle and Harold Turner, and from Margaret Craske, a Cecchetti protégée who is now Tudor's second-in-command at the Metropolitan. Ballet was far from the Cockney boy's native sphere, but it was soon obvious that Antony Tudor had been born for ballet.

He had only a minimum English education, but he could read French and German and play the piano. In 1929 he joined the Rambert school and company, for which Mme Rambert was ekeing out a bare existence in the tiny Mercury Theatre. This was to be known, in the next quarter of a century, as the cradle of English ballet. Ashton's first works had been produced for Rambert, and in 1931 Tudor made his debut at the Mercury with *Cross-Gartered,* based on an episode from *Twelfth Night*. To absorb the right atmosphere, Tudor went to Florence to compose his dances but when he put the ballet into rehearsal in London he found that he had designed movements totally beyond the anatomic ability of his dancers. Undaunted, he began to compose again, with dancers in the flesh.

Cross-Gartered was commended by critics as eminent as Massine, the great man of the day, and Tudor launched one furore after another in London, with the presentations of his ballets *Adam and Eve,* so shocking as to be called lewd, and *Atalanta of the East,* which he set to a score by Seelig, derived from Javanese airs. In 1937 he produced *Dark Elegies,* about the mourning of a fishing village, to Gustav Mahler's *Kindertotenlieder* (*Songs for the Death of Children*). The ballet is danced to a sung accompaniment of Rückert's elegiac poems, and the singer sits onstage.

Dark Elegies caused a controversy because the movement was not traditional dance but had patterns individual in character, like the five *Lieder.* It appeared that ballet was in for another revolution, and there had been nothing so exciting since Diaghilev. In 1923 *Les Noces'* London première had been denounced in the theatre and the press, but championed by H. G. Wells. The controversy raged over Nijinska's odd employment of a wailing, chanting chorus, percussion instruments, and two grand pianos played by four pianists, all, with the danseuse Felia Doubrovska, onstage as part of the ballet.

With *Jardin aux Lilas* Tudor deviated from the known ballet form in costume, movement and character, and the "psychological ballet" genre was born. The critic George Beiswanger later called it "the short-story form of ballet."

Tudor was in the front rank of English choreographers but he was not, from the conservative English view point, the equal of Ashton, because he had wandered too far from the academic principles of ballet. Tudor appeared gifted and inventive, but his native theatre had seen older experimentalists range at tangents in and out of ballet. Some of them achieved reform out of anarchy, as did Fokine's ideals, in the dimension and feeling they gave to Russian ballet.

In this sophisticated theatre Tudor followed Fokine, Nijinsky, Nijinska, Massine and Balanchine, but he owed nothing to their corporate inventions. He was claimed by the Modernists, but his work remained within the traditional ballet métier. Amberg says that the technical foundation of his work is clearly recognizable as that of the classical, academic dance.

At first regarded as a sensualist, Tudor reasonably replied that he was interested in exploring the relationships between men and women. He introduced themes and motives which had not been expressed in ballet, and so was compelled to develop a new vocabulary for their expression. After Tudor, dancers learned to move in a different way: as the visible extension of inner motivation. Gesture was impelled from the deepest sources of the characters and dance became what an older choreographer meant when he said that there is a region of the heart where words and gestures do not suffice, and Dance, and Dance alone, expresses what cries and actions cannot describe. Critics were forced to go outside ballet terminology to discuss Tudor's work. Beiswanger compared it to the novels of D. H. Lawrence and the operas of Richard Wagner. The latter comparison was especially apt, as Tudor evolved a device of motifs and stasis in which movement became an unending flow of expressional dance.

No man in his formative years had more dedicated friends, and these passionately believed in Tudor's genius. One was the dancer Hugh Laing, who created many principal roles in the Tudor ballets, and another was Agnes de Mille, with whom Tudor and Laing formed a small company in England. It was de Mille who brought home to America the news that English ballet had produced an original and lyric choreographer. It was on de Mille's word that Richard Pleasant brought Tudor to America to join Ballet Theatre. By then Tudor had proved himself a dozen times over, but had not been given a company or a theatre. He had taught and composed for pittances, formed two companies that were artistic successes and financial failures, and sometimes had not had enough to eat. His associates found him intolerable to work with, although dancers admired and loved him, slaving for hours at a time to perfect one movement in his strange designs. He could not deliver works on set dates and was often composing onstage before the curtain rose on a première. Even his devoted dancers suffered, because his usage of music and movement were extraordinary and outside their training. He did not, for instance, count.

While he was composing he baffled his friends, but the completed work glowed with a new and striking brilliance when at last it was ready to be seen. Gradually his friends recognized that Tudor was as peculiar, in English ballet, as an eagle nesting among a flock of swans. While his compatriots wished to glide, preen and curvet in the poetic stream flowing from traditional ballet, Tudor aspired to soar and swoop in unexplored vistas of dance. This Richard Pleasant, in America, set him free to do.

At one bound his work spanned all the laborious reforms in dance, combining the traditional and the modern in style and form with new motives and attitudes. The very ignorance of dance that had hampered him initially with *Cross-Gartered* now helped his invention. His inspiration was better than training and his impulse better than dogma. Having himself as sole authority, Tudor moved with infallible ease. His tenets were his own, and therefore subject to no question. While some critics raged against his work the theatres began to be filled with silent people, searching their own selves for the replicas of Tudor's men and women. People were stripped of convention in the ballets, and deprived of subterfuges. Beiswanger declared that the Tudor characters revealed a terrifying splendor of hungry, struggling beings.

In London, out of the necessity of keeping alive and working at his trade, Tudor had been reduced to composing dances for things like *In A Monastery Garden* and *A Chinese Temple Dance.* More happily, perhaps, he choreographed *A Toy Cart,* starring Madeleine Carroll, and *The Happy Hypocrite,* starring Vivien Leigh. In 1937 he choreographed the first television dances in which Margot Fonteyn appeared. But the English reception of *Jardin aux Lilas* was guarded. When it was produced at the Mercury its décor and costumes, original and pretty in the Edwardian vogue, were commended, but a sour reviewer wrote, "If this is a ballet it should be called *Exits and Entrances.*" Beaumont, a dean of English critics, agreed that there were too many comings and goings but, fairly, did not see how they could be avoided, as the ballet depended on an interplay between the dancers.

When *Jardin aux Lilas,* renamed *Lilac Garden,* had its American première in 1940, it appeared at a moment when it could be appreciated. Dance in America had been liberated from old shibboleths, but in England there had been no Denishawn and no dancers like Duncan. No man had set out, as Shawn did, to make his own forte and establish a male ballet. Without a great cause, and an espousal of it, there had been no Graham or de Mille. English ballet was rooted in the Imperial Russian ballet and while it did not become avant-garde in the Diaghilev genre, it incorporated the Fokine expression in the reconstruction it made for its own, individual theatre. Ashton and Tudor, in the forties, evenly divided transatlantic honors. Rambert, who had given Tudor his first chance, retained in repertoire the works he created at the Mercury and for his companies. *Gala Performance* and *Judgment of Paris,* as danced at Jacob's Pillow, appeared in their original form, and the Rambert Ballet's production of *Jardin aux Lilas* effects a totally different interpretation for Caroline than that given in American ballet companies. Tudor is reputed to have offered this role and that of Hagar to Fonteyn, for her interpretations, but to date Tudor's works have not been performed by England's national company, The Royal Ballet.

Loring began in a dilettante theatre but Tudor, with the large and richly endowed Ballet Theatre company, immediately reached a wide audience. In its first seasons the Company presented, in this order, *Dark Elegies, Jardin aux Lilas* and *Judgment of Paris.* The last is set in a *boîte de nuit* and has, like many of Tudor's works, a resemblance to de Maupassant. As *Lilac Garden* the tragedy of manners about Caroline and her lovers became a great American work. Kirstein was said to have called it a ballet with an unmistakable aura of tepid provincialism, but the ballet was danced by the New York City Ballet in 1951, during Tudor's guest tenure, and has been danced by several American casts. The ballet was inspired by Tudor's reading of a story by a Finnish author, Aino Kallas, on the *droit du seigneur* theme. The peasant bride ordered to fulfill her *obligée* on her wedding eve obeys, but takes a dagger into the *seigneur's* bed. The tragedy of a pair of lovers helpless against the mores of their society is the theme of the ballet. Tudor wrote his own libretto and placed the lovers in the Edwardian era, beautifully dressed. The drama takes place in a lilac garden, on the eve of the marriage of the girl, Caroline, to her affianced. At the garden party the guests include Caroline's true love and the woman in Caroline's fiancé's past. Except for Caroline, the characters were named by an enterprising English critic for the principals at the London première, and the use of first names is helpful in narrating the plot.

At curtain rise, Caroline and her fiancé, Tony (the role was created by the choreographer), are awaiting the arrival of their guests. Since the marriage is one of convenience, their mien is polite rather than passionate. Caroline wears a long white dress with flowers in her hair; Tony, a frockcoat with a boutonniere in the lapel. The glass of fashion and the mould of form, the soignée appearance of this lovely couple is in ironic contrast with the emotions that consume them. The score is Chausson's *Poème.*

The guests arrive and among them Hugh (created by Laing), the impecunious young suitor Caroline loves but is not allowed to marry. Another of the guests is

Hugh Laing, Tanaquil LeClercq, Brooks Jackson and Nora Kaye in the New York City Ballet's production of Tudor's Lilac Garden.

Annabelle Lyon, Antony Tudor, Lucia Chase, Nora Kaye and Hugh Laing in Pillar of Fire.

Peggy (created by Peggy van Praagh) a beautiful but slightly *demi-mondaine* ex-love of Tony's. The fiancé is circumspect and practical, but Peggy has no intention of being "sensible." She is still in love, and she desperately intends to hold on to Tony, who means to banish her to his past.

The ballet is in one act, danced to violin and orchestra, and is an epic little comedy of society that becomes tragic for three lovers, Caroline, Hugh and Peggy. Keeping up a pretense of elegant manners, these three now and then encounter each other and behave with propriety, but in between their anguish is revealed as they seek their hearts' desires—Caroline and Hugh longing for each other, Peggy pursuing Tony. At last, never having attained even the dignity of a farewell, they part, and Caroline is left with her fiancé amid the lilacs, unable ever again to bear the scent of their flowers.

Caroline has been danced by Markova, Kaye, Adams and Alonso, and the Woman in His Past by Tallchief, LeClercq and Mounsey.

Never before had dancers become such real people. Never had human emotions been made clearer in dance. Beiswanger noted that the dancers in their lifts were not made godlike, or idealized as in the Classic Dance. They rose only to display their earthiness.

An artistic marriage began between Tudor and Nora Kaye which culminated on April 4, 1942, with the première of their joint masterpiece, *Pillar of Fire,* exactly four days after the choreographer was thirty-three. Kaye had been one of the *corps de ballet,* which she left that same night to rise to stardom as Hagar.

For that ballet Tudor drew his libretto from a nineteenth-century poem, a shocker of its day, *Weib und die Welt* (*Woman and the World*), and used for the ballet score the music the poem inspired, *Verklärte Nacht* (*Transfigured Night*). Months before he went into rehearsal Tudor played the music and related the story to his dancers. The episode concerns a pair of lovers walking in a wintry wood in moonlight. The woman confesses that she had given herself to another man with whom she had not been in love, and who had not loved her. Out of her feeling of being unwanted, at a time before she knew that this, her true love, cared for her, she had deliberately thrown herself away, in anger, despair, lust and bitter pride. The mockery of her present love is that she must bear a child from the wanton incident, and this child whom she now carries is her despair, as is her lost love, walking by her side.

Then the man, her true love, answers her, giving his forgiveness and understanding and illuminating her heart as the bright moon, shining all about them, transfigures the dark night. They have Love itself, says the lover, and the child conceived in hurt and bitterness will be transfigured in a world of love.

Tudor drew the music and theme—transfigured souls in the transfigured night —from Schönberg, but his libretto identified real people, in a certain place, at a special time. The time is of the utmost significance: indicated by the costumes, it is the turn of the last century. We at once understand that the characters belong to a society in which Love, Sin and Duty appeared capitalized in the belles-lettres of the day. The transgressing woman is of the variety Fallen. Unless the time and the society were indicated, the ballet's theme would lose its impact. Hagar in presuffragette, and her only emancipation can come from married love.

She resides in a nice residential district, in a house in the center of its neighbors, of the gingerbread Victorian architecture that symbolizes solid comfort and rigid respectability. Opposite Hagar's house, which she shares with an older and a younger sister, is the house across the way, whose interior veils lascivious secrets. The design is by Jo Mielziner, and the costumes are spinsterish for Hagar and some of the women, sleek for the villain of the piece—The Young Man Across The Way—and girlish for Hagar's Younger Sister, for whom the Older Sister covets Hagar's only Friend, a man who is kind to Hagar but does not know how dearly she loves him.

When the Friend comes to visit Hagar the Older Sister wheedles him into the house to meet the Younger Sister, leaving Hagar alone on the doorstep. Brooding about her fate, a spinster in years but a passionate woman at heart, Hagar sits alone and is accosted by the Young Man, who strolls out of the House Across The Way. She is repelled and fascinated, the more so when she is able to see through the House into its mysterious rooms and at length understands that it is a place of assignation for men and women. Locked up inside Hagar is a world of tenderness and love which she is powerless to release. She needs her Friend to free her from her prison.

But the Friend, coming out of the sisters' house, goes off with the Younger Sister and Hagar's grief is inverted into rage and wild rebellion. When the Young Man again accosts her she yields to his fascination and he, using the tormented emotions of the woman, turns her self pity and longing for the Friend towards himself. Their dance shows how the Young Man, skillful and agile, uses her abandonment to excite and then to seduce Hagar. Forgetting herself and her station in life Hagar leaps, in a great *jeté*. The Young Man stops her in mid-flight, turns her towards him, directs her passion towards himself. Hagar yields, and is held and lifted, her legs spread, her body taut and high. Carried up and out of herself she is borne by passion and the Young Man into the House Across The Way.

The next scene is close to a morality play of the era. Hagar's sin makes her as conspicuous as a belled leper. Having been seen to come from the House Across The Way, and obviously oppressed by guilt, Hagar is an outcast. The sanctimonious detest her no less than those who secretly envy her the visit to the House. Lovers in Innocence avert their shocked gaze from Hagar. Lovers in Experience hate her for having been found out. Overcome by remorse and terror, Hagar flees. Nowhere does she find understanding. The townspeople are offended in their sense of propriety. The loose women of the town mock her. The final ignominy is reached when the Young Man goes by Hagar without recognition, thus informing her how commonplace her seduction was to him.

Eventually, the Friend reappears. His *pas de deux* with Hagar makes him the antithesis of the Young Man. By holding her, forcing her to face him, he prevails on distraught Hagar to believe in his love and understanding. The insistent man and the frantic woman are thus seen twice over, in two separate *pas de deux,* and their characters and motives are made abundantly plain in the dancing. At length Hagar yields to her Friend, and is enfolded and supported by him. Tenderly, but strongly still, they are turned and moved by their transfigured love. At the end they are seen walking into the distance, hand in hand.

The critics analyzed the ballet with care and discernment. Edwin Denby observed that the ballet was complex in device, using three separate techniques of dance: the ballet technique, with controlled gestures, taut leaps and high lifts; a Modern technique—flexible, with impulsive gesture, loose low leaps, low lifts, and movement that exploded into jitterbugging; and a third technique, of the body as in everyday life, unrestrained and at ease—a natural movement. The characters were not dancers, but were seen as persons—men and women in the act of dancing.

Following the tremendous acclaim of *Pillar of Fire,* Tudor created *Romeo and Juliet,* to a score arranged by Antal Dorati from Delius, with Markova and Laing as the star-crossed lovers. The roles were later danced by Kaye and Kriza, and Alonso and Youskevitch. *Dim Lustre* followed, a tale of worldly lovers, more bitter-sweet even than *Lilac Garden,* with roles created by Kaye and

Laing. With *Undertow,* in 1945, Tudor created a clinical dissertation on murder —not of the act of violence alone but of the birth and life of the murderer. The principal character, an Oedipus-figure born to Cybele, is caught helpless in the undertow of human emotions and their causes and effects. The form was less like ballet than *tableau vivant,* with ceremonial pantomime and lyric gesture. Set in a contemporary urban scene, it named the principals as the Transgressor, his innocent love Agniappe, her friend Nemesis, and a psalm-singing hypocrite, Polyphemia. Volupta, a whore, and Medusa, a temptress, are among the strange assortment of characters around the Transgressor. The theme was a powerful and complex one: the Transgressor is repudiated by his mother at his birth. She leaves him to go away with a dashing lover named Pollux, whereupon the Transgressor, grown to manhood, hates the world and seeks to be revenged on it for all his hurts and longings. Surrendering to Medusa in an act of desire, he strangles her in revulsion from all his wrongs from his mother and the world.

Whereas *Pillar of Fire* concerned Hagar, *Undertow* dealt with larger issues of life and society. It was a ballet difficult to understand and uncomfortable to view, but an American audience educated on Tudor's strong and terrible treatises received it with sensitive awareness. Tudor took most of his gestures, as well as his themes, characters and feelings, from life. He appeared to have known some haggard loves and tired hatreds and he was a master at evoking them in ballet.

In 1948, after the première of his ballet *Shadow of the Wind,* Ballet Theatre disbanded for a time and Tudor had a short but not a historic career with the New York City Ballet. In 1950 he went to Denmark, and mounted his *Gala Performance* and *Jardin aux Lilas,* and created *Arabesque* for the Royal Danish Ballet, exerting a marked influence on the national theatre. He worked also at the Jacob's Pillow Dance Festival and in Japan.

Thereafter Tudor became inactive as a choreographer, devoting himself, of recent years, to directing the school of the Metropolitan Opera Ballet. He has been reported to be working on an epic spectacle-drama based on Sibelius' *En Saga,* and created a ballet, *Offenbach in the Underworld,* for a Canadian company, which was taken into the American Ballet Theatre repertoire in 1956. In 1959 he was represented with *Hail and Farewell* at the Metropolitan's first evening program of ballet. In it, Eleanor Steber sang the *Four Last Songs* onstage on a rostrum above the dancers, two of whom were the ballerinas Kaye and Serrano.

The long, barren period which followed Tudor's epic ballets has done nothing to diminish their worth, and even if Tudor creates nothing again as epochal as *Pillar of Fire* he holds his place among the immortals. The boy who began his day every day at 6 A.M. at the Smithfield Meat Market, worked there until 3 P.M., and then went around to earn his dancing lesson in return for playing the piano and doing odd jobs, became the great choreographer. A passion begun in adolescence, in the most unlikely circumstances, out of the most imponderable of fancies, shaped a whole life and helped to shape American ballet. For although Tudor did not compose *ballet americana* he is an inextirpable component of American ballet.

Four of his works might belong to four separate choreographers: *Gallant Assembly, Jardin aux Lilas, Romeo and Juliet* and *Undertow.* His *Pillar of Fire* has obviously influenced other choreography, and his consummate delineation of human passions, with the resulting extension in gesture as the visible expression of the inward feeling, has inspired modern ballet. He has imprinted moments and movements on the stage that are as grand and terrible, as immediate and poignant, as experiences in real life. No narrative could more explicitly describe a woman teetering on the brink of love and anguish than his dance design for Hagar, and Kaye did not glibly achieve the communication. De Mille relates that Kaye was in rehearsal for over a year before dancing the role, and that Tudor so brooded over her that it was impossible to say where composition ended and performance began.

As a teacher and choreographer, Tudor maintains no set device, but employs those he finds apt and eloquent to the moment. He usually works with dancers who are sympathetic to his work, and from a libretto he composes out of an idea or a suggestion from a book or person. In the instance of *Undertow* the libretto derived from a suggestion of John van Druten. Tudor makes his dancers develop fully dimensional characters. In *Pillar of Fire* the dancers imagined the roles in terms of characters, for whose personalities they assumed tastes, manners of speech, behavior, fears and hopes. Out of these personalities, each with an identity as a character in the drama, Tudor evolved dance that was rooted in natural gesture and movement that was an extension, in motive, of the individual. Yet when he was rehearsing Diana Adams in *Undertow* he gave her nothing but instructions for her performance. Only just before the ballet's première did he tell her that she was Cybele in childbirth, whose labor produces the babe that is afterward the Transgressor.

One of the most distinctive aspects of Tudor's work is its understatement. Nothing is fully stated and much is merely implied, and the ballets sometimes have a mysterious communication to the audience, personal and secretive. Although he has incorporated song and dance, as in *Dark Elegies* and *Hail and Farewell,* his ballets are wholly dance concepts. His characters have emotional and intellectual cognizance, but their source is physical. He has broken every canon of traditional ballet and has made some that by usage are now part and parcel of it. The predominant characteristic of his dance movement is control—of physical movements and main effects. To that must be added his own compulsion to seek the nature and motive of every human encounter—a provocative insight into a choreographer who as a man is mild and scholarly, unaffected in manner, outwardly calm. His American contemporaries become involved in their work and show their natures—de Mille is keen and sophisticated, and she can be merry; Robbins' people laugh or leap in animal reflex and the exuberance of movement—but Tudor has a superhuman and steely air, and digests his creations, as it were, from outer sources, rather than from his inner self. Rationally, clinically—sauve in his white coat, eyes unfathomable behind the flashing pince-nez—eminent Doktor Tudor relates only the proven and the true. Observe how such and such mores in this society, one well fed and well dressed, will breed these virtues and vices and cause these heterogeneous little deaths, when lilacs are in bloom! Regard how inevitably as the ancient Fates a life-long frustration, a terrible *desiderium,* a sense of loss, an ardent longing, turns in un-utterable woe as the adductor—the muscle that draws the limb to the main trunk, or axis—thereby casting its helpless victim into the undertow! In these ways Tudor pierces to the heart of the matter and the heart, itself, so pinned, is laid bare to the audience's view.

He has had a greater empathy from Nora Kaye than most choreographers draw from dancers. Kaye totally assumes the personality of Hagar and is the adducent Kaye—the dancer Kaye drawing her muscles to the point where their reflex is not that of Nora-Kaye-born-Koreff but of a woman in a town late in the nineteenth century whose name is Hagar. Even after seeing the Russians and their famed attributes of acting I am struck by Kaye's Hagar, the purest case of transubstantiation on view in contemporary ballet. Other choreographers, as for instance de Mille in *Fall River Legend,* have been content to evoke the individual dancer's interpretation of a powerful role, such as that of The Ac-cused by Alonso, Kaye and Krupska.

Most of the Tudor ballets could be danced in unblocked shoes but the per-formance would have a different expression, since he choreographs for the quick, light, meticulous footwork of the classicist. He has used *pointe* shoes in *Pillar of Fire* apparently to emphasize the feminine nature of the dancer, and his dancers, male and female, have a marked flexibility of the upper back. He does not use rigidity except for a characteristic distortion, functional to the ballet. Strongly dramatic, to the point of fixity and ugliness, his work has also shown a melting tenderness, as in *Romeo and Juliet.* This ballet provided Markova with an ex-quisite role, as Juliet, in which she was ineffably light, quick and unerring as an arrow, and honeyed in sweet, slow-flowing dance patterns. Physical contact as swift and brutal as the rape in *Undertow,* perhaps more dreadful than the mur-der, is transcended by the same choreographer in *Romeo and Juliet,* where the erotic passages have a rapture seldom seen in theatre.

By turns ironic, Rabelaisan, or tender, Tudor has for the first quarter of a century of American ballet beguiled and mystified, stunned and frightened his audiences. Turning human emotions into muscular activity and thereby into dance, he evolved for ballet a union of form and spirit as close as that one be-tween the stage and the street. Not the least of American Ballet Theatre's many honors lies here: in the nurturing of a great individual talent imported into American ballet, and the retention in its permanent repertoire of the works of Antony Tudor.

THE DANCERS

Prima ballerina Nora Kaye was born Koreff, the daughter of an actor of the Moscow theatre, who emigrated with his family to America. Kaye was born in New York in 1920, was a private pupil of Fokine, and studied at the Metropoli-tan Opera's ballet school. Onstage is the most natural place for her, for she has been there from childhood. When she was very small, she played all the elfin roles in opera. Once, as a gnome in Respighi's *The Sunken Bell,* she was held by a singer over a supposedly boiling cauldron, and since her screams were not realistic enough to suit him the singer pinched her until she reached the required pitch of vocal terror. From such beginnings, Kaye drew the power that has made her the great dance-actress of her time.

At fifteen she graduated from the pixie roles to dancing in the operas, and when Balanchine's American Ballet was the resident company she danced in it, resigning when he was displaced. She had a career in musicals and joined Ballet Theatre in the *corps,* when Fokine was auditioning for the Company. Until April 8, 1942, she was a member of the *corps.* On that night, having changed her costume after dancing in *Les Sylphides,* she put on *Hagar's* dress and went onstage in the ballet *Pillar of Fire.* At the end of the ballet she was called the first great tragedienne to come out of her ballet theatre. As a dance-actress she is ranked, internationally, with Sallé. Her range is wide enough to encompass the tortured heroines of Tudor's works and the Russian Ballerina in his *Gala Performance,* and she must be the most sympathetic ballerina of her day, for she has willingly lent herself to some choreographic experiments, like the recent *Tristan* by Ross, which would be hazardous for a less gifted dancer. Although she is constantly made to plunge herself into a crucible of bitter emotion she is a sophisticated woman with a merry wit. The critic Walter Terry relates a delicious anecdote that is wonderfully characteristic. In one performance of *Pillar of Fire* Kaye found herself stranded onstage without the support of three dancers who should have, at that moment, been ready to assist her in some complex lifts. They were in the wings, offering first aid and sympathy to a fourth dancer who had been suddenly afflicted with severe cramp. At last one of the three *danseurs* remembered his cue and dashed onstage, to be met by Kaye, valiantly improvising. As she flew past him, still improvising, the ballerina muttered out of the corner of her mouth, "Say, where the hell is everybody?"

No one is less awed by her position than Kaye, who experiments, sometimes wilfully, against tradition, until she has fathomed a role and feels in her element in it. Her Giselle made the "authorities" frantic, but in its maturity its beauty is vital and new, and so individual that her faithful audiences forget that she is in the distant country of Silesia with that sorry Duke Albert, and understand only the mysterious realm of the heart where Kaye has transported them as Hagar and as Lizzie, as Caroline, and as the poor little predatory Novice in *The Cage.* Her Odette is a live woman, never a bird.

Kaye has danced with the New York City Ballet and the Komaki Ballet of Japan. She became the first American ballerina to dance in Russia under the official sponsorship of the United States State Department, for the 1959 Moscow Trades Fair.

The other dancer in the Company as closely associated with its repertoire as Kaye is the *premier* John Kriza. He was born in Illinois of Czechoslovakian ancestry and began to study ballet, under protest, so that he could build his physique up to the entrance requirements for the Sokol (the Czechoslovakian gymnasium) in Chicago. In due course, he was admitted to the Sokol and in high school excelled in athletics, especially swimming and tumbling. He continued to study ballet, although he intended to enter his father's meat-packing business, and in his senior year he joined a WPA dance project under Ruth Page, studied with Bentley Stone, and found himself engaged as a dancer by the Chicago Civic Opera Company. Next he toured Latin America with the Page-Stone troupe and became a Broadway chorus boy. He was still drifting, and not yet serious about making a career in dancing. One day in 1940 he auditioned for three companies —Radio City Music Hall, the Metropolitan Opera Ballet, and the newly formed Ballet Theatre. He was offered contracts by all three and, on impulse, chose the last. In Ballet Theatre he studied with Tudor and Dolin and had as his fellow members in the *corps* girls named Kaye and Alonso, later his partners as ballerinas. Fifteen years after joining Ballet Theatre, which he never left, Kriza became its *premier*. He is the first American-born and American-trained *danseur* to be *premier danseur* of a major company, and dances the leads of the American ballets, as well as several others. He is the best admired American character dancer in Europe, and in two hundred and twenty-three cities of the United States, and twenty-two cities of eleven European countries, he has been seen as Billy, the Champion Roper, a Sailor in *Fancy Free,* the Pastor in *Fall River Legend,* and Stanley Kowalski in *Streetcar.* In the United States he is lauded in dubious press agentry as the "John Wayne of Ballet" because of *Billy,* and the "Marlon Brando of Ballet" because of *Streetcar.* His wider renown is impervious to this, and Kriza to both. He has partnered the French ballerinas Marchand and Verdy, Tamara Toumanova, and Irina Baronova, and the Americans Alonso, Gollner, Hayden, Koesun, Moylan, Reed, Serrano and Tallchief. And he has partnered Markova. He still dances with an elemental feeling, which sometimes annoys metropolitan critics when he essays classic *danseur* roles, but stands him in good stead when, as in the open air theatres of Europe, he has danced *Billy* in pouring rain with water in his boots.

In style, physique and deportment, Kriza has done a great deal to break down the audience's prejudice against American *danseurs.* He can be properly romantic and tragic as Tancred or the lover in *Winter's Eve,* but above all he is indestructible in his masculine impression on ballet, and has been doing the backflip in *Fancy Free* for fourteen miraculous years.

The second ballerina of the Company is Lupe Serrano, born in Chile and educated in Mexico City. She made a debut at thirteen with Bellas Artes in *Les Sylphides* and was there discovered by Markova and Dolin, on tour, who urged her to make a career of ballet. She continued to study Classic Dance and also studied Modern at Mexico's National Academy of Contemporary Dance, where she performed with José Limon. In 1951 Serrano arrived in New York to study with Vincenzo Celli, auditioned for the Metropolitan and Ballet Russe and was accepted by both, but chose Ballet Russe. She remained with it until it temporarily disbanded, when she returned to Mexico. There she was the first ballerina to dance on television. She later toured with Igor Schwezoff in South America, and on her next visit to New York was invited to join Ballet Theatre and Ballet Russe. She chose the former because of the large repertoire and strong characters and themes, and in 1953 was made ballerina.

Serrano is a great beauty—one of the most striking in contemporary ballet. She has brilliance and femininity, and excellent technique, and moves easily

Lupe Serrano in Les Sylphides.

from classic roles of the abstract genre, as in *Sylphides,* to dramatic ones in *Le Combat.* She is beautiful to see in *Theme and Variations* with Royes Fernandez, and the *pas de deux* from *Don Quixote.* Her forte as a dramatic dancer is matched by her virtuoso ability, and she is especially noted for her *grandes jetés.* In 1958–1959 she was *prima ballerina* of the Metropolitan.

Ruth Ann Koesun is a veteran of Ballet Theatre, which she joined in the *corps.* She is a pretty little dancer, born in Chicago, the daughter of a Chinese physician, who studied with Ruth Page and Walter Camryn. In New York, on school vacations, she was the pupil of Swoboda. She began her theatrical career at twelve, with the San Carlo Opera Company, and specialized in pantomime and Modern Dance. She was attracted to classic ballet in 1931, when she saw her first full-scale ballet by Ballet Russe in Chicago. She joined Ballet Theatre in the 'forties.

A dependable performer, and of the kind that no major company may exist without, Koesun is admirable in many roles. Her repertoire ranges from the Child in *Fall River Legend,* and a hoyden in *Interplay,* to the performance of a particularly lovely Prelude in *Les Sylphides.* Her tenderness and littleness are in vivid contrast with Kaye's dramatic temperament, and the fine *bravura* technique of Serrano.

The Company has developed two notable young *danseurs* in Scott Douglas, a Texan whose father is a sheriff—which amuses the troupe in which Douglas dances as Pat Garret—and Michael Lland, from Bishopville, South Carolina.

Douglas studied with St. Denis and William Christensen, and with Lester Horton, but has been developed into a *danseur noble.* Lland studied in New York with Schwezoff, and from 1945 to 1949 was a dancer at the Municipal Ballet in Rio de Janeiro. Other soloists of note are Jillana Williams, a graduate of the School of American Ballet, and a member for nine years of the New York City Ballet; and Leo Duggan and Ray Barra, protégés of the Christensens, who danced with the San Francisco Ballet. Like Ballet Russe, the Company's dancers are drawn from the American continent. The ballet master, Fernand Nault, is a Canadian, being developed as a choreographer in the Workshop, for which he composed *The Encounter.* Enrique Martinez is a Cuban, and a former member of Alonso's company. He has choreographed not only for his own company's Workshop but also for de Cuevas' company.

The *corps,* traditionally for American Ballet Theatre, is a first-rate one. Its great distinction is its fine discipline and its sensitivity. Seen in ballets like *Les Sylphides,* the *corps* mellifluously accompanies its dazzling principals, but has a rhythmic vitality that, to its pride, the international balletomane describes as "American."

In the 'fifties, American Ballet Theatre presented the great Danish *danseur noble* Erik Bruhn, and in 1957 was rejoined by a former member, the American Royes Fernandez. These two *danseurs* gave American Ballet Theatre the monopoly on *danseur* good looks: these two may quite possibly be the handsomest males in contemporary ballet. More to the point, they are a pair of exciting dancers to see.

Bruhn, born in 1929, was a *solodancer* of the Royal Danish Ballet, for which company he was trained from the age of nine. In 1947, feeling limited by the

Bournonville methods, he obtained a leave of absence from his post and went to England, to study under Vera Volkova, and Stanilaus Idzikowsky, whose elevation and technique were comparable with Nijinsky's. Bruhn's Classic style became superb, and he never sacrificed the virility imbued by the Royal Danish Ballet. He danced in England with the Metropolitan Ballet, and with Ballet Theatre as guest artist on four leaves of absence from his home company. In 1955 he resigned from the Danish organization, forfeiting the pension he was entitled to, and became the *premier danseur noble* of the American company.

Except for Youskevitch in his prime, American ballet has never had a *danseur* to compare with Bruhn. He is indubitably the best of his generation. The very magnificence of his technique makes it difficult to describe. One may only extol it. His technical command is unrivaled, and in this he appears most notable, in America, for his ease and superb style in command of the difficult, like his performance of a series of *entrechats-huit* in *Theme and Variations.* His *tours en l'air,* in an extended position *seconde,* are miracles of elegance. In looks and style, by temperament and in personality, Bruhn is princely. His departure from American ballet left a yawning gap which no *danseur,* foreign or native, has appeared to fill. He returned to the Royal Danish Ballet in 1958, and is certain to play an important part in its new regime, now being evolved under Volkova as *maïtresse de ballet.*

Fernandez is as poetic as any European concept of the *danseur,* and is a remarkable manifestation in American ballet. He is the pupil and protégé of Celli, and he has the graciousness and grand manner of the Cecchetti style, of which Celli is the chief advocate practicing in American ballet. Fernandez has already served a commendable apprenticeship. He danced with Original Ballet Russe, the Markova-Dolin Company, and was the *premier* of the Alonso company on tour in South America, dancing the male leads in *Coppelia, Giselle* and *Swan Lake.* He has partnered Mia Slavenska and Barbara Fallis, and in 1959 joined the San Francisco Ballet on its Near East tour. His style is pure Classic, and his stage presence is the finest among his confrères. Seldom has American ballet produced a *danseur* whose style, forte, temperament and physical appearance have been so marvelously in harmony. Dancing with Fallis, an American (born in Denver) trained at the Sadler's Wells School and under Vilzak, Fernandez was featured at Jacob's Pillow in 1958 and with the Kovach-Rabovsky company on its United States tour. The Fallis-Fernandez *pas de deux* is not surpassed, even by more celebrated dancers, according to the critical assessment.

In its twentieth year American Ballet Theatre possessed the largest and most varied repertoire in American ballet, and the most representative for a national theatre. It had developed dancers who, in the international view, ranked with the best. Its *prima ballerina* is unique, not only in America but in contemporary ballet, where descriptions such as "the Duse of the Dance" are coined in an effort to describe her. Under Kaye are ranked dancers of more than average gifts. The ballerina Serrano is a dancer of passion and technical brilliance, with the promise of a more ample manner than has been the norm for American ballet. Koesun is, in all respects, exquisite. The *danseurs,* to a man, are recognizably of the masculine gender, and range in forte from strong character dancers of an

estimable "American" quality, like Kriza, to the *danseur noble* deportment of Fernandez and Douglas. The *corps,* dancing with the dazzling precision that is an American hallmark, whether at Radio City Music Hall or the Metropolitan Opera, adapts easily from American themes and styles in movement to the "abstraction" of *Les Sylphides.* Dancing this ballet in Warsaw, where Chopin is still worshipped, the *corps* enchanted the Polish audience with its crisp rhythms and "American lyricism."

Here, then, is a company of brimming vitality, with boundless scope, traditionally free to experiment in classic and modern ballet. Most graphically, here is a company that, in a choice of repertoire and by a development of dancers, has achieved a marvelous communication with the international audience. On the evidence of its effects on foreign theatres, some of them in countries adversely inclined towards America, its worth as an ambassador is beyond mere calculation at the box office window. The American Ballet Theatre, whatever befalls it at home, has been taken for nothing trivial abroad. All its twenty full years are not enough to sum up its character and influence. They are the years of its birth and beginning, sufficing only to indicate that America may, if it chooses, produce an indigenous ballet. No company has ever had a more inspired beginning, nor more ardent well-wishers to watch it grow.

Nor is American Ballet Theatre equaled in its contribution and its status. Although it has never completely fulfilled its promise to *be* America's national ballet it comes as close as any company has yet succeeded. It is clearly in need of a home. How paradoxical for the *American National Ballet Theatre* (as this company, by permission of the United States State Department, is billed on its ANTA-sponsored foreign tours) to be more loved abroad than at home! And to be housed, with pomp, in the greatest opera houses of Europe, while at home it must dicker for a stage! But balancing the indignation of its American balletomanes (and these are innumerable) that American Ballet Theatre does not receive state subsidy or civic support, is the contention that this "American" company has moved too far from its original character to be recognized as *the* American Ballet Theatre. The points of contention are that since Loring, de Mille, and Robbins there have been no American choreographers in the Company with equal originality and influence, and that the American ballets in repertoire—*Billy the Kid, Rodeo, Fancy Free,* and *Fall River Legend*—although important, are static contributions which advocate but do not continue to advance the Company's claim to its high office. This claim may only be supported by younger choreographers and new ballets. Both parties must be heard—and must wait, as the audience must wait, for the eventual answer.

Waiting, perforce, are the dancers. A more reticent lot than those of the other companies, they are especially reserved when their company, as now, wavers precariously on the edge of dissolving. But their loyalty and faith to the image held up to them, and by them, is the most notable in their theatre. No body of dancers deserves more respect than the veterans who, in twenty years, have built up the prodigious reputation of American Ballet Theatre. They are not only vitally American but are also tolerant of other contemporary developments, as when on tour they seek classes with foreign teachers, and seriously study museums and

Rosella Hightower and Erik Bruhn in Balanchine's Theme and Variations.

art galleries as extensions of their own profession. The strong characterizations in the repertoire—the largest permanent active repertoire in their theatre—entail thoughtful preparation, much of which the dancers seek for themselves. In Warsaw in 1958 they rushed to take classes from the *maître* of Polish ballet, Stanislaus Woicikowski—the unchallenged character *danseur* of the era—with the same alert and enthusiastic spirit that sent dancers of the Royal Ballet to study, in New York, under the character *danseur* Yurek Lazowski, when they danced *Petrushka* in 1957.

In no other American company has more attention been paid to the confluence of the arts in ballet. The Company has produced the leading ballet artist on the continent, Oliver Smith, and its former musical director, Joseph Levine, conducted fourteen recordings of ballet scores from the Company's repertoire. Its school has regular courses in mime, and includes Classic genres, which are the forte of the teachers Lazowski, Shollar and Vilzak, as well as jazz. The dancers are flexibly attuned to Dance, rather than to one strict form of dancing, and they have appeared in *Circo de Espana* by Carmalita Maracci in 1951, and Dolin's suite for *danseur* pyrotechnics, *Variations for Four,* following its American première on television in 1958. With these, and other varieties of ballets, the Company has preserved the "American classics," in which were first born the indigenous movement, music and art design that accredited American ballet.

I can find no better way to differentiate between New York City Ballet and American Ballet Theatre than to paraphrase the words of an eminent Viennese critic. The first is precisely "Balanchine's company," and an audience must first of all intellectually accept, before it can appreciate, the repertoire of the New York City Ballet. But an audience viewing American Ballet Theatre is struck by nothing less than love at first sight! No civilized audience is unaware of the American West, and Billy, and the Cowgirl in *Rodeo,* require no translation beyond language barriers. Robbins' sailors are as much at home on the great stages of old opera houses as they are familiar in every port of the world. And no human audience sits down to *Fall River Legend, Pillar of Fire,* and *A Streetcar Named Desire,* and finds itself in need of a narrator to explain the mortal events onstage.

We may boldly lay claim to an American ballet at home, and shape it as we will by critical persuasion or by popular tastes, but the real assessment of a national ballet is made by the international audience. No art and no artifact that we have exported has so vividly interpreted America for the world as our American dance, and no Americans have been more admired and loved in the international scene than American dancers. Among them no company has a higher place than the American Ballet Theatre. It has been astutely called America's ambassador of dance.

THE BALLET TROUPERS

Outside the artistic conglomerations of choreographers, dancers, composers and designers, who form the nuclei of "the companies," American ballet has a life in the popular theatre of musicals, television, and films. More than in any of these, it thrives most wondrously on the road.

In twenty-five years, the major ballet companies have found nothing like the opera houses in which European and Russian ballet traditionally reside. The chief opera house in the United States, the Metropolitan in New York, was host to Balanchine's American Ballet and Chase's Ballet Theatre for short and uneasy soujourns and now, after years of mystifying aversion to the ballet, its own school and company have become a fine unit under Tudor. In 1958 its resident choreographer, Zachary Solov, was reinforced by the addition of Alexandra Danilova and Yurek Lazowski, and the Metropolitan announced that full evening programs of ballet would be inaugurated in its opera seasons.

Except for the New York City Ballet's tenancy of City Center—a small stage, governed by economic strictures, and shared with opera and other civic theatre American ballet is of the trouper variety. Indeed, we have not advanced far beyond the status of the Ravels, except that we no longer encounter marauding Indians.

Ballet Russe de Monte Carlo and American Ballet Theatre have executive offices and thriving schools on which the companies appear to be solidly based in New York, but even these two major companies are troupers like all the rest of American ballet. Ballet Russe is the most seasoned, and the most valiant. American Ballet Theatre fares rather more graciously in its foreign travels and circulates to some extent at home but never as constantly and widely as Ballet Russe. However, American Ballet Theatre boasts that it has appeared in each of the old forty-eight states. At home or abroad, these major companies frankly subsist as transients, in whatever makeshift theatre the caravanserai provides.

Two important exceptions are the San Francisco Ballet, which has been pridefully treated by the City of San Francisco and has a school and a theatre of its own, and Ruth Page's Chicago Opera-Ballet which is a part of the Chicago Opera, a first-rate organization, and an independent but unified part of the Chicago Lyric Opera. Established under Page in 1953, it began annual tours in 1955, but it is solidly entrenched in Chicago, where ballet has long been held in high repute. Jacob's Pillow alone is in the unique position of having to solicit no theatre. Instead, companies American and foreign make pilgrimages to the Pillow for the summer festivals. Here Shawn presides over a university of dance in the school, and a variety of dance in his theatre.

Here and there across the United States, ballet is forming youthful traveling organizations that are chiefly the outgrowth of ballet schools or civic symphony and lyric groups. Regional ballet began in 1956 with the first performance in Atlanta, Georgia, of Southern Ballet. These regional groups are thoroughly organized, in contrast with the harum-scarum way that early companies and performing ensembles rushed about the country. They are advised and often directed behind the scenes by authorities like Mme Danilova, and famous dancers like

Karen Conrad, Frederic Franklin and the Jasinskys often hold authoritative positions as teachers, choreographers, directors and dancers. Thus, regional ballet is a serious, solid and businesslike addition to ballet in the United States. It gives cohesion to gifted American ballet students, both choreographers and dancers—and may eventually do the same for composers, artists and librettists. Its nuclei are the semi-retired dancers of the past generations. Many of them are European; most of them have emerged from the past of American ballet, but there are some adventurous strangers who have now been drawn from distant parts, such as the South African dancer Jo Anna, who is the ballerina and choreographer of the million-and-a-half-dollar Poinciana theatre in Palm Beach. Here, in 1958, impresario Frank Hale produced Jo Anna's first full-length ballet, *The Princess,* at a cost of seventy-five thousand dollars, at a première for which seats were priced at twenty-five dollars each. The stage curtains were snowy white and the orchestral music was perfectly tuned. The audience came to the theatre in the indulgent frame of mind of civilized people about to benefit a worthy cultural and civic project. Many of them had first dined in the adjoining restaurant, the Celebrity Room, before they entered the damask-lined entrance to the ornate red, white and gold theatre. The building, and the production of *The Princess,* came from the munificence of one American, the millionaire industrialist Frank Hale. It was like a fairy tale to the rest of American ballet.

It would be almost impossible to enumerate the troupes, large and small, of traditional or of Modern métiers, who make up American ballet. Many of them dissolve so quickly as to leave no real records, but let there be no mistake—they make their minute impressions, and they are as much a part of the indelible ledger that contains the record as the larger, permanent, and better endowed groups. They are, above all, the most courageous—or the most reckless—devotees of American ballet. They remind me, irresistibly, of those hardy creatures who used to fare forth with the Ravel melée of acrobats, ballet dancers and rope dancers. Quite often, now, they are sandwiched in a community hall between a gospel revivalist and a travel-worn wrestling bout. But, as one veteran of twenty-five years or more of ballet touring tells me, *"L'allée est facile*—Pavlova followed elephants at the Hippodrome!" Cheerfulness, real or assumed, is part of the redoubtable frame of mind which the trouper must have as equipment. No dancer tours for fun. The youngest, strongest, most-dedicated weary soon of the gypsy existence, and constitutionally they are ground down in a hard mill of work, and plagued by press critics who comfortably occupy a seat (possibly free) for one performance. The critic believes it is his duty to ballet to hold the dancer to the fine, high principles of art. The plain fact, however, is that the touring dancer cannot perform by hard and fast rules; he dances under a physical and mental strain that would pole-axe a Marine.

However, I am concerned here not with the critics' frequently unsatisfactory view of American ballet on tour but with the effects of touring dancers on American ballet. Without ambulant dancers, America would be destitute of dance arts. The current exploitation of dancing in the movies and television gives, at best, a flat and one-dimensional view of it. Ballet is a dimensional art—movement in spatial design—and unless it is "live" it is, and must always be, the shadow of its substance. No machinery can ever effect a true representation of ballet. The dance goes far beyond commercial and mechanical intermediaries. It remains a personal experience, based on the response of the audience to the dancers. The greatest enjoyment to be drawn from dance on film is its likeness to the "live" article, and an audience would be unable to get even this enjoyment if it had not seen actual performances.

Regional ballet would, obviously, never have been born except under the stimulus of the touring dancers. When we read the memoirs of the "greats" we understand how infrequently the creative urge was born spontaneously, and how often it was inspired by a personal contact so fleeting that the dancer, Pavlova, for example, can never have known what fires she was igniting: only the one inspired knew.

Americans may read in newspapers and magazines that native dancers named Tallchief have been so successful that one, Maria, is internationally accepted as the epitome of her kind, and the second, Marjorie, is the *première* of the Paris Opéra. These statements are understandable to the comparative few who have gone to the City Center theatre in Manhattan to see the *prima ballerina* of the New York City Ballet, or to Europe to see the de Cuevas company or the Paris Opéra Ballet. These achievements become significant to the audience only when Maria Tallchief tours with her company or appears in concerts or when Marjorie Tallchief, with the Ruth Page Chicago Opera-Ballet, or the de Cuevas company, appears on tour in the United States. And this is where American ballet differs from others. In the great cities of Europe, ballet is entrenched—at the Royal Opera House in London, the Opéra in Paris, the Royal Theatre in Copenhagen, and the Bolshoi in Moscow. Ballet in America is a swarming concourse of dance and dancers. No American, however lunatic a balletomane, now says that American ballet exists only in New York. The most that may be said is that New York has established itself as a theatrical center in America. But since it is a physical impossibility to transfer all of its audience to New York City, American ballet has been obliged to travel about the United States.

The readiest answer to the problem of its material state and artistic condition while touring, would be for every major city in the country to support a theatre in which theatrical artists could perform. I use the word *artists*. Meanwhile, we make do with our "troupers" who give us more than our money's worth at the box office, as may be seen by a season's perambulation about the United States.

Small concert groups have produced both dancers of merit and significant new ballets. The Agnes de Mille Theatre developed Gemze de Lappe, who as a child made some appearances with the Fokine company but joined no company. De Lappe made a precedent-shattering turnabout from trouping to legitimate theatre, when she achieved ballerina status in Ballet Theatre as the lead in *The Harvest According.* James Mitchell, another dancer of de Mille's group, is an important example of the new dancer-actor-singer in American ballet. Splendid in physique, masculine in his approach to dance, Mitchell satisfies every ideal of the American audience. Moreover, he is a dancer of skill, versatility, and talent. He rose to stardom in the musical theatre in *Brigadoon,* winning the Donaldson Award for the role of Harry Beaton, and appeared on Broadway in *Bloomer Girl,*

Billion Dollar Baby, and *Paint Your Wagon.* He then went into summer stock theatre and played, to a wide audience, in *Picnic,* and as the Witch Boy in *Dark of the Moon;* in *Carousel,* and *The Rainmaker.* In movies, he danced Curly in *Oklahoma!* and was Cyd Charisse's partner in *The Bandwagon.* On television he has been featured on "Camera Three," "Rendezvous," "The Armstrong Theatre," "The Agnes de Mille Theatre" and "Seven Lively Arts." Turning straight actor, he appeared in *Border Incident, Stars in my Crown, Devil's Doorway, The Prodigal* and *The Peacemaker.* As an actor-dancer, he played five roles in Ben Hecht's play, *Winkleberg;* Mack-the-Knife in a long run of *Threepenny Opera;* Injun Joe in *Livin' the Life;* Jigger in *Carousel;* and the title role of Stravinsky's *Histoire du Soldat* at the New York City Center Theatre. Mitchell is one of the very fine troupers who are an important part of the American tradition.

During the 'fifties, Danilova formed a world-traveled concert ensemble, in which a former *danseur* of New York City Ballet, Michael Maule, matured as a ranking *premier danseur.* He is a South African, who studied with Celli in New York, and made a debut in the musical *Annie Get Your Gun.* He danced with New York City Ballet, Ballet Theatre and Ballet Alonso in Cuba (where he partnered Markova) but although consistently admirable he did not emerge as a star until Danilova chose him for her partner in 1954. Thereafter he become widely known and very popular, and he has been the *premier danseur* at the Metropolitan. Also he is a leading *danseur* in the series, "Great Moments of the Dance," and was the *premier* of the 1958 revival of *Oklahoma!.* As Verdy's partner in *The Princess* he was a star at its opulent première in the Royal Poinciana Playhouse.

Mia Slavenska, one of the first dancers to form a company, established her Ballet Variant in 1948, undeterred by the fact that she had an infant daughter. Slavenska followed the peculiarly adaptable way of American ballet on tour. Her husband, Dr. Kurt Neumann, drove the bus which carried the Slavenska troupe and trappings, and the baby traveled in a basket on the front seat between papa and mama. In 1952, Slavenska formed another company with Franklin, with which Danilova was guest star. For this troupe Valerie Bettis choreographed *A Streetcar Named Desire,* afterwards taken into American Ballet Theatre repertoire. The Slavenska-Franklin company has long since dissolved but *Streetcar* is recorded as a stunning example of the Classic-*cum*-Modern in American ballet. Bettis was the first Modern to create a work for a classic company, with her *Virginia Sampler* for the Ballet Russe.

Streetcar owed much of its initial success to Slavenska as Blanche and Franklin as Stanley Kowalski. This is thought by many to have been the most superb characterization of Franklin's long and celebrated career. Deviating from his frothy champagne roles in the Massine repertoire, Franklin, as noted by the critic Louis Biancoli, danced with a lunging ferocity of grace, and a brooding undercurrent of menace. The ballet—taken almost literally from Tennessee Williams' drama of the same name—is fine theatre, and caused a great controversy. Lauded for its fine characterization, especially by Franklin, it was deplored as "Modern Dance" masquerading as "Ballet." A few incensed balletomanes upbraided Youskevitch, when he assumed the Kowalski role later, contending that it demeaned a *danseur noble.* When American Ballet Theatre took it on tour to Europe a dark-humored member of the press solemnly prophesied it would, with the export of *The Cage,* confirm the foreign impression that Americans were abyssmally decadent and uncouth.

As ballet, *Streetcar* has interesting choreography and décor. Blanche is made to run in speechless flight, as dramatic as a shriek, through shuttered doorways, symbolic of her escape from reality. She meets dream-figures, the Figures of Desire—and the orgiastic revelry would certainly have brought a posse galloping to the theatre in the Diaghilev days. The card-playing scene for Stanley is a little masterpiece of lyric characterization, and the mad scene for Blanche is a great deal more human and poignant than similar scenes of assorted Giselles. Nora Kaye and John Kriza danced Blanche and Stanley for American Ballet Theatre but never quite achieved the rapport of its première dancers. Slavenska's beauty was the explicit contrast to her anguish and her shame. When she turned, *sur les pointes,* in her filmy draperies, she seemed to be the spirit of all vulnerable beauty. And Franklin was the brute, brutal not out of sadism but out of spiritual insensibility. Certainly, in terms of theatre, the notorious rape scene in *Streetcar* was never communicated with such good theatrical form and taste, and with such a start to the senses.

Other distinguished touring groups have brought dance to the general audience that has been of a quality and style far more provocative than simple entertainment. The Ryder-Frankel ensemble dances *The Still Point,* which was choreographed for it and has a classic (with *pointe* shoes) delivery at the New York City Ballet. Robert Joffry's contemporary revival of *Pas de Déesses,* a *divertissement* in which the nineteenth-century goddesses of dance were featured by Perrot, has been in the repertoire of his touring Joffry Theatre.

Present success augurs an increased variety and a widened scope for ballet troupers. A current professional periodical lists more than three hundred ballet artists, of every genre, in solo, duo, trio and so on, up to full companies, a hundred strong and more, who are able and willing to take to the road. The Classic genre flourishes with extraordinary hardihood, while Modern Dance appears to be a penchant of college groups. The American audience, when it goes to see dancing, seems to want exuberant folk dancing or the Classic Dance with its beautiful line and noble deportment—and, of course, with the *danseuse sur les pointes.* The seemingly fragile and exquisite *danseuse,* however incongruously placed on the badly-raked and rough-surfaced stage of a school gym, becomes at once the symbol of Beauty. And her partner, the *danseur,* has now come to be a star in his own right, and is expected to shine spectacularly beside his ballerina.

These beautiful and remote creatures of an art form removed by oceans and centuries from the stages they now inhabit, had beginnings as wonderful as they are strange. Ghosts from the Ravel troupe must smile mistily in the shadows. Much closer in time are the legends of Pavlova on tour and of the early Ballet Russe. People still talk of Shawn's Men Dancers who began to tour in 1933. In 1932 Shawn had begun to teach the art forms of dance to five hundred male students of physical education at Springfield College, and partly as a result of their response conceived the idea of forming a men's group.

In 1933 at Jacob's Pillow he organized a troupe of male dancers. This was so

Frederic Franklin and Mia Slavenska in Valerie Bettis' A Streetcar Named Desire.

Mia Slavenska as Blanche, Frederic Franklin and Lois Ellyn as Stanley and Stella Kowalski.

avant-garde that concert managers and booking agents would not associate themselves with it. The male dancer at that time seemed at best a handy support for the female; much of the audience thought him emasculated. Nevertheless, the Men Dancers set out on tour. Two amateur managers went scouting for theatres. The Men Dancers followed, not too sure if they would dance, never knowing where they would dance, and says Shawn, not knowing how or if they would eat and sleep. But their reputation soon preceded them; and soon their "managers" had no problems with bookings—except to decide where to place the group—and the Men Dancers danced in one hundred and eleven cities the first year. Thereafter, the group toured until World War II, when it disbanded, the majority of its members going into the United States Armed Forces.

Despite the popularity of dance in America, most of the little touring groups fail for one reason or another. Those that survive do so by a combination of stamina and fortitude—a physical and mental adaptability to a rugged life. Also, beyond the act of dancing, they are able to draw responses from the audience. This is not something done only by gesture or plot but, more specifically, by a magnetic quality conveyed by the dancer. It is this powerful attraction that "sells" the dancer.

Despite grueling tours, year after year, some dancers manage to hone their technique to razor fineness. It is inexplicable but true that a dancer hardly able to stand in walking shoes outside the stage door puts on her dancing slippers and dances with grace, finesse and fire on the stage. What is the inspiration? Some of them say, dramatically, that it is "Art," but the most simple (who are often the greatest) have a down-to-earth explanation. They tell me it is muscular control, and nervous reflex. Perhaps the overture is like the sound of a bugle to the warhorse. After a lifetime's service on the stages of the world, moving through Europe and the Americas not city by city, but theatre by theatre, the stage is the only place where many of them come alive.

Few have done so well as Marina Svetlova, and how many have survived as long? Born in Paris of Russian expatriates, Svetlova is one of the Franco-Russe products adopted into American ballet. She was the pupil of Victor Gsovsky in Paris, and of Trefilova, Preobrajenska, and Vilzak. In New York, she studied with Caton. She came to America in her 'teens, and in 1938–1941 was a *soliste* with Original Ballet Russe. In the 'forties she danced with Ballet Theatre in a large repertoire of roles, including *Aurora's Wedding, Graduation Ball, Les Sylphides, Spectre de la Rose, Bluebeard,* and *Pas de Quatre.* In 1943 she was the *prima ballerina* of the Metropolitan.

Svetlova began to tour in 1944. She has appeared all over the United States, in Canada, South and Central America, Israel and India; and is extremely well-known in Europe and in Great Britain. She frequently dances on arty television programs in America and England, and her partners, in recent seasons, when she appeared at world festivals, included George Zoritch and Anton Dolin. Svetlova is a *prima ballerina* in the grand manner, and the darling, for fifteen years, of community concert in America. She epitomizes The Ballet in style and form, and the wonderful creature does this with no accoutrement except the "sets" and lighting she carries in her autobus, in which she travels with her minute troupe: one pianist, a partner in the Classic school, and a *soliste* in Spanish Dance. Svetlova is lithe, chic and striking, and she has outlasted her confrères in the brutal touring circuit because she has the stamina and adaptability, and because—most significantly—she establishes a strong, sure communication with her audience. Svetlova's audience sees a dancer of quality and distinguished attainments, and it is to the credit of American ballet that its audience has educated itself to discriminating standards.

Svetlova is a strong technician, with a sharp clean attack. She is obliged to run the whole gamut of ballet to satisfy individual tastes in her vast audience, and she has a mobile gift in interpretation, from her evocative *Camille* to her fiery *Don Quixote* Variation. She is in turn passionate, vivaciously comic and lyrical. Her community concert audiences are treated to the same Classic form with which Svetlova dances in Europe. She has danced in the four-act *Le Lac des Cygnes* of Sadler's Wells, with the Finnish National Ballet, and at Jacob's Pillow, and in 1958 she was the star of the Paris Opéra-Comique, partnered by Peter van Dijk, a prodigy of the teacher Gsovsky, who is compared with Nijinsky. In America alone, Svetlova has danced for thousands more persons than

Marina Svetlova in Swan Lake.

could be crowded into the largest opera house in the world. Her travels have provided incidental anecdotes that make the history of modern ballet in America as colorful as that of older times.

Regional manners and mores, into the 'forties, were weird and wonderful to foreign dancers. Svetlova, in one of her early rounds, was once pressed to accept a supper invitation.

Bidden to a seat of honor on the stage of the local concert hall where she had lately been a performer in the ballet, she found covers laid for six, and she and her five civic dignitary hosts sat down to sup. To Svetlova's astonishment, an audience of six hundred took their seats in the auditorium, and amiably watched the ballerina consume fried chicken, presumably all for the price of the admission to see Svetlova dance.

In Svetlova's and Shawn's wake have come hundreds of others, foreign and native, uniform only in caliber of performance. So informed and discriminating has the mass audience become that the so-called provincial American stage presents nothing mediocre and, in general, only the best of the various genres. In quality, the very best is expected to have something more: it must, simply, be *special.* A great dancer, accepted as such in the profession, has more than once been lost as a trouper, either by a lack in temperament, or from an incapacity or a refusal to adapt to the rigors, mental and physical, of touring. But when the truly great dancers are also troupers, nothing exceeds their thrilling rapport with their enormous theatre audience. Such were Danilova and Markova—the Markova-Dolin ensemble, originally formed in England, was formed again in the United States in the 'forties—and their concert ensembles. And no one has surpassed Anna Pavlova, the first and the most influential trouper in traditional ballet!

It does not matter in the assessment of a trouper what his special genre is— only that the dancer be special. In the 1958–1959 season two outstanding specialties on tour were the Kovach-Rabovsky ensemble, and Ruth Page's Chicago Opera-Ballet. They toured from coast to coast, a full season of several months "on the road."

Nora Kovach and Istvan Rabovsky are husband and wife *pas de deux* exponents of the Soviet ballet. Their famous escape from their former Russian affiliation is told in the book, *Leap Through The Curtain.* They have caused an American furore, and a European one, and their spectacular form is as widely admired in nightclubs in Las Vegas as it is in the great municipal opera houses in South America. Kovach is a little beauty, a protégée—as is her husband—of Galina Ulanova, who discovered them dancing for the Budapest State Opera and selected them for further training in Russia. Agrippina Vaganova, *prima ballerina* under the czarist and Soviet regimes, and one of the great savants of twentieth-century ballet, taught Kovach in Russia. Kovach and Rabovsky were high-ranking stars of Russian ballet when, sent to dance at a gala performance in East Berlin, they fled at great risk through the Iron Curtain. In the west they have danced with Festival Ballet and Ballets de Paris, and appeared on television and in supper club engagements.

In 1958–1959, under Hurok's management, the ensemble starred the Rabovskys in a program of *divertissements* that emphasized their pyrotechnical style, and included their first modern work, *The Saffron Knot,* by Harry Asmus, which is a lyrical and emotional contrast to such spectacular feats as their bravura *Don Quixote.* The program was shared with a pair of American stars, Barbara Fallis and Royes Fernandez, whose summer appearance at Jacob's Pillow was considered by critic Ann Barzel to be among the best of reigning *pas de deux* executants. The critical assessment was so high and the audience response so enthusiastic, that the program, assisted by two pianists, may be considered a model working arrangement for ballet troupers. It consisted of two pairs of strongly contrasted and excellent *pas de deux* stylists, who were visually exciting. The Soviet-trained Rabovskys danced *pas de deux* from Petipa's *Bayaderka* (arranged by Valentina Perejeslavec), and *Esmeralda* (Beriosoff); *The Saffron Knot,* to Wagner's *Liebestod;* and a *pas de deux* to Gluck's *Orfeo,* by Perejeslavec. The Americans were seen in the peasant *pas de deux* from *Giselle,* Act I; the *classique pas de deux* from *The Nutcracker;* and a jazz arrangement in *Black and White* choreographed by Ray Harrison. By something like magic, two pianos and the four dancers made a *grande finale* of Chabrier's *Espana,* an enchanting little ballet by Perejeslavec, in which characterization, mime, and dance were combined in the great tradition of the ballet. For technical magnificence, for theatrical perception, for good form and glamour in the ballet, no troupe surpassed this minute one in 1958–1959.

On a larger scale, nothing outclassed Ruth Page's Chicago Opera-Ballet, which had a program of Page's "specialty"—the opera-ballet—and neoclassic French ballet. One of Page's works, *Susanna and the Barber,* was ballet-opera, combining (to the delight of the one-third of every American audience which always murmurs that it does not understand what is going on in a ballet) speech and chant, as well as pantomime and dancing in the grand classic genre as a *divertissement. Susanna and the Barber,* taken from *The Barber of Seville,* is a good introduction to ballet for the average audience. Page, with fine theatrical intuition, prefaced every program with a ballet-opera, and contrasted it with George Skibine's *Idylle,* a little gem of a ballet about three horses.

Page danced as the maid in *Susanna,* and was supported by an American master in dance-mime, Bentley Stone. Two American protégés, Barbara Steele and Kenneth Johnson, of the Chicago Opera-Ballet shone in Classic Dance. Other opera-ballets choreographed by Page are *Revenge, The Merry Widow, The Triumph of Chastity,* and *El Amor Brujo.* Her latest, *Camille,* was first performed in 1958–1959. It starred the Skibines (George Skibine and Marjorie Tallchief) on leave of absence from their posts as *premier danseur* and *première danseuse* of the Paris Opéra. These American dancers—he by naturalization, she by birth—are the most admired of Romantic *pas de deux* executants in the European theatre and Skibine is a young and gifted dancer-choreographer of extraordinary distinction in the leading theatres of the world. Marjorie Tallchief has a technique whose perfection has been called "incredible" by English critics generally given to understatement. She is, moreover, a lyric dancer and an actress beyond contemporary compare, whose fluidity of style and subtlety of interpretation have become inextricably one. Utterly devoid of effort or affectation, Marjorie Tallchief literally dances like a dream. She is one of the few dancers for whom no technical appraisal suffices, and for whose artistry ordinary language is inadequate. She, and dancers of her caliber, must be seen in order to be believed. In the 1958–1959 season her Camille became a signpost in American ballet. The response and acclaim were so extravagantly phrased that they read like the grossest press-agentry. I prefer to record here only one response. At the dress rehearsal in Chicago, where Tallchief had learned the role in one week, the members of the Chicago Opera-Ballet wept when Tallchief died as Camille.

On tour, the wet eyes in the theatres large and small were dried during curtain calls. A bit pink about the nose, we then went into the theatre lobbies to share our feelings. All of us who formed the large audience through the states will remain a part of this event—the *Camille* of the generation. Even in these sophisticated modern times the ballet continues to create its golden legends.

Page's company in 1958–1959 also included a star of another magnitude, the ravishingly beautiful Yugoslav ballerina Veronika Mlakar, who turned many masculine theatregoers into balletomanes. Mlakar is a prodigy, first taught by her parents Pino and Pia Mlakar, directors and choreographers of note, and pupils of Laban and Poljakova. Mlakar later studied in Munich, where she was *soliste* of the State Opera, and at Sadler's Wells. At eighteen, she was starred in Cocteau's *La Dame à la Licorne* at the Paris Opéra, and was ballerina of the Ljubljana Opera in 1954. She was *première* of Ballets de Paris in 1955, and starred in a feature-length German movie. In the Argentine, Brazil, Chile, England, Germany and France she is a well-known ballerina. Mlakar was born in 1935. *Épaulement* and fluidity characterize her striking style; her arms are lovely and her back especially pliant. From the swell of her *pointe* to the arch of her neck she vividly personifies Skibine's White Mare in *Idylle*. Her interpretation in dance is such that she seems to respond to mood and music with every nerve of her body.

These necessarily brief descriptions of the two ballet troupes—Kovach-Rabovsky, and the Chicago Opera-Ballet—cannot explicitly record their worth or their effect on the audience in America. But they are splendid examples of what the small unusual ballet troupes can contribute to the American ballet tradition. Consider that two American dancers, of the world-wide distinction of the Skibines, and a foreign star like Mlakar, have not been seen in America under the aegis of major companies. Nor have major companies made a practice of adopting, permanently, dancers of the electrifying effect of the Rabovskys. Yet they become a part of American ballet, and as such make signposts for its developing history, even as Pavlova and her companies and Mordkin's All-Star Imperial Russian Ballet were evolutionary forces in their not-so-distant time.

In a country like the United States, where the democratic principle predicates an individual and widely varied choice, how else should ballet have matured, except in its troupers? Even into our time of jet-propelled air travel and atompowered submarines, by what means could the American audience have viewed the beauties and the prodigies of ballet, and the ballets themselves, in their wonderful and varied array of techniques, styles, forms and themes? How else, save by live ballet itself, with or without elaborate entourages, energetically abroad on the long, long highways with the ballet troupers?

THE BALLETS

American ballet's theme is love, and with few exceptions it has no great artistic or popular success in the theatre unless motivated by some aspect of this favorite subject.

Ranging in style, subject and locale, the choreographic obsession with love is illustrated in the ballets that have become American classics of their kind. *Billy the Kid* and *Rodeo* are drawn out of the Old West, the reservoir of American saga and song; *Fall River Legend* is a somber picture of dour New England. In *Fancy Free,* vibrant color in movement, music and scenic design limns the statement: New York, New York, it's a helluva town! *The Cage* is a glimpse into the abyss that separates life from death by a kind of love.

These are by no means the only classics in American ballet; indeed, the controversy could at once begin that they are not even, in every instance, the best of the genre in American ballet. I have had, for the sake of organization and the size of one book, to omit the ballets by Balanchine and Tudor from this section; and conscious as I am of the vast repertoire and enormous significance of Modern Dance in American theatre, I have not the technical equipment to observe the dance dynamics of that métier.

Judging the American classics only on their talent for evocation or communication, I can find few better designed or more eloquent in the American dance vocabulary than those I have chosen to describe.

In *Billy the Kid,* love is sublime in aspect for Billy and his Mother-Sweetheart. It is the prime factor in social order for the Sheriff, who realizes the signal necessity for becoming his brother's keeper in his first offer of friendship and help to the young Billy and, later, his urgent duty to his community in becoming Billy's executioner.

Rodeo interprets love as the wide-eyed dream of the young, the incurable optimists. The Cowgirl is literally transformed by love, from an emblem Cinderella to a princess with a woman's royal prerogative—where she has not only one suitor but a choice between two. The transformation from Cowgirl to Girl in Red is natural and spontaneous in *Rodeo,* yet it employs an immortal theme. With skill and tenderness the choreographer recreates on a Colorado ranch the enchantment of Cinderella at the ball, and in the character of the Cowgirl defines the touching vulnerability of the young in love.

159

The same choreographer, Agnes de Mille, explores more chaotic love in *Fall River Legend*. Love flourishes as a sturdy plant in inclement weather in *Rodeo* but decays in a malformed growth in Fall River. The ballet's focus is a deprivation of love; the Accused is bereft as child and woman. The aspects of love are the pure, between mother and daughter, and the sweet, between the Accused and the Pastor. In an atmosphere barren and cold, the iron Stepmother and the pallid Father are the negation of love. No couple was ever more lacking in connubial bliss; it is surely impossible for the most erotic imagination to conceive a more passionate intercourse between these two than sitting rocking in the parlor. By an atrocious sterility of passion the choreographer turns the commonplace pair into fatal conspirators against the Accused. They are as ominous as the Furies.

Fancy Free is love in its lightest vein, expressed graphically in the American vernacular. The sailor-boys and the lipsticked girls they pursue so enthusiastically are indigenous to American ballet. The characters are vividly delineated in their meetings and leave-takings, which are as impetuous and abrupt as those of children. They are in love with life, which appears to them as bright commotion and lively music. The intent toward love in the flesh is obscured, or treated as an innocent extension of high spirits, yet the manifold quest is there, under the street light and in the bar. All these ballets are particularly representative of America to audiences in the foreign theatre, and *Fancy Free* most of all. Who but an American choreographer could have recaptured the memory of a summer night in New York, and these winsome cavorting citizens? Consider how differently a foreign choreographer might have interpreted the scene. At least two versions come to mind from the precepts of European choreographers, for whom *les matelots* and *les girls* have irresistible connotations. One would have made French farce out of American love, with a risqué sailor and a bitter-sweet girlish creature; all should have ended, with a *moue* and a sigh— *bonjour tristesse*. Another version should surely have had a foghorn blowing, like Fate, from the unseen river's shore, a darkening of the stage lights and, when the scene was sodden with apathy (or lyrical and pregnant doom) the audience would be shown one lonely rose—dark red, naturally—lying on the pavement under the solitary lamp post. Even had the Barman said not a word we should know, in the audience, that he had twisted the ends of his moustache, shrugged and murmured *"C'est la vie!"* Robbins' boys and girls are not such sophisticated creatures, but have obviously come straight from an American high school into Life in a Big City, where the sailors are swaggering about rowdily in Uncle Sam's summer whites and the girls are mincing about in girlish freedom, with an eye out for the Right Man. Nothing, and least of all sex, swerves them from their conventional course, and the audience knows exactly what happens after curtain-fall—the sailors find another bar and more girls; the first girls go home and rub a nourishing cream into their pores so that they will look beautiful and desirable tomorrow for that lodestar, the Right Man. For the plain but ample reason that Robbins' characters are not evolved out of choreographic whim, but are people alive and abroad in a Big City one summery night, the dancers are able to relate their story thousands of times, in hundreds of cities, without deviating from the reality that Americans recognize and that foreigners can easily understand.

In *The Cage* love is the amoral—the truly desperate—urge to procreation; the birth scene of the Novice, which so appals a few, is the re-creation in dance of an elemental fact. Life and Death are themes of *The Cage*—life impossible of conception other than by some urgent and palpable act of love. The insect nature of Robbins' creatures avoids the grossest implication for the audience that it too, by reason of being, is impelled by the instinct by which life continues. Romanticists may console themselves with the reminder that the design of love and death in mating is peculiar to the caged creatures in the ballet.

The five ballets here described have a creation in common—their choreographers are the librettists, and in three ballets, *Billy the Kid, Rodeo,* and *Fancy Free,* the choreographer danced a première role of importance, forever stamping the roles with the personality of choreographer-dancer. Four of the ballets have scores by American composers, Aaron Copland, Leonard Bernstein, and Morton Gould, and the first three ballets have such integration of plot and music that it is difficult to say where the impetus of the music ceases and the dance action begins. The fifth ballet, *The Cage,* is danced to a composition of Igor Stravinsky, who may be the greatest single foreign influence on American ballet music. He has been associated with George Balanchine's work for three decades and much of what is written about Balanchine and his creativeness describes Stravinsky the artist. An impressive number of American ballet works are set to Stravinsky music. No music could so exactly suit Robbins' stridulating loves and deaths as does the *Concerto Grosso in D for Strings.* The décor of each ballet is by an American artist. Oliver Smith created those of *Rodeo, Fancy Free* and *Fall River Legend,* and in every instance correlated scenic design with dancing so that the characters emerge in dimensions of lifelike scope, in full-scale worlds.

Above all, in dancing, music, and décor there is nothing contrived, but only the necessary, the true, and the adequate. One may almost see an inspired economy in the inventiveness. One must recognize and marvel at the quality, bold and resourceful, ingenuous and also genuine, that never once becomes insipid and never wanly borrows or timidly steals from other influences. The ballets do not, original as they are, depend on the flamboyant intent to be original. They were created for only one reason, and the best of all: like children who are born, they had to burst from their creators as the sum and substance of some heartfelt truth.

BILLY THE KID

Choreographer   Eugene Loring
Composer   Aaron Copland
Scenic and Costume Designer   Jared French

Première—Chicago Opera House, October 16, 1938

The Original Cast:

Billy the Kid	Eugene Loring
Mother-Sweetheart	Marie-Jeanne
Sheriff Pat Garret	Lew Christensen
Alias	Todd Bolender

Billy the Kid was first performed by Ballet Caravan, a Lincoln Kirstein company, and later by Ballet Theatre and Loring's Dance Players. Revived by Ballet Theatre, 1940; revised by Loring for the same company, 1948. In current repertoire of the American Ballet Theatre.

THE STORY

The libretto was created by Eugene Loring after Lincoln Kirstein had given the choreographer *The Life of Billy the Kid,* by Walter Noble Burns, and asked him to see if it could be made into a ballet. Loring was at once interested but felt that the ballet should be done without props (guns, for example) which at first did not seem exciting enough theatre. The libretto for *Billy the Kid* follows Burns' book insofar as it relates the story of the American outlaw, William H. Bonney, who was known throughout the West of the late 'eighties as El Chivato, or the Kid, because his rise to fame and his death all occurred before he was twenty-two. This American knight-of-the-road was no more than a bandit—a little fellow, physically—with a mean temper, who killed his first man at the age of twelve (or possibly sixteen) for a fancied insult to his mother. She was forced off the boardwalk into the muddy street of Silver City, New Mexico, whereupon Billy stabbed to death the man alleged to have pushed his mama.

After this first murder in Silver City Billy fled to Arizona, where he robbed and murdered a number of Indians. After 1877 he joined several outlaw gangs in Mexico, Arizona, Texas and New Mexico and was involved in the Lincoln County War, a fracas between cattle barons and bandits that became so serious a menace to civic order that Governor Lew Wallace of New Mexico offered amnesty to all the combatants in the hope of restoring peace. Billy recklessly refused the amnesty and continued his career as an outlaw until his death in 1881.

The legend of Billy the Kid is based less on his prowess as a gunfighter than on his vicious and unpredictable rage, which insured him a queer protection from even his fellow outlaws. He had a reputation for being fanatically loyal to his friends, but his uncertain temper was even more startlingly triggered than his gun. Friend and foe tiptoed around Billy as though he were a tiger strayed into their midst. Billy was also a lady-killer, especially among the Spanish-Americans of the western states. He played the guitar, was an excellent dancer and a natty dresser, and, despite pronouncedly protruding upper teeth, was considered handsome because of his fine eyes and glossy hair. Above all, he had a tremendous animal magnetism for men and women—the strange kind of fascination that the totally fearless, lunatic personality exerts over sane and sober folk.

His Mexican friends affectionately named him El Chivato and he began to cut quite a swathe in the ranks of lovelorn maidens, from his habit of crashing dances and taking to the floor, where with twirling heels and a courtly manner he swept many a disapproving rancher's wife or daughter off her feet.

When a powerful cattle baron, John Chisun, determined to stop Billy's exploits as an outlaw Billy was holed up at Fort Sumner, pursuing one of his ardent love affairs. Several killings had been charged to him, and he was even accused of robberies that he could not possibly have committed. A former friend of Billy's, Pat Garret, was appointed sheriff and joined a posse of irate Texans led by one Charles A. Siringo. Billy, besieged in a house near Stinking Springs, surrendered after two of his friends hiding with him were killed by the posse. He was tried for murder at Mesalia, and acquitted of one charge, but sentenced to hang for killing a sheriff named Brady. Transferred to the jail at Lincoln, Billy killed his two guards and escaped. He returned to Fort Sumner, obsessed, we may assume, as much by a desire to see his sweetheart as by the intent to lie low. It is said he planned to go to Mexico with the girl. However, Pat Garret and two deputies trailed Billy to Sumner and lay in wait for him near the house of one of his friends, Pete Maxwell, where on July 13, 1881, Garret shot Billy as he was entering Maxwell's door. Neither Billy nor Garret can be considered heroic figures, but in the raw new West that was starving for romance Billy soon became a subject for romantic ballads.

Garret, who was a braggart of note, helped to extol his fame as Billy's nemesis by inflating Billy's reputation as a killer, and legend gorily credited Billy with having killed a man for every year of his twenty-one years of life. Actually, he is believed guilty of committing five murders and aiding in four others. Of the nine, three were shot down unarmed and two (as was Billy) were ambushed. This is the toll of white men; no one knows how many Indians he murdered. Killing Indians in Billy's era was a popular pastime, not murder.

So, by an alchemy of time and romance, Billy the Kid became a heroic figure of the Old West, and the songs that were idly composed to a plucked guitar near a campfire in the desert were far more fascinating than the chilling truth about El Chivato, the cold-blooded (possibly psychopathic) killer.

Kirstein and Loring, with no ambitions to set history straight, employed the legendary quality of Billy's charm and his devilish way with a gun. Kirstein suggested the character of Alias—a stroke of genius, for the presence of this classic symbol of Nemesis gives *Billy* the same premonition of doom that the Ghost gives *Hamlet*. The ballet becomes epochal through Loring's use of a prologue and epilogue, which makes the West itself the heroic theme and Billy and Garret opposing forces in the taming of it. The Prologue and Epilogue have grandeur and pith, and lift the ballet of *Billy the Kid* out of the hackneyed "Western" rut into epic Americana. In typical Western regalia, the characters in the ballet move against the flat and stereotyped scenes with the same size and consequence as characters in classic tragedy.

The scenic design by Jared French evokes the glare and squalor of a mean little desert town in the brawling days of the mid 'eighties. French is superb in his design for the desert scene, making it seem as stark, as lonely and as mysterious as it is in fact, tenanted by the coyote and the cactus—harsh and arid by day, and at night blessed with the same singular softness that, every spring and autumn, magically causes its flowers to bloom.

As Loring wished, no "props" were used and they are not needed; Loring's invention of gesture and style are more than sufficient.

The ballet is divided into a Prologue and Epilogue and four intervening episodes that cover the life of Billy the Kid from the age of twelve until his death. The Prologue and Epilogue are, in synopsis, the story of the westward movement.

The Prologue is set in the desert, a sun-baked wasteland where cacti are the spined guardians of the lonely land. At curtain rise, the sun begins to tear the dark edge of night and into the bleak vista strides a man in the regalia of the American cowboy; he is the embodiment of the Pioneer, the man who tamed the western wilderness. Later in the ballet, the same character dances the role of Pat Garret. As the Pioneer, the dancer uses the expressive gestures of the frontiersman—he appears to drive a wagon train with a lashing whip, or drags the reins of his harnessed oxen to pull the wagon to a sudden halt; with an invisible lasso he ropes his imaginary cattle and works them out of the herd. All is conveyed so clearly to the audience that when the Pioneer drops to one knee and seems to hold his cocked rifle it is obvious that he is on guard against Indian attack.

On the heels of this character comes the wagon train—men, women and children. The Pioneer is their inspiration; the men, working in unison, follow his lead; the women, rejoicing in the promise of a home in the wilderness, sing and dance. The Pioneer at their head moves on toward the West. Heads held high, they press forward.

A darkened stage intervenes between the Prologue and the next scene.

Scene I is a street in a desert town (theoretically, Silver City, New Mexico) where the first settlers have barely pushed back the rolling desert from their doors. Down the narrow street passes an assortment of citizenry. The first man we see is a Mexican who has a proud gait and seems to ride through town on a prancing stallion. He and his people add a foreign note to the throng in the ballet, sometimes gay, sometimes somber.

The good women of the town, in decent, sober dress, their faces demure under their bonnets, go quickly about their business from modest little homes. The men in the street—the Mexican and some cowboys who join him—do not molest these busy housewives in their decorous garb, but they boldly ogle the dance-hall girls who appear to take the morning air, hussies in corselets that emphasize bosom and hip, wearing bright red stockings and high-button yellow boots with high heels. More cowboys catapult onstage and have an impromptu rodeo—they are so full of vigor they cannot bear to sit still on their horses. A group of Mexican girls arrive and saunter about, and the scene is one of several tableaux of people which create a lively atmosphere of a small town in the Old West.

Into this rugged scene a woman enters with a little boy—we know that he is a child by his manner of hanging on the woman's skirts. The role is danced by a man but the skillful interpretation of the mother-and-son roles convinces us that the male dancer is a little boy. This is Billy at the phase of his history when he is simply a child named Willie, perhaps, and he wears a round straw hat and overalls with a patched knee, and is nothing more than a gawky youth. The Mother wears city clothes that would be stylish in the year 1871, and is heavily veiled under her modish hat; she keeps her son close to her side as she walks through the throng in the rough street. It may be assumed they are strangers in town and are perhaps hunting lodgings.

The boy wishes to linger and gawk at the crowd but his mother gently leads him away and off stage. The Mexican dances with the Mexican girls. When Billy and his mother return, walking back along the street, the boy lifts his mother to show how well he can take care of her, she touches his cheek in a caress and the two dance off. The relationship between them is a tender and poetic one.

Suddenly the idle and gay mood of the street changes to a tense one. The Mexican no longer dances and flirts with his young countrywomen but becomes involved in a fierce argument with an angry Cowboy in Red. They fight—balletically, with blows that do not land physically, and they appear to fall but do not touch the ground. The fight grows wilder, tension mounts, and the onlookers are caught up in the quarrel as they realize how serious and desperate it is. Billy and his mother reappear from their wanderings just as the Mexican and the Cowboy in Red draw their guns. The Mexican fires and misses, and the Cowboy in Red sprints away. The Mexican fires again at the fleeing man, who dives into the crowd near Billy and his mother, but the shot goes wild and strikes Billy's mother, who slips lifeless to the ground, trying to support herself on her boy's shoulder as she falls. (Billy's mother's death is, of course, an exaggeration of the actual incident for dramatic effect.)

The horrified crowd seems turned to stone and can do nothing but gape, but the boy snatches a knife and stabs the Mexican in the back, all so suddenly that no hand moves to restrain him. As he turns to rush away a man in the crowd compassionately stretches out a hand to stay him and help him (it is Pat Garret, who at this moment sympathizes with Billy) but the boy is wild with grief and rage and turns away from Garret's extended hand. Swiftly he leaves the scene which holds nothing of his mother now but her corpse. A bystander lifts the woman's body, another throws the corpse of the Mexican over his shoulder, and they exit—but this is not the end of the Mexican in the ballet, for he reappears in later scenes as Alias.

Now the scene dissolves and time flows past the audience's view. The choreographer makes his dancers move in apparently aimless fashion, in circles, and gradually we perceive that each circle on the stage is the completion of another chapter in the town's lusty life—the circling is the passage of years as the seasons move in their everlasting round. At last the scene steadies, and characters come again into focus, and Billy reappears; the passage of time has turned him from a boy into a man. And what kind of man? He has two natures and Loring shows the quicksilver shift between them—light to darkness, sweetness to violence. As Billy enters, he salutes a woman with charming gallantry but within a short time he reveals his vicious self in his soliloquy.

The next scene is the open desert—lonely, arid and symbolic of Billy's soul. He is seen now as a handsome fellow with a jaunty air, in striped black and white trousers, glossy boots and a hat worn at an arrogant angle. He does not merely walk—he swaggers, feeling enormous pride in his lightning draw. He interrupts his soliloquy to practice the pulling, spinning and aiming of his gun—and each time he pretends he has shot and hit a man, deriving from this so terrible a joy that the urge to kill literally lifts and turns him in the air in a spiral of ecstasy.

A posse canters across the desert and Billy goes into hiding; from there he chooses a target among the riders, shoots, and sees his man fall. Again he is seized and lifted and twisted in his spiral of hate.

The stage darkens and the scene shifts to a campfire, where Billy is playing cards with Pat Garret (at this point of the ballet not yet the sheriff). Also present are the Cowboy in Red and some dance-hall girls. In the lonely desert the campfire throws the shadows of the cardplayers into enormous silhouette. Garret idly converses with the others and while his attention is diverted Billy cheats in dealing the cards; Garret soon after accuses him of cheating, Billy denies it furiously, and an argument flares up. At last, angry and disappointed that Billy is devoid of honor even in a friendly game, Garret gets up and strides away from the campfire. Billy begins to bluster his way out of his shame, but his erstwhile friends pointedly ignore him, in obvious sympathy with Garret. This triggers Billy's quick rage and his friends become uneasy. A posse gallops by, a crowd drifts together, and presently a fight ensues. Billy, who has already killed a character identified as a Land Agent, kills a man in the throng and is subdued only when Garret, coming up behind him, sticks a gun in his back. Then Billy is led off, still swaggering, to jail.

With Billy's departure, the crowd seems to draw a huge breath of relief. By now the group has been augmented by townfolk and an impromptu dance begins, to cheerful, robust music. A boisterous and innocent happiness prevails, with only one heart grieving for Billy—that of his Mexican sweetheart who drifts through the rowdy crowd, vainly seeking her lover.

Again, the darkened stage shifts to another scene. Billy is in jail and by exerting his famous charm persuades his jailer to play cards with him. This trusting man averts his gaze momentarily and Billy plucks the gun from the jailer's belt, shoots him, and escapes. We see him galloping across the scene, and when a posse appears and halts to confer on his trail Billy hides in a group of Mexican girls, who shelter him from sight. An Indian guide is delegated to lead the outlaw to a place of safety, where his Mexican sweetheart has arranged to have him hidden until they can slip out of the state and into Mexico.

The Indian and Billy reach the hiding place in the desert and there part, the Indian to return to town. Billy pulls off his boots and throws himself on the ground. He sleeps, and in his sleep he dreams. We see the Dream, the embodi-

ment of a lovely feminine creature who might be Billy's long-lost mother, or his
ideal sweetheart. Like the ghost of the desert twilight, she is clothed in a pale
lavender dress and veiled by a gossamer cloth that covers her face and hair. On
the classic *pointe* shoe, she seems to drift over the ground in an ethereal manner, less of the earth than of the air. Rising from the sandy floor, Billy dances
with his vision. She is tender and yearning; he is strangely remote and ab-
stracted, gazing beyond and almost through her into the dream world that she
embodies. They meet in the attitude of an embrace and yet never quite meet
as a human man and woman might; they dance, with matched steps, but the
dream-woman's longing is directed toward Billy and Billy's toward his invisible
goal. Hauntingly, the woman yearns toward Billy, until the poignant *pas de deux*
ends—more a fading away of the dance than a finale—and the woman vanishes.
Billy lies down again.

Abruptly, he awakens and sits up, alert and straining to hear and see a danger
he has instinctively sensed. And his instinct is right, for the Indian guide has
meanwhile returned with Pat Garret and the two are creeping up on Billy's hiding place. The Indian is now Alias, that awful Nemesis who has been imperson-
ated through the ballet first by the Mexican, now by the Indian guide. While the
silence deepens, and with it Billy's anxiety turns to terror, the night seems to
grow darker, the air oppressive. Billy's nerve, stretched to breaking point, at
length snaps. He speaks, in a harsh, cracked voice:

"*¿Quien es?*"

(It is strange to hear that voice in the theatre. Audiences start, and all the ensuing silence becomes menacing, in conspiracy with the music from the orchestra.)

For a moment, Billy is tense and waiting for a reply. None comes, and he relaxes. We may almost hear his sigh of relief. He takes out a cigaret to calm his
shaken nerve, and puts it between his lips with his old nonchalant grace. He
strikes a match—it lights his face redly—Garret on that instant shoots—Billy
the Kid is dead!

At once, the light increases, and the empty desert becomes filled with sweet
melancholy as Mexican women appear and promenade in a mournful procession, paying their pious respects to El Chivato. They think of him not as the
outlaw and killer but as The Kid. When they lean over him they seem to sigh—
"*Aiyayai!*" and as they move on, drawing their dark shawls closer about their
lips, they may be thought to murmur "*Madre de Dios!*" for the spent young
life.

Such is Billy's epitaph, one of prayers and tears. At this moment, the legend
is not yet made but already in the making, stirred to life by the Mexican
women's grief. The business of the living goes on, and at once the stirring Epilogue begins, taking up where the Prologue was suspended. The Way West continues, Garret again assumes the character of the Pioneer, Billy is left behind as
an episode on the way, and the frontier widens and grows beneath the slow and
tireless circling of the wagon train.

Loring's dancers do not perform dance so much as they create dramatic roles

John Kriza as Billy the Kid.

with lyric gesture—and they do not wear the traditional ballet costume of tights, but are dressed in attire contemporary to the time and locale. The Mexican carries a serape over his shoulder not for effect but to warm himself in the chill desert night. The Indian, in his feathered headdress, wears his moccasins as his prototype did; he does not pose and pirouette but moves with the sure stealth of the Red man. And the cowboys walk as though they have just dismounted from hard-ridden horses. The very gaits of the women fix their characters: the dance-hall girls flaunt their hips and their willowy legs; the decent ladies of the town have straight backs and a modest mien.

Billy's gesture and stance are expressive of the changing years and the altered man—as a boy he is like a colt; as the man he has a terrible grace, pantherlike in its sinuous power. In jail, he is stripped to the waist with black chaps on his legs, a black kerchief tied like a noose around his neck, and black bands on his upper arms, and here he looks more like a magnificent ferocious beast than a brutal man. The aerial leap and twist that presages the murders is a spectacular feat, used with psychological motives.

THE MUSIC

The score for *Billy the Kid,* by the distinguished American composer Aaron Copland, is one of the most evocative in ballet. The narrative becomes immeasurably clearer if it is read while listening to the recording. Few ballet scores have so brilliantly interpreted the characters, the place, and the time of the story.

Copland has made use of strong and definite rhythms in subtle nuances. An unmistakably Mexican air—passionate, yet poignant—complements the Spanish element; a distinct Old English melody and beat, such as we associate with the jubilant, hearty dances of the British Isles, heralds the group dancing of the townsfolk. An oboe is used as the theme for Billy's mother, a blaring trumpet for Billy. The rapid gunfire between the posses and the "bad men" is echoed in trumpet and drum; the street fighting is accompanied by drum beats like blows, dull and thudding. Copland devised a "gunfire" sound by beating the edge of a snare-drum.

At curtain rise, the music comes as though borne on the wind from the desert —mysterious, solemn, faraway. It grows vigorously, and develops the score's focal point: an inspiring processional for the pioneers. At its height, this is cut off abruptly, and gives way to a buoyant tone, informal and rollicking. The rodeo for the cowboys is characteristically raucous Western music; the Spanish undercurrent is romantic and somber. Piccolo and clarinet emphasize the fluting airs; woodwinds waft melodic ones, with strong, nostalgic tones. The street, or group dancing is performed to quick, robust tempo.

For the *pas de deux* in the desert the music employs a waltz measure and embroiders on the romantic theme a sorrowful, dreamy one. When Billy awakens and is gripped by terror, and when he cries out (actually speaking) the fearful "*¿Quien es?*" there is no music at all, only silence and the man's voice out of the lonely darkness.

Following Billy's death comes the lament of the Mexican women. The focal theme then again becomes predominant, in strong, sonorous rhythms, sweeping the pioneers on past the episode of Billy—his death, and his life, immediately seem merely incidental.

Copland's composition for *Billy the Kid* expresses the peculiar echoing wastes of the desert, and it does more—it clearly identifies the people and the place, by the use of brooding Spanish themes and a deliberately jaunty bounce and dash typical of square dancing. He has used folk songs of the prairie in "Old Grandad," and for a romantic theme (as with a twinkle in his eye) that immortal requiem of the cowboy for his horse, "Old Paint." Copland, returning from prodigious early acclaim in Europe, was intent on composing music that could readily be identified as American, and that should not be a copy, however admirable, of another nation's music. In his ballet scores (*Billy the Kid, Rodeo, Appalachian Spring*) he achieved a glorious unity of music and country, with an extraordinary truth and grandeur in the theme of *Billy the Kid.* His poetic concepts have been recognized (in 1951 he held the Charles Eliot Norton chair of poetry at Harvard, probably the most distinguished visiting lectureship bestowed by that university) and *Billy the Kid* is nothing less than epic poetry, in spirit and in sound.

PERFORMANCES

Loring's own creation of the character of Billy in his saga of the Old West is unsurpassed. He was physically able to interpret the dangerous little-man-with-a-gun which stigmatized William H. Bonney in the league of American bad men. And, as almost always when a choreographer dances his own creation, Loring's interpretation had extraordinary fervor and dimension in performance. Onstage, he was often so altered as the menacing Billy that he would cause a momentary chill to a dancer who had, a few moments before, been standing in the wings waiting to go on with the usually gentle-mannered Gene Loring. When Loring, as Billy, turned his back on the audience, that audience watched him with dreadful fascination, forgetful of the other moving dancers. Just so must the real-life contemporaries of William H. Bonney have waited breathlessly for a violent explosion from the little killer.

Loring danced the role of Billy for several years with Ballet Caravan, Ballet Theatre, and with his own company, Dance Players. It was later danced by Michael Kidd and Ian Gibson, but has become closely associated with John Kriza. Loring created the psychological study of Billy, the man; Kriza swaggers and smiles, lifts an arrogant eyebrow and moves with sinuous grace from a hip that bears the symbolic gun, and is Billy, the legend. You have but to see Kriza as Billy in the second act to understand at once why pretty young girls sighed, and nice old ladies cried, all for the love of Billy the Kid.

With Loring as Billy, Lew Christensen is considered to have been the finest Pat Garret. Of recent dancers in the role, Ray Barra brings the most thoughtful and sensitive interpretation to the part of the sheriff. (In 1958 Barra became *pre-*

Eugene Loring as Billy the Kid, *with Bobby Howell as the Mother-Sweetheart, in The Dance Players production, 1941–1942.*

mier danseur with the Stadttheater in Stuttgart, Germany.) The dual role of Mother-Sweetheart has been danced by Marie-Jeanne and Leda Anchutina of Ballet Caravan, and Alicia Alonso of Ballet Theatre; it is an alternate role for Lupe Serrano and Ruth Ann Koesun in current repertoire, from a revision by Loring for Ballet Theatre in 1948. The original production was by Lincoln Kirstein; the first Ballet Theatre production by Michael Kidd. Loring's 1948 revision is that of the permanent active repertoire. Like *Rodeo* and *Fancy Free, Billy the Kid* has been danced in every major ballet theatre in the Americas and in Europe.

RODEO

Choreographer	Agnes de Mille
Composer	Aaron Copland
Scenic Designer	Oliver Smith
Costume Designer	Kermit Love

Première—Metropolitan Opera House, New York, October 16, 1942

The Original Cast:

The Cowgirl	Agnes de Mille
Champion Roper	Frederic Franklin
Head Wrangler	Casimir Kokitch

Rodeo was first performed by Ballet Russe de Monte Carlo, and was revived by Ballet Theatre in 1950, with a première at Rhine-am-Main Air Force Base, Frankfurt, Germany. In current repertoire of the American Ballet Theatre.

THE STORY

The libretto of *Rodeo* is the composition of the choreographer, Agnes de Mille, but the décor by Oliver Smith and the music by Copland are integral parts of the story. De Mille says that the scene is very important, giving characters and theme their actual values. Kermit Love designed the costumes, which set the time at the turn of the last century. The place is a Colorado cattle ranch.

Sky and plain are endless, and the clouds are swirled in semi-arcs. The land at the horizon edge is held apart from the brazen sky by the iron fingers of the buttes. The corral is composed of stark straight lines. Boundless space and the mournful, lonely dignity of the desert surround corral and house. The later indoor scenes are homely and cozy as a contrast with the rugged outdoors, and walls and ruddied windowpanes, the old-fashioned stove and the dishes set primly on a shelf emphasize the idea that the pioneers have made a habitation in the wilderness.

The ballet is in two scenes, with an Interlude, and the role of the Cowgirl is the central one, with those of the Head Wrangler and Champion Roper the principal male leads. The other girl is characterized as the Rancher's Daughter.

At curtain rise, we are in the corral of Burnt Ranch, and the Cowgirl and the two men in her life (the Head Wrangler whom she adores with calflike devotion, and the Champion Roper who is kind to her but evokes no passion from her) are leaning against the fence, watching the distance—a typical attitude for this part of the world. There are nine cowboys onstage, dressed in typical Western clothes, as is the Cowgirl. She is evidently a girl, by her long braid of hair, but wears a felt hat on her head, fastened by a chin strap, and a pair of cowboy boots. There is nothing very feminine and soft about her, not even the braid.

A cowboy gallops up—a dancer so marvelously interpreting the gait of horse and rider that it matters not at all he is not really astride a visible horse. Here is the first triumph for the ballet—the choreographer's invention of gesture which does not descend to coarse pantomime but incorporates in dance movement the instantly recognizable illusion of horse and rider. It is sheer magic for the audience, who see the cowboys lurching with spine-breaking force on the backs of the bucking broncos in the rodeo scenes. Loring and de Mille have both made original use of the illusion of mounted men and prancing horseflesh. Loring's riders, as his Mexican, gallop or caracole onstage, and his posses, when they dance, flee over the sandy desert floor with the wind in their faces. De Mille's horsemen catapult and are thrown about by the huge sweating animals they ride. When the Cowgirl falls, she falls from the sweating back and with very little imagination the audience that sees her lying on the ground may catch, out of the corner of the eye, the flying mane and tail of the horse that has thrown her. Through the years, as these two ballets, *Billy the Kid* and *Rodeo,* are danced by the same dancers in the company, the gestures grow closer and closer in style; certain riding strides that were originally quite different are now identical. This gradual merging of the styles is not astonishing under the circumstances, but what is remarkable is the native creative force that moved Eugene Loring in New York, and Agnes de Mille in London, in 1938, to hit on such similar evocations for American ballet.

With the entrance of the galloping cowboy the Champion Roper and the Head Wrangler leave off their lounging. Business is about to commence. The Cowgirl is at once eager to get into it, but is sternly ordered off. She disobeys, rapidly mounts her horse, and canters off. The business, most naturally, concerns horses, and as the Rancher's Daughter providentially arrives with a group of her girl friends, the men decide to combine business and pleasure and have an impromptu rodeo while they break in some new horses. The girls, including the Rancher's Daughter, are delightfully titillated by this—in this coterie is not included the Cowgirl, because no one on Burnt Ranch thinks of her as a girl. Treated like another man, and at times like a nuisance, the Cowgirl affects none of the men with tender feelings, or a desire to show off, such as they irresistibly suffer at first sight of the Rancher's Daughter and her giggle of friends. Never has the Cowgirl been so brusquely treated, especially by the Head Wrangler. The Head Wrangler ogles the Rancher's Daughter; the Cowgirl languishes for the Head Wrangler. She lives up to her reputation as a stubborn, self-assertive creature by swaggering about in her boots and jumping astride a horse, which she rides as though she were a part of the brute, her body yielding to its every step. Her bright crimson shirt is like a brave red flag as she joins the rodeo. As it starts, the cowboys roughly motion her away so they can show off for the girls from town, but the Cowgirl insists on staying in the corral and rides a bronco until she is thrown. She takes her fall like any cowboy, trying hard to hide the wince of pain and clowning a little as she rubs the spot that hit the ground. She tries to shove her way between the Head Wrangler and the Champion Roper, where they are conversing with the girls, but the first ignores her while dancing attendance on the Rancher's Daughter, and the other walks away to show off his fancy roping for the admiring crowd.

Disgusted, the Cowgirl looks at the cowboys trying to divert the city girls; she would willingly give her opinion of all this la-de-da nonsense except that no one is interested in her opinion. The infatuated cowboys and the demurely coquetting misses are having a delicious time, flirting with each other. These make a charming contrast—the girls in long full skirts, with delicate gestures of hands and tilted heads; the men in the garb of the rugged West—tight pants, bloused shirt, and the big hat canted at a dashing tilt. The Head Wrangler, very conscious of his importance, orders the Cowgirl out of the rodeo and she runs off in tears. She gets little sympathy from the four women of the ranch house, who consider she has made a most immodest spectacle of herself, riding with the men.

Over the corral scene, the light dims to denote the end of the day, and a sweet languor falls on the dancers. The women move softly, slowly, creating the lovely pause between a full day's labor and the mysteriously alive night. Suddenly, in gesture and feeling, they become more feminine still, as certain flowers open only when the sun sinks. The men, by comparison, become bigger, stronger, braver because their attitude is more tender. This is demonstrated in the way the men cross the ground, move toward the girls, surround them in embrace, and move offstage.

Assisted by the music, the dancing now conveys a wonderfully sweet and secretive feeling, and the lighting simulates a glamorous dusk, which holds a promise of the night's bewitching romance.

When the tender twilight scene has melted away, the Cowgirl reappears in search of the Head Wrangler. When she goes to him, he passes her by as though she were invisible. His stride past her, as he goes impetuously towards the Rancher's Daughter, who stands waiting for him, isolates the Cowgirl as a forlorn little figure in the half-light. The Rancher's Daughter and the Head Wrangler, in every step and gesture, are radiant and vibrant; the Cowgirl is like a waif.

She begins a little dance, which we must think of as the ballet conception of singing to herself. We must imagine her as very young, very much in love for the first time, and feeling terribly lonely and in real trouble—what trouble can there be greater than that of not being loved? She sings her little, sad song to herself, because nobody cares about her misery and loneliness. She is so powerless to evoke a return of her love that when the Head Wrangler returns and again passes by her without sparing her a look or a word it is because for him she simply does not exist—except as she did at the rodeo, as a little pest. But the little creature in the rough cowboy garb is a *girl,* and it is that girl who sinks to the ground, going down like a little candle burning itself out, aching with sadness and wishing that she were dead!

Life goes on about her and over her bowed head. The scene ends and the Interlude begins. This is a charming break in the acts, with a décor all its own—a bright blue sky ornamented with magnificent silver thunderheads, the great clouds of the Western heavens. There are ranches in the sky, and the horses are dancing. Four couples appear and perform a rousing square dance, and a Caller cries (in actuality) the stirring square dance calls. The dancers move faster and faster and at last, full of merriment, rush offstage, when the second scene begins.

We are now inside the ranch house, and by a trick of the scenic design this house is made roofless, so that we are reminded of the aching void of blue above. Thunderheads, like archangel's wings, guard the sky. The horses have gone off to their heavenly corrals. And although the harsh flat land is still the same, and the stark shapes of the buttes still rise from the desert, the night belongs to music and dancing, and to love. The men have dressed in their best; the girls have ribbons and flowers in their hair. Even the ranch house is in bloom—the windowpanes flush with lamplight, the dishes shine and glimmer on a high shelf, and the stove almost purrs, as fat and contented as a nice old house cat. The audience looks past this cheery room and sees one corner of an ugly wooden porch and the bleak vista it faces, and then looks back into the heart of the warm, bright room.

As the room fills with merrymakers for the Saturday night dance a bench is moved back to make more space and a fiddler tunes up for the Hoe Down. The dance is the good-humored, half rough one of *Girls to the left and boys to the right—O.K., friends, now don't let's fight!* The Rancher's Daughter, a girl who collects beaux, has two suitors for her dancing, the Head Wrangler and the Champion Roper; she prefers the Wrangler and lets him take her outside to look at the stars. Other couples pair off and begin a waltz. Only the Cowgirl is left out, and she sits on a bench watching the dancers.

A cowboy sits down beside her and just as they are about to strike up a conversation with each other—two lovelorn folk, because the cowboy has been jilted by his girl—the cowboy's repentant girl comes by and forgives him with a smile; at once he is up and after her, the Cowgirl deserted without a moment's hesitation. There she sits, a gallant little figure of woe, until the kindly Champion Roper sees her. To him she is a miserable little varmint, but he is tender-hearted and cannot bear a doleful person at this revelry. He speaks to the Cowgirl to cheer her up, and tells her to get up and dance. She cannot dance—and is ashamed to try. The Roper insists and she gives in; he puts his arm around her and she trembles. It is her first embrace; she weeps. With rough good humor, the Roper urges her to follow his lead and soon enough the Cowgirl finds joy in dancing. She is just beginning to get some fun out of her prowess when she catches sight of the Wrangler and the Rancher's Daughter returning together to the dance floor. Stabbed by a pang of jealousy, the Cowgirl pulls away from the Roper, who then leaves her in some irritation. The Cowgirl, again des-

Rodeo's Interval *square dance against Oliver Smith's famous décor.*

olate, sinks down to the floor. Then, unnoticed by the dancers, she rises and slips from the room.

The dancing continues but very soon a new girl appears, in a bright red dress. (In the original productions of Ballet Russe de Monte Carlo the dress was yellow; Ballet Theatre uses crimson.) The new girl is none other than the Cowgirl, but what a transformation has been wrought! In a dress she not only looks different, but moves in a different manner. No one would recognize her as the waif in hand-me-down cowboy clothes, with her hair bundled into a thick braid. The hair is now free and alive about her charming face. The girls, immediately recognizing a rival beauty, pretend that her dress is much too bright a red to be quite nice; some of them suspect that it is borrowed finery. The men are not in the least bothered by these details—they only know that here is a new and attractive female. The Cowgirl in her Cinderella transformation is thrilled, and sparkles with new charm. A short time ago she was languishing for the Wrangler; now he is quarreling with the Roper as to which of them will have the first dance with the Girl in Red! The quarrel almost becomes a fight. Sheer bliss for the erstwhile Cowgirl, to have not one man suing for her favors, but two! Making a choice, she chooses the Roper for the first dance and as they glide about the floor they make a sweet mutual discovery—they are in love! The moment is as full of exclamations for the little Cowgirl as the sky is of stars.

She is still very young, although no more abused and neglected, and when she is smitten with her new love her awakening is tender and shy. The Roper, disturbed by the sweet emanations of the Girl in Red, kisses her with a kind of jovial aggressiveness, more to spite the jealous Wrangler than anything else. Then, to his surprise, the soft lips he kisses and the scarlet-clothed figure in his arms stir him to a strange, deep joy. They gaze at each other and again they kiss, almost dreamily. In sudden tenderness, they find themselves in love, and create a quiet little world for themselves in the midst of the laughing throng. The moment passes into a larger one of general rejoicing, as the others recognize the implications of the kiss and embrace between the Roper and the Girl in Red. In high spirits, the cowboys lift their girls into the air, and a great soundless shout seems to float up through the roofless house, to commemorate the wooing at Burnt Ranch.

The ballet (whose subtitle is *The Courting at Burnt Ranch*) comes to an ending as merry as the proverbial wedding bell. Only Agnes de Mille, a choreographer who is a woman, could have thought to create the last tender look the Cowgirl turns on the Head Wrangler as she goes off to her happy ending with the Champion Roper.

THE MUSIC

Seldom has there been such unity in music, dancing and décor as there is in *Rodeo*. Once you can picture the world in which the dancers move, listening to the music brings each character into focus in the mind's eye. Copland has interpreted a place that in the daytime is bright and full of heat, and vigorous with the motion of horses and men, but which, with the fall of night, has a plushy softness, like black velvet. The people are the sort whose attitudes range from the rowdy to the sentimental, and they are the kind of people who, when they sing sweet songs, may do so to a horse rather than to a girl.

The ballet begins to rollicking, crashing music, which soon falls to a softer theme. It is followed by the clear sound of galloping horses, and a sudden, spine-cracking pause as the horses are halted and rear and turn. The riders are jerked in the saddles; one is violently thrown, and the music creates a picture of the horses themselves—the great curved necks, the flaring nostrils, the tossing manes.

But when evening falls with its dimmed light onstage, the violet haze in which the dancers so sweetly move is accompanied by the music, here played in five-four time. The music soughs, rustling and murmuring, and in the orchestra the strings are plucked with the sound of the stars coming out, one by one.

In the ballet, there is a long tap cadenza for the Champion Roper, which de Mille created for Frederic Franklin, whose taps are brilliant; this passage, understandably, is not heard in recordings of the score, but is most effective in the dance design.

The second scene has a romantic waltz and a gay Hoe Down, in which the fiddler's arm moves as energetically as the dancing feet. There is nothing lacka-daisical, or what a Westerner would describe as finicky, about the music. Crys-tal-clear, it expresses every changing mood and scene, and people whose emo-tions are as strong and rugged as the shapes and colors of their rough land. De Mille captures a marvelous simplicity and directness, like that of children, for her characters. As soon as the Cowgirl puts on a dress she is *The Girl,* and yet there is nothing heavily symbolic about any character or dance gesture. The ballet is eloquent because it is true, and its vividness comes from the choreog-rapher's absolute certainty and love of familiar things and places. Copland's score, miraculously, has the same clarity and purposefulness. But make no mis-take about its worth, for it is by its deliberate avoidance of the complicated and obtuse and its deliberate employment of simplicity and directness that Copland's score becomes a masterpiece.

Rodeo is a suite divided by the composer into "Buckaroo Holiday"—deriva-tion: "If He'd Be A Buckaroo By Trade;" "Corral Nocturne;" "Saturday Night Waltz;" and "Hoe Down," based on an old tune, "Bonyparte." Agnes de Mille relates that when she was working on the choreography she warned Copland she could not choreograph lyrically, and therefore wished to omit the twilight scene ("Corral Nocturne").

"Too bad," said Copland. "I've composed it already."

It was a gentleman's lie, he had rummaged an old piece out of a drawerful of his compositions and decided it would do very nicely for the evening scene in *Rodeo.* You have only to see *Rodeo,* and listen to the music, to know how wrong de Mille was and how right was Copland.

PERFORMANCES

At the première of *Rodeo,* de Mille danced the Cowgirl, Frederic Franklin the Champion Roper, and Casimir Kokich the Head Wrangler. The Cowgirl was later danced by Lubov Roudenka and Dorothy Etheridge for the Ballet Russe. In Ballet Theatre, Jenny Workman gave the role its closest interpretation to de Mille's, with its wistful, semi-tragic romance. It has been frequently danced in this company by Ruth Ann Koesun, who plays the role more for gamine comedy than pathos. In 1958, the Cowgirl assumed a bright new sparkle in Addy Ador, a Brazilian dancer who joined American Ballet Theatre for its European tour. Slim, long-legged and golden-haired Ador nevertheless infused the Cowgirl with de Mille's original quality of adolescent anguish—the quality that removes the Cowgirl in *Rodeo* from the trite corner of an almost comic triangle and places her among the most brilliantly etched characters of Amer-ican ballet.

But no one has—and no one could have—danced the Cowgirl as Agnes de Mille did in the 'forties, for when she danced it was not as a ballet role but out of her own memories of a certain adolescent—a girl who wanted to be lyrical as a sylphide and seemed condemned to the form of a sturdy little mustang. The Cowgirl's metamorphosis into the Girl in Red may have been the uncon-

Agnes de Mille as the Cowgirl in Rodeo.

scious sublimation of the choreographer's own life, in which the student who vainly sought the *style classique* invented a brand new style of dancing as vivid and startling as a crimson dress. De Mille's Cowgirl was never a stock character, but always a real person to her creator, who saw her as an orphan, in her grandfather's cut-down pants. The dress she wears in the last scene is a borrowed one—perhaps from one of the visiting city ladies. Terribly young, terribly lonely, paralyzed by love and shyness when she is not blundering about trying to be tough, the Cowgirl is strangely tender and vulnerable to romance. And she is so true that she is never clownish.

The collaboration of Copland's score and Smith's décor with de Mille's choreography established *Rodeo* as a milestone in American ballet. It was an instantaneous success with critics and audience. The ballet is admired for its ingenious riding scenes and its jubilant dancing, and is equally notable for its fine characterization of the young girl. The gestures of sinking down and of abrupt and quick turning away from insupportable irritations, the slouching and scuffing—all of these are gestures of the adolescent. These and the awakening of love in the last scene are the fine details in the robust life at Burnt Ranch.

Loring's *Billy the Kid* and de Mille's *Rodeo* are classic examples of the bold and inventive American ballet. *Billy the Kid* is truly a masterpiece, its every gesture telling and revealing. It is epic and profound theatre, and *Rodeo* is simple, genuine life. Nothing in American ballet, within the Western scene, has surpassed them.

FANCY FREE

Choreographer	Jerome Robbins
Composer	Leonard Bernstein
Scenic Designer	Oliver Smith
Costume Designer	Kermit Love

Première—Metropolitan Opera House, New York, April 18, 1944

The Original Cast:

The Sailors	John Kriza
	Harold Lang
	Jerome Robbins

The Girls Who Pass By:

Brunette	Muriel Bentley
Redhead	Janet Reed
Blonde	Shirley Eckl

Fancy Free was first performed by, and remains in the permanent repertoire of the American Ballet Theatre.

THE STORY

The scene is New York but it could be any big city, anywhere, on any summer night, when any three sailors in summer whites meet any two girls who are outwardly free and easy but have their heads very firmly on their shoulders. This is the story of an episode between three such sailors and two such girls. They are all young and characteristically American in their exuberance, sensual innocence, and romantic attitudes. Youthfulness, and a patently American charm, are the main characteristics of this ballet whose music, story, choreography and scenic design were created by young American artists in the 'forties.

The libretto is by the choreographer, Jerome Robbins, and the score by Leonard Bernstein was composed separately. Choreographer and composer worked together by correspondence, putting their creations together only a week or so before the première of *Fancy Free*. The libretto was not contrived, but grew naturally. Robbins had the idea for such a ballet in 1942 and for the next two years, as he toured the U.S. as a dancer with Ballet Theatre during the war, he watched the sailors he saw everywhere. On streets and in bars, he saw sailors practice the "pick-up" technique with horse-play (as two of his sailors do in the ballet with the Brunette) or with a "snow job" (as the third sailor does in the bar with the pretty Redhead). Robbins observed and mirrored every gesture, act and facial expression in *Fancy Free* from life just as, years later, he observed the juvenile gangs before choreographing *West Side Story*. Nothing was devised— not even the way the sailors chew their gum and wad the wrappers into missiles to aim at invisible targets. From the cant of their hats to the soles of their nimble feet Robbins' sailors are the genuine article—the Great American Gob.

The curtain no sooner rises than we recognize New York. Lights shine from the thousand windows of skyscraper apartments, and the glow of a neon-bathed Broadway makes a midnight sunset in the distant sky. The stage is a street in front of a glass-walled bar, with a lamppost as sentinel on the sidewalk. Through the glass we see the barman dozing at the mahogany counter. There is no other sign of life. The scene, although almost deserted, is by some special air of expectancy neither desolate nor calm. Instead, the electric lights in the bar and the street lamp seem brighter than sunshine, and the air shouts of excitement. Untouched by all this nocturnal glamour, the bartender occupies his workaday world; the bar has no more enchantment for him than a desk would hold for an office worker. We have to take stock, here, of the barman, for he is part and parcel of the scene. He belongs, in *Fancy Free,* more to the artist Oliver Smith, who designed the set, than to Robbins' choreography, or to Bernstein's music. The bar and the street are one, for they are the points between which the dancers move in the ballet. There never was a more profitable lamppost, which illumines the wayward loves of the sidewalk; there never was a more useful mahogany bar, over which the barman passes the beers for which one sailor always pays,

John Kriza, Paul Godkin and Eric Braun as the Sailors.

and on which the sailors leap and dance, or fall and fight. The bar stands, in its smug shining height, between the routine existence of the barman on one side and the restless, reckless world of the sailors and their girls on the other side.

Suddenly three sailors appear, in spotless Navy whites, and as they enter the scene comes to life, for these boys dance rather than walk, in a little unconscious strut of bursting high spirits. They actually break into a dance, and two of them seize and lift the third sailor in the air. Jostling and clowning, they are a contrast to the barman, sober as a judge at his bar, reading the evening paper.

For the sailors, the troubles of the night are the passing of time and the lack of girls. They consider the problem of what to do, restless and undecided. One goes into the bar—he thinks better when drinking. The others lounge outside, one leaning propped against the lamppost. Then the two outside join the one at the bar and when they do something as simple as having a beer they turn it into a celebration—it becomes a toast! Slyly, two of the sailors manage with elaborate absent-mindedness to make the third sailor pay for all three drinks.

They chat desultorily. After all, they live on ship together and there is little new or interesting to say to each other. They glance about moodily for some diversion, divide one stick of gum in three, chew, and cogitate. Bored with life, aware that time is fleeting, they lounge until a girl strolls by. At once, they are galvanized into fast action. She is a shapely brunette, with a snaky walk, wearing a tight bodice and skirt. Wow! The sailors lean over at a precarious angle to watch her, nearly falling on their faces; then the leaning frieze melts and they dash off after the brunette. How to get her to notice them? They clown about—mincing along, pretending to walk just like her; they snatch her handbag and play ball with it, performing some tricky passes. The girl is furious—anyway, she pretends she is! At last, almost against her will, she has to laugh at the three gay idiots! There and then she causes a near riot because each sailor believes she has smiled at him and is his alone. Two of them pick her up and hold her high; she acts half afraid, half angry, and kicks, struggles, drops down from their hold and runs away. Two sailors follow in pursuit, knocking down their third buddy in the rush.

When this sailor picks himself up he bumps into another girl. His woes are at once forgotten, for she is a redhead, younger, prettier, altogether more attractive than the brunette who has led his friends on a chase. He apologizes to the redhead and manages, adroitly, to steer her into the bar for a drink to revive her for almost being knocked down by him. Soon they are deep in animated conversation, and the sailor gives his best "snow job," in his parlance—he imitates a zooming enemy plane and the *ratatatat* of machine-gunning; we can imagine his harrowing tale of his many, many narrow escapes from death. The girl is impressed with such heroics—the sailor turns nonchalant as though to say, Oh, it was really nothing! But obviously in war time the poor fellow lives in close company with the Grim Reaper and what can a girl do but make his shore leave pleasant? They get up and begin to dance to the music of a juke box.

The *pas de deux* is in the style of popular dancing. They embrace and are there and then confined in that tiny, lovely private world of two partners alone in a crowded ballroom. The blasé bartender takes absolutely no notice of love blooming under the electric lights. The dance ends with a tender kiss, but this knowing miss takes no chances of being compromised—she carefully wipes her lipstick off her beau's face.

The other three appear—the two sailors and the brunette—but their triumph is short-lived. It turns out that the two girls know each other and fall into each other's arms with cries of joy. In no time they are ensconced on bar stools, their heads close together, deep in a private confabulation that excludes the sailors. The sailors, after all, are momentary diversions, gone with the next tide, but the two girls live in a solid world of yesterdays, todays, tomorrows and the week after next.

Impatiently, the sailors try to break up the girlish chat. It is as hard to shatter as a secret pact. The girls languidly drink the drinks the sailors buy them but continue talking to each other without showing further interest in the boys. The boys begin to knock themselves out, trying to gain the girls' attentions. To do this, they dance, in three Variations.

The first Variation is all spins, leaps, a somersault, some terrific jumps. The sailor does an *adagio* dance on top of the bar and ends by jumping off, turning around, spinning on one leg and ending with one leg extended, both hands behind his back. He is the perfect extrovert.

The second Variation begins on a deliberately softer and more romantic note, with flowing movements, slow pirouettes, spins, and glides. It develops a strong sinuous rhythm, ends on the return to the slow opening. The sailor drops effortlessly to the ground, and poses. He is the romanticist.

The third Variation is a snaky-hipped routine, with exaggerated, almost parodied "Spanish" dance gestures and style—strutting, kicks, small pirouettes, and hands beating in staccato at the sides. The sailor ends on one knee, pretending to be a gallant don. He could either be a show-off like the extrovert, or romantic, according to the mood and the lead he got from a girl.

The girls, even after these efforts to win them, cannot decide which sailor each prefers. To settle the argument between three boys as to which two will squire the brunette and the redhead, the sailors resort to forceful action. In what passes for dancing, they play a kind of grab-bag game with the two girls, who are whirled about from one sailor's clutch to the next, in the frantic form of a Lindy-hop. In the process of snatching a girl into his embrace, one sailor is not above shoving another sailor violently away. Soon the pushing and snatching becomes too wild for comfort and the girls' exhilaration quickly turns to irritation and some alarm. This is more than they bargained for when they entered the bar to have a friendly round of drinks with the sailors.

Meanwhile, the former buddies have digressed from determination to brawling argument. The girls are for the moment forgotten, although they remain the figurative bone of contention. Very much as dogs snarl and prepare to fight the three sailors circle warily, feint, dive and tackle and are eventually embroiled in a real, knockdown tussle. They jump on each other and heave about in a strug-

Paula Lloyd, Muriel Bentley, Jerome Robbins, John Kriza and Michael Kidd in Fancy Free.

gling mass so that the girls can hardly tell one from the other. One sailor is flung off by his two adversaries (all of them are indiscriminately fighting each other, which makes it difficult for any two to really come to a fair exchange of blows) and that sailor is pitched like a ball at the two girls. He strikes their neat legs and down they go, like human ninepins. The sailor pays no attention to them, but leaps up and returns to the heaving white uniforms, into which he dives again.

The girls pick themselves up and dust each other off with expressions of intense indignation. The idea! they seem to say, consoling each other's wounded vanity. They smooth their skirts and, heads high, shocked and furious, they leave the scene. About this time, as one sailor is having his head banged by the other two he sees the girls leaving but has some difficulty in bringing their loss to the attention of his friends, who are so busy methodically smacking him. When at last it dawns on all three that they have been deserted they rush to the door, look up and down the street, and vainly hope that the girls will return. Now they look less like fierce dogs and more like mystified puppies who have lost a bone. But soon their irrepressible spirits rise and having ruefully surveyed each other, clapped each back with a sympathetic hand and affixed their caps at the usual debonair angles, the mercurial three are resigned to a situation that they obviously know all too well.

Back to the bar they go for a drink, in the belief that this timely dram will put things right again. Adroitly, from long practice, two of them manage again to make the third "sucker" pay for the round. They drift back to the street when they have quaffed their beers. One searches his pockets and produces a stick of gum which he divides into three, sharing the pieces fairly among them. Each sailor unwraps his piece of gum, staring into the distance, puts the gum in his mouth, wads up the wrapper and aims it at an invisible target. This is their usual procedure, and has been seen before, when they first arrived at the street corner. The incident has now, we feel, come its full round and the sailors are right back where they started. Strangely enough, their uniforms are none the worse for wear, nor, we shall soon see, are the sailors in body and soul.

While they stand cogitating on the ways of shore leave, perhaps vowing each to himself a silent oath of allegience to these good buddies, whom he will never again betray for anything so unworthy as a girl, a third girl sashays by. She is blonde, with the same snaky walk of the brunette, and the quick unspoken wow! is louder than ever. But the sailors do not at once start the pursuit. Each seems to loiter with elaborate nonchalance, pretending *Who me? Never again!* In reality, each sailor is shrewdly waiting to see if the other two will relinquish the chase to him, when he will have a clear field. Waiting for the first move, they begin to walk in the direction opposite to the blonde's. Their steps grow slower and slower, one at last pauses and looks back, fearful that the girl will get out of sight, and at that moment, the spell broken, all of them react as usual. The chase is on again, as frantic as ever. This time, all three sailors pursue the enticing damsel and the street and the glass-fronted bar are left deserted, under the vigilant lamppost.

THE MUSIC

At curtain rise the orchestra is silent and the first music to be heard comes from the bartender's radio, a blaring blues tune. It is ground out on the air like so much confetti and trembles in almost visible notes under the street lamp's glare. The orchestral music begins with the entrance of the sailors, who dance rather than walk. Their every gesture is frenetic as they fix their caps at devilishly cute angles, wriggle themselves snugly in their sparkling white uniforms, saunter, strut, pose and quick-step. Robbins, in his libretto, defines the music as "fast, explosive, jolly, rollicking. A bang-away start" and this is just what Bernstein has provided. In later passages (again to quote the choreographer) the music is boogie-woogie "with sudden hot loud licks." Syncopation pulses through every note and every dance step and stamps the ballet with its authentic and recognizable American quality.

The first gay and rowdy theme passes into a sweeter tempo and becomes almost moody. A kind of sugared misery lies in the music now, as the sailors contemplate shore leave's freedom and the lack of girls. Time is flying by—there is no real reason for having a good time—and they must have a good time. This is the frantic impulse—to have a good time!

The music is at its best in the three Variations, in quality and character. Under the bland disguise of the starched sailor middies beat three quite individual hearts and it is with the music and the dance interpretation that the sailors reveal their secret selves. The First is proud of his agility; the Second romantic; the Third a bit of a swashbuckler with some Latin fire in his blood. Identical in uniform and attitude, they are quite different in personality. These are not chorus boys, but three gobs on the town.

Bernstein's music differs from many ballet scores that accompany dancing or are interpreted by dancing. The composer is almost wilfully bent on musically describing his three sailors in their Variations, so that with each solo the ballet deviates from its episodic theme and becomes a study in characterization. The overall theme is brash, bold and colloquially American but the music makes a spiritual counterpoint and develops the characters with subtle shadings in the Variations. From beginning to end, the score is apt, and before it begins the tone is set for the audience, with the cry of the blues from the bar. A city is a hungering place, full of empty hearts, it says, but this remark is camouflaged with the confetti spatter of music. Immediately after, the sad and weary mood is dissipated by Bernstein's orchestral music, which seems to echo the crash of the opening gate at the Brooklyn Navy Yard and the rush of gobs and gals that means *the fleet's in*. Then and there, the sailors appear, foot loose and fancy free.

PERFORMANCES

All in the original cast became remarkable figures in American ballet. Muriel Bentley was the Brunette and Janet Reed the Redhead. Bentley was deliciously funny in *Fancy Free* and the soul of malice in *Fall River Legend;* Reed, now the ballet mistress of the New York City Ballet, is the most beloved comedienne in the national dance theatre. The Sailors were John Kriza, Harold Lang, and Robbins, and the roles were later danced with Michael Kidd and Zachary Solov in the trio with the choreographer. Kidd became a great influence on the musical theatre; his ballet *On Stage!* brought him early recognition and he later became famous for his ballets in *Finian's Rainbow, Guys and Dolls, Knock on Wood,* and *Seven Brides for Seven Brothers.* Solov became the principal choreographer for the Metropolitan Opera House.

Paul Godkin and Eric Braun have danced as Sailors with Kriza, and in current repertoire the three gobs are most often portrayed by Kriza, Scott Douglas and Enrique Martinez, and The Girls Who Pass By are Beverly Sims, Ruth Ann Koesun and Patti Schmidt, all of American Ballet Theatre. The dancers may be identified with the narration by knowing that the first Variation is danced by Martinez, the second by Kriza, and the third by Douglas. The *pas de deux* between the Second Sailor and the Redhead is danced by Kriza and Koesun. It is Kriza who pays for the beers as the "sucker."

The dance composition is a fine example of American ballet techniques, with back-flips, tremendous leaps and jumps and spectacular turns and extensions, and is primarily focused on the male dancers. The style is the best of the American genre—athletic, powerful and deceptively nimble, with its poetry of motion dependent on sharp, clean lines and ebullient gesture.

Kriza is indelibly associated with *Fancy Free,* for he has been dancing in the ballet since its première. Quite possibly, he now knows every part of the choreography better than the choreographer. He once did a feat of prompting in the ballet when a Sailor in the cast was taken ill and the understudy was on crutches from an accident. The dancer Fernando Alonso (husband of Alicia Alonso) was commandeered into a sailor suit and went onstage, never having danced in *Fancy Free* before. Alonso went through the performance creditably, for a soldout house, with Kriza leaping, turning and gliding at his side, cuing Alonso in whispers into every step to be taken and every gesture to be made.

FALL RIVER LEGEND

Choreographer	Agnes de Mille
Composer	Morton Gould
Scenic Artist	Oliver Smith
Costume Designer	Miles White

Première—Metropolitan Opera House, New York, April 22, 1948

The Original Cast:

The Accused	Alicia Alonso
Mother	Diana Adams
Father	Peter Gladke
Stepmother	Muriel Bentley
Pastor	John Kriza
The Child	Ruth Ann Koesun

Fall River Legend was first performed by, and remains in the permanent repertoire of the American Ballet Theatre.

THE STORY

The legend of Fall River, Massachusetts, has been perpetuated in doggerel:

> Lizzie Borden took an axe
> And gave her mother forty whacks,
> And when she saw what she had done
> She gave her father forty-one.

The newspapers of the day, in reporting the dreadful crime, made much of two minor facts—that the weather had been the hottest for August in years, and that the family ate a breakfast of cold mutton soup on the morning of August 4, 1892. The family was named Borden, and it was Mr. Borden and Mrs. Borden, his second wife, who were murdered, and one of Mr. Borden's two daughters by his first marriage who was accused of the double murders. The accused, named Lizzie Borden, was tried and acquitted in one of the most famous trials in American jurisprudence. In fact, the murderer was never discovered by law, and Lizzie Borden became the subject of controversy among amateur detectives in her day and into this one. The Borden murder story is a superb who-done-it. We know as a certainty that the Borden family was a divided one; Lizzie had not spoken to her father and stepmother in more than two years before they died. Mr. Borden was respectable and prosperous, but he was penurious; nothing was wasted in that bitter house. The mutton the family ate for breakfast on the day of the crimes was going bad in the heat, but the Bordens were too thrifty to throw it out. Lizzie was a spinster past her first maturity and she lived in a time when a woman of her social class depended on the security of a good marriage, and money. She had neither, and little hope of independence while her parents were alive; presumably, as her father's heiress, she would benefit financially if he and his second wife died.

On the fourth day of that intolerably hot August the Bordens arose and went about their business dressed in the prim clothes of the era, which made all the men look as though they had been cut out of stiff dark cardboard, and all the women as though they had no legs. They came down, one by one, from the top of the house to the lower floor, and sat down to that execrable breakfast. Mr. Borden went to his place of business, returned for lunch, and afterwards lay down in the parlor to have a nap. Mrs. Borden went upstairs. All, as the maidservant later testified, was as usual. By the end of the afternoon the elder Bordens had been murdered and, soon after, Lizzie Borden was accused. But what happened in that house that day nobody knows.

Agnes de Mille wrote her libretto for the ballet of *Fall River Legend* after a theme suggested to her by a friend, Edward Sheldon, the playwright. She says that she was fascinated by the psychology that would persuade a good woman, respected, churchgoing, restricted in a formal age, to commit a double crime of such ferocity and unprecedented boldness—and then never to commit another. In the ballet, de Mille attempts to picture a whole life of stifled and abused love, ending in violence and death. The Accused retraces her past in memory and the audience journeys back into the past through her eyes.

Nora Kaye, Peter Gladke and Lucia Chase in Fall River Legend.

The choreographer, with poetic license, rearranges fact for dramatic significance in the ballet. Lizzie did not die on the gallows, but the Accused is doomed
to hang; the Borden murders were committed in the daylight hours but de Mille
employs the night's passage between two scenes—the murders are discovered in
the following dawn. These things, significant to a law court, are not important
to the ballet where the primary concern is with the tormented passions of the
Accused during her life, not the manner of her death, nor the time of the crime.
In *Fall River Legend* the audience does not go to court to hear the legal testi-
mony against one Lizzie Borden; it adventures with the choreographer into
nameless depths of despair, seeking the soul of the Accused.

The ballet begins in the present, in a *Prologue;* interim scenes are flash-backs
through which the Accused retraces her life up to the present.

The curtain rises on a desolate open field at the edge of a marsh, with a few
broken palings and reedy undergrowth. To one side stands a twisted tree, its
bare limbs streaming as though in a great wind. At the other side stands the
gallows, silhouetted against a greenish sky in which heavy clouds are being
driven by the wind. In a circle of light the Accused stands; she is a neatly
dressed woman, in the mode of the late eighteen-hundreds, and seems incon-
gruous in the wild country, as do her companions, all of them men. Beside the
woman stands a man in clerical dress; near the gallows tree is the hangman, in
a bowler hat. A man, the Foreman of the Jury, begins to read aloud (in actuality) the indictment from the inquest. It is a true bill. The jurors have stated on
oath that the Accused, on August 4, 1892, with a certain weapon—to wit: an
axe—did assault and kill her stepmother and father with twenty mortal blows,
"and therefore the Jury do say that the Accused did kill and murder against the
peace of the Commonwealth." Having thus established murder as being done,
the Foreman continues: "The house in which the murders were committed was
the house in which you were born. You lived there with your mother and father
happily."

The ballet's décor is an extraordinary one, by Oliver Smith, who designed a
versatile set. By removing and replacing sections of the House of the Accused
the edifice becomes the neat parlor of the Borden family, or a church with a
pulpit, as it revolves on its base. When at last the house dissolves nothing of it
is left but the stark frame of the gallows. There are seven scenes.

Scene I, The House of the Accused, stands naked to the street and we are able
to see through imaginary rooftree and walls into the Borden parlor. It is fur-
nished primly, and in the background a steep staircase connects it with the upper and invisible floor. Under the stairs is a little door. The street outside is an
integral part of the scene. The Accused has been transported here in the flesh
(just as we saw her, a full-grown woman, standing near the gallows in the *Prologue*) but she sees all things as they were while she was still a child. People from
that past are discerned. None can see the Accused who, of course, does not exist
then as she does in the present. A young couple and a child appear. They are
the first Mrs. Borden, her husband, and their child, the little girl who once was
the Accused. She looks at them: mother, father, and her childhood self. They

The Accused and her Childhood Self watch the pas de deux *of her father and mother. Dancers Diana Adams, Peter Gladke, Alicia Alonso and Ruth Ann Koesun in* Fall River Legend.

cannot see her, but we do—a woman in a dress of livid green. More than the years separate that woman from her childhood self, the little girl in a white dress with a ribbon in her flowing hair.

The Mother wears a lacy shawl and leans on the arm of her husband; he is tender and attentive. The girl trips about, as idle as a butterfly. The air seems full of sunbeams and the mood is artless, gentle and gay. Strolling people, some in couples, the ladies hanging on the gentlemen's arms, pass in promenade and sociably pause to exchange the time of day.

A woman joins the throng in the street, inconspicuous except for her long black dress and a feather boa hanging about her neck. As she paces towards the Father and Mother of the little girl the air seems to wither; all leisure, peace and good humor flee before the woman, who walks as though crushing beetles with every step. Her ominous presence affects all except the Father, who greets her politely, taking no notice of the rush the little girl has made to him, in obvious horror of the lady in black. She, the lady, is the Spinster on the street, a cold, grim woman, who scolds the little girl for being rude in not greeting her elders properly. The child clings to her father, who seems inclined to reprove her for offending the Spinster. This alarms the Mother, who is a delicate lady; she swoons and is picked up and carried into their house by her husband.

Soon, the Mother recovers and shows her restored strength and gaiety by dancing with her husband. They are still young, and in love, and their *pas de deux* is charming and romantic. The Mother is sensitive and loving to her little girl, sees her standing aside, makes room in the dance for her and when the child rushes gladly to them the *pas de deux* becomes a pretty *pas de trois*. The family life of these three is affectionate and joyous, tempered by the tenderness both Father and Child show the Mother. That lady, lovely, delicate and lissom, has a lyric quality that makes her every gesture enchanting, but she is quickly wearied and soon her weak heart fails her again, and again she swoons and is taken into the house by her husband.

This time the Mother is not easily revived and the Father becomes distraught in his attempts to restore her fading vitality. Passively, he accepts the assistance of neighbors, among them the Spinster in her dangling feather boa. The Father kneels in prayer for his wife's recovery, too distracted to comfort the poor child who kneels with him. The Mother dies and the neighbor women emerge from the house and dress the child in mourning clothes as a sign that she is orphaned. The little girl stands like a doll between them and their busy hands arrange the black smock that eclipses her white frock. The sunlit air darkens and gloom settles on the street. Wracked by the poignant memory of that moment, the Accused falls against the side of the house; a little while before, seeing the child dancing with her parents, the Accused had unconsciously swayed in the dancing, too.

The Spinster appears in the doorway of the house with a great air of authority; the Father kneels at her feet, either in gratitude for her help or because his anguish at his wife's loss has beaten him down. He is totally helpless, bowed, supplicating. The child runs and leaps catlike on his back, clinging to him desperately, in an effort to keep him for herself. With studied calm, the Spinster picks up the dead woman's lacy white shawl, an act of sacrilege to the child. Next the child attempts to enter her house but the door is barred by the imposing figure in black; when the woman will not let the child enter, she has hysterics—the first of the rages that tear her, out of frustration and hate of the woman. The Spinster looks scornfully at the child, and the Father, rising, takes the woman in his arms and enters the house with her. She thereafter becomes his second wife and is no more the Spinster but the Stepmother. The door shuts in the child's face. Her father either cannot or will not help her.

At this point, the Childhood Self disappears from the ballet, as though at the moment of repudiation by her Father she is forever cast out; instead, she will be the Accused, who (in her adult figure) ceases to be the shadowy spectator and is thereafter the actively participating member of the household. For the sake of clarity in this narrative we shall refer to her as Lizzie.

Scene II, The House, shows us the family's joyless existence, with the Father and Stepmother united in their impassivity to Lizzie. These three are seen in the parlor of the house. The Father and Stepmother sit in rockers, holding books before their faces, but they are not reading so much as waiting and listening. Lizzie comes in, seats herself in a rocker between her parents, and begins to rock. They say nothing to each other, nor make a sign. Lizzie finds the silence oppressive and snaps her fingers, rocks her chair wildly, and seems about to erupt.

The house uncannily grows larger to encompass the stage (it is moved closer to the audience) and our attention is riveted to the staircase in the background. Steeply pitched, it has the effect of descending, never of ascending; its ominous character lies in its root shape—that of the gallows.

Lizzie jumps up, mounts a few steps of the stairs rapidly as though pursued, stops, looks wildly around, and then as quickly runs down the stairs again. Her distracted manner causes the Stepmother to incline her head toward the Father and whisper some malicious remark; she is pretending to believe that the young woman is unbalanced. Aware that her distraught behavior makes her sanity suspect, Lizzie makes an effort to be calm, and returns to her chair to rock. But soon the rocking becomes wild again, and the girl jumps up, runs to the shuttered window and stands looking out. The Stepmother rises, follows Lizzie, and pulls the shutter tight, then she pulls Lizzie away so that she shall not look into the street. In despair, Lizzie runs out into the yard. The Stepmother peeps out, to reassure herself that the girl is not meeting someone, then resumes her seat in the rocker. The Father rises, like an automaton, takes the white shawl worn by his first wife, places it about the shoulders of his second wife and stands passively behind her chair.

With another shift of scene, we see Lizzie in the yard chatting with the Pastor. They dance together to demonstrate their meeting and mutual liking and then part, very formally, with a handshake. The Pastor is grave, Lizzie shy. Innocent as this meeting is, it offends the Father, who sternly orders Lizzie into the house. She slowly enters, the Pastor leaves, and once more the three—Father, Stepmother and Lizzie—are arranged in their chairs, decorously rocking. The time passes endlessly, in silence. When Lizzie can endure her tension no longer, she jumps up and this time vanishes through the door under the stairs. She reappears holding the axe.

The Stepmother shrieks and flies to her husband's side and Lizzie gazes at her in surprise at the show of terror. The Stepmother has, in actuality, said nothing, but so real is her fear that the whole world shrieks—the sound is echoed by the orchestra. Lizzie goes out into the yard and with a great supple movement (the first such free and fluent movement she has made) drives the axe blade deep into the chopping block. Then she returns to the parlor, absently wipes her hands, and resumes her place between Father and Stepmother. The scene is, at this moment, just as it was before Lizzie went for the axe, yet everything is changed! The terror betrayed by her parents has informed her of an awful power she exerts over them; it dawns on her that although she cannot win love she can command fear.

Scene III, The Street lies front, with the house retired to the background. Lizzie emerges and sits on the front step, arranging her skirt over her knees. The Father and Stepmother are in the parlor. As Lizzie watches the street she marvels that all who pass have a destination; some people are lovers and walk with arms entwined and faces turned to each other. Of all these only Lizzie is alone, with nowhere to go, and no one to come home to her. *But wait!* something seems to whisper to her. She listens and almost smiles. There seems to be something she must do, something urgent, something important. She leaps up, runs across the stage and confronts the axe in its chopping block. Eagerly, she runs up to it, puts a hand out to it, as though it were a lover met at a rendezvous. The fatal attraction of the sharp blade poised in the wood first draws and then revolts her. She pulls her hand back as though the axe-handle burned it, and falls to the ground. Mesmerized, she keeps her gaze on the fearful thing and slowly creeps away from it.

Her fright leaves her with the arrival of the Pastor, who has brought her a bouquet of red roses. He is courteous and kind and Lizzie blooms under his attention. Love begins to grow between them—shy and timid on Lizzie's part, compassionate and tender on the Pastor's, in the little dance that is their communication. It is interrupted by the Father and Stepmother, who come stealthily out of the house. The woman stares accusingly at Lizzie, intimating that she has been caught doing wrong, and Lizzie gives vent to one of her convulsive childish rages, throwing herself on the ground, kicking and rolling in a paroxysm of furious despair. As the others stand looking at her, she sees the axe and is suddenly quieted. The utilitarian object now assumes a baleful power.

The Stepmother turns the Pastor aside to confide to him that the girl is unbalanced but the young man, although grave and attentive, appears not to be alarmed. Instead, he is more than ever anxious to help Lizzie, and invites her to a church social. Before she can speak, her parents curtly refuse the invitation and motion her back into the house because she is not well. Lizzie, with a strange new dignity, takes her mother's white shawl, arranges it around her shoulders, leans on the Pastor's arm and goes off with him.

Scene IV, The Prayer Meeting, shows us a new Lizzie among the townsfolk gathered at prayer meeting. With the dimming light the house has been pivoted and when the lights come up again the edifice has been transformed into the church, or prayer meeting hall. The Pastor stands among his kneeling congregation, which Lizzie does not at first join out of timidity. She is persuaded to do so by some of the women, one of whom kisses her and reminds her of their schooldays as children. The memory of her childhood, before her mother died, warms and relaxes Lizzie's cold demeanor; she becomes more pliant and moves with more grace. The prayer meeting closed, the congregation divides for social dancing. Lizzie looks on with a half smile, not willing to dance but enjoying the dancing. The church members leave and Lizzie remains alone with the Pastor.

Their communication in the *pas de deux* is intended by the choreographer to depict the Pastor's wrestling for the girl's soul; she pours out to him her tormented fears and hates, none of which disgust him, all of which make him more compassionate and tender. Lizzie returns in mind to her childhood state as she confides in the young man; she turns and turns and delivers herself to his mercy, longing, as a child, to be forgiven and to have her hurts healed. The Pastor becomes her father and protector, gently assuaging her fears, forgiving her wrongs, healing all the wounds of her heart. Many of the gestures in this *pas de deux* are developments of the Mother-Father *pas de deux* in *Scene I,* which the girl remembers. The choreographer has used them deliberately, to express the girl's recollection of a past and lovely time in her life. The music surges with her emotions, and the girl is at first childlike in her trust, lying on the floor curled like a fallen leaf; rising, at the touch of the man's hand; yielding to him as he dances with her, to a rising musical theme. At last they are moving together in wide circles and leaping into the air, evidence of the new strength and freedom that has come to Lizzie from her association with the Pastor. Emancipated now, she again softens and yields, is held and cradled by the Pastor's strong arms, moves with him to a melodious, softened theme of the music.

With the reappearance of the congregation, Lizzie takes her place among them and dances with grace and verve. No girl in the throng dances better, none with such open happiness and spontaneity. The other church members are quick to see the change in Lizzie—the boys partner her and lift her in the air, and the girls, as they pass in the pattern of the dance, touch her hands with theirs and smile at her. Lizzie has taken her place among the young and happy.

Joy is short-lived, for the Stepmother appears and Lizzie's gaiety and confidence at once shrivel. She, who so recently seemed saved from sin and misery by the Pastor's love and understanding, is now shaken by hate and fear and falls writhing to the ground in one of her fits of rage. With hands like claws, she raked the air before her Stepmother in the earlier bout of fury; now the very sight of the dreadful woman paralyzes her, and she swoons at her feet. The Pastor bends to her but is stopped by the Stepmother, who tells him that Lizzie is demented and may not endure any excitement, pleasurable or otherwise. This accounts for her parents' refusal to let her attend the church social. The sane and serious attitude of the wicked woman, so in contrast with her own wild state, makes Lizzie despair of convincing her friends that she is not ill. In her panic she almost goes mad, as her Stepmother meaningfully insinuates she is. The congregation circles the prostrate girl slowly, half in awe, half in pity, and Lizzie at last rises wearily to her feet. She is in rigid control of herself and moves like a sleepwalker. The Pastor gently wraps her mother's shawl about her and the Stepmother, in apparent kindness, takes her hand. Desperately, Lizzie tries to withdraw from that hated clasp and to seek the Pastor but as she yearns to him he is looking the other way and does not see her supplicating gesture. The Stepmother pulls at her hand and Lizzie follows the woman home.

Scene V again returns to the parlor. The Stepmother enters with an air of malicious satisfaction and Lizzie goes into the yard. There she listlessly watches the promenading couples, gazing at them with new insight. She no longer yearns to be among them, for she recognizes her destiny and knows she is about to commit an act so irrevocable it will forever place her beyond the reach of ordinary, happy people. One of her new friends speaks to her but she does not hear, and cannot see. She goes to the chopping block, takes up the axe, and enters the house. Her Father and Stepmother are seated in the parlor and they start up out of their rockers at the sight of Lizzie and the axe. Lizzie looks back at them, and then she covers her face with her free hand.

Scene VI, The Present and the Past are shown superimposed one on the other, at two levels. The lower room is Lizzie's dream, in which she has sought and found her Mother in Limbo; the upper is reality and represents the parlor of the house, where the murders have just been committed. Suspended in the air, the real room has for the time being ceased to matter to Lizzie. We see its disturbed furnishings and its floor, from which the blood drips. Below the fearful scene is one insubstantial but lovely, where Lizzie and her Mother meet. Lizzie is dressed in a white petticoat dabbled with blood, but she appears not to know that the blood has soaked through her discarded dress. She flies to her Mother and nestles in her arms, and they drift tranquilly in embrace. Mother is exactly as the girl recalls her—lovely and lyric in movement, with a gentle face and enfolding arms.

But suddenly the Mother notices the stains on her child's garment, is angered by them, and slaps the girl's hands for being naughty. Then, she recoils in horror, finding that the stains are wet blood. At that moment, Lizzie can escape reality no more. Seeking escape and comfort in Limbo with her Mother, she has been made to recognize her crime. She has sinned so grievously that she has sacrificed earthly happiness with the Pastor and friends and must lose her Mother as well. The Mother, at the dawning knowledge of her child's damnation, begins to weep. And how terrible is the Mother's grief! Now it is the child who must comfort the Mother and Lizzie compassionately embraces her grieving Mother. She is the older by far—old as sin. Compassion cannot heal the breach between them and they now belong to different worlds which not even love can span. The mists rise, the Mother, entreat though she might, disappears. When the mists dissolve, Lizzie stands alone under the blood-smeared floor above. She must return in spirit as in body to that room, to live with the deed and the punishment.

Scene VII reveals Lizzie in the light of the dawning day, and the house on its firm foundations. With the passing of the dark night the sky is red with sunrise. To Lizzie it looks bloodstained. Her neighbors have gathered in the street outside the house, alarmed by the strange noises that have emanated from it in the dark. They speak among themselves, the good citizens, intent on preserving the respectability of their neighborhood. Lizzie appears in a shocking silence, still dressed in her bloodied petticoat. She opens her mouth in a desire to shout and is so held, in a rictus of fear. Since she cannot explain her panic, the excited neighbors rush to the house to find out for themselves. They literally tear the house apart, timber from timber, to expose the crimes within.

Two men return from the shambles, one carrying the bloodied axe, the other the blood-dappled white shawl. Lizzie takes the shawl and lifts it to her lips. The people on the street withdraw from her and gaze at her in horror. All is clear from the evidence and the fearsome story divulged by those who have seen inside the house. Only the Pastor shows sympathy and he draws close to Lizzie and puts his arms about her; she collapses with shame at his touch, and when he releases her she falls senseless to the ground. The neighbors feel no pity— only horror and just wrath—and on their urging Lizzie is revived and led off by arresting hands.

Scene VIII, The Gallows. The house has vanished and only its roof beam and one support of a wall remain, at right angles to each other, to form the gallows. We are again at the point where the *Prologue* ceased and the Accused's mind wandered into her past. The Accused stands as before, never having moved except in fancy, and the Pastor is beside her still. The well-dressed gentlemen, and the hangman in his hard hat, still face the Accused; they are waiting stolidly to see her punished for her sins. A woman and a child come by with other curious people to see the monster-woman who is the Accused; the child looks uncommonly like the Accused as a child; she shakes her little fist at the condemned murderess. Lovers pay no attention as they walk arm in arm, immersed in each other. The end has come and for a moment Lizzie leans her head on the Pastor's shoulder. He kisses her, most gently, and leaves her.

The Accused, left alone, opens her arms to the gallows and embraces her doom.

The ballet employs a great deal of gesture which in parts transcends mute mime, as when in *Scene I* the door is shut in the Child's face, and in *Scene IV* after the dance that is her confessional, Lizzie swoons and comes out of her swoon to find the malevolent Stepmother looking down into her face.

The atmosphere, so much a part of the plot, is created by Oliver Smith's marvelous and ingenious set. Smith has used straight lines and with them he pins the house on the audience's view: the window, through whose shutters Lizzie watches life go by her on the street; the door, through which the Child sees the Father pass first with the Mother in his arms, then with the Stepmother wearing her mother's shawl. The lines like bars imprison the audience's view and the Accused's remembering heart—the window shutters, the flat hard floor, the stairs that never rise, but plunge down from the secret agonies of the upper floor to the ironically neat parlor. There is nothing curved or lovely in that house, except for the formal convoluted chairs in which the characters sit and rock. Over all this—house, street and church—the sky broods, and when it arches over the gallows it is the color of a bruise. Perhaps this is the color of the Accused's heart, swollen with fears and tears, which has been slowly squeezed within her breast.

Fall River Legend is a profound drama, and has an uncanny effect on many in the audience. Not a little of this effect is caused by Oliver Smith, who has created a pretty Victorian chair with a back like a flower and imbued it with such horror than one can hardly bear, after seeing *Fall River Legend,* to sit down in a rocking chair.

The ballet begins on the sound of great musical chords, with an undercurrent of brassy tones. For the reading of the "true bill," actual speech is used by the Foreman of the Jury, who speaks in a dull, mechanical tone.

The music elaborates a small minor theme, as though the Accused softly murmured amid the deeper and sonorous tones.

A low, swinging melody commences, as the past unfolds and the Accused's memory re-creates the scenes one by one. A tender evocation of the past holds a low throbbing, as that of the Accused's heart. There is a tearing away by strident sounds and a joyous lilting melody bears the Accused into the realm of her Childhood Self and the Street in its carefree days. A long musical passage ensues, of deep chords alternated with clear, sweet ones. Plucked strings, bell-like tones, all communicate a full and lovely sense of peace and deep, quiet happiness. This is the ordinary secure world of the Street and through it runs a carousel tune, like a thread of brightly colored tinsel, to accompany the little girl's revelry of dancing; a rhythmic, bold, exciting music propels the little child like a leaf on the wind. The passage ends in crescendo, joyously.

The *pas de trois*, which begins as a *pas de deux*, is a sweeter, fuller passage, with a nostalgic undertone. Borne up on a deep, rich motif, as though Father benignly bent to his womenfolk, is a minor melody; the dual natures of Father and Mother are clear and are swelled by the advent of the happy little child.

The next two scenes are interpreted by a great deal of mime, as is the fifth scene, and the music is subtle accompaniment for the development of the plot and the expression of the loneliness and longing felt by Lizzie as she lives her life in an increasing preoccupation with revenge. When the axe begins to dominate her thoughts the music sketches a whispering, scuttling theme that is the evil, or the madness, which gradually dominates the Accused. It snarls when she seeks the axe. For Limbo, in its veiled intransient mood, the music is unearthly and tremulous.

Scene III, The Street, is danced to music nocturnal and sweet; the choreographer invokes the atmosphere of pianos heard down a street on a summer's night. The piano is used, exquisitely, within the orchestra. For the prayer meeting in the fourth scene the music is built on New England hymn tunes and, in form, is a tremendous fugue, changing its character to one sweet and tender for the *pas de deux* between Lizzie and the Pastor. Gould's score is here—as it is in the opening theme and the fugue—as descriptive as narration. In the *pas de deux* between the Pastor and the girl we understand from the music's discourse that the young woman's heart is slowly opening and unfolding like a rose, as she responds to the man's compassionate love and understanding. The sense of triumph in the Pastor is related by the music, as he moves the girl faster and faster and lifts her higher in a surging, urgent emotion. Purged of guilt, free of suffering, the girl is borne up on a great symphonic swell. Then there is an ebb, the movement of music subsides and the passage ends.

The pace is at once galvanized into a cotillion, spontaneous and energetic. The music and the dancing here, in the communal dance, is meant to express a community sing. The ballet originally included a choir warming up their voices but this part is now deleted from the work.

When Mother and the Accused meet in Limbo the music, as Mother, is at first caressing, and when the mothering roles are most tragically reversed and it is the Accused who must try to comfort the grieving Mother, the music yearns; the sorrowing is melancholy, and we understand that the Accused is too weary and despairing to suffer with passion any more. There is a sense of devastation and unutterable woe.

Into the seventh scene—the house after the murders—this mood endures. The orchestra remains silent; the silence rings. Lizzie moves in a void of horror, her gestures those of a sleepwalker, her gliding steps muffled; her face is white as bone and wears a lost and stricken look. The first sound in the silence occurs with her appearance on the doorstep, around which her neighbors have gathered. Disheveled, in a shift dappled with blood, she presents a frightening spectacle. She opens her mouth and clutches with her hands at the empty air, and the music shrieks. Cymbals clash in deafening cacophony to illustrate the young woman's terror, and then the music gushes by in headlong volume, bearing the Accused's panic in its sounds.

The return to the *Prologue* scene, where the Accused faces the gallows, is accomplished to majestic music, as accompaniment for the procession of townspeople who pace by to see the Accused receive her just punishment for her crimes. Like the mood and mien of the throng, the music is pious and solemn, but another note intervenes, which only the Accused hears—the sounds of breaking and falling away, as if a great edifice, or a whole life, were disintegrating. There is a thundering chaos of great chords, a climax of reverberating notes, and silence like total demolishment of sound and motion.

This is the first ballet score composed by Morton Gould, who is distinguished in American music as a composer, arranger-pianist, and conductor. He is well known for popular music.

PERFORMANCES

Fall River Legend is widely considered de Mille's masterpiece. It is a massive work in theme and emotional content, and the dramatization is excellent: the tension endures from the beginning to the end of the ballet. Much of de Mille's work is robust, and her sense of humor inclines her to precipitate intense emotion into a sudden and climactic joke, but in *Fall River Legend* she creates no pranking humor to distort the profound emotions, and the ballet is a graphic revelation of one side of the choreographer, as it is of one style of American ballet. To move with such surety, skill and perception from a *Rodeo* to a *Fall River Legend,* and from a *Fancy Free* to a *Cage,* as does another choreographer, Jerome Robbins, proves a depth of feeling and a breadth of social conscience as remarkable in the native choreographers as their gifts of inventive dance forms.

The role of the Accused was created by de Mille with Nora Kaye in mind;

Kaye being on tour at the time of composition, the role was developed on the dancer Dania Krupska, a student of Catherine Littlefield, who had been de Mille's assistant in several Broadway shows. (Krupska created the role of Laurie in the first touring company of *Oklahoma!*) At the première, Kaye was ill, and Alicia Alonso danced the part of the Accused, preparing for it in only eight days under the direction of Krupska, who danced the role herself only once in public performance. Kaye subsequently added the immortal Lizzie to her great roles. In *Fall River Legend* and *Pillar of Fire* she achieved her unrivaled stature as a great dramatic ballerina.

Alonso, Krupska and Kaye each had a different interpretation of the role. Krupska went to the gallows as a real-life Lizzie might have done—grimly accepting justice like a Calvinist New Englander, and aware, with iron down her spine, that it was she and no other who had erected the gallows on which she must hang. Working directly with the choreographer in the hours of creation, Krupska received the imprint of the dynamic de Mille, whose choreographic design is built on living dancers and their reactions, and Krupska's sole performance was a rare and wonderful delineation of choreography. Her stoic death was in dramatic contrast with her tormented life and loves.

Alonso's interpretation was most beautiful in the tender scenes with the Mother, and she faced the gallows with thrilling piety and renunciation, looking more like a serene martyr than a sinner come to an inevitable end.

Kaye, in the *pas de deux* with the Pastor, gives an exquisite interpretation of the woman-child, and reaches histrionic heights in dance when she performs a love-duet with the axe. She expresses a fascinating and frightening perversion of passion, with the axe in the masculine role, in a terrible compound of love and hate, triumph and fear. Appearing on her doorstep in her bloodied chemise, with her wide-opened mouth and clutching hands, Kaye has the impact on her audience of a thunderous report or a piercing scream.

And when Kaye is about to die, she does not do so stoically or serenely, but with a Russian anguish, and a Russian relish for doom. Passionate and abandoned, betrayed by Love and Hope, Kaye stands trembling at the gallows' foot, and the audience trembles with her, too.

Muriel Bentley and Lucia Chase have given memorable performances as the Stepmother; Bentley's was notable for its venomous savoring of power. The boa around her neck hung there like a gorged snake, and her white face and glittering eyes gave her a witchlike beauty; she was a spinster with a horrifying seductiveness for the Father. Chase's interpretation is a marvel of scrupulous detail. She makes the Stepmother more human, with a niggardly spirit and a maddeningly smug righteousness. The Accused is hated by both of these Stepmothers, but while we feel that Chase's Stepmother gets no worse than she deserves we are inclined to fear that Bentley's ghost haunts the scene long after the Accused is led away.

John Kriza danced the Pastor and has continued to do so for American Ballet Theatre, and the impressive dance-actor James Mitchell has also interpreted the role. The Mother is one of the most beautiful roles of Diana Adams, who made her debut at sixteen in *Oklahoma!* and was developed under de Mille into a poetic dancer. Ruth Ann Koesun, a small and fragile-looking dancer, has been the Accused's Childhood Self since the première of the ballet.

For a television performance of *Fall River Legend* in 1957 Kaye danced the Accused, Adams the Mother, Kriza the Pastor, Chase the Stepmother and Koesun the Child. The Father, originally performed by Peter Gladke, was played by Dimitri Romanoff. *Fall River Legend,* in abbreviated form, was an "Omnibus" production in which the ballet depicted the psychological motives behind the Borden murders. The other half of the program consisted of a discussion by attorney Joseph Welch of the dramatic re-creation of the celebrated murder trial.

THE CAGE

Choreographer	Jerome Robbins
Composer	Igor Stravinsky
Lighting of Scene	Jean Rosenthal
Costume Designer	Ruth Sobotka

Première—New York City Center, June 10, 1951

The Original Cast:

The Novice	Nora Kaye
The Queen	Yvonne Mounsey
The Intruders	Michael Maule
	Nicholas Magallanes

The Cage was first performed by, and remains in the permanent repertoire of the New York City Ballet.

THE STORY

The choreographer based the libretto on the biological behavior of the genus *Orthoptera,* and the dancers are costumed in macabre garments and move in febrile gestures to suggest the species praying mantis. The behavior of the characters in the story is symbolic of the mantis and the spider whose female, after mating, kills and consumes her mate. Human parallels are to be found in mythology and pagan religion—for example, the Amazons of Cappadocia, the warrior women who founded a nation in Asia Minor, and who used men only for breeding purposes.

Most disconcertingly for the audience of *The Cage,* the theatre becomes pitch dark before the ballet begins. Footlights briefly flare up and then go out; all that is glimpsed in that brief illumination is the still curtain. Even the lights in the orchestra pit are put out. The orchestra is silent. At the New York City Center theatre, where *The Cage* is an annual event, the regular balletomanes sit like children waiting to hear a familiar but still terrifying ghost story.

The curtain rises suddenly, and the stage appears dimly lighted. One may suppose this to be dawn, or the beginning of Time out of Chaos. There is nothing to be seen but a giant web of multicolored strands; this is *The Cage*. As it rises, apparently of its own volition, it reveals a close-packed swarm of creatures, clinging together in foetal oblivion. The light grows brighter and the swarm loosens about the nucleus, the Queen; she is in the throes of birthing. Grotesque in her pain, her body arches, her knees bend, and from between her rigid legs her attendants draw forth a swaddled form.

At once, the Queen revives and strips the membrane from her progeny's body. The new-born mantis lies on the ground, under the cage, crouched in a foetal position. Her body is wrapped in tangled viscera and her face is still swathed; she lies as though lifeless, but her mother, the Queen, towers over her, extending her taloned arms in a protecting arc. Twelve of the attendant mantes begin to dance (*en pointe,* which gives the dancers, in their weird costumes resembling the carapaces of beetles, an air both sinister and exquisite). The Queen joins the dance—which is obviously a ceremony to honor her, since the other females bow and gesture toward her.

The ceremonial dance ended, two of the attendant mantes drag the still form of the newborn creature to the Queen, who bends and tears the last piece of membrane from the thing's face and head. Until now, the newborn mantis has lain somnolent and blind, but it is to be noted that the dance of celebration has taken place only after the first caul has been ripped from the Queen's progeny— she has first assured herself that her progeny is female, and need not be put to death. The infant mantis is now ready to be initiated into her feminine novitiate. She appears pleasing to her mother, the Queen, who lays a hand in benediction on the Novice's head, before she and her attendants steal from the scene.

Wet with uterine fluid, the Novice lifts herself and looks about her world. She has short, ragged dark hair, plastered to her delicate skull and framing, with its points, a face of strange beauty. Cheeks and lips glisten in the dim light; the eyes are large and set in markings that exaggerate their lambency and size. At first, she is almost comatose. When she begins to move it is tremulously, as the newborn tests its uncertain strength and balance. Her movements are spastic, but grow, with every moment, to a surprising power. She squats, rises to full height (*en pointe*), and claws the unfamiliar air. Instinctively vicious, she attacks nothingness with rapier thrusts of her taloned arms. Growing accustomed to her new element, she begins to move about, but awkwardly, with bent knees far apart, and arms extended from her sides. She is grotesque and even a little comic, but growing, growing in her strength and her instincts.

Suddenly she is attacked by a male intruder, who rushes up behind her and seizes her about the middle. The Novice writhes in his grasp but the Intruder holds her fast, drawing her close to him. Thus held, she appears to bite or sting him, for he suddenly releases her and drops on the ground. At once, the Novice falls full length on the Intruder and in a death-clutch more rigid than the Intruder's first amorous one they roll over and over, thrashing the ground. Soon the Intruder expires and the triumphant Novice rises from her embrace and stabs him in the breast (she does so by placing the *pointe* of one foot on the chest of the recumbent Intruder, so that she appears to pierce him with the pointed, elongated foot). All the Novice's movements have now become quick, neat and precise; she is a strong, sure and graceful thing. Next, she straddles the dead or dying Intruder, seizes his head between her knees, and crushes it. Her talons clench and her body arches, with the strain and the ecstasy of making her kill.

A wild happiness pervades her; instinctively, she knows she has done some greatly consequential act. Rising, she turns the Intruder's body over with the *pointe* of her foot, as though contemptuous of his staring death's face. She begins her first dance. She is strong, free, dominant—this is what her dance relates about her, as she prances in a kind of march. Each time she lifts a leg the knee rises high, each time she thrusts it down it is with the force of pistons moving and driving her limbs with limitless power. She throws her head back and opens her mouth wide, in a shrieking paean of rejoicing.

The Queen-mother returns with her tribe, and swaggering in self-approbation, the Novice kicks the dead Intruder. Her fellow mantes salute her and drag the Intruder off to one side to devour him at leisure.

The Queen now embraces the Novice as a sign of her regal pleasure, and the Novice assumes a preening quality, full of the pride of the neophyte who has successfully passed her first test. The mantes recline on the ground, with an indolence insolent in its security. Although they are female, of the supposedly weaker sex, their conduct is fierce and their attitude conspicuously confident. An emanation of masculine calm and repose emphasizes their Amazonian nature, a paradox of sex and habits. The choreographer has defined the nature of the inhabitants of *The Cage* as clearly as though he hired a narrator to explain it to the audience. Lolling at their ease, the creatures from *The Cage* have the exact male, warriorlike aspect of an encampment of men—an immediately recognizable Spartan manner. And Spartan love is suggested in the way the female creatures pair off, two by two, as they rest; this, too, violates the concept of femininity and accents the masculine humor of the insect-women.

Suddenly their fine senses are alerted—another intruder is stalking the cage. The couples part with dispatch; the light dims; all are intent on the Queen. At her signal they all vacate the place except for the ignorant Novice. When the Novice realizes that her tribe has left and begins to follow them, she is caught and held by the new intruder. The intruder is, as was the first, a male, and clasps the Novice with predatory love. At first, the Novice reacts by struggling and then she becomes prey to a strange feeling that affects her as strongly as did her instinct to kill when she was attacked by the first intruder. In her great seeking eyes the form of the second intruder becomes that of the Suitor.

The struggle turns to an embrace. As they clasp and unclasp their arms and legs the courtship becomes a *pas de deux*. The Novice sharpens her talons as

Nora Kaye and Nicholas Magallanes as the Novice and her Suitor in the love scene from The Cage.

Nora Kaye and Nicholas Magallanes at the death of the Intruder in The Cage.

though for a murderous onslaught, but this is simply a physical reflex, for she is bent on love, not death. Even in the throes of love she is rapacious.

The Suitor supports the Novice across his knees, and she appears supine and yielding; when they fall apart they at once turn to face each other, meet again, and entwine their talons. The dance grows more languorous on the part of the Novice, dominating on the part of the male. The Novice has abandoned all her fierce resistance, and suffers herself to be borne back in the Suitor's arms. He grips her between his legs, she turns her face up to him, and their arms lock them together. In a paroxsym of love, the Novice's delicate feet drum the ground, as the Suitor becomes her mate. So they remain, until the approaching hive startles the intruder, who only then releases the Novice from between his knees.

They are lovers still and as the light dims they try to conceal themselves from the Queen and the attendant mantes. The taut, driving force of the Novice has altered in the throes of love to a brittle gracefulness, but suddenly she is no longer desirable to her suitor, who recognizes in the approaching creatures of the cage the awful identity of his new mate. Revolted and terrified, he thrusts the ardent Novice from him into the presence of her Queen.

Immediately, the hive is upon him, and the Queen clasps the Novice in her talons, while the other females seize the intruder male. The mantes swarm up and over the Suitor, climbing him (as Balanchine says) "like ants on a stick of candy." When the swarm descends from the Suitor, he falls down as though life has been sucked from him. The Novice, all this time gripped by her mother and compelled to see her Suitor's fate, now tears herself free and flies to the body on the ground. She falls on it, straddles it with her legs, slides herself beguilingly over it, as though to imprint and transfuse it with life again. In her emotion she ignores the rest of the swarm. Again the mantes advance on the Suitor, snatch him from the Novice and bear him aloft as a trophy. The Novice, young, untried, weakening, squats disconsolately and looks on.

At this moment, the Queen gives a sign to her attendants and some of them, who are not engaged in carrying the Suitor, run to the Novice and lift her high— so high that she is raised higher than the Suitor. Thus elevated, the Novice's female pride returns; she is no longer a submissive and almost cajoling bride but a cruel and potent femininity. The Suitor is not dead and stirs slightly. The flicker of life arouses in the Novice her fierce and primary instinct and the lust to destroy the male becomes paramount. She sharpens her talons, quickly, expertly, and deftly strikes, killing the intruder-suitor with one blow.

The mantes lower their burdens to the ground—the triumphant Novice; the murdered intruder-suitor. The swarm can hardly wait for the Suitor to succumb. They begin at once to slide and crawl over him on the ground. There is no sign of life left in the corpse, but the Novice must ensure the death, and perform the ritual. As she did with the first male intruder, she straddles her Suitor, grips his head between her knees, and cracks it. Her body and face are contorted; the murder spasm is as violent as the spasm of love. The Suitor's body contracts and then straightens, laxly. Some of the eager mantes roll him over and over, like a log, while other excited members of the cage leap over and around him in a bacchanalian dance.

The Queen advances with her wild and regal air toward the Novice, and embraces her. The Novice has well passed her final test—the ordeal of love—and is a true creature of *The Cage*. She has mated, and then killed her lover, whom she now recognizes only as a means for perpetuating the tribe.

Queen and Novice dance a *pas de deux* of triumph and exultation. The cage descends slowly, and the mantes gather beneath its multicolor web. The necessary acts have been accomplished: the Queen has birthed, the Novice has been

The triumphal dance of the women in The Cage, *with Nora Kaye as Novice and Yvonne Mounsey as Queen, in forefront.*

tried. She has mated and killed and will now return to the cage until her birthing times comes. Motionless and quiet, the swarm draws about the nucleus of Queen and Novice, waiting in proud serenity for the cage, which at length falls and covers them, hiding and protecting all the hive from view.

The ballet of *The Cage* is exceedingly difficult to perform, requiring extraordinary strength and muscular control in the principals, the Novice and the Suitor. She turns *sur les pointes* and *en plié* and assumes some Interpretive, or Modern Dance forms. In one passage, the Novice seats herself at the edge of the Suitor's bent knees, and extends her own legs, full length. When she embraces the Suitor with her legs in a predatory insect love-grip, the Suitor must support her entire weight about his hips.

Despite all these acrobatics, nothing about *The Cage* appears athletic. Its horrific theme and disturbing implications absorb the audience's mind as much as the bizarre costumes intrigue the eye. The strenuous gymnastics of the mantes are all toward a profound purpose and a fearful end.

The costumes are the work of a dancer, Ruth Sobotka, and the lighting—of more than average importance to the ballet—is the work of Jean Rosenthal; these stage devices transform much of the dance action into vivid characterization and plot. Rosenthal's lighting has the interpretive quality of the music—by the dimming and lightening of the scene the audience perceives the ebb and flow of feeling in Robbins' grotesque-characters. The costuming establishes the insect identity of the dancers and grants the shrinking audience respite from an abominable empathy with the characters. Robbins has keenly observed the model for his Novice. It is a habit of the lady mantis to clean her paws delicately while, in good appetite, working her jaws, and the movements of stamping (especially in Kaye's interpretation) have the exquisite ferocity of the mantis, poised on a leaf and flexing her elegant limbs. The mantis' limbs are large and strong, armed with powerful spines, admirably adapted for clasping the living things on which the *Mantidae* feed. In the Novice's moments of love, and at the kill before feeding, Robbins has meticulously incorporated an insect nature within the *danseuse* form. The addition of the multicolor ropes which form the web (an almost sentient thing in the ballet) gives a secrecy and an added horror to the hive, or swarm. Seldom are human beings more thankful for being human than the audiences who see Robbins' creatures vanish into *The Cage*. For a moment after the ballet ends, the theatre plunges into the same primal dark out of which the ballet begins.

THE MUSIC

The Cage is danced to the *Concerto Grosso in D for Strings* by Igor Stravinsky. The curtain is lifted and the cage revealed in silence so eery that the cage, or web, seems a living organism. The cage rises and the tableau of the clustered hive is posed—then the music begins, with three piercing notes on the strings. After the birth of the Novice the music becomes martial and to it the twelve *en pointe* mantes dance in solemn praise of their Queen, who has borne another female.

The awakening of the Novice is accompanied by a slow and melodic passage, in tempo with the gradual flexing of the awkward young creature. When she is attacked by the first Intruder the orchestra utters a loud burst; the music then moves in rapid, rhythmic attack and, in crescendo, describes the battle, quietens at the death, blasts when the Novice contemptuously kicks the body of the male.

There is a musical lull while the mantes retire in couples to recline, and an almost drowsy inflection in the music matches the pulsing light of the rest hours. The mantes' antennae vibrate in the music's wild, sharp notes when danger is felt and the dimmed light is a counterpart of the music's sound when all, at a sign from the Queen, steal away and leave the untried Novice to the second intruder. The music warns the Novice, who distractedly kicks her legs to its rhythm when she is captured by the male. Gradually, the music changes with the Novice's emotions, and flows in a yielding and melodious stream as the new instinct of love activates the thin juices of the mantis' scaled form.

The rising volume of the music and its rhythmic tempo inform the ear in the same way that the dancers' movements inform the eye of the course of that weird passion.

Again the music alters, the lights dim, and the orchestra creates a loud, chirring sound that seems to emanate from the advancing horde of mantes. The music is from here wild and grand—not melodious or emotional—contributing through the aural sense an understanding beyond what the horrified eye perceives. The music relates, without emotion, sounds like forces, representing nature in its most ruthless economy of plan—love not so much animalistic as it is intent on creation and nothing more.

It is helpful to hear the musical score before seeing *The Cage* for the first time, because the music redeems the gross female aspect of the ballet and discloses the ballet's real theme: rapacity for life. It might be useful to study Stravinsky's ideas, since this ballet is an interpretation of his music—a reversal of the usual process. Stravinsky has sought to return the art of music to its very source, stripping it of all that is superfluous to show what is timeless, objective and remote. The *Grosso in D for Strings* writes the plot of *The Cage* as with a diamond stylus. Blazing with a hard, white beauty, it sings of survival under enormous stresses and the primal instincts to survive and procreate.

The music is also evocative of insect characteristics in the whirring and chirring noises that express from the orchestra pit the activities and emotions of the hive. Especially effective is the moment when the Novice kills, shivering in rapture—and the music shivers, too. Particularly important is the visual and aural confluence of the ballet and orchestra at the moments of climax in love and death, and the shriek of the music which amplifies the Novice's paean of triumph.

A moment before the cage begins to descend on its creatures, the music ends.

PERFORMANCES

The Cage was first performed on June 10, 1951, at the New York City Center, by the New York City Ballet. Nora Kaye, then on leave of absence from Ballet Theatre and fulfilling an engagement with the New York City Ballet, created the role of the Novice. Yvonne Mounsey was the Queen, and the male intruders were Michael Maule and Nicholas Magallanes.

After Kaye left the New York City Ballet the Novice role was given to Melissa Hayden, who continues to dance it in the current repertoire, with Magallanes as the second male intruder, the Suitor.

The Cage has been praised as the finest example of modern ballet, in which the Classic technique is combined with the strong emotions—and some of the styles—of Interpretive or Modern Dance. It has also been denounced as the shocking excrescence of a decadent and perverted society. Some Americans consider it worthy of being classed with *Le Spectre de la Rose* and *Le Jeune Homme et la Mort,* and call it the most serious sociological work to emerge from the American ballet theatre. Others have been affronted by its matriarchial significance as a reflection of American society. Now and then there is a feeble attempt made to censor such dance action as that of the Novice's birth and mating, or to enforce an edict of "for adults only" on ballet performances.

When the New York City Ballet went on tour in 1952, the European reception was mixed. At the august Paris Opéra *The Cage* was viewed on a program which included Balanchine's austere classics *La Valse* and *Bourrée Fantasque,* but the cosmopolitan audience gave Kaye as large an ovation for her Novice as they gave the ballerinas in the other ballets. *The Cage* was suppressed in Spain because it was considered immoral. In Italy it received undiluted praise, and at a grand reception for the company at the Palazzo Serristori in Florence a sweet little old lady invited Kaye to come and see the mantes the lady kept as pets, because Kaye, in *The Cage,* so perfectly reminded one of a beautiful lady mantis.

The Cage offended the English critics, whose conservatives were shocked, while the more blasé dismissed it as "needlessly brutal and ugly." One English critic described the ballet as "elevating human beings to the level of worms."

The Germans thought it an interesting debate on American sociology, and a Russian expatriate writing for the Scandinavian press declared it a waste of the only American ballerina of dramatic worth, Nora Kaye. In The Hague, the scheduled first performance was summarily banned, until Robbins said he would withdraw all his other ballets in protest, whereupon *The Cage* was allowed to be viewed.

The greatest mystification was felt, abroad, about a choreographer who enchanted with *Fancy Free* and charmed with *Interplay,* and then created *Facsimile* and *The Cage.* A positive clue might have been found in the opinion of people who knew Jerome Robbins well. Tanaquil LeClercq, a good amateur photographer, contributed to a magazine a picture of Robbins (in which he looked the perfect young man of distinction for a cigaret advertisement) with the caption, *Jerome Robbins, so many people in one.* Robbins, meanwhile, busied himself after *The Cage* with his *The Pied Piper,* a work considered to be "typically American," although the classical dancers in the New York City Ballet had to take lessons in the Charleston before they could writhe and twist through the new ballet.

The years since 1951 have brought more praise than condemnation for *The Cage,* and interest has been revived for audiences at home and in foreign theatres, who saw the original Novice by Kaye, in the later one by Hayden.

Kaye gave an unequaled characterization of the Novice as an innocent, ruthless entity. Seen under the close scrutiny of an opera glass her face had a transfigured look; the glistening skin was not so much stage make-up as the glaze of her fantastic beauty. It is doubtful if any other contemporary dancer could give a more realistic performance of a lady mantis in love; she managed to convey the positive feminine gender of the Novice. Kaye's interpretation had an unfathomable eroticism; in the lull following the mating scene there was the sense of debauch. And Kaye's angulated dances in the Novice's awakening, and in *pas de deux* with the Suitor, had a strangely touching quality—one almost thinks of it as a sweetness, incompatible though that quality might be with the character. She was something young and brave and fierce, trying to learn to walk, and later falling in love. If a mantis may be believed to feel disconsolate, then Kaye was disconsolate as she squatted while the other mantes snatched her Suitor and raised him aloft as the hive's trophy; if a mantis may be believed to feel more than hunger, then some tenuous emotion was conceived when Kaye slid her body along the prostrate Suitor, devouring him with love who was destined to be devoured as food.

After the New York première the critic Anatole Chujoy wrote that *The Cage* was violent, bitter and outspoken; that it was not a pretty work and not for children; and that the implications of its comment, unpleasant to contemplate, are wider than those abstract ones of the animal kingdom. Yet Chujoy, and most critics, felt the ballet to be an exciting work of beautiful savagery and thrilling choreography. A woman critic, Doris Hering, saw the ballet as born in bitterness and misogyny, leaving no hope and admitting no ray of light—yet containing so much creative power, so much rich life force, that it could not for one moment be called a work of negation.

Above the clamor of critics and audience about the ballet rose the universal acclaim of the dancers, especially of Kaye as the Novice and Mounsey as the Queen. The Queen and her attendants were wild in looks, with matted, tousled hair, but savagely impressive. Mounsey, a dancer of great skill and authority, was commanding and imperially sure. She brought to the modern ballet role of the Queen the undisputed feminine force of Myrtha in *Giselle*—a force quite implacable and cool, beyond human understanding. If in Myrtha it is a supernatural one, in *The Cage's* Queen it was nonhuman.

The first Intruder was danced by Michael Maule, who seemed appropriately boyish and adventurous. He was quickly dispatched, as an adolescent would be outmatched, contemptuously, in a too dangerous game. Magallanes seemed maturer, and was less the daring adventurer and more the desiring male. Whereas the death of the first Intruder occasions a start of surprise and horror, it has not the affecting tragedy of the Suitor's murder, and in this role Magallanes, with his dark and serious looks, has a romantic authority and sadness.

Melissa Hayden as the Novice is handicapped by the première magnificence of Nora Kaye, in exactly the same way as Hayden, herself, imposes a handicap on all other dancers following her in the role of Clorinda in *Le Combat*. Hayden's interpretation of the Novice is more energetic and less erotic than Kaye's—she is, as it were, more mantis and less lady. She is wonderfully agile in the straddle-legged and bent-kneed postures, and suitably nimble in the insect love affair, and in her slick, jagged coiffure her face looks omniverous. Both dancers portrayed the Novice with a terrible appetite—I should say that in Kaye it was to love, and in Hayden it is to live.

The Cage marks a milestone in ballet, and not only in America. At the turn of the century it was the Europeans who shocked the Americans; the century had hardly crossed its meridian when a young American choreographer of the "typical" bounding joy of *Fancy Free* was astounding Europeans with *The Cage*. He had, by coincidence, composed dancing to music by that "madman" Stravinsky, whose *Rite of Spring* in Nijinsky's première caused a riot in the theatre. The conductor, Pierre Monteux, recalls that the Parisian audience of *The Rite of Spring* jumped up and beat their neighbors with fists, canes, umbrellas and whatever came to hand, and then turned against the dancers and the orchestra, throwing everything available at them until the gendarmes arrived. At City Center, when *The Cage* had its première, the audience was well-behaved and although the theatre went dark, and the orchestra incomprehensibly played no overture, no raging anger was precipitated. The audience even applauded *The Cage* at the end. Not three decades before, an American audience could not sit without having the police called to protect their morals at The Ballet. I wonder if there were, in the audience of the City Center theatre on June 10, 1951, any who had occupied another theatre in that same city in 1917, when *Narcisse* had so horrified the proper throng that it was thereafter banned from performance as "an iniquitous example of European decadence, that will corrupt the morals of our clean American youth."

THE CHOREOGRAPHERS

Great dancers are immortalized by great choreographers, and no one knows the choreographer better than his dancers, who are his tools and founts of inspiration, and in the course of every ballet are likely to become his pride and despair. These objects of fearful joy have remarkable opportunities for observing the tribal propensities of choreographers, and it is largely through their knowledge that I have drawn the biographical sketches of the four Americans who represent the native creative force: Lew Christensen, Eugene Loring, Agnes de Mille and Jerome Robbins. A Russian, George Balanchine, and an Englishman, Antony Tudor, exert the most significant foreign influences on American ballet. In their lives and times, and in the prolific repertoire they have created, we find the Present of American ballet.

The six have widely divergent theories and ideals, and highly individual methods. Some are democratic, others autocratic. One or two of them strive for empathy with the dancers while creating the ballets; others require, and demand, nothing less than absolute obedience. Most choreographers believe that they were born, not made, but one American choreographer, Eugene Loring, maintains that choreography is a technique to be learned and taught as a part of professional dance.

In other national ballet theatres there is generally one strong governing influence that often lasts for generations. Petipa in Russia is an example. In American ballet there are several strong and energetic influences, many of them independent of each other, and the most notable of these are the precedents of Loring, de Mille and their artistic heir, Robbins; the Neoclassicism of Balanchine; and the revolutionary psychological ballets of Tudor. Out of their own passionate convictions the choreographers have literally developed special breeds of dancers. The Loring dancer is the Greek in ballet—a professional artist with no emotional prejudices, and no recognition of divisions between music-dance and poetic gesture. He is akin to but separate from Tudor's dance-actor. De Mille and Robbins, like Loring before them, bring stage and street into dramatic cohesion. The characters developed by the American choreographers are usually people of urgent commitments and intense emotions.

Tudor goes beyond the stage and the street into the realm of the subconscious, and his ballets are not so much unsung operas and speechless play as explorations of the human heart. Separate from the active embroilment with life is Balanchine's work—sanguine in its Classic form and avant-garde in theme and invention. He has a signature flourish—a Balanchine ballet is in full scope as soon as the curtain goes up—and his choreographic designs involve his dancers in extraordinary athletic feats. Form in spatial design is Balanchine's great forte, and his musicality imbues his genius for form with beauty. He has invested the old, old Classic technique with a new and sinewy power.

Traditional to American ballet, perhaps because there are more *danseuses* than *danseurs* at hand, the choreographers are more concerned with women than men. Of the ballets described here only one, Loring's *Billy the Kid,* does not pivot on the female of the species; and among the choreographers only one, the feminine de Mille, consistently employs men of exaggeratedly virile appearance. There is seldom a marked difference in size between male and female dancers but de Mille chooses men of exceptional size and masculine deportment such as James Mitchell, and women with the pliant, lithe, childlike appearance of Gemze de Lappe and Bambi Linn.

But the most significant thing about the choreographer in American ballet is that he has developed his art in a commercial and competitive theatre, while choreographers in other countries have developed under dilettante patronage. Consequently, the most successful of the American choreographers have competed in the popular and the legitimate theatres instead of restricting their talents to a small and esoteric society. To succeed in the wide American theatrical métier they have had to create for "popular" theatre with the same conviction and devotion to ideal that they compose for the "legitimate" ballet stage. The audience they have reached is the huge, independent and argumentative general audience of the United States. Their contemporaries have continued to work in national ballets governed by a presiding influence, often as dominant as were the influences of Petipa on the Russian and Bournonville on the Danish ballet. Indeed, it is still the Bournonville influence that characterizes Danish Ballet, and the Russian theatre is dedicated to the frozen principles of its archaic splendor. The Royal Ballet of the United Kingdom reflects the artistic tastes of its founding choreographers, Ninette de Valois and Frederick Ashton. Serge Lifar, for three decades, exerted absolute rule in the Paris Opéra Ballet.

In contrast with the luxury in which omnipotences create, American choreographers must compete to exist. Except for Robbins and Balanchine of the New York City Ballet and Lew Christensen of the San Francisco Ballet, they have no theatres of their own. Instead, they must pioneer in whatever métier is offered to them: the legitimate theatre, musicals, movies or television. They are most often hired, like craftsmen, to design for a spectacle whose theme and characters are already set. Few of them are ever given the time and environment to create out of artistic meditation, and so energy and a positive genius for the expeditious have become the working requirements for the American choreographer. Balanchine—and he one of the few to command a theatre of his own—has commented that he is a chef who must cook up a bill-of-fare every season, on demand.

Precarious as such an existence is, American choreographers contrive to express themselves, and with considerable fluency and conviction. What they have done in the circumstances is nothing less than wonderful—they have, with their contemporaries, created the contemporary repertoire that is American ballet. Despite the inevitable fallow periods that interrupt a career, as in Tudor's case, or the elegant trifles that embroider the prodigious, as in Balanchine's, the first group of American ballet choreographers give every evidence of bountiful future years.

All that has been done on the ballet stage that is daring and new in the past twenty-one years has germinated in Loring's work, as is obvious when we study the works: the theatre piece, *The Great American Goof;* the intermingled Classic and Modern Dance forms of *The Man from Midian;* the social conscience of *City Portrait;* the psychological study in *Billy the Kid.* The robust impulse of folk dancing that is even now animating American ballet in the wake of the Russian influence originated in the first works of Eugene Loring and Agnes de Mille. The character and tempo of American dancing had not been fully formulated until *Billy the Kid* and *Rodeo.* With increasing audience participation in theatre, and the new American intent to create a graphic and inspired repertoire, it is significant that *Prairie,* created in 1942, combined the poetry of Carl Sandburg and the music of Norman dello Joio with Loring's choreographic interpretation of a great American movement—The Way West.

A summation of the past's accomplishments will serve to indicate the creative sources of the contemporary repertoire. It is Jerome Robbins, the choreographer of *Fancy Free* in 1942, who has, in the nineteen-fifties, widened the concept of ballet in musicals with *West Side Story.* And George Balanchine, the avant-garde desecrator of the Metropolitan in the 'thirties, is now avant-garde Balanchine, a savant of the 'fifties. The Metropolitan itself, under the impetus of choreography, has at last begun to found a ballet tradition in opera for America.

Although the fact that they are the "first" surrounds them with an aura of sanctity, the first American choreographers still remain a vigorous part of the tradition they founded. We will not know, in our time, who exerts the greater permanent influence on ballet, Balanchine or Tudor, but it is certain that Balanchine's development of Neoclassic dance and the American technician are comparable to the achievements of Petipa in Russia and Bournonville in Denmark; and Tudor has, in his lifetime, become the preceptor of forms as revolutionary as Fokine's. Choreographers like the Christensens are a different but nonetheless contributing power in American ballet. They represent the closest equivalent we have to dynasties like that of Vestris, Taglioni and Karsavin.

In the lives and times of the American ballet choreographers lies the substance and the spirit of American ballet, and those described here are examples of the native creative force and the foreign imported influence on which our heritage is based. If we were to divide the choreographic kingdom we should designate for Balanchine the mountain top, lofty and cold, to which we must intellectually aspire, and we should reserve for Tudor the wide province of the human heart. For the native choreographers—Loring, de Mille and Robbins—we should choose the crowded city street and the dusty desert floor, and all those portions of the realm filled with rampant life. Balanchine and Tudor build with air and fire, and the American choreographers with flesh and blood.

LEW CHRISTENSEN

The Christensen theatrical dynasty is represented today by the three brothers whose names are associated with the San Francisco Ballet, William, Harold and Lew. Their lineage and dance dynasty goes back a hundred years to a Danish emigré named Lars Christensen, who danced and fiddled his way across the United States. He settled in the Mormon community of Salt Lake City to teach the violin and dancing, and in the nineteen forties his influence was still evident in his descendent Peter Christensen, who traveled with small dance troupes through the American West and Midwest. Peter's brother, also a dancer, who taught ballet and ballroom dancing in Salt Lake City, had three sons, William, Harold and Lew. The boys were tall, blond and spectacularly good-looking. As a part of their general education, they learned to dance.

William, the eldest, began his studies under his Uncle Peter and was later the student of Fokine. Harold studied under Balanchine and Vladimiroff at the School of American Ballet. Lew took his first lessons in Utah from his brother William, and his uncle, Peter. The three brothers represent the confluent styles of Fokine, the master of interpretation, and Balanchine, the master technician. From their father and uncle they inherited an American derivation of the Danish dance tradition. In their work they have been resolutely dedicated to the Classic Dance of traditional ballet.

The Christensens are an inseparable part of the San Francisco Ballet. Founded by Adolph Bolm in 1933, before the Ballet Russe became a resident American company, it boasts of being the oldest company in America. Bolm, the first choreographer, established the company as an auxiliary to the Opera. It is now independent as an organization, but still dances the Opera's ballets.

William, born in 1902, was a successful dancer who into the late nineteen forties appeared on Broadway as the partner of Ona White. He joined the San Francisco Ballet as *premier danseur* in 1936, and two years later became resident choreographer. Under his direction, the company produced such full-length classics as *Coppelia, Swan Lake,* and *The Nutcracker,* and gradually grew into a full-scale organization, resident in San Francisco and touring the vicinity. To the ballet-hungry West, the Christensen Era brought dance of Classic caliber, which never deteriorated despite the competition and proximity of Hollywood, where ballet has often been less than ideal. In each tour, the company widened its influence and soon became the standard for ballet on the West Coast. Recruiting students when they were quite young, and training them in the theatre as an extension of the school, the San Francisco Ballet developed some very good, and very youthful dancers, many of whom were at once lost to other and larger companies.

The second Christensen, Harold, was educated at West Point and at the University of Utah, but gave up his studies to go into vaudeville. Later he danced in Balanchine's company at the Metropolitan and in Ballet Caravan, creating the Motorist in *Filling Station.* From 1941–1946, Harold danced with the San Francisco Ballet, and in 1942 with the Opera. Today he is the director of the San Francisco Ballet School.

Lew, born in 1908, is the third Christensen, and was the *danseur noble* of the family. His masculine beauty in Balanchine's *Orpheus* and *Apollon Musagète* startled early American ballet audiences, to whom the epitome of male dancing was Pavlova's partners and the *danseurs* of the Diaghilev company. Bolm, Mordkin and Kosloff were remarkably handsome, with virile personalities, in the Classic genre, as Shawn was in the Modern or Interpretive, but in Lew Christensen American ballet had found a native prize for classical roles and was understandably exultant about it.

Graduating from high school, Lew joined his brother William and three girls from his Uncle Peter's school and toured the West in an eight-minute program of dances in the vaudeville circuit. The troupe was successful and survived for seven years—a phenomenal life for a dance ensemble, then and now. When William left the act, Harold took his place. During that time, Lew continued to study and had lessons with one of William's teachers, Mascagno, whose forte was the mastery of *tours.* Later he studied under Fokine.

In 1935 the Christensen brothers reached New York with their little troupe and appeared in the musical, *The Great Waltz.* Balanchine and Kirstein saw the musical and invited Lew to join the company of The American Ballet, then resident at the Metropolitan. Lew, continuing his studies at the School of American Ballet under Balanchine and Vladimiroff, became the company's *premier danseur,* and danced in Balanchine's *The Bat,* and in *Card Game.* His greatest acclaim came from his roles in *Apollo* and *Orpheus,* where his size and looks made him especially impressive.

He next set about making history for the American ballet with Loring and William Dollar, in Kirstein's company, Ballet Caravan, and his first ballet—with an American theme—was *Pocahontas.* It was with *Filling Station* in 1938 that he emerged as an American choreographer of the first rank, and showed his distinctive style—a commingling of the playfulness and sharp clarity that seem essentially American, with a sense of design and deportment derived from the classical tradition.

The same clean lines and satire without malice that marked *Filling Station* in 1938 are to be observed in *Octet,* in 1959. In the first ballet Christensen directed

Lew Christensen as Mac in Filling Station. *Ballet Caravan production, 1938.*

his gentle irony at the contemporary scene and the ubiquitous American gas station; in *Octet* he satirizes conformity.

Lew Christensen has the gift of characterization and a gimlet eye for types, and in no other ballet has he so hilariously reminded the audience of the composite lives of stage and street as he has done in his minor classic, *Filling Station*. The première of this ballet, danced by Ballet Caravan, cast Lew as Mac, the hero; Loring as Ray; and Harold Christensen as the Motorist. Marie-Jeanne and Caccialanza alternated in the role of the Rich Girl. In 1953, the New York City Ballet revived *Filling Station*, with Jacques d'Amboise as Mac, Janet Reed as the Rich Girl—one of her great antic roles—and Michael Maule as the Boy Friend. The revival was hailed for the memorable performances of this trio. The ballet remains in the company's repertoire.

Filling Station does not have an involved plot, as in the *ballet d'action* type of theatrical dance, but it is not abstract. It is, instead, episodic, and the choreography sharply and cleanly characterizes the dance roles and the dance scene as native American ballet.

Mac, the mechanic and attendant at a filling station, starts a typical night's work. In rapid succession he has a series of visitors, for the filling station is a busy place. A Motorist who has trouble finding his way with a road map arrives with his nagging wife, a perfect back-seat-driver type, and a daughter who always needs to interrupt the journey to find a rest room. This trio provides much of the robust comedy of the ballet. They are followed by two truck drivers, Roy and Ray, who are friends of Mac, and as soon as these three young men meet they break into boisterous dance antics, showing their youth, high spirits and camaraderie.

The gaiety is subdued by the appearance of a State Trooper, who (we have the feeling it is not for the first time!) sternly warns the truck drivers against speeding. Roy and Ray blandly deny any wrongdoing and appear—or try hard to, anyway—to be a pair of sober and sedate people.

When the strict State Trooper departs, hilarity again breaks out in the filling station. A young man and a girl (she is listed as a Rich Girl) totter in; obviously the Girl has had several drinks too many. The unfortunate Motorist and his nagging wife and daughter have just completed a dance pantomine of domestic strife when the drunken couple reel in. The Girl is blissfully sure she can dance—indeed, it is plain to see she thinks she can float on air. Although she can hardly stand on her feet, she insists on dancing with her escort. Their *pas de deux* swells to include a *pas de trois* improvised by the irrepressible Roy and Ray, and the good-humored and agile Mac. The Motorist returns to the scene alone, and the Girl takes an immediate fancy to him, plunging into his arms and insisting that he dance with her. He cannot, for his shrewish wife and whining daughter bustle in. But the infectious madness of the Rich Girl and the athletic bonhomie of the young men thaw the ice and soon everyone is doing the "Big Apple," a popular dance of the nineteen thirties. Even the henpecked Motorist has a good time, for a change!

Into this lighthearted scene comes the ominous figure of a hold-up man, the nineteen thirties' "gangster" of fact and fiction. When he appears, he behaves in stereotyped fashion, lining up his victims, commanding them to lay out their valuables, then turning out the lights so that he can escape in the concealing dark. Mac, our hero, slips outside in the confusion, to get a flashlight; single-handed, in the best tradition of heroes, he will capture the gunman! The nervous Gangster stops in his flight and shoots wildly, accidentally killing the Rich Girl, but the State Trooper appears just in time to apprehend the criminal.

The essentially comic tone of the ballet does not die, even though the music becomes a dirge and the corpse of the Rich Girl is borne solemnly from the scene: as her funeral cortège parades by, the Rich Girl rises from her supine pose and blithely waves farewell.

The filling station empties, the furore ends, and Mac is left alone. He deftly tidies his station, looks around with the alert, efficient glance of the competent worker, and then picks up the day's newspaper for a look at the news. Now he will have a breathing space until the next flurry of visitors arrives to bring movement and perhaps excitement to the scene.

Wit and humor and buoyant energy permeate this ballet. It was realistic as an American scene, and even now, decades later, when we no longer dance the "Big Apple," it is still topical. Its freshness is sustained by its depth of characterization, often quite satiric. It never deteriorates into slapstick, although the humor is antic and robust, and all the dancing was based on the Classic style, although it interpreted music that was distinctly American. When Virgil Thomson created the score for *Filling Station*, American music began its strong and wonderfully effective collaboration with American ballet.

That same year, 1938, Christensen danced the role of Garret in Loring's *Billy the Kid*. Balletomanes of the day say that the role has never again been danced as Lew Christensen interpreted it. Critic Ann Barzell wrote that the role was distinguished not only by superior dancing, but by the strength and goodness that Christensen radiated onstage. One of the American dancers of the early American ballet says, "We only realize now what we had, in those times, in Loring and Christensen, when we go into the theatre and see the present-day *Billy the Kid*. It has become a theatre piece, very fine in its way, but this is not what it was when Loring and Christensen were Billy and Pat Garret. Loring and Christensen were not of the breed of dance-actors that came after them; they were the characters of good and evil incarnate, set against the scene of The Way West. You see, these two boys did not know they were making, or helping to make, a national ballet—they only danced, and they danced what they believed in, very much as inspired children instinctively reach for the truth of the matter."

Perhaps Christensen's apex as an American dancer came in the ballets Loring choreographed, in roles that Loring created on Lew Christensen for such ballets as *Billy the Kid* and *Prairie*. They were roles of heroic proportions, which Christensen's size and deportment suited to perfection. From all the recollections I have gathered from people in the profession and the audience, Christensen's great charm as a *danseur* lay in his good technique, fine physique, and handsome face. He learned to project onstage and was a dynamic performer, especially in epic ballets. Barzell records for us that he had "gentleness backed by great force, and serenity born of assurance; he moved with dignity and grace, but was never bold and aggressive." And he could characterize national concepts without becoming pedantic because he was so patently, in looks and mien, the apotheosis of the Good Guy, or the Hero. Above all, he never seemed to feel foolish while dancing, as did so many male dancers of the English-speaking world at that time. "He danced," one of his contemporaries has written for me, "with the kind of frankness and seriousness that foreigners used to associate with Americans. Lew Christensen was as close as American ballet ever came to producing the knight in shining armour." This observer of the young Christensen refers especially to the *danseur* in his *Bach Variations,* and in Balanchine's *Apollo* and *Orpheus.*

The witty Christensen next turned to a surprising work in his *Jinx,* first performed by Dance Players (in which Christensen was active with Loring) in 1942. It is a macabre and melancholy ballet, which has been revived by the New York City Ballet.

Set against a circus background, the central figure is a clown who brings death and disaster to everything he touches. A Girl in Pink and a boy who is a Bareback Rider are lovers and the Jinx, by the merest contact, kills the boy and then the girl. Janet Reed, Francisco Moncion and Herbert Bliss have danced the revival; Reed and Christensen appeared in the first performances.

It is now impossible to judge how much Lew Christensen's mature talent as a *danseur noble* might have outweighed his development as a competent choreographer. The early promise and the American quality he showed as a *danseur noble* was all too soon checked by his entry into the Army. After his period of service he turned to choreography and organization, rather than to the continuation of his *danseur* career. But he has been evidence of what the American male dancer may achieve in that premier role of ballet, the *danseur noble.*

In Hollywood Christensen danced with Vera Zorina in *On Your Toes.* He also traveled with the American Ballet Caravan to South America, danced in Tudor's *Time Table,* and collaborated with the choreographer José Fernandez on a ballet called *Pastorela.* He choreographed *A Midsummer Night's Dream* for the San Francisco Ballet. Meanwhile, Loring's Dance Players had been disbanded and the Balanchine-Kirstein companies dissolved, and Christensen, who had married the ballerina Caccialanza, a protégée of Cecchetti, perfected his style and worked with his brothers in San Francisco. In 1948, he became choreographer to the San Francisco Ballet, and in 1951 succeeded William as director, a position the oldest Christensen had held for thirteen years. At the same time, Lew remained a director of the New York City Ballet, a connection he had formed as ballet master with its parent company, Ballet Society.

On the invitation of the University of Utah, William formed the first company and theatre of their kind in a college, where he continues to work, propagating the Christensen legend. He is among the least esoteric of the American ballet "greats," with his skill as a teacher equaled only by his generosity. Professionals say that he may be picked of all that another dancer might hold secret; such as how a *danseur* can make a heavy motion look light without becoming distressingly ethereal, how to get the most out of a phrase, or what an individual contribution will give the staged scene.

The San Francisco Ballet School is unique in that it extends into the San Francisco Ballet Company. The teaching in the School, and the repertoire of the Company, are more or less the indissoluble developments for the student, and I have chosen to discuss them together, as the singular theories and contributions of the Christensen brothers.

Beginning with William, the tradition has been set for the Classic *danse d'école* in the School and the *danse noble* in the Company. William Christensen and George Balanchine may be the only men in America who are able to make ballet exercise into performances. William, in the classroom, is a paragon of form whose ease and style make his students despair, even while they inspire them. Under Harold, even the beginning classes have a cadet corps discipline, a quality rare in a school in America. The youngest students have a crisp sense of propriety, and the Positions are the objects of passionate absorption. As a result, the San Francisco Ballet has produced some infant prodigies. Among the stellar alumnae is Jocelyn Vollmar, the *prima ballerina* of the Borovansky Ballet in Australia. William's celebrated pupils are Vollmar, and Janet Reed, the most famed of the classical comédiennes, and his sister-in-law, Ruby Asquith, Harold's wife. They have been ballerinas of the San Francisco Ballet, and *solistes* of rank with other and larger companies. Harold Lang and James Starbuck were trained by William.

Girls are admitted to the School from the age of five. Boys begin at eight, and sometimes younger. By the time the dancers are twenty they have had a minimum of ten years of training and some experience as performers. Early training under the Christensen discipline seems to establish an easy command of the Classic technique, and the San Francisco Ballet Company is notable for its effortless style. Also, the dancers, with very few exceptions, are entirely produced by the School and live within the radius of its influence. They have a regional quality of good looks and healthiness that evokes comment about them and California, much as if they were a natural resource.

After the student of the San Francisco Ballet School graduates into the advanced class he must pass on to the stage to complete his education as a dancer. He does so in the repertoire of the San Francisco Ballet, beginning with minor parts as understudy, and as part of the corps, gradually advancing through the echelons of the repertoire just as he moved through the ballet classes in the School. The maturing student-dancer continues his rigorous training in ballets that are the tried-and-true training ground of the *danseur noble* and the *danseur caractère*. The active repertoire includes versions of *Swan Lake* and *Don Quixote*, for whose *pas de deux* the dancer must achieve the ultimate standard of technique. First in a version by William, now in one by Lew, the Company has excelled in a full-length *Nutcracker*, which it takes on tour every year during the Christmas season. In the West, the San Francisco Ballet's *Nutcracker* has long been a gala tradition. William has also restaged *Swan Lake, Coppelia,* and other classics, and choreographed *Chopinade,* an original version of *Les Sylphides.* Most of the repertoire is Lew's work, choreographed especially for the Company, along with ballets by Balanchine and William Dollar.

Con Amore, created by Lew in 1953, has become one of his best known works, and is danced, under an exchange policy, by the New York City Ballet and the San Francisco Ballet in the same way that Balanchine's *Concerto Barocco* and *Serenade* are shared by the two companies. A ballet about love, as the name signifies, *Con Amore* is in the best Christensen style, with beautiful visual form, impeccable taste and a fine satiric flavor.

To music by Rossini, a band of Amazons frolic under the command of their Captain. A male Bandit invades the scene, and the ladies are bewitched by the intruder. It is he who repulses the Amazons, until they force him to his knees at musket point. Having parodied these terrifyingly importunate females, the choreographer wisks us off to the next scene—that cliché about the lady whose beaux all called on the same evening. The dance pattern is not a cliché, however, as the lady distractedly packs her bulging closet with her suitors. Receiving them, one after the other, into her boudoir, the lady stuffs the closet with a Man-about-town, a Sailor and a Young Student. Last to arrive is the lady's Spouse, but instead of the expected denouement we are again faced with the unfortunate Bandit of the first scene, still on his knees before the angry Amazons.

Amore, the Goddess of Love, arrives in a chariot, ready to take care of the contretemps of Scene I, but she is at once summoned to deal with the domestic confusion of Scene II. Both scenes now appear on the same stage, so that the audience may enjoy Amore's dealings with the two situations. Drawing her bow, Amore shoots her deadly arrows at all the men in succession, whereupon each of these wounded gentlemen promptly falls in love with the female nearest to hand—the Bandit with the Captain of the Amazons, the Spouse with his own Lady, two other men with two of the warrior-maidens. The Student, until now a bashful swain, collects Amore herself.

The ballet is light in mood but has some exceptionally difficult dance passages, especially for the Captain of the Amazons. The Bandit (who is sometimes billed as a Thief) must spin and soar in his Variations. This is a role which Jacques d'Amboise has fulfilled with thrilling feats of elevation. The Man-about-town is sometimes billed as a Rake. At the New York City Ballet, where it has had its greatest success, the Captain of the Amazons has been one of the best roles of Yvonne Mounsey.

In teaching and repertoire, the San Francisco Ballet excels as a traditional ballet company. Since his association with it in 1948, Lew has emphasized the importance of music, and the ballets he composes are danced to the works of Bach, Britten, Mendelssohn, Mozart, Rossini, Schubert, Tchaikovsky and Vivaldi. Commissioned by the University of California, he choreographed the ballet *Lady of Shalott* in 1958, to music by Sir Benjamin Britten.

Until recently, the San Francisco Ballet's handsome reputation was regional, but in 1956 Ted Shawn presented the Company at Jacob's Pillow, and at once the national press accorded it paeans of praise. Conrad Ludlow, one of the soloists of that season, later joined the New York City Ballet.

The first and most dazzling impression for the audience was the Company's youthfulness, the beauty of the girls, and the clean-cut good looks of the boys. Shawn describes the Company's style as pure Classic, and critics everywhere have commented on the mastery and ease of its Classic technique. Because of its rare homogeneity of training, the individual members have a uniform style. "They do not appear like a set of dancers congregated into one company," a dazzled foreign critic commented. "They look unlike any other company we have seen. They are a *race* of dancers." They are, in fact, the Christensen product, in School and Company. They are not typed by the Christensens, but they are the distinctive products of the Christensen methods—one of which is the somewhat earlier than usual age for beginning ballet training. The training is classical, and the Christensens, to a man, are classicists. Lew, following Balanchine's influence, makes the music determine the dance. In artistic policy, the San Francisco Ballet under Lew has not featured stars, but aimed for an overall starry atmosphere of general competence.

The teamwork is exceptional and the Company has a youthful air of sparkling sweetness. This youth and sparkle create *vitesse*—an expression for velocity, fleetness, the easy, rapturous soaring of a bird. In its quintessence it is a quality that only such unsophisticated dancers are able to diffuse, so it seems providential that the best, or most advanced, of the San Francisco Ballet's dancers move on to larger companies, as have Conrad Ludlow and Christiane Bering, the former to the New York City Ballet; the latter, in October 1958, to de Cuevas' company. Such losses, far from being irreparable, support the Company's energy and youth.

Although the Company does not have a roster within its ranks it recognizes the theatre protocol of stars, and in its tours employs strong personalities, like Jocelyn Vollmar, the *prima ballerina,* and the *danseurs* Leon Danielian and Royes Fernandez. These give stability and character to the individual ballets in the repertoire, and provide the central motivation from which the dancing extends.

The Company's dancers are by no means obscured. On the contrary, their style is enhanced, in the proximity of more mature dancers. Two girls are especially fine—Nancy Johnson, who excels in *tours* in legato; and Sally Bailey, whose line and extensions are remarkable. The boys have a typical "American" look; Dick Carter and Gordon Paxman, for example, have the same frank and amiable air as the Christensens. With these young dancers American ballet has a chance to endow all the old classics with new life. A Giselle is often so mature in years before she can support her role that the character lacks conviction. This is even more true in the case of Prince Siegfried, who in many productions seems a man surely old enough to know better. While American ballet can produce classicists like those of the San Francisco Ballet we shall receive a clear vision of a *young* Prince enamored of a Swan Queen, or a *young* peasant girl going mad for loss of love. We are so often condemned for an American lack of lyricism in ballet that the Christensens' work thereby becomes all the more exciting. Their possible influence on the Romantic era in American ballet is beyond present estimate. Striving only for the acme of classicism, these teachers may have marked the beginnings of a new epoch. Their men, alone, are an extraordinary contribu-

Conrad Ludlow, now of the New York City Ballet, in Lew Christensen's Masque of Beauty and the Shepherd, *for the San Francisco Ballet.*

tion, as in the case of Paxman, the ballet master, who was a sports champion in school. They are building a masculine grace on athletic lines that may well become the hallmark of the American *danseur noble.*

All this is an echo of Lew Christensen's background, preserved by him and his brothers as a legacy for American ballet. The world-wide prestige now accruing to the San Francisco Ballet comes in part from the people of San Francisco, who support the school and the company resident in their city. But most of all it comes from the work and ideals of three men, the Christensen brothers.

EUGENE LORING

Eugene Loring was born in Milwaukee, Wisconsin, to parents whose own grandparents had emigrated from Germany to America. He lived during his early years in a small fishing village on a little island in the Milwaukee River. His father, a saloonkeeper, was a trainer, on the side, of professional boxers. Loring's first love was athletics and dancing. He does not remember that he was ever taught to dance, or that, on a certain date, he began to learn to dance. He remembers only that he always danced.

Attached to his father's saloon (and Loring makes it clear, in his dry way, that it was a saloon, not an old world inn, or tavern) was a dance hall, and every Friday night the fishing village gathered there for a fish fry and dance. Young Loring danced with such gusto and skill that he soon earned himself local fame. And he danced everything he saw, in the popular and the folk genres, and made his own improvisations on them. It was all in fun, for a good time, but the invention and the catholic taste for dancing became characteristic of Loring. He is a democratic choreographer, who refuses to consider any one form of dance as the best, or the most perfect, type of dancing. Instead, he puts to his own original use the Classic, the Modern, and the Ethnic, using whatever seems valuable to the theme of his ballet. His casual attitude toward some of the most sacred cows of the Classic and the Modern Dance may perhaps be traced to the Friday night dance hall days. You do not have a good time at a fish fry if you are a snob.

The elder Loring gave up his saloon but young Loring continued to dance. He also became, in school, an excellent swimmer, and an actor in theatricals. The family was a poor one and Loring was the second of five children, so as soon as he graduated from high school he went to work for his living. It was the time of the Great Depression—jobs were hard to get and hard to keep—but Loring managed to become a young gentleman of some substance. He worked in a hardware store in Milwaukee and soon became head of his department, and he acquired a savings account in the local bank. He might have remained in this happy niche, except that he continued to dance, and to act.

Loring had joined a little theatre group called the Wisconsin Players, the same theatre in which the celebrated dance-mime Angna Enters worked before Loring's time. The Wisconsin Players attempted dance and drama and very soon Loring was an enthusiastic member of the company.

He was small in stature, not impressive enough in size for heroic masculine roles of stock theatre, but he was adept at characterization and he was also exceptionally strong and agile. And he was a musician. The Loring parents were unable to give Loring much formal education, but they equipped him with two attributes that were to stand him in good stead: a training as a gymnast, and a training as a pianist. His father sent him to a German gymnasium in Milwaukee where Loring became a good tumbler, and his mother made him take nine years of piano with a teacher who not only taught him to play the instrument but also made him study theory, harmony and counterpoint. Loring learned to read full orchestrations, and still scans orchestra scores as easily as other people read books.

The Wisconsin Players had as their director a Russian, Boris Glagolin, who had been an actor in his own country with the style and popularity of John Barrymore in America. When Glagolin became the director of the amateur theatrical group he began to produce some extraordinary work, of a caliber that would be avant-garde even today. In their naïveté and enthusiasm the Wisconsin Players scarcely realized what Glagolin demanded of them, but they were willing to do their best. Glagolin was interested in Loring and set him to performing certain roles in the plays, and certain chores in the theatre. Loring not only danced and acted but began now to master stagecraft, and to understand Glagolin's conception of the actor as a trained interpreter of feeling who did not depend solely on speech as an actor, or on gesture as a mime, but employed the best and most eloquent tone and movement for his role. Glagolin demanded of his actors individual interpretations of their roles, and he refused to let the Wisconsin Players depend on dialogue alone, or on pantomime; nor would he permit them to model their performances on those of other actors, even when the patterns were set by the most acclaimed actors of the theatre. Every actor had to move or speak within his role as though the character were the extension of himself—the role did not stop short at the spoken word, or the deliberate gesture. And when the role required dancing, the dancer was the actor, extending speech and gesture into dance.

Very soon, the Russian director had imbued Loring with his ideals. More, he set Loring to dance designing, not only for himself but for others in the company.

The gay and innocent attitude toward the Dance began subtly to change as Loring set about mastering the staging of it. Wryly, he looks back on that early choreography and wonders how bad it was—but he had begun to choreograph, and he was working with the choreographer's tools, the dancers. As a fledgling engineer begins awkwardly on his graphs, so Loring began to pattern dance design. Often, he was dismayed and amused at the difference between the fancy and the fact, but gradually he learned how to impose his ideas on the bodies of his dancers.

From Glagolin, too, Loring derived a new and profound idea of dance as a supremely interpretative force—the lyric means of acting. Dance ceased to be exuberance and pedal skill and became an art within itself. The little Milwaukee boy had never heard of the exciting ballet revolutions under Noverre and Fokine, or of the stages created by Petipa and Diaghilev, until Glagolin described them to him. Loring hurried every day from his job in the hardware store to his apprenticeship under Glagolin, who would tell the eager boy the stories, and describe the dance design, of the ballets like *Petrouchka* with which Fokine had dazzled Europe. *Petrouchka* is to ballet what *Hamlet* is to drama—a great tragedy—and hearing about it thrilled Loring. He wanted to learn how human emotion could be portrayed in dance and determined to study ballet for an understanding of the Classic genre.

Loring tried to enter a local school of ballet, but the teacher was pessimistic about teaching a boy. Loring persisted, the teacher reluctantly consented, and Loring entered his first ballet class as the only male student. The experience was brief because everyone was acutely uncomfortable. Loring learned nothing about ballet technique in Milwaukee.

In 1934, while appearing in a production of the Wisconsin Players, he was seen by the members of a touring stock company who were playing in Milwaukee. Three of them, total strangers to Loring, went backstage after the performance and insisted that Loring come out to supper with them. Then they sat him down in the restaurant, and insisted that he go immediately to New York to study dancing.

The prospect excited Loring, but he was dubious about it until one of the stock company actors told him she knew Lincoln Kirstein, who had just organized a school of ballet. She promised to write a letter of introduction to Kirstein, begging him to accept Loring as a student in the School of American Ballet. Loring was just nineteen, and he had never been out of Wisconsin, but he gave up his promising job at the hardware store, drew his savings of two hundred and fifty dollars out of the bank, and went to New York. He was immediately accepted into the School of American Ballet, where he began his study of Classic Dance under Balanchine and the other famous teachers of the faculty, Muriel Stuart and Pierre Vladimiroff among them. When he had barely mastered the rudiments of the art, and before he thoroughly understood the peculiar terminology, he showed such gifts that Balanchine invited him to join the American Ballet, the first performing group to emerge from the School. Then, after two and a half months of study, Loring heard that the great choreographer of *Petrouchka* was auditioning dancers in New York. With youthful temerity, Loring presented himself at Fokine's studio and asked for an audition.

By chance, Fokine granted him one at a time when there were no other dancers about and the intrepid two-and-a-half-month veteran ballet student encountered the Father of Modern Ballet in circumstances as farfetched as any in romantic theatre.

"Perform for me," said Fokine, in his heavily accented English, "a double pirouette."

"I can't do a double," said Loring, honestly. "I think I can do one, perhaps."

"Do wan," agreed Fokine, expansively.

Calling desperately on all that he had learned at the School of American Ballet in two and a half months, and supported by all he had learned about movement in dance and athletics all his life, Loring performed a pirouette.

"Ah," said Fokine, without enthusiasm but without distaste.

"Now," he said, matter-of-factly, "we try wan—and a half."

"I know I can't do one and a half," said Loring, positively.

"Well, then," said Fokine, composedly, "we make it maybe wan—and a little bit. Not half, no? Well, *half of half,* eh?

"Try!" he said, in a suddenly stronger voice, and with such conviction that Loring, praying he would not make a fool of himself and fall flat on his face, obeyed.

"*Eh, bien,*" commented Fokine, politely. He surveyed Loring's neat small figure, and the sleekly muscled gymnast's legs. "I think . . ." he pronounced oracularly, "we try wan, and a little bit more than half of half." He sounded so confident that Loring meekly obeyed—and succeeded. He soon got easily to one and a full half, and was urged by Fokine to try the *leetle bit more* than the full half. Ah, this was better! Fokine appeared to feel that they, he and Loring, were achieving something of consequence. After a few more tries, he decided that Loring could begin again with one pirouette, and, that performed, he called for one and a half—*wan* and a little bit more than half, and so on, until Loring, going further and further each time, was turning two easy pirouettes on demand, and going beyond these . . .

When the audition was over it was that and something more, for only in later years did Loring fully realize that Fokine had been a tired and embittered man who did not care to work with students unless they were advanced in the Classic technique. He had little patience with the basic grind. He did not supervise the barre exercises in most of his classes, but came in after his dancers had performed them under another teacher, and went at once into rehearsal. Loring was an unknown and untrained dancer, little more than a beginning student, but he radiated his intense will to dance, and he had the twin skills of musician and gymnast. Some spark in the young Loring had stirred the old man into encouraging the American dancer.

"I must have been mad!" Loring muses now. "Imagine a nineteen-year-old, straight out of a hardware store in Milwaukee, auditioning for Fokine!"

But the lessons at the School of American Ballet had begun to shape his natural gifts, and the training in the gymnasium and the piano, and under Glagolin, had formed for Loring a reservoir of skills, mental and physical. He already understood rhythm and movement, and he had begun to invent steps and gestures. There was needed now a basic discipline and a development in the dance métier, and these he assiduously studied at Balanchine's school.

Fokine took Loring into his company at the Lewisohn Stadium, and then at the Capitol Theatre in New York, and soon this aspiring American dancer was appearing in the Russian ballets, *Prince Igor* and *Schéhérazade,* which had made history for Diaghilev's Ballets Russes. Loring continued to work hard and steadily at the School of American Ballet, and when Fokine called auditions for a revival of his ballet *Carnaval,* which had been danced in Diaghilev's company in

1910, Loring begged to audition for the role of Pierrot, which had been created by Adolph Bolm.

"No," said Fokine, and then, watching the stricken look on Loring's face, he added mischievously, "No—because I have something better for you. Audition for Pantalon!"

So Loring danced Pantalon. After the performance, Fokine wrote on Loring's program: *To the greatest Pantalon of them all.* And Cecchetti had danced Pantalon!

Loring still cherishes the program—and he treasures his association with Fokine, who impressed on him that dance was lyric feeling, the very visual soul of man. In the work of Fokine and Loring there are marked similarities: both introduced pliancy into the rigid Classic technique, the more eloquently to make use of the instrument of feeling, the dancer; and both employed the *danseur,* rather than the ballerina, as the leading character in ballets. Instead of using frivolous and fantastic themes, they employed strong, dramatic ones, with lyrical force and continuity as clear as narration.

Loring later danced the title role in Fokine's revival of his 1916 ballet, *The Sorcerer's Apprentice.* He had, within the surprisingly short time of one year, risen to soloist rank, in ballets where the roles combined dance and pantomime. He danced with The American Ballet Company under Balanchine, and appeared with the group when it was the ballet company at the Metropolitan Opera. He was a soloist and choreographer with Kirstein's Ballet Caravan, creating *Harlequin for President, Yankee Clipper, Billy the Kid* and *City Portrait* for this company. He went with the latter company on tour and saw the locale of *Billy the Kid* for the first time, while dancing the title role.

He and some members of the company stopped in an obscure little town in New Mexico, where they had been told they could view some of the possessions of the legendary outlaw. The museum, if it could be dignified by such a title, was a tiny place in which were purported to rest the gun and other regalia of William H. Bonney. The dancers sought out the honorary curator, who had to be coaxed from his home to open up the "museum." There he lectured them as he showed his exhibits, on how Billy could not have been left-handed (as some of his legends recount) because the gun was fashioned for a right-hand draw. To the old codger the dancers were just a bunch of Eastern dudes. He had probably never seen a ballet and, in any event, the dancers did not divulge their real interest in Billy the Kid. At the end of the lecture, as the dancers were about to leave, one of them asked the old curator what Billy had looked like. The curator eyed them all, one young man after the other, and then pointed to Loring.

"Like this 'un!" he said emphatically. "He's the one who could pass for Billy!"

And leaving him ignorant that this was the ballet creator and interpreter of Billy, the Ballet Caravan dancers left in haste, to smother their laughter.

Loring's career had matured with extraordinary success. A member of Balanchine's company and a Fokine dancer, both within a few months of going to New York—a soloist, after only one year's ballet training, on the stage of the Metropolitan Opera House! And, above all, a choreographer with Kirstein's

Ballet Caravan! If he had stopped to think about it he would hardly have believed the reality of the events that had precipitated him from a hardware store in Milwaukee to the opera house of New York—but he was too busy working, and studying at the School of American Ballet.

With some other dancers—Agnes de Mille, Mary Heater, Michael Kidd and Paul Haakon—he shared a rented studio and exchanged lessons. These were the days when Americans regarded dancing as though they themselves had lately discovered it. They could not get enough of it, and tried to budget for lessons from the best teachers, and to see how many lessons they could fit into one day. Agnes de Mille recalls that they used to work in the little studio for two hours every morning and often she would spend another hour or so drinking coffee and talking to Eugene Loring. She recalls that she did most of the talking, and Loring listened. He is remembered as being a very quiet young man, with a low voice, and a calm, almost gentle manner—but he was a great choreographic talent of the native theatre, who had created the first important American ballet at the age of twenty-four.

He was intent now on choreography and worked at dancing chiefly to understand the possibilities and limitations of the human body in dance. His contemporaries remember his elastic strength and his patience. At the end of a lesson when most of the dancers were hanging pallid and sweating against the barre the former gymnast turned dancer would be perfectly at ease. Loring was small, neat, compact and indefatigable. He had blond hair, cheeks that went into deep indentations when he was angry or amused, and a pair of powerful legs. In the athlete's body were the musician's trained sense and the creativity of the dancer-choreographer. There are some of his contemporaries who believe that Loring is still unmatched as a *danseur caractère*. If the role required it, Loring could look six feet tall.

Loring weathered the lean years of American ballet. There was still a strong prejudice against male American *danseurs,* and these had to stomach the opprobrium of effeminacy, as the *danseuse* endured the slur of immorality. Apparently few in the audience realized the physical prowess required of the male dancer to perform his dances and to lift and support the *danseuse,* a human woman despite her air of feathery lightness. Public admiration for a weight lifter was a great deal more general and impassioned than that for a *danseur,* although, as Youskevitch has been heard to remark, there is many a *danseuse* weighing one hundred and thirty pounds with whom the *danseur* must appear incomparably gay or noble.

And the economics of dancing has seldom been worse. Until AGVA (The American Guild of Variety Artists) was established in 1939 as a trade union for dancers, the dancers were not paid for rehearsal time. Until the nineteen forties a dancer in the *corps de ballet* received less than forty dollars in weekly salary, after deductions.

The compensations were hope and youthful enthusiasm, and the fact that in those days lessons were to be had very cheaply from the best teachers. Besides, as the dancers commented in happier times, one jumped better on an empty stomach—it gave one a feeling of lightheadedness in space. With such euphemisms they comforted themselves, and meanwhile had lessons and danced for fun whenever they could.

When Ballet Theatre was organized in 1939 it seemed to American dancers and choreographers that their profession was on firm ground at last. Loring joined the company as a choreographer and soloist. His first work for it, *The Great American Goof,* had a libretto by William Saroyan, and its subtitle was *A Number of Absurd and Poetic Events in the Life of the Goof.* It was an early manifestation of the same fellow who would later crop up in one guise or another as the Ugly American, in his inept journeys around the world. Loring, who danced the Goof, choreographed a dance drama that was considered a daring and ingenious piece of theatre. Although it was a failure with the audience and was dropped from Ballet Theatre's repertoire, in retrospect it is seen to have set the precedent for the contemporary ballet-play where dance and speech are combined. Saroyan's book was serious in intent, but avant-garde in nature and too misanthropic to appeal to the American ballet audience of that day. In the ballet's unpopularity, Loring's inspired choreography and the excellent dancing by Loring and Antony Tudor and Lucia Chase were largely overlooked. Yet the critical assessment was remarkably high, and John Martin called it admirable and moving and George Amberg said it was an outstanding performance, and a "splendid failure." When Ballet Theatre revived *Billy the Kid* that ballet had instant and wide acclaim, and was lauded for its poetic subject and vivid characterization. Billy in life and legend was a central figure with whom the audience felt more empathy than the Goof.

When Ballet Theatre was passing through one of its slack spells, in the winter of 1941, Loring organized his own company, sponsored by Mrs. Winthrop Palmer. He called it the Dance Players, to emphasize his intent to use lyric movement or dance interpretively. Lew Christensen was the associate choreographer, and also danced, as did Loring. Others in the company were Janet Reed, and Joan McCracken, who had danced with Catherine Littlefield and was later a featured dancer in the musicals *Oklahoma!, Bloomer Girl* and *Billion Dollar Baby.* Among the men was Michael Kidd. Dance Players had a tour in the spring of 1942, and a season at the National Theatre in New York, and went into residence to rehearse and perform at a summer theatre in New Hope, Pennsylvania. After an autumn tour in the same year, which terminated at Trenton, New Jersey, the company disbanded. Its repertoire had included *Billy the Kid, City Portrait, The Duke of Sacramento, Harlequin for President, The Man from Midian,* and *Prairie,* by Loring, and *Jinx,* by Lew Christensen.

Dance Players, as had been Balanchine's company Les Ballets 1933, was a seasonal company. Its dancers were not confined to the Classic technique, but merged expressiveness, or interpretation, with lyric movement. The ballets were of dramatic content, rather than of elegant or complex designs alone. The company was well received, on tour and in New York, and seems to have elicited as much wonder at the youth of the dancers and choreographers as it did for the merit of its dancing and repertoire. After the disbandment of Dance Players

Janet Reed, Bobby Howell and Michael Kidd in Loring's The Man from Midian.

Loring returned to Ballet Theatre, but he very soon left this company, which was then undergoing difficulties in its management and its fight for survival in the theatre.

Loring wanted to produce *The Man from Midian,* a ballet about Moses, to a score by Darius Milhaud. He had originally presented the ballet, in his Dance Players, to a score by Stephen Wolpe. Instead, the management of Ballet Theatre—Sevastianov had taken Pleasant's place—proposed that Loring compose a ballet to the music and story of *Show Boat*. Loring disagreed, and shortly thereafter decided, with typical American gumption, that if there was a demand for ballets of such character he might just as well compose them for the commercially rewarding stage. In 1943 he went to Hollywood, on a six-month contract as resident choreographer with MGM. The ballet contingent in New York sat down to wait for the return of the prodigal. Instead, Loring settled in Hollywood, and founded the American School of Dance. Here he began at once to exert his influence on the tastes and education of the American audience in the ballet theatre.

Ballet in America now has a richly varied existence. The choreographers who have worked within all its media—the legitimate theatre, musicals, films and television—have naturally exerted the largest influence on the audience. No choreographer in the popular media—and Loring was among the first and most brilliant of these—has influenced more than Loring the caliber of choreography, the virtuoso demands of the dancers, and the education of the mass audience. Any one movie in which Loring has worked presents a full scale *divertissement* of style and dance movement, especially in his use of the male dancer.

In *Funny Face* there is notable dancing by a male *corps de ballet,* and a fine *pas de trois* in a Left Bank café for Audrey Hepburn and two male partners. In *Silk Stockings* Charisse's talents are put to good use in ballet technique and mime, a high point being her solo as Ninotchka, when she strips off her dark, drab Soviet clothing and exchanges it for the symbolic silk stockings of the capitalistic western fashion. In this film there is also "Russian Ballet," for which Loring has utilized the Classic technique, and he has created a spectacular *divertissement,* with a male *corps de ballet,* that would do honor to any ballet on the legitimate stage, in the idiom of traditional Russian dance.

Loring is conceded to be the master of gesture in American ballet, and to possess a peerless sense of theatre. His work is marked by a sublety that employs economy; he will discipline and if needs be sacrifice his own most inspired dance designs for proper effect. His ballets are notable for the drama and cohesion of plot and dance, and for heroic cognizance, marked most clearly in *Billy the Kid* and *Prairie*. These two are considered to have had the same significance for American ballet as *Petrouchka* and *Coq d'Or* had for European ballet. A great deal of what Loring did, and did first, has become the common usage and standard for American ballet. In *The Man from Midian* the dance ranged from the ballet *pirouette en attitude* directly into a Modern "fall." In *The Great American Goof* he and Saroyan originated a new American form for ballet, the "balletplay." Loring's daring, imagination and vision became more and more evident with the development of the theatre in which he pioneered.

It is of singular importance to American ballet to observe the life and times of this pioneer, an epitome of native creative forces. The influences of Glagolin, Balanchine and Fokine on his trained musical and athletic abilities developed the individual who was to be the first of the great American choreographers. These were the exact forces that were to develop American ballet: the influence and heritage from Russian and European teaching on the remarkably agile physique and the strongly rhythmic nature of American dancers, combined with the Americans' personal creativity.

No other American choreographer has more instinct and skill in the craft of theatre than Loring. The *Billy the Kid* which he staged for television is still the most plastic example of contemporary American *ballet d'action*. His use of the symbolic, as in *Prairie*, is unequaled in poetic terms and good taste. A man of parts, he revealed his actor's training in the composition and oral narration for the "Omnibus" production of *Billy the Kid*—still the best of its genre.

Among the young pioneers in American ballet no one, and Loring least of all, fully assessed the worth of *Billy the Kid* in 1938. It was taken at face value as what we should today call an "adult western," although actually Loring was anticipating the implications of psychological theatre by two decades. He also anticipated the "psychological" ballet of Tudor, whose work in the genre established him as a master in the ballet delineation of emotion.

In every description of *Billy the Kid* there is some mention of the tremendous swirling leap that precedes each of Billy's murderous assaults, and balletomanes continue to marvel at the choreography. It was dictated by Loring's ever-precise and passionate concept of movement as the extension of feeling. What he has deliberately given the audience is the ballet exposition of schizophrenia. The almost spastic galvanization of Billy into this swirling leap bears such graphic relation to real emotional and nervous frenzy that any person who has worked with dance therapy or with the mentally ill must at once recognize the indication. Patients with *grande mal* epilepsy, especially the very young ones with strong, agile and muscular bodies, have seizures that lift, twist, turn and catapult the flesh with tremendous mental and nervous impulses. It is possible, I am sure, that a schizophrenic emotion may "look" very much like these physical manifestations. Curious to know what had inspired Loring, at twenty-four, to choreograph such movement for Billy, I asked him his reasons. "I wanted," he said, "to show the white-hot force that drives an apparently ordinary, and even likeable person, out of his everyday self into a state of feeling which, extending into action, moves the person to the final violence—murder. I had read I don't know how many newspaper stories of people, charming and romantic as Billy Bonney appeared to his friends, who went berserk occasionally, and afterward returned to their apparently normal ways. I believed that the overt act had its invert picture, and it is this picture, of schizophrenic rage, that I wished to show. Billy's leap and aerial turn are performed as an extension in movement and gesture of his inner feeling; a feeling white-hot, piercing, and erupting with blinding speed, which transformed El Chivato into the murderous outlaw."

Loring's great precedent for American ballet was his use of the simplest and most evocative dance designs. In *Billy the Kid* he created an epic out of a realistic background and genius in characterization. An episode of truth was related, and the force of evil exorcised, without triteness or loss of fine theatre. In *City*

Portrait and *Prairie* Loring demonstrated his keen social sense, but without the bitterness and malice that the Moderns were inclined to develop in their strong human themes.

City Portrait, in eight scenes, sketches a tragedy of urban life, leaving it open to the widest application by identifying the characters not by name but by type. In Scene I the Daughter of a meanly-housed city family occupies The Street, that haunt and refuge of tenement dwellers. Scene II, the House, is a cramped and confused place, a dwelling only in name and a travesty of "home," from which all the family members fly to escape the one person constrained to stay there, the nagging mother. The Daughter snatches her soft moments under the street light, against the side of a building, with a boy friend as miserable as herself, who comes from a tenement as joyless as her own. Because they are blindly seeking something more than they have, aching with a dull sorrow for their condition in life, the Daughter is not a playful companion, and the boy tires of her melancholy. He leaves her to search for a companion who will serve as anodyne for his own misery.

Scene after scene—Street Sewer, Waiting in Line, At an Office—conveys a dull desolation and an impotent anger, and through them the characters die, little by little, as their souls shrivel. In The Street life goes repetitiously by, and the Daughter stands and sees her younger sister going the same way she has already passed, as each girl is driven out of the family house to seek love in the street. There have been no more wolfish characters than the Drug Store Cowboys lurking at the corner of the tenement world, waiting to decoy the girls with an empty promise of light and laughter. In the final scene, The Crowd, the family disintegrates in the city.

Loring had a knack for making the audience uncomfortably aware of truths in *City Portrait* and *The Great American Goof,* so that only the judicious critics, and a small coterie of balletomanes, remember the significant contributions of these ballets. *City Portrait* was first created for the American Ballet Caravan in 1939, and then revived and reworked by Loring for his Dance Players in 1942. *The Great American Goof* was produced by Ballet Theatre, which preserves *Billy the Kid.* Yet there are a number of balletomanes who remember with the greatest praise Loring's *Prairie,* based on a poem by Carl Sandburg, and some of these feel *Prairie* to be more epochal than *Billy.*

First performed by Dance Players, *Prairie* was created on the dancers Janet Reed, Lew Christensen, Eugene Loring, and Bobbie Howell, with a première at the National Theatre in New York, April 21, 1942. As much as *Billy, City Portrait,* and *The Goof,* it reveals the particular enthusiasm and personal affinity that Loring felt for American life which made John Martin describe him as the first really original artist to rise in the field of the American ballet. But, as Amberg points out, Loring had also to solve the delicate problem of transforming authentic and documentary data into genuine dance and Amberg reminds us that it was Loring's professional discipline which made him avoid empty acrobatics and stunts; his sense of humor which made him avoid the sentimental cliché; and, above all, his fine sense of theatre which preserved him from the danger of literal

Janet Reed, Lew Christensen, Eugene Loring and Bobby Howell in Loring's Prairie.

storytelling. He used all his skills as an actor and a dancer, but first and always he had an original and inventive gift for expressing characters and situations in dance.

Prairie is arranged in four movements, the first of which pictures The Homesteaders in pioneer times. The scene is the Middle West, and the spirit is one of high adventure, whose fervency and restless seeking are balanced by the American economic dream. The ceaseless and urgent quest moves the pioneers on and on, leaving few, actually, to be The Homesteaders, the parents and offspring of the new settlements. The Second Generation is seen in the second movement. Life has become dull and routine, and a daughter of one of the pioneer families, bursting with energy and hereditary restlessness, urges her generation to forsake the countryside and move into the cities. The movement away from the prairie is finally so wide and wild that even the Daughter shrinks, momentarily, from the uprooting of the young people, but borne helplessly on the storms she has evoked, she is moved with the others from the prairie.

In the third movement, Another Beginning, the Daughter is shown friendless and lonely, aware that she is cut off from her people and her land. She weakens and droops in the alien climate, until her savior arrives. He is the Man from the prairie, who lifts her up and teaches her to walk again. Together, they return to seek the old people and the old ways, but not as prodigals or in resigned desperation. They go as enlightened people. In the fourth movement, New Cities and New People, the prairie is regained as the fount of the people's strength and wisdom.

Prairie is wider in scope and more profound in implication than *Billy the Kid*. Loring uses poetic abstractions without becoming coy and sticky, and there is dignity in the symbolic figures of Man, Father, Mother, Daughter, and the significant Land, or the prairie. The academic ballet style is used, and the dance is formal in design but fluid in movement. Costumed imaginatively by Felipe Fiocca, it was beautifully danced to a vivid score by Norman dello Joio.

In *Billy the Kid, City Portrait* and *Prairie,* dance has the same classic quality as literature, in revealing places and times in America. They are masterful ballets because the choreographer does not resort to cliché, nor parrot glib philosophies, and because he never uses his acrobatic dexterity purely for decorative effect. Working with both realism and symbolism, Loring has unerring good taste, and a fine sense of theatre. He employs none of the rude shocks of some forms of "realism." His characters develop the themes in dance with natural behavior and gesture. With classical aplomb, they transfigure the poetry of *Prairie*. In bare feet, and with a ceremony of arms and wrists, they make true and evocative the story of Moses in *The Man from Midian.* These and all else that Loring has created lie half obscured by the enormous popularity of *Billy the Kid.*

Loring's memories capture the whole exciting story of American ballet. He has an excellent memory, and a detached regard for the opinions of his detractors and his fans, and manages to mix warm sentiment with his sense of ironic humor. Apparently self-effacing and modest to a fault, he is in reality a stubborn and independent person, with the peculiar artistic serenity that supports his principles without confining them. His idiosyncrasies are all in his ideals of training the dancer. Loring dancers will tell you, half in pride, half in mischief, that he has a fetish for neck-rolling exercises, as a sort of therapy for his cherished Kineseman's spiraling force in dance. He writes well and wittily, and advocates a catholic use of dance forms in American ballet but he is not a revolutionary against the Classic ideal. Far from it, he employs the Classic technique freely when he feels it useful and eloquent, and his school system is based on classical ballet training methods.

Dance is, to Loring, eloquent action, but the action must spring, as part of its technique, from the dancer's heart and mind. Loring's dancers are taught to examine their own emotions in figurative situations that compare with those of the characters they will interpret in the ballet. From the dancer's analysis of himself, Loring persuades the dancer to give a personal interpretation of the role he has invented, in the choreography he has designed. He never composes a ballet purely as dance design, in an orderly or grotesque arrangement of physical shapes and movements, but he uses every dancer, and each group of dancers, as units of the total sum of the ballet or dance number, *for the visible extension of feeling,* either of a mood or idea, or the lyric interpretation of a story. Because of these ideas, Loring does not separate traditional ballet, or the Classic form of dancing, from other forms.

Yet he must not be thought of as a revolutionary or controversial choreographer, intent on chaotic upheaval in either the Classic or Modern Dance forms. He is, most truly, a completely original and independent choreographer, making use of the movement he finds most lyrically communicative in his inventions of ballet.

In appearance small and slight, little aged by time, Loring seems reserved and almost shy, with a gentleness that masks his determination. He has an astute knowledge of the contemporary scene, especially as his school is the training ground and classroom for most of the noted dancers who find themselves in its vicinity. He is able to keep a shrewd eye on the international scene through these classroom dancers and his guest teachers.

On the subject of his work, Loring is an intelligent, thoughtful and frank conversationalist who never retreats into esoterics. He will make every effort to define his principles and methods and seems particularly free of "attitudes" towards dance. One is at once struck by his quite American penchant for the scientific, or workmanlike view of ballet, compared with the vague and evasive language sometimes used by foreign *maîtres,* which often borders on *préciosité.* He regards *Billy the Kid,* his acknowledged masterpiece, with the same detachment he shows for any ballet by any choreographer. Far more passionate are his feelings about the future of American ballet. This he believes is largely dependent on the professional's acceptance of continuous change in real life and in theatrical forms. Realizing that we are in the process of developing a tradition of American ballet, he feels that our theatre must also remain contemporary in its communication, or fall into the decadence and sterility of other and older national ballet theatres. And his theories of how to grow without narrowly confining our métier are those he practices in the training of the dancers, actors and choreographers in the American School of Dance.

Putting his hope in training, rather than in the creative urge that at first moved him and some others, Loring believes in an early, long and scrupulous training for the ballet professional in a university of dance, where the development of mind and body proceed together, in one indissoluble course. He believes that training is the basis of all creative work in choreography, and interpretation in dancing.

As a choreographer, Loring is able to work with more ease and dispatch than many, because he has devised a system of dance notation, "Kineseography." He long ago mastered the limitations and possibilities of human movement, and with his Kinese-man he can plot spatial design like an engineer with his own tools. Where most choreographers require hours of trial and experimentation—and many more hours of rehearsal—with a company of dancers, Loring goes into rehearsal with his ballet in Kineseograph, and begins at once to translate the dancers' individual response and interpretation into theatre. When he is working with dancers trained in Kineseography, as many are, his rehearsal time is further shortened. The dancers take copies of Kinese notation of the ballet for individual study as a sort of "homework," as actors study their scripts before coming into working rehearsal.

The Kineseograph of a Loring ballet is only the bare beginning, however. Dance is also speechless theatre, requiring the highest qualification of acting, and beyond the step and the gesture Loring and his dancers together explore the substance of the theme in the ballet and the character of the dancer's role.

All this makes Loring a composite of scientist and idealist. He praises Lincoln Kirstein and George Balanchine for their enormous contributions to American ballet, and admires the musical phrasing or the Classic technique of this or that contemporary choreographer and dancer, and yet, above all, he remains a force within himself—strong, independent and unique. As an artist, he is monumental in American ballet because of the sum of his gifts and works.

AGNES DE MILLE

The foremost woman choreographer in American ballet was born Agnes George de Mille, in New York, and grew up in the West. In 1952 the first volume of her biography, *Dance to the Piper,* described her childhood and her struggle to become a dancer and choreographer. In 1958 she published a second book, *And Promenade Home,* in which she told about the first years of her dazzling success on the American stage. De Mille is as gifted a writer as she is a choreographer and all biographical sketches are pallid compared with her autobiographies, yet even these do not entirely describe her. For instance, in *Dance to the Piper* she tells us that she was of middle-class family; actually, by heritage and breeding she belongs to an aristocracy of intellectual and theatrical significance. Her uncle, the late Cecil B. de Mille, was the single most famous man in the contemporary American theatre, and her mother's father was Henry George, the American economist and social reformer, author of *Progress and Poverty,* the most popular book on economics ever published in the English language.

The writing of Henry George is characterized by simplicity of diction and lucidity of thought; in dance, his granddaughter has demonstrated the same aptitudes. George was a radical and reformer in society; Agnes de Mille was one in American ballet.

She began to study ballet when she was thirteen, and by chance: her sister Margaret had fallen arches and an orthopedist prescribed ballet lessons. The two little girls were sent to the Kosloff School in Hollywood. Theodore Kosloff had been a member of Diaghilev's company and his school was grandly named the Kosloff School of Imperial Russian Ballet. One of the teachers was Vera Fredova, from Pavlova's company, and under Fredova Agnes de Mille began to study the Classic Dance.

It was a difficult study for the child, who was trying comparatively late in life to master a physical technique that begins, ideally, when the child is five or six with gentle rhythmic exercises, and introduces the peculiar ballet Turnout and Five Positions when the student is seven or eight. De Mille was now approaching adolescence, and frightening changes were going on in her body. She had been a lovely child. Ted Shawn, who knew her from the age of six, recalls her beauty and grace, and photographs have captured the lyric quality and the dramatic feeling of the little girl. Until her teens she was slender, with pretty, delicate features. Suddenly, the airy little sprite became imprisoned in the short frame that was, to her despair, to be her total height, and she found herself encased in puppy fat, with broad hips and short arms and legs. At this time she took no comfort from the fact that she had tiny hands and feet—she wore a size one-and-a-half *pointe* shoe and could barely reach a full piano octave—but felt a stranger to her new body. The little nymph with exquisite, arched feet now inhabited a clumsy, alien body.

The despair of this fleshy disguise was one she had to bear alone. She lived among energetic, successful and temperamental people to whom there were far more important things than a little girl's adolescent plumpness. Annie de Mille was a busy and dedicated woman; William de Mille, with his brother, Cecil, was engaged in developing the new motion picture industry in Hollywood. The other de Mille sister, Margaret, remained pretty and gay. The house where this family lived was thronged all the year round with fascinating cosmopolites of the theatre, all of them scintillating with charm and good looks. In this brilliant coterie Agnes de Mille turned, as though overnight, into the Ugly Duckling.

Her passionate love of the dance began when she saw Pavlova, of whom she wrote, *My life stops as I write that name.* Her absorption in the theatre had begun before that, for her father was a playwright, as his father had been before him, and her natural love of acting was nourished by proximity to Hollywood. At first, she was determined to be an actress; her grandfather had been associated with David Belasco and Mrs. Leslie Carter and the legitimate stage seemed the simple extension of her life. She changed her mind about acting after she saw Adeline Genée in New York, whereupon she declared to her parents that she must at once commence the study of ballet, as she had decided to become a ballerina. She was a very little girl and her parents, naturally, took no notice of this whim. In any event, as de Mille was to discover, her parents would offer her no encouragement in becoming a professional dancer.

Agnes de Mille at twelve, as dancer-choreographer in a lyric mood.

However, from the time she saw Genée, Agnes de Mille began to dance, and she did so straight out of her heart and head and without guidance. She was allowed to perform her little dances for the family and friends and her mother made her costumes, but her father took no notice of this childish talent. In Los Angeles, she saw a performance of *Les Sylphides* by the Diaghilev dancers, and instantly visualized herself as one of those ethereal creatures. The sylphide became the symbol of beauty and aerial power to her, the supreme bliss of her spirit. Then she saw Pavlova, after she had started semi-weekly lessons at Kosloff's School, and her longing was crystallized into a determination to dance.

At first she was the worst in her ballet class, and the training was hardest for her, but she bore the humiliation of awkwardness and the physical pain of breaking her developed body to the rigorous training, and through the shame and the agony contrived to find ballet exercises profitable and inspiring. Her teacher, Fredova, would enthusiastically praise a pain as a "good" one. In between training her students, Fredova talked to them about the glittering dynasty of ballet—all the wonderful ballerinas and *danseurs nobles* who had become immortal on the international family tree of ballet—and the little de Mille listened and cherished the hope that someday her name would shine among them. Above all, she wanted to dance. It was the chief thought in her head, which was covered with thick, red curls. And with redheaded tenacity, Agnes de Mille determined to conquer the theatre.

She seems to have been wide open to all sights and sounds, sensitive to the flicker of a leaf as it fell—the sound of its falling, the sight of its turning in the sun, gold on one side, green on the other. She drank in her world with the pores of her body, feeling and not knowing as yet how much she felt, but storing it all up, to make dances out of it. When the family moved to California, she fell in love with the West, drawn to it because it was her mother's home. She has written an essay, "Games," in which she describes how she played in the canyons in the twilight, and in *Dance to the Piper* she relates how she was affected by the desert shapes and colors of the frontier land. How deeply these things impressed her were shown in *Rodeo* and her other ballets about the West, which she created years after the impressions had been sealed within her child's heart. In *Rodeo,* the audience was said to smell the sweat of the horsemen; I know that after I went to live in the West and saw *Rodeo* again I distinctly smelled the odor of the desert after rain, as the sagebrush smells in the evening. De Mille's extraordinary empathy as a choreographer has worked magic for her audiences; of all the American choreographers she has most often, and most successfully, made use of simple and everyday actions, direct human emotions, and genuine scenes.

Aside from dancing, Agnes de Mille's great love was for her father, the "Pop" of her memoirs. He was a handsome, charming, brilliant man, and she longed with all her feminine soul to make him proud of her. She had chosen, by the saddest contrariness to his opinion, to be a dancer; he had the clearest contempt for the dancer as a person of no consequence to art, and he almost broke his daughter's heart when he told her a brutal truth about the dancer—that he ceases to exist the moment he sits down. Her mother was more tolerant, and let her dance for a friend of the family, Ruth St. Denis. The audition was vaguely observed, and de Mille continued in her own way, stubbornly pitting one part of herself against the other. Her mother brought up the two girls strictly. They were encouraged to be dutiful, and circumspect in behavior—perfect little ladies. Mrs. de Mille was herself a most steadfast and noble woman, ever aware of her legacy of greatness from her father, Henry George—not an easy woman to live with, but an ennobling person to know. The de Mille girls had freedom to run and play, but, compared with other children, were made to live very sheltered lives. Agnes de Mille lived excitingly in her imagination, which was so fervent and inventive that she dominated her sister and their playmates, becoming playwright and leading lady in the plays she was forever staging, and choreographer and *prima ballerina* in the dances she performed under a banana tree in the backyard. She tried to teach herself theatrical dance by poring through books and magazines and, before she became a Kosloff student, passed through a happy chrysalid period, dressing after the Grecian manner of Duncan in draperies, or more opulently in her mother's idea of an Oriental belle. She was, at this stage, the beautiful, lively child, pleasing to adult eyes, and these games were considered self-expression and so indulged.

The Kosloff student, practicing in agony and grim earnestness, was a different sort of person, and a quite tiresome one. She must have exasperated and grieved her parents, who saw a plump and awkward child bent on breaking her body to an archaic discipline, determined on a profession that they considered of no intellectual and artistic worth and of rather raffish reputation. And in her ballet class the de Mille girl no longer dominated her contemporaries, and was not thought brilliantly witty and entrancingly pretty, but was the slow and dismal end of the line. Abashed at her inadequacies, she crept to the tail of the class.

When Mrs. de Mille realized that her child was determined to dance she had a *barre* put up in her own bathroom for home practice—there was no mirror in which the practicing student could see her flaws—but insisted that the piano lesson which preceded the ballet class was more important, and as a result de Mille was late to dancing class for three years, twice a week. When she graduated from high school and found her father still adamant in his refusal to accept dance as her vocation, she gave up ballet and entered the University of California at Los Angeles. Bringing to her college studies the same fierce intensity she had given ballet, she graduated *cum laude* at nineteen. During these years, she danced only as a student, arranging dances within the curriculum for her classmates, but in her sophomore year, when she volunteered to dance for a benefit at the college, she set foot on a stage for the first time.

At college, de Mille was told by well-meaning friends that she did not have a dancer's body and should concentrate on trying to become an actress. Like de Mille herself, these people thought of the dancer as something fragile and aerial, in the tradition of the classic Diaghilev ballerinas they had seen, or as someone lyric and seductive, like Duncan and St. Denis.

De Mille pretended that she had given up dancing, but continued to think of nothing else. And already she had become excited at her own discovery of the source of dancing, which her education had shown her had origins in the histories of all peoples. She created a skit on jazz and its relationship to African jungle dancing, and her father complimented her on it. With swelling heart, she visualized a career of working with William de Mille in movies. To her dismay, her father took her idea to Kosloff, who choreographed for Hollywood productions. De Mille realized that although she was grown up her father still could not accept her desire to dance as anything more serious and permanent than a child's fancy. Reaching an impasse between her two loves—her father and the dance—she returned blindly to ballet and the excruciating task of breaking herself again to its discipline. In her college years her body had grown less pliable and more fleshy. In her heart she knew what she still fought against admitting; she was never to be a classical technician, one of the lovely and aerial sylphides. Yet people thought that she could dance—at least, one young man thought so. He was one of Margaret's beaux, a handsome and successful movie actor named Douglass Montgomery. When he came upon de Mille dancing by herself, for herself, he enthused over her gifts. But he advised her to renounce traditional ballet and to make her own kind of theatre.

With the assurance of this handsome and confident young man that she had a future as a dancer, de Mille's misery became more acute. Until now, she had danced obsessively. Now Montgomery gave her confidence that, with half a chance, she could dance as she wished, on a stage, for thousands of people in the audience. And suddenly, her father capitulated and said she could try for a professional career in dance. Had her father only just remembered that he had given up engineering to become a playwright? The stage was his daughter's real and natural habitat. She had lived her whole childhood making believe; she was in truth making ready to take her rightful place in her world.

But nothing miraculous occurred; instead there was bewildering hurt and change. After a long and apparently idyllic marriage the de Milles shocked their daughters and friends by getting a divorce. Grief-stricken but stalwart, Annie de Mille took her daughters to New York and set about storming the theatre. Agnes had created a repertoire of concert dances, for which her mother made the costumes, and with these she auditioned for theatrical managers. She had to combat total indifference to her style, which was new to the Broadway stage of the day, and endure a patronizing as Cecil de Mille's little niece and the child of those nice William de Milles—what a pity about the divorce! Her mother rented halls, and relatives and friends came to see Agnes dance and told her she was enchanting, but no impresario hurried to put the de Mille name up in lights. She was thrilled that audiences enjoyed her work and continued to dance in hope and drudgery, and in drudgery and disappointment. The thought began to gnaw on her that she was marked for failure, and that she was ruining her mother's life and pauperizing her. Never lacking in a sense of drama, she began to be the martyred shell of her dreams, taking a sardonic and gloomy relish in despair.

She began again to study ballet—a sound, sure discipline for mind and body. Something about the torturous daily class put iron into her body and her spirit, and she became strong, and aloof from her fears and wild hopes. In 1928 she made a most auspicious theatrical debut in New York, in the company of Jacques Cartier, and found that in comedy she was a great hit with her audiences. It startled her, for she had not altogether given up the idea of being a sylphide.

A small but estimable artistic reputation began to accrue to her, and in 1929 she joined Adolph Bolm's company to replace the *prima ballerina* Ruth Page. Bolm had been Pavlova's partner and he regaled de Mille with anecdotes about her star ballerina, and de Mille heard from Bolm's piano conductor, Louis Horst, about a new American dancer named Martha Graham. On the tour de Mille danced three of her own concert pieces and on her return to New York rushed to see Argentina. Profoundly moved by the great dancer, she was appalled at the contrast between Argentina's dancing and her own. More than ever aware of her limitations and faced with her mother's dwindling finances that were being spent on her career, de Mille grew despondent—but was still obsessed by the will to dance.

The Black Crook was revived in Hoboken, and she was hired to choreograph it, and to partner her she hired a dancer, Warren Leonard. Until then, she had danced in solo. *The Black Crook* did not make her fame and fortune, in the way it had done for Marie Bonfanti and Rita Sangelli in the eighteen hundreds. De Mille danced to an audience providing counterpoint to the orchestra—there were catcalls, whistles, drunken singing, and a barrage of peanuts, popcorn, beer-coasters, chewing-gum wrappers and programs. She stuck it for a time, felt she was getting nowhere on the wrong side of the Hudson, and resigned. Out of the experience she had received long admiring columns in the Sunday *New York Times* from the dean of the dance critics, John Martin, and collected a broken nose when her partner inadvertently kicked her in the face, "due to my absent-mindedness," she relates, while they were dancing.

There followed a run of night clubs of the third-rate variety, private parties and movie houses. Whenever de Mille went onstage she made an audience laugh at her comic dances, and when the audiences responded to her she felt that she was making the dance communication she so longed to give them. Nothing lasted, though, and every engagement ended without a real foothold on the stage.

With Warren Leonard, she braved Hollywood and had a great artistic success; even "Pop" applauded when she came out in her yellow *tutu,* swinging a watering-pot. She danced the first piece she had composed for concert work, the *'49,* in which she sacrificed all her youth and charm to appear in a sunbonnet and a calico dress limp from the Western sun. A strangely gaunt and defiant dignity permeated the work. It was startling to know that this was the little (but no longer very plump) de Mille girl who was so mad about dancing. A man named Oscar Hammerstein saw her dance in Hollywood and informed her she showed marked talent; the problem, he added, was how to use it. That was twelve years before *Oklahoma!*

The Hollywood concert was a *succès d'estime* and an almost total financial failure. De Mille went to Europe. She danced her concert pieces in Paris, Brussels, Copenhagen and London, amassing a mixed bag of theatrical experience which she has emptied, with singular good humor, in *Dance to the Piper.* In London she laid the foundation of her real recognition, and with such success that I often encounter young English balletomanes who believe that Agnes de Mille is a British choreographer seduced away, like Tudor, by the blandishments of American ballet in the early nineteen forties.

In London de Mille got excellent reviews and an invitation to dance at the Mercury, a joint drama and dance theatre run by Ashley Dukes, the playwright, and his wife, Marie Rambert. Rambert conducted a ballet school and was in the process of forming a company. De Mille gave a series of concerts at the Mercury and studied under Rambert. Her classmates at the *barre* were some obscure young people named Pearl Argyle, William Chappell, Walter Gore and Hugh Laing. Some of the dancers wanted to choreograph: they were Andrée Howard, a girl, and two boys, Frederick Ashton and Antony Tudor. De Mille returned home on Christmas Day, 1934, confident that she was ready to win honor in her own country.

In 1924, Mrs. de Mille had been active in raising funds to pay off the mortgage on the Hollywood Bowl; in 1934 she arranged for her daughter to stage a concert in the Bowl, for which the de-Mille-girl-who-dances was to be paid two thousand dollars. Wild with enthusiasm, de Mille composed suites for eighty dancers, costumed them, and rehearsed for two months. The dress rehearsal was superb but catastrophe came at the première, when the Bowl was packed with an expectant audience. Because the money, which at first seemed munificent, could not stretch to two stage managers, she hired one; he was delegated to herd the performers, and the electrician was left alone at his switchboard. The performance began, but the lights stayed dim, and strain as the audience might it could not see what was going on on the one-hundred-and-four-foot width of the Bowl's stage. The frantic stage manager ran up and down the aisle, in hope of getting through to the electrician, who sat in his box on the other side of the hill. That gentleman, having turned the lights on for the first cue (bare visibility) calmly sat out three hundred and sixty dollars worth of his service, while the dancers danced, praying that someone would understand what was happening and correct the lighting disaster. The audience, a restless fifteen thousand, waited for what they did not quite know. Only one of the concert pieces was satisfactory (news having at last been carried by a maddened stage manager to the electrician) and the newspapers the next day headlined the Bowl's offering with DE MILLE GIRL FAILS. Worse, the cost of three months' work—composing, costuming and rehearsing—was a thousand dollars more than the two thousand de Mille had been paid. It took her mother's last bond to make up the deficit. Probably the hardest bill to pay was the three hundred and sixty dollars to the electrician.

As she has done at every hiatus in her career, de Mille threw herself on the *barre* like a martyr on the rack. She went back to Kosloff for lessons and studied under the Spanish classicist Carmalita Maracci, and she went to the Perry Studio where she gave classes in pantomine and began experimenting with her theories of gesture. Her lessons with Maracci were the most inspiring. Maracci is a unique personality in American dance, whom Ted Shawn has called "dancer without passport" because she cannot be typed as a Modern or as a Spanish dancer and is, as John Martin calls her, the possessor of the most beautifully styled Classic technique anywhere to be seen. A descendant of Spanish, German, French and Italian forbears, Maracci was raised in the Sacramento Valley. She did not use any set discipline in her classes, but every day she taught her students to do one single thing they had not done before. So, using work as the panacea for pain, de Mille marked time and went on dancing.

In England, she had taken a course in Pre-ethnic dance from Arnold Dolmetsch at Haslemere, and now she began a gradual and original integration of Ethnic and Classic Dance, developing her ideas of gesture. She had no idea that she was creating her own vocabulary of ballet. A young man named Richard Pleasant answered the telephone and kept the studio bookings at Perry's and he used to hang about and watch de Mille as she taught and worked. She could not bear to be watched and barred everyone from the class except the students, but Pleasant persisted and because he was unobtrusive she let him stay. He confided to her that someday he meant to have a ballet company of his own. She hardly listened to him. She had other and more serious things on her mind.

In 1936, de Mille was hired for the MGM production of *Romeo and Juliet,* with Leslie Howard and Norma Shearer. She worked under the different requirements of the cameras but succeeded so well that the producer, Irving Thalberg, invited her to choreograph for another picture, *Marie Antoinette.* A future in movies seemed about to open to her, but three months later Thalberg died. A more immediate tragedy to de Mille was that all her beautiful dances for *Romeo and Juliet* had been cut, or edited beyond recognition, before the film was released. The dances had cost a hundred thousand dollars to film, and had been good. When the choreographer saw the cut version of the picture she was physically sick, as though she were adrift on a rough sea. The simile is apt: Agnes de Mille at that time looked at her life much as a sailor views a shipwreck.

She was nearly thirty and she felt she was getting old and reaching nowhere, either as a woman or a dancer. She took on the job of choreographing for a Broadway musical, *Hooray for What,* a title that she could have used for her autobiography up to that date. It was to afford her little satisfaction as a choreographer, but a liberal education in the American theatre. She had to work with chorus girls who were the favorites of pasha-like backers of the show, and the clear intent of the management was sex, rather than dancing. The girls were hired to appear in the show and to provide what the business manager called a little loving on the side. De Mille quit after a series of humiliating incidents—she was by then incommunicado with her dancers, on the management's orders—and went back to New York during the out-of-town tryout. At two in the morning one of her dancers telephoned to gleefully announce that the business manager had broken his back while climbing onstage to tear a costume from one of de Mille's dancers in *Hooray.* The dancer who delivered the news was Kay Thompson, who was later to create *Eloise.*

De Mille returned to London and the Mercury, and her friendship with Tudor and Laing. A friend loaned her a house and she worked there with twelve girls, composing a suite of American dances. The English, affectionately disposed to the "American dancer, de Mille" from her first appearance, were delighted to have her back. She was feted by great society figures and her work was lavishly praised. One of the two foremost English Ballet critics, Arnold Haskell, wrote the newspaper headline THANK YOU, AMERICA, FOR DE MILLE. It was considerably more inspiring than DE MILLE GIRL FAILS.

She gave concerts, on which she cleared expenses and consolidated her artistic success, and continued to develop her original approach to gesture in dance. She was intent on marking the basic difference between the stylized and the genuine, and searched continuously among the ethnic and folk dances of England and America in order to, as she says, reach down to the bones of the matter. Only when she had arrived at the source of a gesture did she attempt to translate it into theatre. When she choreographed for *Oklahoma!* she made her boys take lessons from an American country dance expert on how to bow to the girls, and how to offer their hands to them. On such details, with infinite care and respect, she was building a craft of choreography that would turn dancers onstage into real and living people.

In London that year, 1938, she began to compose a concert work on the American cattle country. She knew it well—its pale, dun-colored ground, its blazing sun-lit sky, its black velvet nights—and remembered the rhythmic gestures of men on horseback and those same men, dismounted and limping in their run-over high-heeled cowboy boots, when they moved over the ground. Her principal dancer was Peggy van Praagh, who later became director of the junior Sadler's Wells Ballet. The concert piece was first performed in London that April. She called it *Rodeo,* and years later she took from it all the gestures that she put into the first ballet that made her famous in America.

In this year, she gave a series of concerts with Laing as her partner, at the Mercury, and received consistently fine notices. She began to work under Tudor, in a new ballet called *Dark Elegies.* It was a new phase for her, because she had never worked under another choreographer before, and she believed that Tudor found her neither quick nor adroit, while he, in turn, baffled her because he did not count. However, he was patient and rehearsed her in private and she danced in the pre-mière of his ballet, which was considered a fine work. She thought Tudor was without peer in the ballet world, and formed a company with him and Laing, called The Dance Theatre, to which she contributed her savings, her repertoire and her costumes. They parted when they agreed that their styles contradicted each other's, and in 1939, with war about to be declared, the English refused to renew her visa. Her farewell concerts were danced at the Westminister Theatre with Laing as her partner. She commissioned a ballet from Tudor, *Judgment of Paris,* with costumes and libretto by Laing. It is a satire on the Greek legend of Paris, and de Mille created the role of Venus, which she later danced for Ballet Theatre in the United States. It was comedy, in which de Mille excelled.

Returning to New York, she resisted her mother's wish to live at home and took a Greenwich Village apartment which she could not afford to furnish. In its empty rooms she began to compose the dances that she put into the later *Oklahoma!, One Touch of Venus, Bloomer Girl, Carousel* and *Brigadoon*—the ballets that established her as the most brilliant choreographer in the musical theatre. She had a piano, and when friends called they sat on the piano bench or the bed. After *One Touch of Venus* she bought a French Provincial chair for thirty dollars and set it in the middle of the bare floor, to sit in when she was feeling depressed. She would put her hands on the arms of the chair and draw some of its classic beauty into herself.

Until her success in *Rodeo,* which coincided with her falling in love with the man she married, Agnes de Mille was a creature of contradictions. She was an intensely feminine woman, generous and tenderhearted, bound to a profession of ruthless rivalry and no security. When she began her career the American theatre was far worse than it is now, and the dancer was hedged in a narrow void between people like the business manager of *Hooray for What* and nice people who thought all dancers were immoral and perverted. At any time, in any country, there have been few women choreographers and Agnes de Mille became one in America while theatrical dancing was a dubious profession in the popular opinion. She had to fight for every inch of her career, first against loving parents who were shocked and disapproving, and then against the theatre itself, which forced her into a masculine belligerance that was totally foreign to the real feminine softness of the fighter. A core of toughness and her obsession to dance, and to create dance, preserved her from all the insults and injuries of her career. Sometimes she realized that she was growing older and passing up the time, and the opportunities, for love and marriage, but she always turned her back on such opportunities because to have accepted would have meant withdrawing from the theatre. She thought of her whole life as a failure, and yet she did not consider herself defeated.

In New York, she took stock of herself. Gone was the lovely child, the lyric dancer, the girl who was going to put the de Mille name in lights on the American theatre's marquee. Even her family had given up waiting for the brilliant child to achieve her promise of greatness.

There was no more money and she could no longer rent recital halls, so she went back to the ballet *barre* and took classes at Carnegie Hall. She gave two lessons a week at the YMHA in New York, and joined with some other dancers to rent a studio for five dollars a week, where they gave themselves lessons. The boys, from Balanchine's company, were Paul Haakon, who had been a *premier danseur* of a Balanchine company, Michael Kidd and Eugene Loring. There was a dancer named Mary Heater from Seattle, who had been in the *corps de ballet* of Ballet Caravan, and later joined the *corps* of Ballet Theatre. These five were stern taskmasters with each other and all of them benefited greatly from the mass teaching. They were all obsessed with the desire to dance, and trained to do so, but at that moment they had no audience to dance for except each other. Two of them enjoyed the rapport to the extent of making it permanent. Heater and Kidd got married.

Martha Graham was the most talked of new dancer. De Mille met her, saw her dance, and fell entirely under her spell. She calls Graham one of the geniuses of modern dance. Graham would not let de Mille study with her, but became a fount of strength and encouragement and, with Pavlova, de Mille's great inspiration.

To the foundation of classicism to which she still held, taking the daily lesson as therapy for mind and body, and all the absorption she retained in ethnic dance, she now added the influences of Modern Dance, merging them with her own feelings and beliefs, which she has never been able to divorce from her work. Her early recognition of Tudor's strange and wonderful work convinced her that ballet was moving into dimensions unbounded by past theories, but she could not know, as yet, that her fierce preoccupation with the genuine, her stubborn fight against trickery in pretty dance forms, would set the style for her native theatre.

Every penny that de Mille earned in the little concerts at the YMHA and from teaching she used for theatre auditions, but the summer of 1939 came and almost went without change. A friend recalls her as a hurrying figure with a perpetually harried look which occasionally gave way to one of sardonic mirth. Her sense of humor survived, but was drawn thin and apt to become sarcastic; it was as though she wore a feather in her cap, one badly bent and bedraggled, but a feather, nonetheless. Since the career would not change, the careerist did. With bitter resolution, de Mille took what she considered a sensible attitude towards herself. She had never cared, in the least, for her looks offstage, to the distress of her pretty sister and dainty mother. Now she began dressing in her sister's castoff clothes, and went to an orthodontic surgeon and had her teeth straightened—on credit, because she had no money. She was punctual for appointments and tried to look calm and collected, even when she was mentally composing ballets while giving a fair imitation of being a sociable body. Outwardly, she conformed to something closer to the pattern of correct behavior than her old brusque and eccentric air; inwardly, she lived in a secret world where, when she was happy, she was composing, and where, when she accepted failure, she settled into an oblivion of despair.

The American theatre had changed while she was in England. The Balanchine-Kirstein companies had excited a great deal of interest in New York and the Ballet Russe de Monte Carlo, the most famous company in the world, had become an established favorite in America. Other dancers were dancing. In New York, the most celebrated ballerinas were Danilova, a Russian, and Markova, an Englishwoman. Martha Graham, an American, was making history for Modern Dance. England had thanked America for de Mille but at home she was still the orphan at the feast. She stood, like such an orphan, with her face pressed to the glass around the theatre she longed to enter. She had talent—and had been so informed on two continents—she worked hard, was patient, and had done everything except compromise her ideals, but these fairy virtues had brought her no reward. There was no spell she could cast to bring her success.

Then an unlikely Prince Charming came along in the person of Richard Pleasant, the gangling young man who had hung about her classroom at the Perry Studio. He was magically transformed into the impresario of Ballet Theatre, a brand new company, for whom he was hiring dancers and choreographers in gross lots. There was an English Wing under Anton Dolin, and a Russian Wing under Michel Fokine. The American Wing was to be made up of Eugene Loring, who had created the first American ballet, *Billy the Kid,* and Agnes de Mille, whom the English and Europeans had enthusiastically hailed as an "American dancer."

The happy shock that Ballet Theatre wanted her was followed by the unhappy one of being told that she was not to dance, but to create dances for others. She still believed that her great hunger was to dance, and she fought Pleasant for the right to perform, at least in her own ballets. He would not consent, and, her pride broken, de Mille agreed to join Ballet Theatre as a choreographer. Pleasant wanted to invite Frederick Ashton to join the company—he had choreographed Gertrude Stein's *Four Saints in Three Acts* in New York in the 1933–1934 season. De Mille, knowing that Ashton was working with the Sadler's Wells Ballet, advised Pleasant to get Tudor, instead. Pleasant imported Tudor, Andrée Howard, and Hugh Laing—and now de Mille got a lesson in the necessarily ruthless condition of creativity. Tudor and Loring, who best knew her abilities, shut themselves off on their rehearsal stages. The bitterest thing was when Tudor gave her première role of his *Dark Elegies* to Lucia Chase. De Mille had thought that this was one of the few roles in Ballet Theatre's repertoire that she would be allowed to dance.

She recalls that she became extremely nervous. Inspiration was the fire in which she could forge her work, but there were also the mechanics of work. At that time there were no schools of choreography, no classes in which a dancer with a ballet in his head could learn to translate that invisible pattern into a working design for the stage. All was by trial and error, depending on the limitations and possibilities of the dancers. The choreographer entering the rehearsal studio was faced with what de Mille calls the materials of the craft: creatures called dancers, patient, disciplined, neat and hopeful, in chaste black woolen practice uniforms.

She had had nothing like such tools before, and although her heart leaped at the chance of using them she recognized what little experience she brought to the task. She writes, in *Dance to the Piper:* "My brief and frenzied flurries with commercial troupes of mixed prostitutes and chorus dancers had not helped me build a technique of composing and rehearsing . . . But now I was being given a real chance."

There would be no excuse if she failed. Ballet Theatre was the richest and the biggest company to be formed in America. A choreographer had only to express a wish to have it satisfied—or so it seemed. Since she was not to dance her own creations, de Mille turned from her forte, comedy, to a ballet genre new and daring for her—an avant-garde experiment with a Negro troupe.

She chose for her score the *Création du Monde* by Darius Milhaud and began to compose her *Obeah. Black Ritual,* or *Obeah* is the black magic of the Trinidadian Shango, the old Dahomean religion from which *Caliso* derives—and, in turn, the dance and music now called calypso.

Obeah was the longest ballet de Mille had yet composed, twenty-five minutes. It was developed on dancers whom de Mille actually taught to dance, even as she rehearsed them. There was then no school or stage for serious Negro dancers, for Katherine Dunham had not yet appeared. De Mille recruited her dancers by audition. She says they were without dance technique, without rehearsal discipline of any kind. Worse, they were badly nourished, and fainted from hunger at rehearsal. She had to do more than train them to dance in *Obeah*. Ballet Theatre had to keep them warm, keep them fed, and de Mille taught them to move as she wished.

The piece depended greatly on the leading soloist and for this role de Mille chose a very beautiful dancer. While she was rehearsing, a dancer she had not auditioned came to the rehearsal hall to offer de Mille her services. Her name was Katherine Dunham. De Mille decided to risk all on her previously chosen *soliste,* although the girl lacked timing and projection. She was to learn from this experience that these were the two things a choreographer cannot teach, because they depend on deep psychological involvements.

The Negro *corps* hired for de Mille by Ballet Theatre was without precedent, and Ballet Theatre commissioned for *Obeah* a superb Caribbean background as the décor. George Amberg praises the ballet, and calls it an even more courageous experiment than Loring's *Great American Goof.* De Mille was not literally ethnic in *Obeah* (the title was used allusively) and she puzzled the audience, as Loring did with his avant-garde *Goof.* The audience at American ballet in 1942 still expected dancing to be romantic or fantastic, danced lyrically or in fashion *caractère,* and always on the tippy-toe. *Obeah* was given three performances in a season studded with premières by ten choreographers, among whom the competition was cruel. The little American Wing labored in contest with Fokine and Nijinska. The English Wing was soon dominated by Tudor, but remained supported by Dolin's accomplished romantic genre. It can have been small consolation to the two American choreographers, Loring and de Mille, that their ballets that season were considered admirable failures. A critical concensus now ranks both *The Great American Goof* and *Obeah* as fine works. They failed because they were too much in advance of the developing tastes of the American ballet audience.

Smarting under the failure of *Obeah,* and the knowledge—that followed with the tremendous popular triumph of Katherine Dunham—of having turned down the soloist who might have saved her work, de Mille saw her troupe of sixteen Negro dancers disbanded. Worse was to come, in the dreary round of misfortune to which she was growing accustomed. Ballet Theatre, which had begun so auspiciously as an "American" company, could not find American theatres to dance in. These were monopolized by the big American booking companies, who believed only in the *ballets russes* as the kind of dancing that could jingle the box office cash register. Lucia Chase made herculean efforts to hold Ballet Theatre together, but with no theatre bookings it was impossible to do so. The company existed, but only in a tenuous relationship between its members and the organization. Several of the company went their separate ways, although the majority were drawn back, later, to the nucleus of Ballet Theatre.

The company's real American significance, in the first few years, lay in the revival of Loring's *Billy the Kid.* When Loring left to found Dance Players *Billy* remained in repertoire, but Tudor was the acknowledged, and the undisputed, influence on the company. Following the première of *Pillar of Fire,* Tudor dominated Ballet Theatre until he resigned from it to join the Metropolitan Opera.

De Mille next created a broad and pungent satire for Ballet Theatre: *Three*

Virgins and a Devil, in which she developed four masterful characterizations of the Devil and the virgins Priggish, Greedy and Lustful. The ballet gave a first chance to a soloist named Jerome Robbins, but was only quietly received. An independent impresario, Lucius Pryor, engaged de Mille to organize a troupe, which he financed on a United States tour. It was de Mille's first national tour. She went to Hollywood and raised seven hundred dollars, the first money she had ever borrowed. Her mother's income was depleted, and de Mille was determined not to accept more from its little hoard. With borrowed money, she costumed a troupe of five dancers, and paid all expenses, and the money covered these only because the troupe made the costumes and copied the music. Besides, de Mille undertook the complicated details of paper work, and learned the jargon of ballet's office routine. It often kept her up until dawn, after having danced at that evening's performance.

She was wildly happy, although her troupe danced six nights a week, and on a different stage every night. Louis Horst, the conductor she so much admired, was in the troupe; so was Joseph Anthony, later to become noted as the director of *The Rainmaker* and *The Lark.* With a repertoire made up of de Mille's concert pieces, the company danced in college auditoriums and small towns, and every performance was an unqualified delight to audiences who traveled three hundred miles to see the dances that de Mille had created out of their own prairies and hills. Winding up the tour in Chicago, de Mille's troupe played against the most formidable competition in her theatre, Ballet Russe and the reactivated Ballet Theatre, and sold out every performance. Now she knew that people liked her dances—especially the people she wanted to reach, whom she called "the people of America, the ordinary people." They simply loved to see dancing and were not oppressed by the balletomane prejudice that it must always be *ballets russes.*

Back in New York, life ground to a full stop. The war was at its height, and her mother had begun to have serious heart attacks. Oppressed by her financial failure in the theatre, worried by her mother's failing health, de Mille resigned herself to the inevitable: she would give up dancing and get a job where she would earn a regular salary. She chose Macy's as the place to give her security, but meanwhile she went to the daily ballet class at Carnegie Hall. Free of her ambitions, she no longer punished herself for her inadequacy as a classical technician—she kicked as high as her head and jumped like a boy. She danced, in fact, like the Cowgirl in *Rodeo,* who was not yet created.

One day, on her way to class, someone told her that Ballet Russe was looking for an American ballet. She went home and wrote a libretto, elaborating on the dances she had composed for her *Rodeo* suite in London in 1938. She submitted the ballet and it was accepted, and when she was told to choose her composer she chose Aaron Copland. A very tall young man, with hair as red as hers, was the scenic designer. He was Oliver Smith, who was to become the most celebrated scenic designer in American ballet. These three, in dance, music and scene, were to create the immortal characters of *Rodeo, or The Courting at Burnt Ranch.*

Then the fight began. Ballet Russe wanted a piece of charming rustic Americana; de Mille was determined on the realistic and the genuine. She refused a red barn which, although picturesque, would have been an anachronism in the Colorado desert where she had placed the people in *Rodeo*. The title did not please the Russians, who suggested *Colorado Pastorale*. De Mille quailed, and managed to squash the idea. Next it was suggested that Nijinska should try her hand at a *ballet americain* full of cowboys, while de Mille tried hers with a Russian fairy tale. Despite all this, de Mille's *Rodeo* went into rehearsal.

The male dancers, the "boys" universal to ballet regardless of their ages, ballet styles or nationalities, were, to a man, *les danseurs*. They had graceful wrists and could push themselves off the ground into the air, but they had no relationship with the ground, which the classical technician uses only as a step into his aerial sphere. De Mille required of these dancers a real relationship with the ground: they were to walk on it, ride imaginary horses over it, and fall down on it. She forced them to squint against an imaginary sun, and to sweat under it. When they were not bucked by broncos, or precariously perched in the saddles of galloping horses, they were constrained to walk on the rolled-over heels of their dusty boots, with the stance of tired men crotch-sprung from the saddle.

This went on in the Hollywood studio of Maracci while Ballet Russe was rehearsing for the new season. Men who had spent a lifetime learning how to leave the ground now rolled on it, thrown there by a horse—and not gracefully, or with classic dignity. *Danseuses* who prided themselves on their *pointe* work begged for a series of *fouettés en tournant,* and were bidden, instead, to squaredance. The rehearsals were supervised by a choreographer adamant in her requirements, and the gloomy company resolved that she was a madwoman.

No choreographer had ever asked them to grovel on the floor, far less fall off invisible horses with such force that they went away with cracking headaches; the girls were used to the czardas and the mazurka, but not to the calls of the American square dance. Did this choreographer, they muttered to each other, know what ballet was? What had she created? Something about Negroes, someone remembered, and, also for Ballet Theatre, some little thing called *Three Virgins and a Devil.* How would these compare in history with the works of Massine, the choreographic ideal of Ballet Russe? Massine had created *Le Beau Danube* and *Gaîté Parisienne.*

He was rehearsing his ballets in an adjacent studio, and de Mille's courage nearly deserted her at the competition, and yet when she entered the room the dancers stood and waited for her to precede them—even the great Danilova. At least the Russians knew what it meant to be The Choreographer.

The Russians were most mystified about de Mille's work, and the American and English dancers only a little less so. The choreographer's partner, luckily for her, was the incomparable Frederic Franklin, an Englishman who had cheerfully danced in an American flop called *Ghost Town* in 1939. Meticulous in the European ballet protocol that ordains a choreographer as an inviolate authority, Franklin tackled every new de Millean gesture and urged the rest of the company to follow suit.

To tell the truth, the company could have better satisfied the choreographer if they had been able to understand her. "Bob!" de Mille ordered, and when they stared at her she shrieked: "Bob! Bob!" She wanted them to bob and curtsy in the square dance. There was a great hubbub and she howled at them to be quiet. "And *bob!*" she implored, with all the force she could muster. One Russian "boy" stepped forth: "But Madame, which Baub, *please?*" There were four dancers named Robert.

Despite all this, the ballet began to shape up, and the *danseurs* and *danseuses* vanished into the cowboys and the city girls of *Burnt Ranch.* The Head Wrangler who lounged like any idle cow-poke on the corral fence was Casimir Kokitch, Danilova's husband: above all, he was an excellent character dancer. The Champion Roper of that Colorado scene had been born in London and had begun to study dance in Liverpool. De Mille transfigured them all, and at the première when the curtain rose there were the authentic Western articles standing squinting into the simulated Western sun. When the curtain fell, the ballet was a rousing success and the de Mille girl had made good, as all the newspapers blazoned the next day. An excited balletomane rushed up to Annie de Mille and cried, "Aren't you proud of your daughter?"

"I've always been proud of her," said Mrs. de Mille. "Always. When no one hired her. I'll go home now and start the coffee."

Thus, suddenly, Agnes de Mille's life changed forever. *Rodeo* was described as the kind of ballet Mark Twain would have written, if he had run to ballets. Ballet Russe went on tour and *Rodeo* was a triumph wherever it was seen. In Los Angeles, figures from the despairing past came to make the triumph complete: "Pop," Warren Leonard, from *The Black Crook,* Carmalita Maracci, and Richard Pleasant, who had left Ballet Theatre and become an artillery captain in the U.S. Army.

A new world opened to de Mille, which she has described in *And Promenade Home,* using for the title the square-dance call with which the caller summons the dancers back to the original figure in the dance.

And de Mille became a household word in America, with the galaxy of ballets she created for the musical theatre. Although *Rodeo* is the most popular of her ballets for the theatre, her masterpieces are *Fall River Legend* and *The Harvest According,* both of them created for Ballet Theatre.

The Harvest According has a New England scene and the dancers are costumed in fashions from the time of the Civil War. The music is by the American composer, Virgil Thomson, and the theme is from Walt Whitman's lines:

> *Life, life is the tillage*
> *And death is the harvest according.*

De Mille, as is usual in her work, created through the eyes of a woman. The ballet motif is a circle, and variants of a circle, seen in the ring of womanhood in birth, the ring of the children's games, the ring of the folk dancing. The larger circle is life into death: birth, growing up, dying—the loss of men at war—and birth again, as life continues and the cycle is renewed. The childbirth is not pain and danger alone, but an occasion of pure magic as new life is drawn from the womb; so the woman in labor is shown as not crushed by suffering but exalted. The Games are more than just that: they are savage contests that test the strength and development of individuality among children; the adolescents strain

apart and are drawn close again, as they recognize themselves as a group. War comes like thunder clouds, passes, and life is renewed.

De Mille had long wanted to compose a ballet on the Civil War and had made concert studies and compiled notes, but after many years when she began to compose *The Harvest According* it took life of its own, and changed from a dramatic episode in history to a lyric work. The major historical incident was almost submerged in the more engrossing and vital aspects of life itself. The ballet has been mistaken for an American vignette, but it has a far more universal intent, involving as it does birth, growing up, going off to war and dying—conditions not particular to one people but universal to all peoples.

In style, the ballet is uniquely American, employing Freestyle, Classic and Modern forms. The choreography was dictated by communication, not by dance styles. Although it was produced in 1952, after the precedent had been set in *Billy the Kid, Rodeo* and *Fancy Free,* there were some die-hard conservative balletomanes who sniffed and declared that this was not ballet. They meant that it was not the Classic or traditional form of ballet, but they failed to understand that de Mille did not intend it to be—she was expressing, in dancing, her concepts of life, and of men and women. To do this, she trampled down all the barriers between the separate and jealously guarded dance forms; she did not mean to be stylized and was not intent on being stylish. When the old sufficed, she employed it, and where its vocabulary faltered she expressed herself in modern language.

De Mille put the dancer as a Child *en pointe,* to achieve the tiptoe quality of exuberant joy peculiar to childhood, but in the Games the boys stood on their heads, which classicists do not do, and literally sprawled through the air in their big jumps, in the happy gaucherie of the adolescent. One dancer turned cartwheels, and also *en pirouette;* the girls, *en pointe,* fainted and fell backwards until their shoulders touched the floor, then leaped upright.

As she had done in *Rodeo,* de Mille worked with dancers in a traditional ballet company for *The Harvest According,* and with the young dancer Gemze de Lappe, whom she has trained in her special theories of movement, gesture and interpretation.

Others in the ballet—which was created for the Ballet Theatre in its Metropolitan Opera season, October, 1952—were pure classicists like Ruth Ann Koesun. All the dancers under de Mille ceased to be dancers and became her people —men, women and children.

Her women were involved with fundamentals, the evocation of which demanded gesture beyond those of the narrow confines of ballet *port de bras,* so she used gestures closer to the Modern style. For a demonstration of anguish, the women did not delicately *bourrée* in the agitation of a *Swan Queen* but fell to their knees, and moved about on their knees, writhing and twisting in an access of human grief or suffering. She points out that the technical ability of the dancers was remarkable in the difficult choreography she devised for showing the vital functions of birth and death. The degree of dance technique involved was no less than for the most complex traditional *divertissement*—only, all the gesture was human, not idealized in classic style.

Ruth Ann Koesun and Kelly Brown in de Mille's The Harvest According.

No longer obsessed with *la sylphide,* de Mille evoked fleet young women in *Harvest,* who moved as the wind moves over the prairies. When I saw these young women dance in San Francisco the walls of the theatre fell away and an illusion of our vast American spaces was created onstage. And when the girls in *Harvest* stood still they were not in *pose,* the static position of the ballet *danseuse,* but were standing thinking, with tears in their eyes, of the boys gone away to war.

Virgil Thomson's score for the ballet includes a cello concerto, a symphony on a hymn tune, and passages from his opera, *The Mother of Us All.* Although the original works were written as separate compositions and at different periods, they were arranged in a homogeneous score by the composer for *The Harvest According.* The ballet has mistakenly been described as an extension of de Mille's Civil War Ballet in *Bloomer Girl,* but only the time and locale are the same—the music, costumes and scenic design are new and different, as is the basic emphasis and style.

The Harvest According has been called de Mille's most mature work, and is the ballet in which she has most nearly succeeded in freeing the choreographer from the woman Agnes de Mille. Yet even here it is clear that she will create nothing in dance of which she is not deeply aware. Her own child was born in 1947. She waited until she had experienced a birth-pang before she set the pattern on the floor for a dancer.

This is the key to Agnes de Mille, who wrote of herself and the choreographers Tudor and Loring, "we danced what we knew about." Coupled with this fidelity was a profound, spiritual understanding of dance, which is—however disguised—a paramount characteristic in the native choreographers, and most clearly evident in Ted Shawn, who exchanged a vocation in the ministry for one in dance, but kept his work a vocation, nevertheless. De Mille defines dance as gesture with meaning—and the dancer is that creature she finds in the Bible: *. . . and God said, Let the waters bring forth abundantly the moving creature that hath life. . .*

Writing as eloquently as she creates dance, she has won great literary honors for her two-volume autobiography and several articles for leading magazines. Her first book, *Dance to the Piper,* remains the best-selling book ever written by a dancer, and has been translated into four foreign languages. Since 1956 she has had conspicuous success as a national television figure, especially in her "Omnibus" series on ballet.

In her ballets for the legitimate theatre de Mille has chronicled her own emotions, suffusing her characters with such sincerity that they are dramatic figures of her life, as well the plastic words with which she writes of the world. In *Rodeo* the Cowgirl is the same little girl, with the thick red curls and the stout frame, who longed to be a sylphide when she could best be a spirited little mustang. In *Fall River Legend,* it is no trick at all to read into Lizzie's hunger for love the choreographer's passionate quest for recognition as a dancer. Her ballets are based on feminine projections, with a woman as the central figure, and she has an aversion to the symbolic as being false to reality.

Her choreography is based on her knowledge of folk dancing—a considerable repertoire, since all peoples have histories of dancing—and her own highly original and intensely personal gifts. In the lyrical exploration of feminine emotion she is unsurpassed in the contemporary theatre. Whereas Balanchine's classical dancers are the physical, or visible, extensions of music, de Mille's dancers are people, whose actions and emotions are conveyed to the audience with such simplicity of phrasing and economy of movement that they have a marvelous lucent quality.

She must always work with dancers who are sympathetic to her ideas, because she is a democratic, not an autocratic choreographer. She usually starts work on a ballet with three or more of her dancers—people she has trained in her theories of gesture and interpretation—and creates the ballet out of their emotional and physical reactions to her ideas. On the other hand, Balanchine and several other choreographers work out the ballet before they go into rehearsal and require nothing but blind obedience from the dancers.

A de Mille ballet begins by consuming the choreographer and is then communicated emotionally to her dancers, who tell of exhausting but inspiring sessions with her. When the work goes well, de Mille's joy and energy transports them about the studio; when she is balked, either by herself or by a dancer's inadequacy or withdrawal, she suffers acutely and is by turns furious, despairing or anxious. Inevitably, the dancers achieve an emotional rapport with the choreographer. Dominated by the theme, they unconsciously submerge themselves into the de Millean creation and appear as radiantly alive people onstage. This is particularly true of her women, who are always partnered by exceptionally virile dancers. For instance, Bambi Linn and Gemze de Lappe, two of her favorite dancers, have a fragile, childlike purity, and in the arms of a dancer like James Mitchell are lifted and held and shown off with immense masculine strength and tenderness. De Mille's young girls open like flowering buds in her ballets, and are imbued with an extraordinary combination of innocence and sex. Her *pas de deux* have the same unearthly feminine compassion that is evoked, for instance, in the "white" scenes between Odette and the Prince in *Swan Lake*.

Her classes at the Ballet Arts School at Carnegie Hall in New York are taught by her own system. Her dancers learn to breathe, walk, and run, and to employ her vocabulary of gesture—a language to which she continues to add from her perceptive observations of people. De Mille travels widely around the world, and continues to study and work with superlative zest. Remaining active as a choreographer, she also finds time to lecture and produce television programs on ballet. Her history of dance will be published in the near future.

Agnes de Mille is in appearance a small, compact woman with a very feminine air. The little girl who mourned her lost childhood beauty grew into an intelligent, handsome and extraordinarily accomplished woman. Recalling her as a dancer in London, one of her contemporaries describes her as "perhaps not very pretty, but sometimes most beautiful onstage and off." She had, as Marie Rambert said of her, a Dionysian quality, which she has superimposed on many of the female dancers in her ballets.

Gifted as de Mille is as a writer, she is never more autobiographical than as

Agnes de Mille with Gemze de Lappe and James Mitchell rehearsing Gold Rush *for television production, on "Seven Lively Arts."*

a choreographer. Her intense nature still bears the imprint of Annie de Mille's exalted spirit. Fearful of self-pity the woman de Mille has affected the choreographer de Mille: in the midst of emotion, she has been compelled to divert the dance into the antic. Only in maturity as woman and artist has she become more fluent in expressing feeling, and in using elements so fundamental as to become symbolic, especially in love and anguish. One need only compare *The Harvest According* with *Rodeo* to see the difference.

Grim as her struggles were, phenomenal as her success is, she retains characteristics that are attributes of her work—an enormous affinity with suffering and joy, and a fearlessness that overthrows traditions and eventually vanquishes prejudice. Invulnerable in her artistic scruples, she has become one of the most significant influences in the theatre. Well within her time as an American theatrical performer, she has lived to see the dancer leave her paradoxical state of obscurity and notoriety to take her place as *prima ballerina* on an equal with any opera diva. With characteristic caustic humor, de Mille has recreated in the musical, *Goldilocks,* some of the people she outlived on Broadway—the vamps, the mashers, the men-about-town and girls-on-the-loose.

By doing what she believed in, and by believing in what she did, she helped to develop American ballet.

JEROME ROBBINS

Jerome Robbins was born in 1918 in New York, to immigrants named Rabinowitz. His father was in the corset business, and the family had no theatrical connections, except in Robbins' sister, Sonya, a Modern dancer. Through her he became interested in dance, although his first work in the theatre was with puppets. He studied Interpretive Dance with Sonya Robbins and Alyce Bentley, and Spanish and Oriental dance forms with Hélene Veola and Yeichi Nimura. He also took lessons in drama and voice, and learned to play the piano and the violin.

Robbins graduated from a Weehawken, New Jersey, high school at seventeen, and attended the University of New York for one year with the idea of becoming a chemist, but lack of funds made him give up college. He began to study dancing in earnest despite the disapproval of his parents, who felt it was a poor way for a man to earn a living. A friend says of Robbins: "If Jerry had really meant to be a chemist, he would have moved heaven and earth to stay in college. When he made up his mind to become a dancer, he found a way." He still had no money, but he had ballet lessons all the same, beginning his training under Ella Daganova, who gave him three classes a week for cleaning her window blinds. His study of Classic Dance was continued under Hélene Platova, and later under Eugene Loring and Antony Tudor.

In 1937 Robbins joined the New York Dance Center of Gluck Sandor and Felicia Sorel, where, he says, he learned a great deal of what he now knows of the theatre, and between 1937 and 1941 he worked in the Yiddish Art Theatre and did his first choreography in small revues for Max Liebman. One summer, when he was a mere beginner, he was hired as one of a group of dancers to entertain the guests at a camp called Tamiment, in the Poconos. The director of Camp Tamiment is said to have looked his entertainers over with godlike authority, and commanded: "So all right, go make the guests happy." Robbins and Co. did their best to fill the order, and one of the girls did so well that she was put in charge of the group. She was a young dancer who had a certain theatrical air, having made her debut at the Metropolitan in a rather unorthodox way. Small as was Lily Pons, she was still not small enough to be hauled about in a sack in *Rigoletto,* so this duty fell to a child student of the Metropolitan Ballet, who used to be stuffed into the bag whenever *Rigoletto* was performed, and dragged convincingly about the stage. Her name was Ruthanna Boris, and Camp Tamiment serenely employed her services that summer, all unknowing that she was to become a ballerina and one of the few women choreographers whose work—such as *Cakewalk* and *Cirque de Deux*—would be taken into the repertoires of major companies. The Camp Tamiment guests as casually employed the young man who was to become, at home and abroad, the hugely acclaimed American choreographer, Jerome Robbins.[1]

Robbins became a chorus boy on Broadway in the musicals *Great Lady, High Hat Revue, Keep Off The Grass* and *Stars in Your Eyes.* While dancing in *Stars in Your Eyes* he auditioned for Ballet Theatre with some other aspiring unknowns named Alicia Alonso and Nora Kaye, and all were accepted. The next year, 1941, he became a soloist.

De Mille tells us that when she was composing *Three Virgins and a Devil,* she wanted a boy who could do an intricate jazz bit, and none of the *danseurs* in the company could. Someone told her about a boy named Robbins, who could count anything in music, no matter how intricate, or in whatever dance idiom. Robbins arrived, and de Mille taught him a little solo under a chandelier in the Fifty-third Street mansion, later the Theatre Guild, where Ballet Theatre was holding rehearsals. The solo he did as The Youth in *Three Virgins and a Devil* was quite a hit and people began to notice the Robbins boy. He later created the Spanish Lover in Fokine's *Bluebeard,* Benvolio in Tudor's *Romeo and Juliet,* and Hermes in Lichine's *Helen of Troy.*

After Robbins joined Ballet Theatre he could not get enough of his craft. His contemporaries say that he used to stand in the wings, and dance all the solo roles while the male dancers were practicing or performing onstage, often to the annoyance of dancers who would nearly knock him down coming and going about their important affairs, and swear at him for being a nuisance. When Ballet Theatre went to Mexico Robbins begged Fokine for permission to rehearse with the group of *danseurs* understudying Petrouchka, and Fokine consented. These *danseurs* stood in three rows, and Jerome Robbins was always in the last row, at the end, where he was kicked and elbowed, half by accident, half on purpose. But Fokine watched him, and one day in Mexico City the great choreographer put the American dancer into the role of Petrouchka. That same year Jerome Robbins danced Petrouchka on the stage of the Metropolitan Opera House in New York. As time goes in ballet, it was scarcely a hop, skip, and a jump from the time Robbins had been swopping three lessons a week for cleaning window blinds.

His first great success was in the happiest and most romantic tradition of the theatre. On the morning of April 18, 1944, three young men, all twenty-five, awoke and went about their business. By nightfall they were famous in New York as the choreographer, composer and scenic designer of the ballet called

Fancy Free. Their names were, respectively, Jerome Robbins, Leonard Bernstein, and Oliver Smith.

The ballet that they jointly created has had more than seven hundred performances in fifteen years without losing one whit of its vitality, and it has immortalized the great roles of the three American Gobs created by Jerome Robbins, and the dancers John Kriza and Michael Kidd. Ballet Theatre dancers have cut their teeth on the sailors in *Fancy Free,* just as, in Ballet Russe, other dancers have done in Massine's and Fokine's ballets.

The little masterpiece of lyric and contemporary Americana was conceived in 1942, while Robbins was on tour with Ballet Theatre. The country was full of sailors and other military personages. None intrigued Robbins more than the gobs.

Fancy Free launched Robbins as a choreographer, in which calling he excelled his career as dancer. Not a strong technician, having come late to the Classic métier, he compensated in ballets like *Aleko, Bluebeard, Petrouchka,* and *Tyl Eulenspiegel* with a fine interpretive gift. He could easily have developed into a first-rate character dancer if he had chosen, but who in the audience would pine for Robbins the dancer, after Robbins the choreographer had emerged from the chrysalis? The man who might have made a fair chemist has become a talented choreographer, concocting some of the liveliest mixtures in American ballet.

Robbins' catholic education in several dance forms, his total freedom from ethnic and classical schools, and his own originality, precluded his confinement within a single genre. He used, as did Loring and de Mille before him, Classic and contemporary dance, employed natural gesture instead of the stylized ones of traditional ballet, and made frank use of jazz idioms—in this he was soon followed by his contemporary Michael Kidd—but Robbins experimented in dance forms with such good taste that his ballets are accepted as Ballet by die-hard balletomanes.

He was ably assisted in some all-American works by the music of Bernstein, Copland and Gould, and by the scenic designs of Oliver Smith. The entire collaboration was so outstandingly modern and inventive that Robbins' American ballets appear overseas as hallmarks of our native theatre.

Interplay followed *Fancy Free,* and Robbins moved at once into the popular theatre of musicals. While at Ballet Theatre he created *Facsimile,* strikingly danced by Nora Kaye in the leading role. As wide a gulf separates *Interplay* from *Facsimile* as the one that divides Robbins' *Cage* and *Pied Piper.*

Interplay, danced to the *American Concertette* by Morton Gould, against scenery by Oliver Smith, uses children's games—leapfrog, follow-the-leader, and so forth—in a rondo of dance movement ranging from Classic to contemporary American. The ballet begins to raucous music, and four boys and four girls participate in the first movement, "Free Play." The costumes by Irene Sharaff are simple tights and jerseys, with sashes. There are no footlights in the first scene and the audience first sees the dancers in frieze, silhouetted against the backdrop. Their positions create the hard, shallow impression of a poster advertisement for "jive." In "Free Play" one boy dances a solo, the others play leap-frog, and then all four join in a Variation. Ballet pirouettes and arabesques are boldly used in the jazz theme. "Horseplay" is an extension of the same theme. Some dancers sit, some stand, and an audience accustomed to the ceremony of the Classic stasis has the eery feeling that it has strayed into rehearsal hall—these charming young people lounging about stage are hardly doing a ballet! In keeping with the mood, one boy dances alone, as though practicing or improvising. He doesn't seem to be a very serious student of the ballet; his dance is full of comic undertones and he ends up on his knee before two of the girls, as though parodying the grand gesture of the *danseur* in Romantic ballet.

"By-Play" is a change of mood—romantic, but not in the accepted Classic genre; its love affair, in a *pas de deux,* is told with a torch song. Carried away by the music—obviously not by their emotion—a boy and girl dance the *pas de deux*. They are clearly motivated by the mood of the music. Impersonal (one may imagine them chewing gum) as strangers, they meet, embrace and wander in a maze of love, true to the mood of the *pas de deux*. The music stops, the dance ceases, and the partners, dissolved, resort to the childish behavior of their peers. This is a wonderful exposition of American innocence and insouciance— or, at least it is so taken by the European balletomane! Now the boy and girl "horse around." The boy pretends the girl is a wheelbarrow and propels her about the floor, on her hands, exactly as though she were. They suddenly embrace, in a clutch like a wrestling hold, then they sit down, holding hands, looking like somebody's good children.

"Team Play" is just that—the dancers divide, take sides, and each side has a captain. They go, in football parlance, into a huddle. After this, the contest begins.

One boy from each team competes to see who can do the most turns. Two girls, mounted *en pointe,* join the fun. The dancers, despite the use of classic *pointe* shoes, behave like "teen-agers." They turn cartwheels and rush about the stage, not in classical design, but as free and exhilarated as ice-skaters. For a *grande finale* the girls rush madly forward, as though to command the stage, and pose, front. The boys, instead of appearing in *danseur* positions noble and tender behind the girls, fall on their faces, slide through the legs of the standing girls and grin engagingly at the audience as though to exclaim: "See there! We made it farther front, after all!"

Facsimile, miles apart in theme from the gay *Interplay,* is held to be "American" in manners by the foreign audience, which inclines to the belief that Americans are mechanized body and soul. *Facsimile,* however, was intended to typify human boredom, as old and tired as sin. The theme is ennui.

The problem may be that of too much leisure. The ballet program informs us in the words of Auden, *Small inward treasure does he possess who, to feel alive, needs every hour the tumult of the street, the emotion of the theatre, and the small talk of society.* The creature of small inward treasure in *Facsimile* is the Woman, in which role Kaye has expressed such attrition of soul and predatoriness of sex that the little ballet itself becomes a treasure. In its way, it is better than a sermon on putting leisure to good and profitable uses.

The curtain rises on a beach, in a scene made dreary by the Woman who oc-

John Kriza and Nora Kaye in Jerome Robbins' Facsimile.

cupies it. She wears a bathing suit but obviously will not go in swimming. The music is lonely and low and expresses the emptiness inside and around the Woman. She goes into her bathing tent and amuses herself by dancing with her own shadow. By the act, she is revealed as a child. However, her movements, and the sharply etched contours of her body, remind the audience that she is a woman. A Man comes drifting into the scene. By his attitude he is as aimless as the lady in the tent, whose dancing shadow at once catches his listless eye. The lady emerges and they meet. Pavlov's animals would be more stimulated. The Man and Woman are so far removed from elementals that they have lost, with their more divine instincts, the quick sexual response. Here we have a jewel-like characterization of people of their sort: they have experienced every emotion of which they are capable, and sensation alone remains, but even that is mechanized. Like a pair of robots, they make passes, say the expected things, and knowingly proceed through all the usual angles. There is none of the rich-bodied and full-flavored flirtation of the sailors and their girls. These two are sterile, incapable of contributing or experiencing a thought or a feeling in their casual meeting.

Already bored with each other, they see another person coming along the beach. It is a second man and now the triangle is complete. The Woman revives considerably from her attack of boredom. Like litmus paper, she takes on color from the proximity of violence. Unfortunately, the second man is not quite as worldly as the pair. After a while, the rote of flirtation having been duly observed, the Woman finds that her two swains will not summon up the energy to duel for her. They indicate that she must make the choice. Reluctantly, because she hates to relinquish one in case the other is even more of a bore, the Woman chooses the second man. And now a spark ignites in the first Man. At last something occurs to which he can react with some genuine feeling. He drags the pair, the Woman and the other man, across the beach, and a kind of a fight ensues. They all three writhe about like snakes on the ground. The Woman soon has enough of this, separates herself from the groveling mass, and cries *"Stop!"*—The word is spoken with stunning effect on the startled audience.

Sheepishly, the men obey. The Woman, selfishness paramount, makes sure she has not been disarranged too much by the coarse tussle. The final "angle" is tried by the first Man. He affects wounded sensibilities and pretends that the Woman has hurt him deeply. The second man, less jaded, or more impatient, simply gives up and admits he doesn't care. They separate. The Woman, again alone, again lonely, begins to stroll aimlessly along the empty beach.

The designs for the scenery of *Interplay* and *Facsimile,* both by Oliver Smith, have one thing in common—they are stark in architecture. The feeling is something else. In many American ballets the décor is far more important than the audience realizes. *Divertissements* from classics may be viewed against anonymous backgrounds, but to separate Robbins' happy adolescents in *Interplay* from their scene, or his neurotics in *Facsimile* from theirs would be a mistake. In *Interplay* the spare, bold décor is entirely in keeping with the playfellows, granting them space uncluttered by inanimate objects. The décor, in fact, has the antiseptic air of a well ventilated day-nursery for energetic youngsters. *Facsimile's* setting is more elaborate—irregular pilings mark the shore line, and a bathing tent stands to one side—and yet it is emptier. By a mysterious means Oliver Smith has made the set in *Interplay* free to the playful tenancy of one cast of dancers, and on an open beach, contrasted with the blue enormities of sea and sky, he has confined three miserable wretches in one of the more desolate and arid corners of hell.

There is a mystery, also, in fathoming the choreographer who moves between *Interplay* and *Facsimile.* He has such keen, fresh knowledge of the people in *Interplay;* from what knowledge has he plumbed the cynicism of *Facsimile?* A creature of light and shade, Robbins embroiders his ballets with his own moods and observations. Because he is an American born and bred, the conclusion is irresistible for the balletomane: Robbins is delineating America, in the latter part of the first half of the twentieth century. As such he becomes a commentator on our society. Americans have little conception how seriously his ballets are taken, as comments, in the foreign theatre, but they may get some idea how profound they appear by noting the imitation-Robbins that appear as Modern Ballet in Europe. There he is held by many to be a greater influence than Jooss in his time. The Government, obtuse to American Ballet as a national art form, is more alive to the effect of American ballet on foreign audiences. *The New York Times* reported that *West Side Story,* a smash hit in London, was scheduled for a European tour under State Department-ANTA sponsorship but would not be sent to Moscow, on the advice of American diplomatic officials who expressed concern that the juvenile delinquents, The Jets and The Sharks, of *West Side's* "gangs" might be exploited as anti-U.S. propaganda.

Robbins served an apprenticeship as a dancer that stands him in good stead as a choreographer. Besides Petrouchka, he was Alias in *Billy the Kid,* and alternated with Laing as the Young Man in *Pillar of Fire.* He danced in Massine's *Aleko, Boutique Fantasque, Capriccio Espagnol,* and Fokine's *Carnaval* and *Russian Soldier.*

When he first went with the New York City Ballet he danced première roles in most of the ballets created for that company, and was Balanchine's Tyl with remarkable fidelity to character. His interpretation of roles in his own ballets are, like Loring's, unsurpassed. He is a fine actor but, besides his choreographic talent, his chief asset is an unrivaled theatrical intuition.

Two aspects of his ballets are immediately notable. The first is the composition, which is a masterpiece of interrelated dance, character and mood, and dynamic projection of the choreographer's intent. There is not a Robbins ballet that requires program notes for comprehension. The other distinguishing aspect is his continued use of the antic young and the most enervated and sterile of civilized peoples. This alternation (which is marked by proximity—*The Cage* and *Pied Piper* were produced in the same year) and Robbins' personality, are likely to create a legend around this youngest of the first great choreographers in American ballet.

The dark and intense young man, who is still thought of as "Jerry" by his colleagues, despite his great attainments, is the key to his ballets. At times, he seems to permit glimpses into himself; at others, he presents such varied impressions of Jerome Robbins that the general opinion about him is a potpourri of roses and thorns. He is sometimes described as a serious artist, strongly attached to his native country and theatre, and dedicated entirely to localized or contemporary themes that bear directly on America—sometimes as a young and enterprising talent who occupies a theatre made by Loring and de Mille, exploits it, but can make no move beyond it into really historic landmarks for ballet. His friends and admirers admit that he is hard to know, but insist that his preoccupation is from artistic concentration. His detractors have added up a list based on their wounded self-esteem, and declare that Robbins is hard by nature, self-centered by intent, and artistically limited. Inasmuch as he will be no more than forty-odd in the coming decade, he must be allowed one or two decades more before the account may be fairly balanced.

Meanwhile, we have the Robbins ballets, some constituting bold denials of others, a few frightening us with bogies of the modern world. He makes us fear ourselves, pity ourselves, and then chuckle at the types among us, from which he has lavishly drawn for *The Concert*. Who at the ballet has not been to Robbin's *Concert?* It is subtitled *Or The Perils of Everybody*. This is the ballet:

A typical, incongruously-assorted audience attends a concert, and we see their secret dreams and fantasies. The impression is that people are funny—hilariously, sadly so, when caught unawares. Listening to Chopin, while looking at the dancers doing so in *The Concert,* is a shattering experience and a verbal description cannot possibly convey the impact of this ballet. An audience must make up its mind, in the theatre, whether the exposure is sardonic or amusing, wicked or compassionate.

The Concert was produced by the New York City Ballet in 1956 and was revived for Robbins' 1958 touring company, Ballets: U.S.A.

Robbins has done nothing more noble and beautiful than his *Fanfare*, to Benjamin Britten's *The Young Person's Guide to the Orchestra.* The dancers are ranked in colors that identify the instruments in the orchestra—blue for woodwinds, orange for the strings, yellow for brass, black for the percussion instruments. Each dancer has an emblem of the instrument he represents embroidered on his costume; every dancer's head is crowned. At the first sight of this beautiful throng the audience is impressed with a sweet strong dignity. It is as though Music itself had massed in its ordered rank of sound. A narrator introduces the instruments: the Woodwinds appear; a Piccolo and two Flutes dance a *pas de trois.* Clarinets perform a *pas de deux.* The *soliste* Oboe dances in *adagio.* The Bassoons are a comic pair.

Now the Strings appear; the Violins, first and second, are girls. A *pas de deux* for the Violas follows. Cellos are girls, and a boy is the Bass Fiddle. The Harp is the ballerina of the piece, dressed in white. Brass and Percussions file by: horns, trumpets, tuba and trombones; drums, gongs and cymbals. All has been grand, with an unearthly beauty and sweetness. In movement, the dancers repose upon the air. Here and there, Robbins' free and irrevocable force exceeds the classic bounds, as when the Bass Fiddle boldly mimes. And with the entrance of Brass and Percussion what a wonderful unity there is between music and dance! Wonderfully we have visual and aural boom, rattle, crash and bang!

The narrator decides that the orchestra will play a fugue. He summons the Woodwinds, the Strings and the Brass. Their performance mirrors perfectly that of the orchestra in the pit, and the dancers embody all that we know and love as the sound and nature of these instruments. For a finale, the percussion returns.

The four great founts of sound in the orchestra are now grouped, and the orchestra plays Purcell's mighty *Fugue.* Before our eyes the music becomes visible. It is a most noble, a most majestic sight!

I feel slightly irritated that this ballet is called *Fanfare,* rather than *The Guide* that it is. Young persons would be admirably served, and their elders worthily employed, in observing *Fanfare* as a guide to music, and to dance. I cannot think of anything in American ballet more beautifully designed to do this for us.

Fanfare is the ballet that ardent balletomanes point to as justification for their belief that Robbins will outgrow the purely antic and topical, and turn to ballets of substance, comparable to the traditional classics. There is a consensus of opinion that he deliberately avoids classical composition because in his present company his contemporary works contrast pleasantly with Balanchine's Neoclassicism. Certainly there is already a division in the dancers of the company, some of whom prefer to dance in Robbins' "Jazz ballets." But to relegate Jerome Robbins exclusively to the métier of Jazz is to confound all that he has done and all that he gives promise of doing. Certainly his repertoire has proved that Robbins the choreographer is an erudite and perceptive person.

After turning out an inconsequential beach picnic, with mosquitoes, in *Jones Beach,* he produced *The Guests,* a ballet about intolerance. It was not the most finished of ballets but it had some moments of great feeling, as when hands touched, and its meetings and leavetakings are exceedingly interesting to note from the choreographer of *Fancy Free.* Such range of subject requires understanding of an extraordinary degree. *Age of Anxiety,* as monumental as *The Cage,* is set to Bernstein's second symphony of the same name, and both music and dance derive from *The Age of Anxiety: A Baroque Eclogue,* by W. H. Auden. Bernstein's notes describing his work state that the essential line of poem and music is the record of humanity's difficult and problematic search for faith.[2]

Robbins states that his ballet differs from the poem and the music and explains it as an episode in which four people, in search of the meaning of life, exercise their illusions in a quest for security. Presumably, the "security" is whatever the individual audience's ideal may be.

True to Auden's poem, the ballet shows the stages of man, from birth to death, in seven Variations. These follow a Prologue with a modern urban scene. The cast is made up of one girl and three men. They are strangers, and are obviously frightened people, but what their separate fears are we do not know, until they move through the stages of life, and the ages of Man.

In the first stage—*the infant, helpless in cradle*—a dancer learns to walk and talk. The second Variation is by the girl, who advances, warm and joyous, to meet the world. In the third Variation following the poem, the four adventure into love. Auden says: *With a multitude I made the long Visitor's voyage to Venus Island.* The fourth age is that of man in competition with the world and his ideals.

Grown, aware, blessed—or cursed—with wit and will, he must choose his way in the world. Between dream and reality is he deceived or does he deceive? The problem is his alone.

And in the fifth age, having chosen material things, the dancers pay the price. All that is elemental has been refused, and on schedules and timetables the human beings rawly born in the first stage become the mechanized robots of the fifth.

Man has, by now, as the poem described, jumped—*and is judged: he joins mankind.* . . .

The sixth age is the sum of the fifth and fourth. From it the life's total is resolved. The four dancers have an argument as to a choice between two fates: having come to the robot stage in the city, shall they yield to it? Or is it better to fight against it, in the hope of something better? The four split in dissension, solving nothing. A man gives up entirely, yawns, assumes a position close to the foetal one, and absolves himself from all responsibility. Gradually, hope is abandoned. With it goes even cleansing rage. In the final negation, a dancer walks out into the City as though invisible—the people who pass him by do so unseeingly, bound to their own schedules and time tables. Frantically, the man tries to reach someone—anyone. The effort deprives him of all strength. He falls. And is immediately, in a businesslike manner, toted away.

A figure crosses the stage dragging a long swatch of black crepe. The funeral emblem. The last little civilized rite. Man is dead, no longer individual.

The seventh stage brings all four dancers together again, and again they are timorous and groping. Four figures, their counterparts, appear—but these four are masked. On a dream journey, seeking happiness, the four are surrounded by other masked creatures, who imitate or mock every gesture of the four and *their* masked twins. Taking partners, the original girl and the three boys wander in a maze, lose their way and each other, and emerge wrung from a horrible dream-state into reality. Here they recognize only each other and, strangers no more, meet now as friends.

In quartet, they worship a figure designated as the All-Powerful Father. He is huge (because he is mounted on stilts) and imposing (he looks strong, but he is only tin). Thinking him a god, the crowd surrounds him but the audience will perceive that the towering figure is *carried* by his followers so that actually they support him, not he them! The tin god is overthrown when the girl, in dancing a paean, reaches out to him and he collapses, ignominiously. This ends the passage called The Dirge.

A Masque follows, during which the four, to the stimulus of jazz, in dance like jive, try to "live it up" in a colloquial *danse macabre.*[3]

In the Epilogue one man expires, the other three try to succor him. Nothing is resolved, no problem is solved, and so they part. But just before they disappear, from four opposite corners of the stage, they turn and bow to each other. Each, in the acknowledgment of the others, has given meaning to his anxious age.

The Girl in *Age of Anxiety* is one of the most powerful roles danced by Tanaquil LeClercq, who also danced the girl in *La Valse*.

Robbins is preoccupied with social conditions in *West Side Story,* which uses

Todd Bolender, Francisco Moncion, Hugh Laing and Tanaquil LeClercq in Age of Anxiety.

the New York slums and their "gangs" in a modern concept of Romeo and Juliet. Puerto Ricans and native Americans are the prototypes of the Montagues and the Capulets. He originally meant the characters to be Jewish-Catholic protagonists in New York, in 1949, but by the 'fifties the "gangs" were more apt. (The theme was used by Balanchine in the 'thirties, in a musical called *Golden Follies,* whose locale was a Manhattan East Side tenement district.) In 1958 Robbins appeared on a television discussion of the theatre and religion, in which his *West Side Story* was used as an example, with excerpts from the musical as illustration.

Between 1951 and 1953 he worked in Israel, and was instrumental in bringing the national dancers of Inbal to America, under the American Fund for Israel Institutions, in 1956.

Loring and de Mille, who have known him from his beginnings, speak fondly of him. Their affection and pride are his best criteria in the cut-throat politics of the competitive theatrical world. De Mille has gone on record as saying that Robbins has not yet begun to show his strength. The onus of love and pride that Robbins bears places on him a staggering responsibility to American ballet.

By temperament he is reserved, or shy. In appearance he is dark, slight, handsome, with a rather imperial air. His personality is striking, and he has a smile that warms the backstage world but he is also a martinet, according to the dancers who work with him. They know him for a perfectionist, and since he is a dancer of character and an actor, he fully perceives how his creations must be portrayed. Some of the less hardy souls who work with him are abashed by his fury of concentration.

His dancers are a breed got out of Loring's precedents, and they have evolved into the dancer-singer-actor type. Whereas in other musicals the dancers are the visual extensions of the singers and actors, in *West Side Story* character and performer are one. These Neo-American dancers are the most flexible instruments in Robbins theatre. Many of his contemporaries think he is the most progressive and greatest stylist in American ballet. And there is a large section of the audience that would like to keep Robbins young and antic, and let the profundities of ballet remain the prerogatives of other choreographers.

These are, in the main, the balletomanes who believe that topical and regional American ballet, as seen primarily in musicals and films, will establish the most active contemporary ballet theatre in America. They believe that on the international scene we must dance with energy and great showmanship, in the Robbins' style, with idiomatic use of Jazz and Modern forms, in order to have a recognizable American métier.

Others in the audience, unconcerned about American ballet in the foreign view, are simply prepared to relish, ad infinitum, Robbins' exuberant dance, and his light but sharp statements on the times.

He has what is defined as a "boyish" period which often dwells astringently on love. His girls are hoydenish; his lovers dance less with themselves than with shadows and mirrored reflections. He has a predilection for hand gestures, in *The Guests, The Age of Anxiety, Pied Piper,* and in *New York Export: Opus Jazz.* If not a questing hand, a yearning hand, it is a hand disembodied as in *Piper,* or in *Opus Jazz* when his dancers, in two lines, lift their arms and with spread fingers hold their hands in what a reviewer calls an "oddly ecstatic" gesture. His love affairs in *pas de deux* have a certain similarity. The participants are almost symbolic of separateness: they do not mesh, but remain strangers in the most intimate meeting, and part with no apparent grief.

Of *Pied Piper,* which has utterly nothing to do with Hamelin, the *pas de deux* to Copland's *Concerto for Clarinet and String Orchestra* has best survived. The rest now seems repetitive, because we have seen its facsimilies and imitations many times since 1951. In its première years at home and abroad it had passages almost indecent to the audience's eye. Full of horseplay, its dancers twitch as though galvanized by St. Vitus rather than jazz, and a girl rides a boy's back in what would be a *bacchanale* in Grecian draperies in a classic dance, but is fun-and-games in contemporary clothing. Other boys, possibly contemporary "wolves," lunge at the girl riding the boy, and their quality of male rapacity is suddenly turned to frivolity as they fall back, crouch and take aim with thumb and forefinger, in the ways of little boys with mock pistols.

The *pas de deux,* especially when the girl is danced by Diana Adams, is so tender and lovely that no matter how many times the ballet is seen the movement always seems to be interrupted too soon! Among the other dancers of *Piper* is a girl who holds up her arm and shakes the hand on it like a little animal; it then seems to shake with a life of its own and to possess, with its galvanic shimmy, the body of the girl.

In *Afternoon of a Faun,* which is laid inside a ballet studio, a boy in practice clothes replaces Nijinsky's sylvan one, and performs calisthenics on the floor in lieu of eating grapes on a summery hillside. The nymphae are replaced by one girl, primly practicing at the barre. The *pas de deux* is ascetic compared to Diaghilev's Arcadian production. Mallarmé's poetry and Debussy's music are evocations one of the other. The American afternoon's idyll simply deals with Boy and Girl. They have no poetic frenzy but a fine athleticism and they enjoy looking at themselves in a mirror, not in each other's eyes. They dance, keeping watch on their form in the studio mirror, and when the dance is over they part, with a little kiss on the cheek. Romance here is cool, fresh, and prettily narcissistic.

In *Opus Jazz* there is a *pas de deux* called "Passage for Two," in which Modern Dance is mingled with some of the cantilevered forms Balanchine uses. The boy squats, lays his cheek on the girl's thigh, and cantilevers her across his knees, with her empty outstretched arms reaching into the air at one end, and her wide-apart legs spanning the air at the other end. Opinions are divided on "Passage for Two": is this typical of a regional, contemporary Americana that will shortly be passé or become obtuse when removed from its locale—or is Robbins actually documenting his times, and exploring, in dance, the society of young America?[4]

Afternoon of a Faun, The Concert, and *Opus Jazz* were all seen in Ballets: U.S.A., the company Robbins formed in 1958, to appear at Gian Carlo Menotti's Festival of Two Worlds, at Spoleto, Italy. Ballets: U.S.A. was sponsored by the Catherwood Foundation and ANTA, and the company numbered sixteen dancers in Europe. There it had a tremendous success, first at the Spoleto Festival, which was primarily to bring young artists together, from Europe and America, and then at the Maggio Festival in Florence, and at the Brussels World's Fair.

On the company's return home, with the addition of two more dancers, it had such a hugely popular New York season that it was booked for a seventeen-week tour through the United States. The general audience, however, did not find it exciting and the company disbanded after its fourth week on tour, at a loss of seventy-five thousand dollars. Road companies lead a precarious existence, too often dependent on the incitement of advance publicity. The home audience's loss was the foreign theatre's gain. In 1959, sent by the State Department-ANTA Cultural Exchange Program, Ballets: U.S.A. had a four-month tour of Europe and represented American dance at the second Spoleto Festival. The company was augmented by Muriel Bentley and Michael Maule.

When Ballets: U.S.A. had its successful New York season it was part of an unofficial Jerome Robbins Festival in that city. At the same time the American Ballet Theatre was dancing *Fancy Free* at the Metropolitan, and two musicals of Robbins', *Bells Are Ringing* and *West Side Story,* were playing on Broadway.

In 1958 Robbins announced the establishment of a foundation, named for his mother, Lena Robbins, to assist young choreographers who could not otherwise produce their works. Since the greatest difficulty for the choreographer, especially as a novice, is the finding of a theatre with a stage and a trained company, the Lena Robbins Foundation will be a great boon to the profession. The foundation is destined primarily for choreographers who are not eligible for the other and larger grants offered in American Dance. It also will set up a film library and record important contemporary dance works and the contemporary interpretation of the classics. In short, it seeks to do much of what Lincoln Kirstein's Ballet Society set out to do in the 'forties.

Whether a more mature Robbins means a less profound, or a less jovial Robbins as choreographer, only the coming decades will tell. Meanwhile, American ballet looks hopefully to the "boy wonder" of the era for works even more prodigious than those he has already composed. That he feels his responsibility keenly is attested to by all who know him, friends, and less than friends. Grave or gay, he has marked the theatre with his personality. A colleague closely associated with him declares, "Jerry will resolve his career, but not in terms of 'career.' He has too much humility as an artist to think of his work by that word. He will work into his full maturity as a choreographer by a process as simple, persevering, and happy as he became a dancer. He has been called a genius and he may in time prove beyond contention that he is one. After all, the years mean precisely this—in the past he has done marvelously well. In the future nothing is likely to stop him from doing even better."

In truth, as the 'fifties come to an end, Jerome Robbins occupies the center of a boundless horizon. He is the Man of the Hour in American ballet; he may be that personage in all modern ballet! Outside the United States he strongly influences his contemporary theatre, and Roland Petit is accused of drawing heavily on Robbins' ideas and precedents.

But inspiration is the common currency in choreography, and Robbins can easily spare his influence to others, as he has been able to profit by those before him in American ballet. As the new decade of the 'sixties opens there is every evidence that Robbins and his theatre will progress into years of achievements as great as those recorded in the past.

THE SCHOOLS

In ballet, the "school" is not the place where a dancer attends classes as a student. It is the system of teaching under which he is trained to dance. Traditionally, all Classic Dance schools are founded on the *danse d'école*, and have a standard vocabulary. But variations occur in almost every school and these differences, major and minor, can be seen in the performances. It is tacitly accepted, by the international ballet professional and the audience, that there is a "school" of the East, and a "school" of the West.

The "Eastern" or "Slavic school" employs a system of training practiced by Russian ballet and by the ballet theatres influenced by Russia, such as the present Polish ballet.

The "school" of the West embraces every other national theatre. And large indeed is the embrace. Tolerant and eclectic, it reaches from the fount of the *danse d'école* to the Neo-Spanish ballet, and includes the Danish ballet after Bournonville, the Franco-Russe style, and the English ballet derived from the Imperial Russian ballet. It contains the American ballet. Beyond these acquired and stylized forms it embraces the indigenous classicism of the Basques whose national dancing has provided movements assimilated by ballet. *Pas de basque,* in its many variations, is, literally, the "step of the Basque." This occurs in many variations in ballet, and by a mysterious process of absorption appears in the third act of the classic ballet *Le Lac des Cygnes,* executed by Odile at the end of her solo.

In France, Denmark, England, Russia, and the other great nations that support ballet theatres, there is a standard of teaching, and a uniform style, or national "school." In American ballet we have no standards except those set by various teachers and companies, which are of course separate and private enterprises. In competition, several large and successful teaching establishments in the United States of America claim to have specialities of teaching. For example, the ballet school of the Metropolitan Opera Company in New York advertises itself as the "Only school of its kind in the U.S.A." It is under the direction of Antony Tudor. Another school, established at the Metropolitan Opera House Studio, is titled "School of Russian American Ballet," and is directed by Boris Novikoff.

These are just two of innumerable schools in the United States, all autonomous, except for schools designated as branches of a main one, such as those in Denver, Oklahoma City, Cleveland and Indianapolis, affiliated with the New York school of the American Ballet Theatre.

This sort of education for the professional dancer in American ballet is one that American dancers take for granted. It confuses the student from abroad just as the international "school" system of ballet might surprise Americans. English ballet is closest in age and theatre to ours, so it is useful to observe the "school" of the British dance in contrast with our own.

The school attached to the Royal Ballet comes under its jurisdiction but there are innumerable other British schools established as free and private enterprises, like ours. The difference is that the standard of teaching is uniform as defined by the Royal Academy of Dancing. Established in 1920, it maintains a standard of excellence in operatic or theatrical dance throughout Great Britain and the Commonwealth, and its business is to conduct examinations (which it does, all over the world), award scholarships, and proffer lectures, demonstrations, classes and conferences to its members. Graduates are entitled to use the letters A.R.A.D. after their names. The R.A.D. has a residential Teachers' Training College, which awards diplomas (L.R.A.D.) and grants scholarships. The scholarships go in four Overseas divisions to South Africa, New Zealand and (two) to Australia. Among other awards are the *Pavlova Casket,* the *Plender Cup,* and a scholarship to the school of the Royal Ballet. Independent of R.A.D. but closely associated with it is the Imperial Society of Teachers of Dancing, whose system of examinations has furthered the excellence of theatrical dance throughout the British Empire. The Society also grants awards for children's choreography and holds annual dance competitions, limited to students under twelve. The Imperial Society of Teachers was originally established in 1904 and in 1924 incorporated the Cecchetti Society, founded in London in 1922 by Cyril W. Beaumont.

Among the most important of the free and private enterprises, as distinguished from the government-subsidized school or the Royal Ballet, is the Arts Educational School, which gives students a complex training not only in dancing and the arts and crafts of the ballet, but a general academic training which includes vocational subjects. Its premise, of course, is that a general education furthers the student in the vocational education of ballet. The A.E.S. has three divisions —a Junior, Middle and Senior School—and it is co-educational. Students are admitted at the age of eight, and after four years of training appear in performances, not as professionals but as part of their student education. This is in certain ways similar to what is done by the Christensens at the San Francisco Ballet.

American ballet has no official national ballet company, and no established "school," but has organized, of its free will, certain standards of training for teachers of dancing. These groups, autonomous and self-directed, with their varying principles and directives, include the American Society of Teachers of Dancing, Inc., Cecchetti Council of America, Inc., Chicago Association of Dancing Masters, Inc., Dance Educators of America, Inc., Dance Masters of America, Inc., National Academy of Ballet, Inc., National Association of Dance and Affiliated Arts, Inc., and the Texas Association of Teachers of Dancing.

The American groups teach all forms of dancing, but the English schools, excepting the Imperial Society, are exclusively concerned with "operatic dance."

The teaching in American ballet is not by an official "school" but by a network of teachers in schools, some attached to companies or performing organizations, most of them subsisting on a round of daily or weekly classes, without stage privilege in a theatre or any performance outlet for their student body except an annual "recital."

Most of the latter schools do nothing except instruct students in the exercise of ballet positions, movements, and the rest of the standard vocabulary, and—usually for "recital" purposes—teach them routines or rehearse them in excerpts from ballets. For the past two decades Americans have "taken ballet lessons," either by going to a daily, weekly, or bi-weekly studio class, or by being collected by itinerant teachers commuting from one region to the other. Even in large, established, successful schools, where the training in the classroom exercise of ballet is of good caliber, student education in the ballet as an art form is seldom included. "Taking ballet" is a rather different matter from studying for the ballet.

The first attempt to establish a university education—with the standards of a university—for American ballet was made with Denishawn, and is continued by Shawn in summer session at the Jacob's Pillow Dance Festival, whose Silver Jubilee year was 1957. Since then, with the increased prestige of ballet in the theatre and in the audience's estimation, other and extraordinary developments have been made such as the department at the University of Utah under William Christensen. Modern Dance and a great deal of folk dancing is included in the curriculum of many American universities and is taught in the colleges and high schools. Nevertheless, the general attitude toward ballet is that a dancer must "learn how to dance," master the difficult and complex science, and thereafter enter a company or join a group, where he is related to, but not an integral part of, the other arts and all the crafts of the ballet.

In state-supported ballet, of the variety accepted as "national ballet," there is an annual or seasonal candidacy, where judicious choice is made by trained teachers and anatomic experts. Just as the national company's dancers are salaried and pensioned, occupying the rank of civil servants to the government, so are the students uniformed and disciplined in the cadet corps regime. For an understanding of what this would signify in America, we may imagine a facsimile of a West Point, an Annapolis, or an Air Force Academy, set up as the American National Academy of Dance. There the candidates would be subject to medical and scholastic entrance examinations, would proceed through their study by grade, graduate by protocol, and be integrated into the profession for which they had received a long, explicit and diversified training by experts and pedagogues.

In lieu of a national academy of dancing we have recognized an academic standard of training for ballet that is essentially the practice of the Imperial Russian Ballet—the same style that our English cousins have incorporated into the "school" of English Ballet. This is the basis of the Franco-Russe academic ballet, with subtle differences in physical characteristics and in artistic interpretation, and it has begun, under Volkova of the twentieth-century Russian ballet, to permeate the antique form of the Bournonville System in the Royal Danish Ballet.[1]

The three major companies in the United States have schools designated by their executive boards as "official." All are in New York City. They are the School of American Ballet, the official school of the New York City Ballet, the School of Ballet of the Ballet Russe de Monte Carlo, and the Ballet Theatre School of the American Ballet Theatre. The rosters of the schools' faculties are indicative of the teaching that has produced American ballet's many-faceted style.

The School of American Ballet has been used in this book as an example of the Classic teaching, and its faculty has been named. At the Ballet Russe school teachers include Edward Caton, Leon Danielian, Casimir Kokitch, Maria Swoboda, Anatole Vilzak, and Frederic Franklin. The Ballet Theatre School, directed by Lucia Chase, offers classes in jazz by Matt Mattox, and employs as teachers William Dollar, Yurek Lazowski, Valentina Pereyaslavec, Ludmilla Shollar, and Anna Youskevitch. These teachers, and their contemporaries on faculties of major schools in America, are the link with the European and Russian heritages from which we have drawn the American ballet. The second-generation scions of that inheritance are, even now, dispersed about the world, dancing or teaching and impressing their own influences on the international scene. Some of the influence stays at home, to more graphically delineate American ballet.[2]

Of special consequence in the training of dancers is a school like Ballet Arts, Carnegie Hall, New York, whose faculty list indicates the variety of dance education to be drawn on by the student. The teachers include Agnes de Mille, Vladimir Dokoudovsky, Gemze de Lappe, Vladimir Konstantinov, Vera Nemtchinova, Yeichi Nimura, Dorita Ortiz, James Starbuck, and Nina Stroganova. Combined, they constitute a symposium of dance, from American to Oriental, from Jazz to Classic.

It is impossible to briefly indicate, far less to properly catalogue, the independent teachers and schools of dance in the United States of America. Some of them choose to teach in only one genre; the majority teach in several. The most remarkable aspect of the teaching in American ballet is its position of respectability in liberal arts schools. Butler University in Indiana, for instance, combines a liberal arts education with professional training for ballet, and offers a college major in dance. To appreciate this, one must remember the time (described in this book in *The Beginning*) when the dance was derelict of honor and the dancers, except for the notorious "stars," were "the disgusting rabble" of the *corps*.

It is not so long ago that Jacob's Pillow was about to be seized by the town of Becket for unpaid taxes, that civic power refusing to consider the Pillow as an educational institution and taxing it as a dance hall. By the end of the 'forties the Pillow was granted tax exemption, recognized by the United States Treasury and the Commonwealth of Massachusetts. Now, in affiliation with Springfield College, the Pillow's summer school courses are credited on graduate and undergraduate student levels. A history of the national dance, in the proverbial nutshell.

Nowhere, at any time in ballet history, have there been so many students, both boys and girls, and in no country are there more dance students now than in the United States of America. Until now, American technicians have been mostly women, and the American product is easily recognized in the international theatre. She is noted for extraordinarily long and gifted legs and for her unusually lovely face. This prettiness of feature is sometimes made alarmingly uniform by a predilection among juvenile *danseuses* for bobbing their noses and thus effecting the stereotyped profile dictated by Hollywood and fashion magazines. Our natural characteristics of physique have inspired American choreographers in the ballets: a very long, high extension and a strong, clean *pirouette* are two of our splendid hallmarks in the Classic genre. Our natural sense of syncopation has apparently influenced the dance tempo, even beyond the dance interpretation of American ballet music. This is strikingly evident in the works of choreographers who use dance as a counterpoint to music, or who have invented distinct dance tempos. These American aptitudes and attitudes have helped to form an "American dancer."

THE TEACHING

Of course the training, or teaching, of the dancer is the foundation of the dance. In American ballet, as in all others, Classic Dance is the basis of technique and choreography. In training and in performance, ballet has an international vocabulary, governed by rules that are universal to this art form. The strictest law is that of the Turnout, the peculiar stance in which the dancer's knees are turned out from the hip at an angle of ninety degrees. The feet are then set in a straight line, in Positions One to Five, and the ballet Positions and some of the corresponding *ports de bras* are copied from the stance and gestures of fencing. At its inception the art of ballet was developed on men, courtiers of the French royal houses, and the ideal is impeccable form, or "line," superb control in stasis and *adage,* and brilliant speed and effortless strength in *allegro*. These, in a standard of performance universally accepted as perfection, are the "technical" attributes of the Classic Dance. "Interpretation" is described by one school of thought as "feeling" or "expression" in dance, and by another—strictly adhering to the austere beauty of the Classic Dance—as the dancer's personal thought, while dancing to choreographic command.

The Turnout is neither natural nor easy to perform, and the Positions are acquired only after study and practice. These basic Positions involve a great deal of time and work for the student, and are the established points of artistic perfection for the professional dancer. The ability to leap prodigiously into the air, to cover a lot of ground at top speed, or to dance or leap about on the tips of the toes are by no means the basic aspects of the art of ballet. A large number of healthy children do these things in play, and some exuberant adults have the strength and energy to perform similar feats. When the student begins the study of ballet he undertakes a slow, arduous, scrupulous and demanding task, whose exercises have been for almost four hundred years used in developing the untrained body into *the dancer*. There are no short cuts and, however dedicated the student, there are physical and mental impositions that forever "type" him as the dancer. Beyond the physical aspect, the capacities and limitations of the dancer are ruled by psychological involvements. These factors govern the dancer's timing and projection, and the actual interpretation or expression of his dancing. Schooled in an implicit obedience to the choreographer, the dancer still creates with his animate self the artistic and the emotional movement that is dance. This is where dancing differs from sports and athletics, and unless the audience in the theatre or the reader of the book about ballet understands the difference, the point—the very essence—of dance is lost.

But the dancer's understanding of his profession, or vocation, comes first and it is as much the business of the teacher to impart a knowledge of the property of dance as mankind's first true art as it is his duty to explain the Positions One to Five, in the seven definitions of movements: *élancer, étendre, fouetter, glisser, plier, sauter et tourner*. Next comes the teacher-and-student investigation of the physical capacity and limitation of the student. Very often, this types, to a great extent, the kind, or character, of dancer that the student may hope to become. Some dancers, with almost superhuman will (and often with physical exercises prescribed by anatomical specialists in ballet) achieve physical developments, as when a ballerina, for example, adds, literally, an inch or more to her neck for the approved long and willowy look.

Fat, as such, is not a problem to the serious and sensible dancer, but muscular development can be, and bone structure. There is an esthetically standard ballet dancer—well-proportioned, with a neatly placed head, and a natural air of meticulous lightness. In the "ballerina" the type is associated traditionally with a look of deceptive fragility, and an almost spiritual beauty—a beauty dependent not on facial contour, but on the kindled spirit of the dancer. The ballerina is not anything so simple as a female dancer performing traditional "ballerina roles," but a woman dancer of mature artistry. Dancer and woman both make the ballerina.

In ballerina roles there is an enormous degree of technical skill, requiring physical strength not in keeping with the ballerina's deceptive fragility. She is, by tradition, *sur les pointes,* and must assume this deliberately unnatural pose as though her *pointes* were the normal extension of her human foot. If she is lucky, she has a naturally sturdy point to her foot, with all the toes approximately the same length.

The pretty little foot, with tiny ankles, delicate attenuated toes, and a lovely swelling arch, is not always the strong, sound foot for the dancer. When a great ballerina has such a foot her choreographer adjusts the ballets to her style and type. Fonteyn, for instance, is matchless in Ashton's superb "lifts," where her miraculously pure, singing "line" is shown. It would be folly to set the great lyric ballerina on tiptoe for the sheer purpose of whirling and leaping about *sur les pointes,* as seems often to be done with the virtuoso Tallchief, who has *pointes* of steel that cut designs as sharp and glittering as diamonds. The differences in dancers are those subtle differences in jewels—one is a diamond, another a pearl.

About once in a generation a first-rate "all round" ballerina emerges. This is the dancer who can dance any role of ballerina caliber. Most dancers are typed by character, physique, style, temperament, and all the flesh-and-blood and mental involvements that compose the human being, while dancing. The flesh-and-blood characteristics, such as a dancer's pretty hips—making her small, narrow, unobtrusive in her "line"—irrevocably govern the dancer's style and forte. The dancer with the pretty hips encounters difficulty in achieving the perfect Turn-out, and she may never attain the strength she requires in *adage,* especially in long, high *arabesque.* Since "line" is the esthetic motive, and the *arabesque* the most beautiful of poses, the symbol of sustained and arrested flight, this predicament of physique is one that many female dancers futilely strive to overcome. When, in contrast, the dancer has extraordinarily strong hips and back there may be a physically poor line. If the dancer has indulged in strenuous sports, or perhaps played an instrument for many years, a palpable defect spoils the line. One gifted dancer, who studied the French horn while a dance student, developed such a large rib cage that the protruding ribs ruined her shape for ballet.

There is a fallacious idea that a child with a physical abnormality will remedy the defect by studying ballet. Very often, the disability is made greater, or another one added. The study of ballet is not one to be lightly undertaken by a child, or easily assumed as a profession. Only the trained teacher can understand these things and, in his professional integrity, follow all the teaching precepts.

The role of the teacher in ballet remains paramount. He is the link between the past and future, and the students are the preparation for the present history of dancing. The best teachers try not to impose their personal emotions and physical characteristics on dancers, but almost always fail in this attempt, since their energy and skill are the forces that transform the dancers bodily into the plastic words of dancing. When a great teacher is also a great choreographer he literally turns out his own breed of dancers. This Svengali relationship is always recognizable in the Classic Dance and very often among the Moderns, for all the vaunted "freedom" of expression that the latter genre proclaims. Agnes de Mille has noted that her dancers start off with the right foot, because she is right-footed and right-legged. Martha Graham kicked her left leg, spectacularly, straight up at an angle of one hundred and eighty degrees, and made the personal idiosyncrasy a style for her pupils. And the dancers turned out under George Balanchine, from the School of American Ballet, have the high chest, straight back, and proud deportment of the Imperial Russian ballet artists, with a characteristic tightness in the arm socket. Line is the forte of all the classicists, and while someone like Balanchine develops his genre in spectacular *allegro,* a teacher such as Vecheslav Swoboda developed magnificent *adagio* properties in many of his pupils including the ballerina Gertrude Tyven. In subtle emphasis the teaching develops marked styles, some quick and sharp, others soft and opulent.

Over a period of twenty-five years or so, teaching has bred the recognized American dancer. He evinces, roughly, two characteristic strains—the American Classic, and the American Freestyle. The styles do not contradict each other, and often, in the merged training of the individual dancer, complement each other.

Separately, the styles are the subject of controversy among balletomanes and modernists, and until recently the dancers developed prejudices against all other genres but their own.

Economic pressure, rather than persuasive education in democracy, has destroyed this infantile prejudice. Hollywood is not altogether undeserving of its maligned character, nor does television scrupulously produce dance in its proper spirit and sphere, but these two mammoth entertainment industries, plus the requirements of the American "musical" theatre, have caused the most precious of the dancers to eschew their private snobberies. Simply in order to survive, the American professional has become a jack-of-all-genres in dance. It is a happy dancer who has a "specialty," bred out of a dynamic personality and an extraordinary gift or ability, that can be projected in the enormously broadened theatre of ballet: musicals, movies and television. But the sheer necessity of earning a living, of drawing a regular salary, has driven the contemporary dancer to accept and to practice a comprehensive dance métier. Out of necessity, American ballet teaching has resourcefully invented formulae that, in a single school, qualifies a student dancer as the "American Professional Dancer." It is of special note that the best and the biggest of these schools have established the Classic regimen as the discipline of classroom exercise. Some, still stubbornly teetering on the brink, protest that a Classic training is nullified by training in a Modern school, or that both genres, Classic and Modern, adversely affect the style and good form of ballroom dancing, in its theatrical presentation. This contention has become less topical recently in the dance periodicals, and when it rises it is castigated with some saber blows from the right and left—by both classicists and modernists. As this twain has met in some particularly stimulating ballets, and yet its component parts are now more than ever distinguishable in the theatre, we may assume that any form is possible in American ballet!

While the half-hearted "feints" and "parries" desultorily make press "salutes," theatrical professionals are engaged in more serious business, like that of getting an education. Whereas a dance education is subsidized by national ballet in other nations, the American dancer must earn his for himself.

The cost, providentially, is ridiculously cheap. I know of first-rate low-cost instructors in ballet who are not only well trained and suited to teaching (the latter a vital point in the teaching of ballet) but who continue the onerous business of a semi-professional career. These people do not teach a student for two dollars or so an hour out of the determination to become rich; they do it—never realizing their altruism—out of a feeling of duty to their profession, and an ever-growing exasperation over the waste and the want in American ballet. There are experts in ballet, in our so-called materialistic and competitive United States, who work themselves to a point of physical exhaustion, and past the stage of patience with the times, literally giving themselves to preserve the ballet in America. Unfocused, autonomous, restless and largely obscure, these teachers have no central organization, no national significance, and only some localized advantages for the American ballet theatre. When we realize that more than half the great dancers of the past generation have been absorbed into American ballet, from Pierre Vladimiroff, Diaghilev's *premier danseur* and a partner of Pavlova, down to under-studies—among them Nijinsky's, now a teacher in Florida—we may readily under-stand why the American technician has become the marvelous instrument he is. The only wonder is the lack of concern and of organization in this best-of-organized nations. With some executive guidance, the concentrated teaching profession in America would undoubtedly produce an academic standard beyond all that we have yet attained, perhaps comparable to the best known in the centuries-old history of the ballet.

The remarkable student of the ballet in America is the most enthusiastic student in the world although he studies a profession only now beginning to have social prestige, in which there is still the most impoverished of economies, and no national academic or theatrical recognition. If he became a dancer in Denmark he should be of the highest consequence. In Russia, I am informed, his prestige would rival and in some instances surpass that of the scientist. In England he would be assured of his teacher's qualifications, and he could obtain an integrated dance education. In France his status would be enhanced by his attachment to the Modern school which has produced the *enfant prodige* of the controversial Charrat-Petit caliber—or by his position as a *petit rat* in the *Académie*. [3] Here, there are six divisions of boys and girls, uniformed, segregated and, according to tradition, "persecuted for their own good by their betters." The girls wear hair ribbons of dark and light blue, pink, yellow and white, as though these were badges of extraordinary merit. They are, in fact, novices in ballet, and so attach to their vocation and to themselves a dignity beyond anything yet accruing to the American student. Money could not purchase the equivalent of this status, and it is worth examining, because it remains, in the graduate dancer, part of the bred-in-the-bone training for ballet. To explain the difference between the school traditions of American students and all other students of ballet in the national theatres, I quote the opinion of a French child studying for a year in the United States: "Here there is much trainment, of varieties. Here the dancer is free, but he is not sure. Here there are stages for dancing, but not yet *le théâtre*. And here a student and a dancer is without *helix*." By "helix" the child means "place"—that high place that is one's own, and like no other's.

Homeless as the American student is in the international *hiérarchie*, he is possibly the most accomplished and certainly the most facile of his contemporaries. Indignantly refuting the necessity for anything like a "school tradition," many of the Americans have told me that our dancers jump higher and turn faster than any other dancers, except possibly the Russians—and anyway, a Balanchine dancer has better Positions. Incontestably, our girls jump like boys and our boys jump like giant cats, and we have a meticulously placed and steel-strong Position. Praiseworthily, we dance almost as we danced in the 'forties, for something close to joy, with something amounting to passion. These are attributes the American brings to the ballet. Choreographers in this, as in every age, are not easily come by, but American dancers in ballet are of a uniform grade—topnotch. A study of the process of training proves that (and in a time when the young are glibly vilified for being indolent and undisciplined) very young boys, and girls who are still children, willingly undertake the vocational instruction in ballet which requires patience, pride, and a fervency and discipline awesome for a layman to contemplate. The student dancer must give up all the frivolities of contemporary society. He begins to observe a regime that he knows will never get easier: it will always get harder, with sterner demands and more responsibilities, demanding a kind of devotion comparable to the strictures of ancient chivalry.

Inasmuch as American ballet students have no national "school" to which to give their allegiance, they nourish crushes on a variety of systems, each belligerently supporting one genre as the best and the only legitimate one for American ballet. The reliance on a "tradition," which is essential for the novice and almost always supports the graduate, makes a dancer prone to *isms*. Among the classicists a state of mind prevails frequently called *balanchinage,* which is to George Balanchine's credit and demonstrates his position *par excellence* in the American Classic métier. After observing student attitudes and complexes for the past sixteen years I find that the least prejudiced are the Freestyle dancers, who employ all forms of dance as educational or theatrical styles, but do not rigidly align themselves in one genre. The Freestyle is becoming the rule rather than the exception for American ballet. Even in the classicism of the New York City Ballet, Robbins' works demand a comprehensive dance skill. In the school that most closely approximates a dance university, Loring's American School of Dance, the Classic genre is still the absolute basis for the dance discipline, and the student begins with the Turnout and Positions just as he has always done in traditional ballet classroom exercise. Yet such is the eclectic nature of American ballet, and the influence it exerts on training, that Anna Sokolow, the American Modern, has held classes at the School of American Ballet—while *prima ballerina* Danilova, and the English lyric *prima ballerina* Beryl Grey, have been guest teachers at the American School of Dance.

By coincidence, these two schools stand physically at opposite points of the compass—the School of American Ballet in New York, and the American School of Dance in Hollywood. I have chosen to describe them as examples of training because I have firsthand knowledge of their practices and the principles of their theories. My choice is of necessity limited to only these two schools, but in no way disparages the contributions of all the other excellent schools of dance in the United States, although the two schools I discuss in detail are, in my opinion, unsurpassed in their special genres and the most significant examples of the Classic and the Freestyle training.

THE SCHOOL OF AMERICAN BALLET

The School of American Ballet—known as "Balanchine's school"—was first established in Connecticut, but the location was found impracticable and it was moved to New York. By an amusing coincidence this most strict and austere of traditional schools was for a time housed in the old Isadora Duncan studio—that fount of Free Dance and rebellion against "tights" and "toe shoes." This school is as near as we have approached to the St. Petersburg ideal of training for the ballet. The chief difference is that the School prescribes for the students only in classes, and does not give an integrated education in general subjects and in the whole science and art of dancing. This is still a felt want, as has been discussed, and contributes to a pernicious anemia in American ballet.

The background of the School's teachers is the best indication of the School's tradition. Balanchine's own education in dance is illustrative of the heritage of ballet that has been transfused into the western theatre.

Teachers in the Imperial Schools occupied positions of honor and importance. The student came under a jurisdiction as strict and detailed as that of a religious novice. Boys were uniformed like cadets, except that they wore the lyre as insignia on the tunic collar and cap. Girls wore dresses of different colors that indicated their graded ranks. They lived—sleeping, eating, and studying—like votaries in secular form and actually had almost monastic and convent existences. Some of the children came from homes of wealth, where they had been waited on by maids and footmen, but at the Imperial Schools the ballet alone was royal, and all else served it, especially its noviciates. Ballet classes began in the morning and continued until luncheon; in the afternoon until four there were studies in the subjects that constituted "a general education." The subjects included religion, languages, music, singing, drawing, design, and fencing. Before the early supper juniors took a dancing lesson from a senior student, similar to the *petite mère* to whom a *petit rat* at the Paris Opéra attached herself. The ballet "godmothers," and their facsimiles among the boys, conscientiously watched over the students' progress.

The regimen never became slacker—it only grew more demanding. When the students reached senior grade they no longer went home for holidays but attended a kind of summer ballet camp. Here the girls were taught to sew and were allowed, as recreation, to read good books and to go on rambles in the woods.

The students, Balanchine included, were invariably as miserable as only the young are under strict discipline. All the "old ones" to whom I have talked seemed to have been thrust into the ballet and they went in kicking, scratching and bawling, in futile rebellion. A few wondrous creatures of burning inspiration, like Pavlova, approached the ballet as an altar to serve. The rule was, I have been told in so many words, that the students felt themselves to be martyred and the *barre* to be the rack. The whole of the first year was spent in mutiny and anguish.

Having been persecuted for a year, they found that all their misery would, if they had shown qualities of value to the ballet, entitle them to the honor of enduring more of the same. By the mysterious chemistry of the young human animal, the second year student at once believed himself a personage and looked with polite pity on his fellows who had been disqualified. The trial period passed —something like a test in the Age of Chivalry—the students assumed the suave demeanor of the aristocrat: they had by then become indoctrinated in the ballet. This meant that they had begun to master the formula of performance and the perception of the art, and they were now prepared to believe themselves the best of a theatre where their art is the oldest—so old that it is older than man himself.[4]

The core that nourished the ballet for the students was the theatre. They were a part of the Maryinsky, school and company, and passed into the Imperial Ballet after graduating from the Imperial School. Often the first entrance into the theatre was a simultaneous birth and baptism for the dancer. A candidate to the Russian school, then and now, might be a protesting child who passed a medical examination and went on trial for a year. Thereafter he was sorted like a pea, for size, color and substance, to define the character in which he could best serve the ballet. In the tuition of experts, savants not of theories but of practices in dance training and performance, the student matured into the dancer.

This is the training that existed under the czarist regime, and it produced artists like the teachers at the School of American Ballet: George Balanchine, Felia Doubrovska, Anatole Oboukoff, and Pierre Vladimiroff. It produced Pavlova, under whom another of the teachers, Muriel Stuart, was educated.

This is the training, in substance, that still is followed for Soviet ballet. It has produced the best known Russian ballerina of the West, Violetta Prokhorova, and two of the junior teachers of the School of American Ballet, Helene Dudin and Antonina Tumkovsky. Under precepts of this training were produced the spectacular Hungarian *pas de deux* specialists Kovach and Rabovsky, and the recent Polish emigrants Edmund Novak and Irina Kowalska.

I feel that it is more profitable to describe the system that bred the teachers than to attempt a technical analysis of the dance taught. Here we shall sketch a portrait of the Imperial system rather than hold an autopsy. American ballet is founded on that system of classicism and although we may move far and fast from it, it remains the basis of our ballet theatre. We have built on enduring materials, as we may see by the evidences of longevity and fire in the Russian emigrés themselves.

Alexandra Danilova has charted for me the graduate Choreographic Technicians of Leningrad. The female dancers were Alexandra Danilova, Maria Semenova, and Galina Ulanova. The male dancers were George Balanchine, Vachtang Chaboukiani, and Alexei Yermolayeff. With the exchange of visits between Russian and American artists the significance of this becomes clear even to the non-balletomane. Only Balanchine and Danilova left Russia for the West. Only American Ballet now possesses Balanchine and Danilova. There is hardly a theatregoer who does not recognize that Ulanova stands for the epitome of Russian dance. Chaboukiani became the greatest *danseur* in the Soviet Union, was twice the recipient of the Stalin Prize, is a choreographer, and directs the Ballet at Tiflis. Semenova was long considered the greatest classicist in Soviet ballet and was made an Honored Artist of the Republic. Yermolayeff was three times the recipient of the Stalin Prize, and is titled People's Artist R.S.F.S.R.

The modern ballet classicist is a product of three contributory styles, the French, the Italian and the Scandinavian, confluent in the Imperial Russian ballet. The American student taught by Balanchine and his contemporaries is a lineal descendant of the centuries-old tradition, and as dancer and teacher eventually makes himself one with it.

The teachers Doubrovska and Vladimiroff (who are married to each other) were Diaghilev dancers of note. Doubrovska is remembered in London for her roles in *The Sleeping Princess* of the 'twenties, as the Fairy of the Woodland Glades and Florisse in the *Bluebird* Variation. As a dancer, she was light, buoyant, with a special feathery quality of her *pointes*. She was a *soliste* at the Maryinsky, and in Diaghilev's company created a number of roles in ballets by Nijinska and Balanchine. In 1938–1939 she was the ballerina of the Metropolitan in New York, under Boris Romanoff. Doubrovska is noted for her classes in *pointe* work, and has been on the faculty since 1948.

Vladimiroff was the successor to Nijinsky as *premier danseur* of the Maryinsky. He later joined Diaghilev as a soloist and was the *premier danseur* of the opulent London *Sleeping Beauty*. Pavlova's favorite partner, he toured with her, and was the partner of Karsavina. His aplomb and deportment are aristocratic, and he specializes in men's classes, and in exercises in elevation. In bearing, he is the model of the *danseur*. The *danseur* in *pas de deux* is not an exhibitionist bent chiefly on proving that dancing is a man's game; he is the epitome of all the profoundly masculine qualities established as masculine virtues in real life. The *danseur* must impart nobility to his role, and appear as a strong male in attitudes tender, passionate, courteous, and sweet, toward the lady with whom he is dancing. In this deportment more than in the Turnout, he becomes the *danseur,* as separate from—although not always contrary to—the male dancer of Modern and Ethnic dance. A *danseur noble* is the Male Lover, idealized, and as such, hardly mortal. Vladimiroff has been imparting the art of this delicate, difficult and demanding role to male students at the School since 1934.

After Vladimiroff left the Maryinsky his place was taken by Anatole Oboukoff, who joined Blum in 1935 and Diaghilev in 1939. He married Nemtchinova and organized and danced with the Nemtchinova-Dolin Ballet in the late 'thirties. He came to America in 1940, and has been for several years on the faculty of the School. With Vladimiroff he has taught innumerable American dancers, including Christensen, Dollar, and Loring.

The English Muriel Stuart was taken into Ivy House by Pavlova at the age of eight and studied under Ivan Clustine and Cecchetti. She was also a student of Uday Shankar, who produced *Radha-Krishna* for Pavlova and taught in her company. In America, Stuart was the pupil of Martha Graham and Carmalita Maracci, and studied dance composition with Louis Horst. She had a more versatile training than most of her contemporaries in the classical tradition and danced in Pavlova's company from 1916 to 1926. In 1925 Pavlova commissioned a ballet for her protégée, *Ballet Schubertiana.*

In 1926 Stuart moved to San Francisco and founded a school; in 1930 she was *maîtresse de ballet* for the Chicago Civic Opera and staged *Faust, Thaïs* and *Judith.* She taught in Los Angeles from 1931 to 1934, when she joined the School of American Ballet. She has long exerted her particularly mellifluous influence on American dancers including those in her summer classes at Jacob's Pillow, and she has written a textbook, *The Classic Ballet,* that is widely used. The faculty is typical of the peculiar poetry of teaching in the ballet. In appearance outside the classroom, Balanchine, Doubrovska, Vladimiroff, Oboukoff and Stuart are like any persons of their generation, except that they walk and stand with considerably more ease and dignity—but once in their own environment, in the classroom where they rule, they become ballet's legendary force, the battery that, behind the scenes, sparks the dynamic performance onstage. Here, in its elemental strength, is The Ballet.

Dudina and Tumkovska are graduates of the State Choreographic School at Kiev, and Tumkovska studied post-graduate under Vaganova at the Leningrad State School. Their promising careers were interrupted by the Axis forces in World War II, but they survived and came to America, where Tumkovska joined the School of American Ballet in 1949. She had been a *soliste* in Russia, dancing at the Kiev State Opera, the Bolshoi and the Maryinsky. Dudina was the *première soliste* of the Kiev theatre, and also danced at the Bolshoi and the Maryinsky. She appeared later in Germany, Austria and France, as Solskaya, before her marriage. In 1952 she was the *première danseuse* of the New York City Opera, and joined the School's faculty in 1954. As products of the current Russian ballet system Tumkovska and Dudina have inherited the tradition of the Imperial Russian Ballet.

The curriculum of the School of American Ballet is administered by Balanchine as Chairman of the Faculty. The School is a non-profit educational institution administered by Kirstein as Director, and Eugenie Ouroussow as Executive Director. It is a large school, serving both its registered pupils and the peripatetic professionals, and is the official classroom for dancers of the New York City Ballet. Regular classes are conducted all the year round and in summer, beginning in July, there is a special six-week session for professional teachers and out-of-town students. At this time there is usually a heavy enrollment of professionals in recess from companies.

In 1959, the School celebrated its silver jubilee, and the occasion was marked by a memorial exhibit and lectures at the New York Public Library. In its second quarter-century the School's principles remain those of its founding: it is an academic classroom for the ballet—not a dance studio of the average genre in the United States. The student is expected to be a serious one, and the School does not enroll those who want to dance as therapy for obesity or physical malformation. There are separate divisions for adults and children. The Children's Division was begun under the late Kyra Blanc, and a full year's scholarship is awarded in her honor at the end of a school year. The admission age for children is eight, and the program, begun each October, is relegated into four divisions. Third and Fourth Division students participate in the graded courses in Labanotation, under the tutelage of Ann Hutchinson.

The regular courses at the School are Academic Ballet, Toe, Men's Classes, Adagio, Variations, and Labanotation, and they are divided into nine graded classes, called Divisions, which separate students not only according to age, or

George Balanchine in 1947 teaching a children's class at the School of American Ballet. The boy is Edward Villella, who joined the New York City Ballet in 1957.

physical development, but also according to aptitude. The division for beginners teaches the correct placement of the dancer's body in ballet. In the Intermediate Division the complex ballet movements, in quickened tempo, are mastered, and in the Advanced Division technical demands are increased and the *enchainements* become more fluent and of longer passages. A fourth division is designated as Professional, and here the stress is laid on virtuosity, brilliance and style. This division consists of professional dancers, and includes the senior graduates of the School.

The student requirements are strict. Following a series of interviews, the typical student is admitted only if he is in excellent health (periodic medical examinations are recommended for all students, although the School does not hold them as part of the curriculum) and the student is observed on a trial basis for the first few months of instruction. He will have been accepted at the School only if his examiners think him young enough, or flexible enough, to assimilate the academic training. He will have, ideally, a well-porportioned, well-coordinated body, feet and legs that easily assume the Turnout, and a natural gift for movement. The School does not teach music but recommends its study to students and welcomes those with musical aptitude. Usually, the young student begins with two lessons weekly. The more advanced student takes six to nine lessons a week. The attendance requirement, strictly enforced, is three academic ballet lessons a week, and for the student bent on a professional career a class a day is *de rigueur*. Each year, some graduates of the School are taken into the company of the New York City Ballet, and the remainder are readily absorbed into other companies in America and Western Europe. American dancers and teachers abroad have an immediate cachet if they are graduates of "Balanchine's School." At home, they dance in every theatre from Radio City Music Hall to the Metropolitan Opera. The Children's Division regularly supplies young dancers for the casts of ballets, chiefly for *The Nutcracker*. Since the school year 1957–1958 a course in dance notation has been included in the curriculum, taught by Ann Hutchinson, the author of *Labanotation* and the co-founder of the United States Dance Notation Bureau, established in 1940. The graded courses in Labanotation are taught for one hour per week to students enrolled for the full school year. In these studies students learn to analyze, notate and compose ballet movements.

From the very first class for the youngest students, there is a striking atmosphere of seriousness both in the authority of the teachers and in the respectful attitudes of the students. Beginners are restricted to soft, flat ballet slippers, and the girls take an equivalent of three years' studies and must show a particular standard of mental and physical development before being promoted to toe-shoes for *pointe* work. At the end of the school year the faculty determines whether a student may enroll for the ensuing year, depending on physical qualifications and progress, and the student's conformity to rules and regulations. Unsatisfactory progress, and a student attitude and deportment that conflict with the standards of the School, are sufficient reasons for dismissal.

The authoritative status of the School enhances its reputation. It is the only one of its kind, and has no affiliate branches, as does the Ballet Theatre School. Its close link is the New York City Ballet, and the students' gain in watching the company in daily practice and rehearsal is obvious. Scholarships are necessarily sparse, as the School is not endowed and subsists on its own funds, yet from full scholarship the School has produced ballerinas Marie-Jeanne and Tanaquil LeClercq. Its bright new alumni include Allegra Kent, and d'Amboise and Villella.

A graduate dancer of the School is, essentially, a Balanchine dancer. *En attitude* and *en arabesque* the aplomb is marked. Movement has a cleanly athletic quality—not to be confused with an acrobatic one. In Balanchine's coruscant ballets the dancers excel in delicate *pointe* work, *batterie,* and *gargouillade.* Some of the girls, like Patricia Wilde, have a bold and exhilarating command of space that instantly brings to mind the fabled Maywood. The Parisians declared that

Balanchine rehearsing Agon, *in 1958, with dancers Arthur Mitchell and Diana Adams. Jonathan Watts in background.*

Maywood danced like a *danseur,* so amazing were her prodigious leaps and *allegro* abilities. Tallchief performs miracles in dance, like the *entrechat-huit,* which few male dancers achieve, with studied precision, rather than as an occasional and freakish feat. Tallchief jumps and performs a *tour en l'air* and lands *en pointe,* and, to borrow Walter Terry's apt description, dances in a pyrotechnical command of movement as the soprano sings in a pyrotechnical ascension of sounds. The *danseurs,* many of the younger now beginning to show marked qualities of elevation, have dignity and presence, and an awareness of space that grants them an unerring and gracious movement. Their dancing is characterized by a uniform magnificence of pose, far exceeding the norm for the American company, where, unfortunately, some of our finest young *danseurs* are allowed to assume poor postures in repose.

So conspicuous is the graduate dancer of the School of American Ballet that his very particular stance and gait are sometimes misconstrued as affectations of Balanchine's teaching. This is a characteristic of the Classic—not an affectation of the teaching in the School. The aim of the School is to develop *danseurs* and *danseuses* of the Classic genre. The women rise on their toe-tips, as though the *pointe* shoe were the natural extension of the foot, and they and their partners move in the patterns of the traditional ballet, which are not the ordinary ones of real life. Modern Dance classes have been held at the School, conducted by Merce Cunningham and Anna Sokolow, and Arthur Mitchell now teaches Jazz, but the pervading climate is that of the Classic Dance—precise, strict and noble of deportment. The presiding influence is that of George Balanchine, not as the avant-garde choreographer, but as the unquestioned pedagogue of his day. It is Balanchine and his associated faculty who define the nature of the School.

Its prestige is founded physically on the faculty, but it endures because of its principles, to which its founder Kirstein adhered out of respect, and which its spiritual head, Balanchine, established as the extension of his own training. The School of American Ballet is dedicated to the effortless performance of the difficult, and for the purest idealization of the human form in spatial design. Its system is a tried and true one, existing for hundreds of years, founded on beauty and strength and a sense of order. It is an incorruptible system, to which the students strive to adapt themselves, and its rules, as *danse d'école,* are those that the ancient Greeks defined: "the excellent becomes the permanent." For this reason, the system creates the kind of theatrical dance and dancer distinctly recognized among all others and exclusive to its principles, known as the Classic.

THE AMERICAN SCHOOL OF DANCE

In 1948 Eugene Loring leased a tall, old-fashioned white stucco building on Hollywood Boulevard and began a school of dance. Situated near the celebrated

corner of Hollywood and Vine it is only a block or so away from Grauman's
Chinese Theatre, whose pavement is a mosaic of hand and footprints signifying
the birth of movie stars. Loring's school was started to supply dancers to the industry, whose catholic demands for dance styles and dance specialists have greatly influenced the lives and times of American professional dancers.

Some of those in movies and musicals began with a Classic training. Nijinska
had a notable school in Hollywood, and among her students were the young Tallchief sisters, Gwen Verdon, Cyd Charisse, and, later, Allegra Kent. Three of these
are ballerinas of the legitimate theatre, Verdon is a star of stage and screen, and
Charisse is a Hollywood luminary in dance and drama.

The professional in Hollywood or in musicals and television had to be more
dynamic, plastic and versatile than most ballet artists. He could not indulge in
prejudices and esthetic vanities, but his theatre was well paid, in comparison with
the ballet theatre, fairly consistent in employing dancing and elastic in its use of
dancing. To survive, the Hollywood professional learned how to dance anything
the director or movie choreographer demanded. He might move from a movie
about King Arthur to one about juvenile delinquents. The movie moguls had
early grasped the importance of dance as a pleasant diversion in the movies and
they found choreographers to create stately measures for characters in escoffions
and houppelandes, or jitterbuggers with sloppy slacks and sweaters and twirling
skirts. From the minuet to Rock-'n-Roll the screen cavorted or writhed with
nimble dancing. In between, national characteristics were stamped in dance dyes
as brilliant as Technicolor: with the crook of a finger, the director could summon
Cossacks or dervishes, hula girls or American hoofers for a buck-and-wing, and
fling them pell-mell among the tribulations or triumphs of his featured players.

One of the universities from which the marvelous technician of many genres is
drawn is Loring's academy, aptly named the American School of Dance. Although
only a decade old, it is the most famous school of its kind.

When Loring was choreographing for the musical, *Silk Stockings,* he held auditions for dancers in New York. They were going into a show for which Loring had
choreographed Russian Character, Classic and Jazz, to emphasize the plot and
characterization of the story. The auditions began and the dancers gathered. Some
were Russian character dancers and very proud of it. They would dance nothing
but character dances. The haughtiest were the classicists, who appeared to suffer
when Loring asked them if they danced Jazz—they would not so demean their
Art. As for the Jazz specialists, they stoutly resisted anything as effete as ballet, or
as "folksy" as character dancing. Despising all worlds but their own, four hundred
dancers auditioned for *Silk Stockings* and from this number Loring managed to
extricate one small company to dance in the show. He has lived to see his ideal become the practical necessity not only for the popular theatre but for a great deal
of legitimate ballet.

The American School of Dance still occupies the old-fashioned white building
on Hollywood Boulevard, and is still directed by Loring. It is operated on a thesis
of dance as expression. There is no partition between technique and interpretation, and its technical command implies the perfect gesture and movement for the

moment and mood. Ideally, all the arts and crafts of ballet are integrated in an education that is directed at forming an instrument for lyric communication with the audience. Movement is the primal force in the dance, and to Loring, as to Noverre, "a step, a gesture, a movement express what no word can say; the more violent the sentiments it is required to depict, the less able is one to find words to express them. Exclamations, which are the apex to which the language of the passions can reach, become insufficient and have to be replaced with gesture."

Loring's dancers lyrically portray their feelings and thoughts in character, and his dance relates to the plot or theme of his ballet.

Loring had a clear idea of his ideal dancer and he went about formulating his own system of education that would produce this paragon. The school that began with daring experiments in theory and practice continues to be adventurous and energetic. Traditions are understood in the School, but are studied for the historical, sociological and philosophical significance in dance. No tradition is worshipped, and the attitude is practical, never devout. Democratic in its acceptance and use of all forms of dance, the School is well named, and has been called by writers "Loring's wonderful American School of Dance." In accord with Loring's belief about the dance itself, the educational precepts in the School remain contemporary, to prepare students for the changing theatrical concepts of the times.

The education is thought of as "technic," and the graduate student is the Loring "technician." One uses the word in its dictionary content, which means that the Loring dancer is "efficient, and able to produce the desired effect or service without waste of time or energy."

This student technician begins in an orientation class, an exploration of *What Is Dance?* Comprehending it as a fundamental instinct for rhythm, as the first of mankind's arts, as the expression of all peoples in special lyric forms and styles, the student has no prejudices and no alignments with one form or style. He then commences his integrated education for Dance, rather than for Ballet.

His curriculum covers techniques, theory, choreography and Kineseography. He takes more classes in academic Classic Dance than in any other one form of dance, because Loring feels the Classic Dance to be the best exercise in discipline and development of the dancer. Theory classes cover the general knowledge of dance, the structure and concepts of dance, dance terminology, and music. The "technics" absorbed in classes are in graded classes of ballet—men's ballet, *pas de deux,* free style, rhythm and jazz, character, and dramatic dance. The basic idiom is that of the traditional ballet, which Loring considers the most graphic and precise in terminology.

Loring believes that choreography, like dance, can be taught—recognizing, of course, that great choreographers are gifted in that art. His own system of Kinese is a form of dance notation, and separate from it he has classes in choreography, which his students study to better understand and perform dance, as a musician studies harmony and counterpoint to execute musical compositions in a knowledgeable manner. All students at the School take classes in choreography, whether or not they intend to work as choreographers. The study involves an understanding of the limitations and possibilities of the human body, and the recognized values of movement and gesture as expression and communication, related in space and tempo. Other facets of the choreography class are these:

The Creative Process: how other artists create. Not limited, by any means, to artists of the dance, or even of the theatre, this embraces notable figures whose major contributions have been in arts and sciences.

The Sketch Method: ideas realized in general form, comparable to the economy of communication made in some of Picasso's works.

The Block Method: the use of isolated steps and gestures, comparable to the use of separate bricks, to compose a feeling or an idea, in the same way that the bricks could be used to build a portion of a wall.

Directional Choreography: a student conceives an idea and then communicates it, recognizably, by directing the class himself—literally, an exercise in dance design which forces the student-choreographer to become aware of the possibilities and limitation of his materials, i.e., the student-dancers.

Emotional Choreography: dance as the pure extension of emotion, but in its theatrical sense, i.e., with power in communication and good taste in form.

Gesture: in its ballet significance, *to express, or mean.* This alone entails intensive study in a wide range. Nor does Loring limit it to the regular faculty, but invites guest teacher collaboration. Broad Pantomime has been taught by a circus clown. The *Telling Gesture*—eloquent communication without the aid of props—has been demonstrated by actor-mimes in the styles of Jean Louis Barrault, Marcel Marceau, and Fernandel. Nothing too simple is despised, and "Real Gesture" is studied, as in entrance and exit. Nothing is too academic for consideration, and "Stylized" or rhythmic, gesture is practiced.

"Kinese," from kinetics—the science of movement—is the study of the possibilities and limitations of the human body in their relationship to elements of time and space. It gives its name to Loring's system of dance notation, Kineseography. This form of dance notation is taught precisely as what it is: the writing and the reading of dance movement. In it exercises in movement are ingeniously explored. The student is debarred from bringing personal prejudices or "traditional" conceptions to the dance. Instead of pedantically stating "the torso must be plumb with the leg in arabesque" as is the rule of *aplomb* in Classic Dance, teachers and students sometimes spend an entire class period discovering the possibilities, and the limitations, of a particular phase of movement and gesture.

Loring's precepts are, as the King of Siam was wont to say, "very scientific." His Kinese-man has a plumb line that passes through the body at the hip. The plumb line is constant, whether the Kinese-man is vertical or horizontal. Kineseography establishes four categories of movements on the key dancer, or Kineseman: Normal, the ordinary undramatized posture and emotional projection of the human being; Extravert, in which stance the feet are turned out in the Classic, or traditional, ballet position; Intravert, the turned-in stance; and Emotion—the character of the gesture. No movement in Kineseography is devoid of meaning: Extravert is "open, with confidence"; Intravert, "closed in, or lacking in confidence."

Eugene Loring students of the Workshop's Dance Players, 1959.

Kineseography is simple enough to be studied by twelve-year-old students at the American School of Dance, where it has been in practical use for seven years. It is complex enough to notate dance movement for ballets, and dancers familiar with it can read it easily and clearly for a pre-rehearsal understanding of their dancing, as actors read their lines. At the School, young students in the teens employ Kineseography to write dance compositions in the same way that an English Lit. student occupies himself with language compositions. Teachers and students are enthusiastic about Loring's Kineseography. Its preciseness leaves no doubt, and students like it because it is simple to master, and clear to express, when they compose. Above all, it satisfies, in its fourth movement, Emotion, the requirement to express feeling—which no one is ever allowed to forget in Loring's academy of dance.

In teaching Kineseography, and in the text of this name in use in the School, Loring emphasizes that the system of dance notation is explicitly *a statement of the choreographic intent,* as a musical composition on graph is the notation of the composer's intent. The performance of the dance, like the performance of the musical composition, passes from the creator to the performer, as interpreter. Loring believes that students of dance and music must first acquire technical command of their art, and then develop artistry in interpretation. The performer has both.

The dancer, as an individual interpreter of dancing, is developed at the School through an integration of art and artist. The relationship becomes the identification of the student as the performer. In some ways, by the exploration of dance, the students at the School are involved in the study of the humanities. Loring's concept of The Dance Theatre embraces a relationship between music, drama, poetry and rhythm. It requires an understanding of literature, art in color and design, sculpture, and engineering. Since he believes emphatically that in exploring a dance culture we perceive a national history, his school actually inquires into history, philosophy, and sociology.

In all the teaching, the premise is this: movement has identity with feeling. The dumb, the blind, the lame, make movements in an effort to communicate. The idiot, incapable of speech, makes gestures. The mad, withdrawn into a realm outside of reason, betray inchoate feeling with gesture. As a technician, the dancer is expected to comprehend these things, and as a Loring student he must discover, from within himself and in observation of others, the nuances of gesture, and their relationship to feeling. The dance technician will then, in Loring's premise, be immediately obedient to choreographic command—but he must, always, observe personal identity in characterization. The actor and dancer, to Loring, is not a performer parroting speech and movement; he is the theatrical artist who is trained to express, within his métier. As such, he is as much a creator in the theatre as the playwright and the choreographer.

I observed a class in choreography in the school that had just completed a study of Medievalism. Loring now expected the students to know the period—in costume and in architecture, in attitudes of philosophy and in the declaration of its art principles. This last category, alone, covered not only music, but painting, literature, and the developments of sacred and secular dance. Loring will not tolerate the performance of the gavotte by students who do not relate its derivation to a country dance of the fourteenth century, as he will not countenance a player in doublet and hose who, with no other attachment to the Elizabethan period, professes to act in a Shakespearean repertory. The ideal Loring technician is aware, as part of his training, of the source of movement in dance and of the significance of gesture in normal life, and in the stylized form of the theatre.

There is no separation of what are usually called "dancing" and "acting in dance." One encounters students in the School in classes where dancers are being taught how to act, and in the class on Music for Dancers finds professional actors side by side with professional dancers, studying rhythm, tempo, and the elements that affect dance. In the School there is a consistent exploration of movement—of the acts of falling, rising, descending, ascending, extending, bending, twisting, turning, gliding, darting and jumping. These form a rondo, and all excursions into action, movement and interpretative forms return to the concept of dance as lyric expression.

The Loring principles of dance make a clear division between dancing with a meaning, or the Fokinean theory of ballet, and "abstract" dance in the theatre. Loring believes in classroom exercises in dance genres—Classic, Modern, Primitive, Jazz and all the others, and encourages a comprehensive vocabulary for the student—but he maintains that a classroom exercise must be staged for demonstration purposes, not as the theatrical dance. The theatrical dance he believes is a form of expression, and as such should lyrically express, in its multitudinous forms, the passing stage scene, and the contemporary world.[5]

The system of training in the School is based on the Classic Dance, but beyond its precise exercise it is used in dancing only when it is useful, and when its style and special Turnout and movements are eloquent of the choreographer's theme, or a characterization in dance. It must be remembered that this is a school for the professional who must command the eclectic, not the special dance. In the competitive theatre (Loring is not attached to one company) he feels that there must be a clear differentiation in sexes, and I find that the Loring *danseur* has some of the characteristic virility of the male dancer of Character and other genres. In Academic Ballet classes the male student masters the techniques (the vocabulary and deportment) of the classical *danseur,* and of the segregated men's ballet of traditional schooling. The graded classes of Freestyle are co-educational, but stress, for the male dancers, a masculine approach to dance. This applies to character dancing, ethnic dancing, and other types. Loring is a choreographer with a predilection for strong male characterization, as in his *Billy the Kid.*

The School's academic ballet classes are separated into Children's, and the Professional curriculum that begins with the orientation class: "What is Dance?" The Classic standards are as prescribed by the genre—which does not recognize mediocrity of performance. Both the Children's and the Professional classes are graded in five classes each. Loring's preferred system is Freestyle, and most of the students pass from an Academic Class (with a change of shoes) to one in Progressive Jazz, exchanging the Chopinesque measure of the first for the frenetics of the *Man With The Golden Arm.*

Under the classical teachers (some of them with the older semantic and crisp accents of English ballet) there are classes in *pas de deux,* for partnering and supported *adagio;* classes for girls in *pointe* work and Variations; and classes especially for boys. The female students are encouraged to develop finesse; the males a powerful technique and a masculine manner in interpretation.

Classes in contemporary dance include "Basic Jazz," in which the terminology, and the isolated functions of movements are studied; and "Advanced," in which interpretative work and demanding theatrical routines are taught. The "History of Jazz" symposium traces the dance from its New Orleans roots through ragtime to rock-'n-roll, segregating them as "Dances of the 'Twenties," "Dances of the 'Thirties," "Dances of the 'Forties," and "Dances of the 'Fifties." These cover the Charleston, Blackbottom, Lindy, Big Apple, Shag, Swing, Bop, and Progressive Jazz.

Ethnic dance is taught by teachers direct from the sources, drawn to America from the British Isles, the Orient, and the Slavonic countries. Courses have been held in the dances of the British Isles, India, Israel, Bali, Java, Japan, the Sudan, and Mexico. Russian Character Dancing is a regular course, as are Primitive, Afro-Cuban, Modern, and Spanish. In the latter course there are classes in Spanish Ballet, and in Flamenco. Teachers whose names are noted in the theatre include Danilova for the Classic genre, John Gregory for Progressive Jazz, Devi Dja for the dances of Java and Bali, and others, but Loring prefers not to advertize "name" teachers in order to discourage hero-worship in the student, on the premise that this establishes mannerisms in dancers. So that his students will not acquire predilections and prejudices in dance, the faculty and the guest teachers are rotated. Students seldom know in advance who will preside as the teacher of the day's class. The exception is made only for the children's school, in the primary grades. Here it is evident that the youngest students are being encouraged to express as they dance. They are carefully watched for "dance quality," as well as for precise development in Classic exercises, and the traditional terminology of Positions and movements is taught from the beginning.

Under the system of rotating classes, the student's progress is followed on graphs, the teacher of each day's class adding an entry for the purpose of informing the next teacher what errors must be corrected and what weaknesses must be strengthened. This method also keeps a record of the over-all progress of a class. When a teacher notes on the graph that some time has elapsed since a particular exercise was performed, the class is set to doing it. The student works not towards one teacher's idea of perfection, but towards a teaching symposium's demand for perfection. Loring encourages his regular faculty to continue in professional performance, and draws freely from visiting professionals, because he believes that the students must recognize the theatre and be prepared for active participation in it. He finds that the continuation of a theatrical career prevents academic supervisors from becoming stagnant and losing touch with the contemporary stage—for which, naturally, they are preparing the students.

The American School of Dance is open the year round and besides its regular student enrollment is the classroom for the peripatetic dancers in the profession, who, when in Hollywood, take the daily class that is *de rigueur.* In the anonymity

Dance Players in Dance Is a Language, *from Loring's "Omnibus of Dance" demonstrations.*

of practice clothes, the dancers famed on stage and screen (like Leslie Caron, Cyd Charisse, Taina Elg, Mitzi Gaynor, Roy Fitzell, Renée Jeanmaire, James Mitchell, Roland Petit, Gwen Verdon, and Violette Verdy) share the barre with students whose hope it is to be the stars of tomorrow. Loring has a library of books and art objects, and hopes, eventually, to found a Dance Archives for the city of Los Angeles. Summer classes do extensive art study, to familiarize dance students with form and line in relation to space. Mobiles are built and used in experiments to establish relationship, for the dancer, with space. With forms made from paper and wire, the students first study the structures from all angles, and then study the structures' shadows on ceilings, walls and floors. Tireless invention of movement and form in spatial design, would summarize this curriculum. Loring feels that it is basic for the School to remain tolerant of dances and theatrical concepts, vigorous in its explorations of the limitations and possibilities of drama and dance, and receptive to new and changing artistic ideals. Inevitably, he says, some experiments work out less than satisfactorily but no experiment, for being discarded, is considered a failure. The very act of experimenting proves fallibility; and each experiment is profitable, as an exercise in exploring a theme. Pressed for one hard and fast precept for this school Loring admits that it is the refutation of timidity and prejudice, of any principle that would dictate, "Let us do nothing new, for fear we do something wrong."

Eminently practical, he finds that his best practices have come to him out of necessary invention, as his Kineseography, which he developed lying on a beach one summer, supposedly sunbathing but trying to solve the problem of incorporating mood and movement precisely, in one economical gesture, when he made dance notation. His Kineseography is used now as a textbook in the School and for his choreography, and he is evolving a new textbook of dance terminology—a catholic dictionary of dance that ranges from the Classic vocabulary of *arabesque*, *battement* and *plié*, and so on, to the vernacular of the Progressives—*shorty-george*, *fish-tail*, et cetera. In any terminology, traditional or contemporary, Loring interprets the technique of dancing for ballet as *the entire range of human movement*, for the expression of all thought, feeling and narrative.

As a teacher, Loring is patient, just and scrupulous, undeviating in preparation, and such a disciplinarian that students are occasionally taken aback to discover the steel under the usually mild manner, and the sharpness under the gentle tone. He conducts a martinet's examination, with a strict panel, from which the academic ballet students are graded. The School holds National Scholarship Examinations, and supports a workshop, presents a Special Teacher's Course, and in the 1959 curriculum added classes in Indonesian Dance, Dramatic Dance (with Tchouky Mattei) and Dance through Applied Art. All classes, remarkable to note, are observed for dance quality and classroom deportment. A large section of the student body comprises high school and college students and while these are in the main intent on dancing as professionals after graduation, all agree that attendance in the School automatically enriches the liberal arts content of their general education.

Loring is too modest to claim students of his system, although both Michael

Kidd and Jerome Robbins are listed, categorically, as his pupils (q.v. reference books, ballet dictionaries, etc.) and from the School have come Ernest Flatt, the inventive choreographer of television's long-lived "Hit Parade" Dancers, and the gifted Modern, Matt Mattox. Loring agrees that the American School of Dance has not existed long enough for critics to assay its influence on American ballet, but if one criterion suffices to explain its principles it may be this: here no student simply performs the *arabesque*. Instead, the student learns to comprehend the *arabesque* as line and form related to space—not only as it appears in the dimension onstage for the audience, but in perspective, and from all angles. The purpose in the training of the dancer is the realization that he is an animate creature, concerned with a wondrous and delicate engineering of balance and in an infinite variety of design.

The School is the only one of its kind, and has no branches. It has no endowment and subsists on its tuition fees, from which it defrays operations and scholarships. Annual examinations award two full-annual scholarships, two half-annual scholarships, and four quarter-annual scholarships. These are open on a national basis, not restricted to students of dance schools, and are held in summer. The School's academic examinations are opened in January of every year.

The link with theatre is made in the workshop, which approximates a company, and besides producing groups for demonstration and concert it provides a company for experimental work by choreographers—among these, Merce Cunningham.[6]

From the current student body Loring has drawn the nucleus of a performing group, The Dance Players, for whom he has created a small but choice repertoire. The company is not of the caliber of gifted amateurs seen in "recitals" but has a flexible style and theatrical suavity that puts it on par, if not above, some of the troupes accepted as "companies." In 1959 The Dance Players had great success in Loring's children's ballet *La Boite à Joux Joux* (*The Toy Box*) commissioned by the Los Angeles Music Festival and later danced for metropolitan and university audiences; and the troupe was lauded for its "omnibus of dance" productions, such as *Dramatic Dance Works of Tchouky* and *Dance is a Language*. The Dance Players have already achieved a reputation in university dancing and civic festivals in the United States and Canada.

By geographical situation, the School's regional students are peculiarly representative of Occidental and Oriental Americans. The Dance Players is a veritable melting-pot of American national derivatives, whose physical inheritance and rhythmic qualities lend piquancy to the dancing. Notably, the boys of the School are masculine, and the girls have an engaging femininity, and the uniform technical standard is first class—but it is obvious that Eastern antecedents produce boys with a quick, adroit elasticity and girls of elegant suppleness, while the Western characteristics develop remarkably handsome males, of fresh and candid appearance, and some girls whose svelte good looks have the striking litheness of thoroughbreds. In their comprehensive types and temperaments it would be hard to find a more representative group of dancers who could be labeled MADE IN THE U.S.A.

LOOKING AT AMERICAN BALLET

There are as many angles to American ballet as there are facets to a jewel, and we must be prepared to see it not from a single view, isolated as American dance theatre, but within the panorama of contemporary ballet and the history of dance. Dance itself has historical and esthetic categories and is traced socially, philosophically and technically. Ballet is a comparatively young development in dance, and ballet itself is centuries old. As Americans, we dance not only in obedience to the *danse d'école* of the Classic style but in the ballroom, on the street, and in ways which we have invented ourselves. It has become obvious that we are representative of America when we dance, and that often our dancing is the most eloquent and joyous converse our country holds with foreigners.

As Americans we are proudest of being free, and we have reason to be proud of our freedom in dance. Making use of the Classic as a superb foundation we have profitably commanded an eclectic choice of all other styles. Our only danger seems to lie in a chauvinistic preference for one style in which a distrust of feeling and warmth of expression makes us appear too bent on the difficult and showy. The criterion for American ballet is pedantically set by self-designated authorities, but it is not one universally held by the American audience, as is to be observed by comparing the printed statement of this faction with the tastes and temperaments of audiences throughout the United States.

The most boldly sketched view of the ballet appears in newspapers and magazines, in reviews written by reporters who are journalists by profession and, one assumes, balletomanes by preference. Many of the most oracular statements in the past have been made by writers whose sole concept of ballet was dancing on the tiptoe, and there is surely no happier development in American ballet than the literacy and discernment of present reviewers. The best of these keep themselves free of personal attachments onstage, profess no authority, and content themselves with describing the ballets and compiling judicious estimates of development in the ballet artists.

For the Restoration theatre, critics were the self-assigned arbiters of the performance, who outstayed the performers in the theatre and vocally determined

305

the merits of the play. The most that a ballet reviewer may hope to do is to describe the dancing and comment on it intelligently, and his comments are bound to be more intelligent if he has a sound knowledge of the subject. We are fortunately well past the days when the minor sports writer was promoted, or demoted, to "covering the ballet" between affairs in the arena, but there are still comparatively few reporters trained to recognize and to note the passing scene of the ballet and compare it with what has preceded it, and what exists as contemporary in the international dance theatre. Writing about dancing, beyond the bald description of the ballet, requires an evocative talent. The ideal combination might be the factual and judicious writing of George Amberg with the poetic descriptions of Edwin Denby and Marianne Moore. The best that the individual writer may hope to produce is an awareness in the reader of the articulate movement, shape and color of the ballet, and the sound of its music. If he animates the printed page with life he can engender in the reader a realization of ballet—not only as a design for dancing, but also as an integration of all the arts of the eye and ear, combining, besides, the grand art of illusion known as theatre with the engineering that is stagecraft. A ballet, seen and heard all in a series of flashes, is grasped only when remembered as an experience in thought and feeling. It is this memory, like a camera record, that the writer seeks to capture and give to the reader.

The large newspapers and news magazines employ dance reviewers who are uniformly informative, and as many of these are strong personalities the timid in the audience attach themselves to their vigorous opinions. Few of the reporters have trained for ballet as has Walter Terry of the *New York Herald Tribune,* but they write wittily or well, and draw bold reflections of American ballet. The kindest of them are unfailingly enthusiastic, and even the manic do ballet a good turn. In the theatre a spirited controversy is sound publicity. It is difficult to remain just while becoming excited over your subject, and some reviewers are such ardent balletomanes that they become attached, to the point of obsession, to a particular genre, company, or kind of dancer, and the comment then becomes authoritative—either worshipful or excoriating. Both kinds of views, and the comments they provoke, are highly entertaining reading.

THE VIEWERS

It is for entertainment, rather than for guidance, that the audience reads such ballet reviews, and this is a marvelous difference between American audiences and those of other countries.

In the theatrical centers of Paris, Moscow, Copenhagen and London, as in Milan, Florence, Edinburgh, Berlin, Vienna and Tokyo, a small stratum—a balletomane audience—evaluates and issues statements about the ballet. Nothing of the sort exists in American ballet, where the balletomane is a peculiarity. Here it is the *audience en masse* that holds the purse strings and chooses what it wishes to pay for in the theatre, as well as in the supermarket. We have no state opera house. That institution, with its ballet company, ballet politics, and claques in the audience and in the press has traditionally ruled the ballet theatre elsewhere. Such authorities have traditionally been full of personal vendetta.

Of even more interest is the fact that the general audience at the ballet in America is not the same audience that is guided and overawed in the dramatic theatre, where a handful of critics make or break a show at the première. No critical review has yet succeeded in making or breaking a ballet in America. New York is the center of dance activity in the United States and its dance criticism is largely syndicated by local newspaper reviewers when the ballet companies go on tour, but more and more the local reporter is writing about what he sees and what he feels at the ballet. This kind of reviewing may not be exact in terminology, or even literature, but it has a wonderfully fresh and pungent flavor, and it proves a new vigor in the dance and a new interest in the American audience.

The most important view is the opinion of the audience, because this is what supports ballet. We Americans do not go to the theatre with as much passion as our fellow balletomanes in Europe but we go, nowadays, with a discriminating taste. While we have lost the early wonder that sent us backstage to examine the magic shoe or boot of the *sur les pointes* dancer we still respond with admiration and, even, joy. The American audience, in lieu of a puissant authority, has determined the standard of excellence in dance performance, and it has done surpassingly well, as we have noted. This American prerogative is not a recent one—in the nineteenth century Americans were able to decide, for themselves, between the quality of dancers like Ciocca and Morlacchi, and the puerility of a "performer" like Lola Montez. The American audience is, like all such audiences, independent, capricious, mischievous, and responsive—and it is impervious to sweet reason, esoteric diatribes about esthetics, and unctuous pedagogues. The theatre and the press exert absolutely no control over this huge, wayward child, which Hammerstein has called a "black giant."

The audience will look with interest, and without aversion, at anything at all in première, but the most avant-garde of themes and styles is incapable of altering an American taste for the qualities of the old "classics"—the sumptuous décor, the melodious music, and dancing that frankly includes feats of activity. We feel strongly, like Prince Wolkonsky, that ballet dancing should have a meaning. The plot may be thin if the characters are strong and the action moves swiftly and well. We are slightly mystified by "excerpts," but indulgently applaud if they are pyrotechnic or full of lyric feeling. Although American ballet persists in the Diaghilev programming—several short ballets to a performance—the American audience has great enthusiasm for the full-length ballet, in the fine panoply of the Petipa style.

The audience in American ballet theatres is accustomed to spectaculars on television and colossal productions, with casts of thousands, in the neighborhood movie house. It stubbornly associates ballet with the grand manner of theatre.

What the American audience wants is what it buys. In the ballet theatre it spends from fifty dollars a ticket for the Soviet's Bolshoi Ballet at the Metropolitan in New York to three dollars a seat in Mobile for the Ballet Russe de Monte Carlo.

The Nutcracker by the New York City Ballet regularly grosses fifty thousand dollars a week when its seasonal appearances are made in New York and Chicago. The returns have been undiminished from the time of its première in 1954. In the same season Balanchine created for the New York City Ballet a work called *Opus 34,* set to Schoenberg's *Begleitunsmuzik zu einer Lichtspielszene (Accompaniment for a Motion Picture).* This ballet has been called a "cosmic message" of the Atom Age and is remembered by the dilettante audience of the avant-garde. Although I do not have access to its box office "take," it is not in active or permanent repertoire.[1]

The audience will fill the theatres to standing room for *Giselle* when it is danced by Alonso, Chauviré, Markova and Ulanova. It fills the theatre, every two years, for anything in which Fonteyn dances. It continues to go in droves to view the "American classics," especially *Billy the Kid, Rodeo* and *Fancy Free.* These examples are representative of the general audience in the United States. Regional audiences have strong preferences, not for ballets but for individual ballet dancers, and this affects the ballets in which the favorite dancers are "stars." It also affects, needless to state, the "take" at the box office and the parity of ballet. Here is where American ballet is forced to strike a precarious balance between its marketable commodities and its artistic policies.

The local favoritism of "stars" is not so evident in New York, where the three resident American companies hold not one dancer but the whole company in focus. Here, too, are first seen all the foreign and imported influences and styles of dancing, except for those that come first to Jacob's Pillow.[2] But in the West the ballerinas most admired are Alonso and the native daughter Maria Tallchief, who was born in Oklahoma and brought up in California. In Florida, Verdy will arouse the same excitement among "fans" as Borowska stirs in Los Angeles.

When the sumptuous national companies of the Royal Ballet, the Royal Danish Ballet, and the Bolshoi Ballet appear, audiences from the Metropolitan in New York to the Shrine Auditorium in Los Angeles fill theatres to overflowing. Three companies playing at once in New York have set records for ballet and, I am sure, for the taxicabs that rush avid balletomanes from one theatre to another during the intermissions.

THE ECONOMY

Although American ballet is recognized and its artists have given proof of creative and interpretative gifts, it is hard-pressed to exist. From the time of Catherine de' Medici the dance theatre has been subject to the whims of the rich, and much of its life force has been drawn from people who never pointed a toe or mounted a stage. Few patrons have been more generous than the wealthy Americans who patronize ballet.

The Marquis de Cuevas lost eight hundred thousand dollars when he formed his short-lived International Ballet, from which he drew, at immense costs, the succeeding de Cuevas companies that have been titled Grand Ballet du Marquis de Cuevas, and the International Ballet of the Marquis de Cuevas. In the 'thirties Philip Leidy helped to support The Philadelphia Ballet—he was the husband of Catherine Littlefield. Chicago's ballet theatre owes a great deal to Ruth Page's husband, Thomas Hart Fisher. Lucia Chase is reported to have expended $2,250,-000 on the first decade's support of Ballet Theatre—set down in figures it has its full round savor! Julius Fleischmann, of Fleischmann's Yeast, donated lavish sums to Ballet Russe de Monte Carlo. Kirstein and the Warburg family gave large contributions to the New York City Ballet.

The box office sometimes grosses handsomely, as when, in fourteen performances, Ballet Russe's 1959 Chicago season drew more than one hundred and fifteen thousand dollars.

Despite these sums, American ballet is penurious because of the astronomical costs of producing ballets. Too often there is a ruinous deficit between the plus of "gifts" and "take" and the expenditure for the mounting of the stage and the support of the artists and craftsmen.

Unlike those in other theatrical professions, such as the motion picture industry, the "stars" in ballet do not devour its profits. Far from that, dancers dance more for love than lucre. In *And Promenade Home,* de Mille describes the rewards of choreographing for the musical theatre, whose economy is a great deal more munificent than legitimate ballet's. The dancers are scarcely better off than the other theatrical artists, and at that their lot has been improved in the *corps* by AGMA. In the 'forties, a dancer took home less than forty dollars a week after deductions. Tallchief received all of fifty-five dollars for touring Canada in 1942, and this included overtime. Now dancers actually get paid for rehearsal—half-time, in pay ratio. In 1959, AGMA contracts stipulated $95 per week, and $104.50 for an out-of-town performance. In 1960 AGMA specifies increases, respectively, of $100 and $109.75. AGMA has also provided a "seniority" clause by which the *corps* member gets a one-dollar increase per annum, after the first year, for three years, and a two-dollar increase after the fourth year. The *corps* member has then had it, literally. In five years he can expect a total raise of five dollars a year over the minimum salary—and there his economy and his "seniority" must rest.

Solistes and *premiers* get anything from a hundred dollars a week up; dancers of ballerina roles usually begin at two hundred dollars and now and then rocket to a thousand dollars. The norm is five hundred dollars a week, in season. The salary scale for the soloist is purely a matter of bargaining power between the "star" and the management, and does not come under AGMA contract. This means that the "star" hires an agent, a percentage man, who bargains for the best that the traffic will allow. A ballerina of Hayden's position gets a thousand dollars a week, but I have known excellent dancers, carrying the responsibility of a "ballerina" status, who received from two hundred to three hundred dollars, depending on how the tour grossed and the management was inclined.

All these rates are on seasonal ratio, and "seasonal" ballet in the United States means precisely this: the dancers, like school teachers, are only partially employed in the course of a year. They never receive a pension. They get no vacation pay. In England the Royal Ballet does not yet have a pension plan, or a retirement age, but it employs its dancers, full pay, during performance season, rehearsals, and vacation periods. The English dancer has a year-round job in the national ballet. This applies to the senior company at Covent Garden, and the members of the junior company resident at Sadler's Wells.

The conditions for American dancers are quite different from those of nations whose ballet is a cultural force, and a national pride and responsibility.

At the Paris Opéra, dancers are on annual contracts and are eligible for pension between thirty-five and forty. At the Bolshoi Ballet retirement on pension is permitted for the *danseuse* at thirty-seven, and for the *danseur* between forty and forty-five. Teatro alla Scala, at Milan, has a contributory pension plan whereby dancers deposit four percent and the management sixteen percent towards the retirement allotment. The Royal Theatre of Stockholm pensions women at forty-one and men at forty-five, and pensions are computed at sixty-five percent of salary at time of retirement. The Royal Danish Ballet has a graded salary system, increases in salaries for dancers who marry, a paid two-month annual holiday, and engagements on a lifetime basis from which dancers may retire at forty— on three-quarters of the salary at time of retirement.

American dancers, from *corps* to stars, are simply "laid off," and seasons may vary from six to twelve weeks. Although they receive no vacation allotment, they must, of course, maintain their form for the next season, which means that they continue to take a daily lesson and rehearse roles in a repertoire that must be made more and more comprehensive with the years. The prerequisites considered ordinary necessities to labor are not even granted to the "unionized" *corps.* Vacations are farcial by that name. The dancer often works harder between seasons, when he goes on tours or hires himself out to municipal centers as ballet master and guest dancer. Cashing in on the star names they have built in the big companies, the *premiers* and *premières* are engaged by concert or municipal managements, or create touring ensembles, in which they expend a great deal of energy. Hayden and Eglevsky and two New York City Ballet soloists toured with *Quartette* in 1959. Earlier, the ballerinas Novak and Tyven formed a Ballet Russe ensemble and toured, dancing, turn-and-turn-about, the ballerina excerpts from *Swan Queen* to *Glove Seller.* Some of the stars are captured for movie sequences. Many of them are placed incongruously in television backgrounds, not as dancers but as distractions for the audience tired of gazing at a singer's tonsils. Orchestras and choirs have not the visual attributes of dance, and dancers, often in full ensemble, are hired to dispel television inertia. These excursions into popular theatre, in which the "musical" theatre grants the best position if not the best pay, popularize dancers with large audiences but often prove exhausting to the dancers. At the start of a season the big companies often seem fagged and ragged. Only after the "season" has been operating for a week or so, and the company has begun, out of its mystic force, to nourish its members, does the sure and brightest glow begin to be diffused. For all the proverbial stamina of these magnificent workhorses, the exhaustion and the ever-present hazard of accidents deplete the ranks, season after season. Strained tendons, twisted ankles and a general lessening of "tone" or form result from the grueling tours, and the new seasons often begin with disastrous gaps in the ranks. In the 1959 season the New York City Ballet's ballerina repertoire was for a time carried entirely by Patricia Wilde and Allegra Kent, with Hayden with an injury, and Adams and Tallchief on leave. Few in the audience recognize the superhuman heights to which a dancer must rise on these occasions, and only now and then does the more carping "critic" take cognizance of the facts.

The companies are incapable of doing more for the dancers, since from season to season they barely hold their organizations together against the tide of ever-mounting costs of materials, labor, and living expenses. The New York City Ballet is the only company which, so far, has not been forced to disband for lack of money, although it has been near that point on at least one occasion. It pays a token rental of one dollar per annum for its theatre but must depend on the box office gross to mount its stage. It received a 1953–1955 grant-in-aid from the Rockefeller Foundation to City Center of Music and Drama, in the sum of one hundred thousand dollars, to be applied against the costs of creating and producing new works. Balanchine, its Artistic Director, long accepted no salary as his personal contribution to the company's economy.

Ballet Society, Inc. continues to function as an organization and helps to support the company. It solicits contributions of any size towards its maintenance of the company. Ballet Russe de Monte Carlo draws its chief subsistence from Ballet Foundation, formed in 1939 by Julius Fleischmann and associates "for the promotion and development of American Ballet." American Ballet Theatre is one part of the Ballet Theatre Foundation which supports company, workshop and school, and like its sister companies solicits gifts of any denomination. All such contributions from the public are tax-deductible as charities, and it is charity that actually supports the economy of the national ballet theatre. The money comes from gifts for companies, workshops and schools, as contributions of largesse from patrons, in ten dollar bills from people who quietly and humbly associate themselves with the national theatre. And chiefly it comes from the queue that stands outside the box office window.

Now and then in a crisis galas and special lecture demonstrations are arranged to benefit a company in dire straits, as was done for American Ballet Theatre in 1958 and 1959 with the première performance of the Metropolitan season and art expositions at the New York museums and city library.

In the absence of a federal government subsidy, the financial onus for American ballet rests entirely on stage and civic support. The requirement here is for money, first of all, and for edifices designed to house a stage and the audience. Regional ballet seems to be beginning to stimulate local pride and may manage to secure theatres, as Jo Anna's school and company in Palm Beach has secured the Royal Poinciana Playhouse. New York is likely to remain the greatest central power in American ballet with its gigantic Lincoln Center, which will occupy an eleven-acre block, containing a complexity of theatres, from a new

Metropolitan Opera House planned to seat thirty-eight hundred to a recital hall for six hundred. These theatres will produce opera, symphony, repertory drama, concert and dance, in a lively and harmonious association of the arts, around an open plaza. Scheduled for completion in 1963 it may become the landmark for the next quarter of a century of American theatre and American dance.

Besides its Lincoln Center (whose cost is estimated at seventy-five million) New York's Local 802, the American Federation of Musicians, is negotiating with the New York State government for the creation of a permanent agency to foster music and the performing arts. The plea could hardly be addressed to an ear more sympathetic than that of New York's governor, Nelson A. Rockefeller, the same person who, in the 'thirties, called on Lincoln Kirstein to organize American Ballet Caravan for a South American tour. The wording of the plea made by Local 802 expresses the needs of all our theatrical arts: that we are woefully lacking in cultural areas and lagging far behind other civilized nations, where artists have had the benefits of official aid and encouragement with which to develop and support their national theatres.

The ambitious New York projects have already begun to excite national competition. The cry of *Are we going to let New York have all the glory?* will be a crusading challenge for cities large and small throughout the United States. It is a strange paradox that the United States has more material wealth than any other nation and fewer cultural centers than any other civilized country. New York is the only metropolis with theatres, museums, galleries and libraries comparable to those of major European cities, but its location precludes its ever becoming the natural hub of theatre in our enormous terrain. However colossal a project for theatre becomes in any one region it must, because of the size of the country, leave a large part of the audience outside its sphere. An increase in theatrical facilities on a nation-wide scale is the imperative need of American theatre. In this need, nothing stands more impoverished than American ballet, and few native resources promise so much joy to their supporters as this one would if it were allowed a tradition and a home in America.

THE ARTISTIC RESPONSIBILITY

When the American ballet is no longer an orphan taking its luck on the road, but is housed like the opera companies, what then? It already has won a mass audience, the largest and most amiable that ballet has ever commanded. When the theatre is filled with the expectant audience, what does the stage propose to offer?

The repertoire and the choreography will depend upon the quality of the dancing, for the dancers are the visible outward sign of all that ballet contains.

The basic human materials, students in schools and trained dancers in search of a theatre, are governed by the tastes of the audience. The American audience will vociferously applaud energetic male dancing, especially in Character, Ethnic and Primitive genres, but it still is nervously apprehensive about the classical *danseur.* He is, traditionally in ballet, the man who dances in company with the *danseuse,* and the epitome of his style and classic caste is the rare *danseur noble.* Most of the old calumnies against this European and Russian apparition in the American theatre have largely died out—some were that he was physically weak and mentally deficient—but one charge persists: that the *danseur* is sexually perverted. The charge of homosexuality is not laid against the male dancer of the acrobatic, eccentric, ballroom, tap or jazz styles; it is not attributed to any and every male dancer in the Modern genre, and seems never to be attributed to the folk dancer of the caliber of the Moiseyev group, or the Afro-Cuban and Oriental dancers. Mercifully, it has never touched the American Indian dancer. Fathers once absolutely forbade their sons to study for the ballet, and they still are averse to it for fear it develops a tendency towards homosexuality and general depravity. There are homosexuals in the theatre, worldwide, but it is erroneous to believe that the training for the Classic Dance induces emasculation and perversion.

In the theatre the homosexual is drawn to the disguise, the costuming and make-up, and to the excitement of public adulation. We do not, in the audience, have an antipathy to the Shakespearean actor in doublet and hose, to the Restoration player in curls and a plumed hat, or to the Greek, half-naked, in a *chiton.* We approve of the acrobat, in his skin-tight garb, which the *danseur* borrowed for his *maillot.*

Bared flesh, or flesh tightly sheathed in revealing garments; wigs, exotic facial expression in make-up, and the stylized gesture and stance, are well known to us in theatre, circus and sports arena. We grant a maleness to all the men who participate in plays, sports and other forms of dancing than the Classic.

The fact is that there is no greater percentage of homosexuals in ballet than there are, proportionately, in other professions, or classes of males. As Kinsey reports, the greatest percentage of homosexuality exists among cowboys and matadors. But the fact alone does not dispel the prejudice, and it is the artistic responsibility of the ballet theatre to create a position of significance for the *danseur,* so that the audience may come to recognize him as the male instrument in dance, rather than the emasculated *porteur* of the *danseuse.* To do so, we shall have to develop a repertoire in which the *danseur* has roles of significance; and in order for him to perform the repertoire he shall have to have, as a student, proper training to dance as the male in the theatre.

Choreographic recognition is long overdue the *danseur* in American ballet. He has, from the inception of the Classic Dance, been supremely male—so much so that for some time he prevented women from entering the sacred precincts of the ballet, and, when he permitted female roles in repertoire, himself danced them *en travesti.* Until the Romantic Era the *danseur* was the "god of the dance." After the Taglionist and Elsslerite factions finished quarreling the theatre contained only *pas de dessées.* All the ballets began to feature *la ballerina*—but it is worth remarking that even in those times of pallid anonymity for the *danseur,* his role in love was not misconstrued. The choreographers who created *Giselle's* Albrecht and the Swan Queen's Prince had no obscure ideals of Platonic affection, and these characters are not given to neurotic introspection. Hardly a Hamlet-complex occurs in the classics—the *danseurs* are genuine Romeos, to a man: impulsive, passionate, and persuasive.

Odette's Prince, by *Act III,* having met Odile, is a promiscuous fellow. The

Students of a men's ballet class at the American School of Dance, 1959.

most gloomy Freudian will hardly suspect good, faithful Benno of pederasty. All the princes, lords, peasants and other masculine characters in the "classics" have a roistering—not to say a libertine—charm. They support the ballerina in adagio, and catch her in her fish-tail dives with the rapturous masculine attitudes of Leander yearning for Hero across the Hellespont, or some Montague climbing a balcony in search of his Juliet. Sometimes bad, always divinely mad, the classic heroes are the same swashbuckling chaps of the "costume" drama and the "period" movie. Some of them, no doubt alarmed when the *pas de dessées* became the vogue, may have seen what would come about, and began to wear little moustaches, as did Saint-Léon. We may come to that, if the badge of beard and moustache will aid in the re-establishment of the man in ballet.

A common complaint, usually from the men in the audience, is that the *danseur's* traditional costume of "tights" should be changed for something more contemporary and less "like a suit of long underwear." There is a certain hilarity, to the unaccustomed eye, in seeing grown men dressed, or costumed, for baseball, so the revulsion from the *maillot* is not only because it may appear ridiculous but more precisely because it is thought strange and weird. But the tights have a number of purposes. As practice clothes, they reveal imperfections in exercise to the eye of the teacher, and they absorb the sweat in which the working dancer is liberally bathed. The wool *maillot* keeps the overheated dancer from chilling, and thereby prevents him from suffering muscle cramps. On the stage, during the Classic Dance, the feats expected of the *danseur* in his Variations require him to be dressed like an athlete or an acrobat.

The best education for the uninformed audience in the character of love in the ballet, and the qualifications of sex or gender, still lies in seeing the classics, and their contemporary prototypes. I notice that American audiences, of both sexes, and all ages, take it for granted that the classical dancers of Russian and Danish ballet are virile, and when Michael Somes of the Royal Ballet embraces his English ballerinas the same attention is given to this fine and princely *danseur noble* as the audience gives to the tenor in the Verdi opera. The foreign *danseurs nobles,* in the classic ballets—especially when these are *ballet d'action* with a gracious plot, character and décor—are considered romantic and eminently masculine. The American *danseur,* extracted from the sumptuous ballet and placed inconspicuously in a character abstract, in a ballet cerebral, appears suddenly—to the audience—to be effete. The connotation of effete then becomes effeminate.

The precise artistic responsibility of the American ballet is not to decide whether or not homosexuals shall be allowed to dance in the theatre. It is that the *danseur* should be presented in ballet with a masculine significance. Discussing this aspect of ballet with Russian and European professionals I find that in the foreign theatre the *danseur* subordinates his personal prejudices and predilections to the classic theory of masculinity in dance. Whatever he may be offstage, onstage he is *le danseur.* And inasmuch as the foreign theatres still retain repertoires which explicitly define genders and love in the ballet, the normal and permissive emotional states of sensual love are developed in the ballets. For an example, consider the repertoires offered by visiting national ballet companies—those of the Royal

Ballet, the Royal Danish Ballet, and the Bolshoi Ballet. And note that the *danseurs* of most significance in American ballet—the Danish Erik Bruhn, the Franco-Russe Eglevsky, Youskevitch, and Zoritch, and the American Kriza, are emphatically male, not only in attitude and character but also in repertoire.

In the ballet, love, like every other emotion, must be conveyed with lyric movement and gesture. Man, in his normal world, is expected to be tender and courteous to his mistress, as well as passionate. He must, ideally, both conquer and protect the female. The same male prerogative allowed in novels, operas, and plays—and the exact attributes he is adjured to cultivate by marriage counseling bureaus and hygienic lectures on his love life—are those he must employ in dancing. His training fits him for this *danseur* technique when it is properly given.

The *danseur* technique develops the attributes of the prize athlete—balance, coordination, endurance, flexibility, judgment of distance, a feeling for or understanding of space, and precision of movement. The main difference is that the *danseur* does not compete—he must appear to command all these virtues effortlessly, and as normal attributes, rather than as training for a contest of skill and brute strength. If, before a display of *entrechat-huit,* an official like an umpire bustled out on the stage and addressed the audience through a megaphone relating the records already set and tempting the present one, the audience would respectfully observe the form of the *danseur.* Bruhn and Youskevitch might become the subjects of sagas like *Casey at the Bat.* But Classic ballet precludes exhibitionism—its forte is an excellence of performance, *comme il faut.* Its technique idealizes the *danseur* and the *danseuse.* When the repertoire fails to give them significance as the supreme male and the sublime female of the Classic genre, then the repertoire has failed in its artistic responsibility to the dancers and to dancing. This applies to situations, or plots and characterizations, tragic and comic, anguished and joyous. The connotation in all emotion and action must remain clearly male and female, or the audience is confused, and the ballet is obtuse.

Largely, the American audience's contempt for the *danseur* is the audience's ignorance of dance as the first art of mankind. Insufficiency in normal education predicates the ignorance. Perhaps all the companies should preface their pretty, glossy souvenir books every season with Havelock Ellis' words: "Dancing and building are the two primary and essential arts. The art of dancing stands at the source of all the arts that express themselves first in the human person. The art of building, or architecture is the beginning of all the arts that lie outside the person; and in the end they unite. Music, acting, poetry proceed in the one mighty stream; sculpture, painting, all the arts of design in the other. There is no primary art outside these two arts, for their origin is far earlier than man himself; and dancing came first."

There is an imprimatur of virility on the American Indian, the African and Maori chieftain, and the Spaniard. When dancers, costumed as these, drum the earth with their feet, leap into the air, gyrate or click their heels, their masculinity is valid for the American audience. Here because we have not had a tradition of nobles and peasants in their attires through the centuries, the tunic of the Sugarplum's Cavalier may not appear to clothe the *danseur* as a brave, noble and triumphant fellow. When we are exposed to *The Nutcracker* as children, the Cavalier is perfectly credible as a male—he is as male as Clara's *Nutcracker* princeling. The man and the boy are recognized easily by children. For this reason, if for no other, American ballet must emphasize the romantic male in repertoire, either by revivals of the old works, or by creations of others as vivid in the incorporation of sex in the dancers male and female.

The most obvious audience reaction to male dancing has come in the American response to folk dancing, and the dance of the genre *caractère* in the Classic métier. The Moiseyev troupe and the *danseurs* of the Royal Danish Ballet and the Bolshoi Ballet, are notably masculine in style, figure and the approach to dance. These companies produce spectacular male technicians, who excite American audiences to wild applause. We have such technicians, except that for every ten boys trained in our system, the Danes and the Russians train twenty and forty. The difference is in the theatres—in one the male dancer has honor, in the other none.

A boy in the United States who wishes to become a dancer cannot easily develop his talents. He may the more easily become a crooner by practicing in the bath, but for the dance, in any genre, he needs floor space—and training under a teacher. He should begin his preliminary training between eight and ten, or his form and technique will seldom become the standard of his foreign confreres. The few exceptions, like Youskevitch, have been athletes and unusually gifted dancers who, coming comparatively late to the Classic métier, have mastered it to the *danseur noble* qualifications. Now and then, as in the case of Alan Howard, parents will give a boy lessons from early childhood. More is required. Howard, for instance, was sent to a private school so that his education could be concentrated in liberal arts; he was given lessons in French, and music, and sent regularly to dancing class, promoted from one school to the next, and with teachers of uniformly excellent caliber. This early and well defined education better prepares the American boy for dancing in the Classic métier. He should enter a company as an apprentice at about fifteen or sixteen, to begin to learn a repertoire, and he should, ideally, have already begun an education in stagecraft and ballet's associated arts of opera and drama. This applies equally to the girl. Both these young people will have, ideally, completed their normal, or general education past the regulation high school period. They now know as much as they need to know as apprentices. For the rest of their lives as dancers, they must be prepared to learn by studying the arts and crafts of their profession, and by slowly and sensitively absorbing human experiences for the growth of heart and mind. Only by the employment of thinking, feeling artists is art matured.

But even when this ideal condition prepares the student, as the *danseur* in the American theatre he is often the forgotten entity in choreography—or, even more pathetically, he enters the classic roles so tentatively that his masculine authority is negligible. He is accomplished in technique, enriched in mind, but awkward in the spirit of his maleness. The emasculated *danseur* spirit is caused by the consciousness of being suspect in his national theatre. Unless the *danseur* is accepted

Alan Howard, Chicago born and trained, premier danseur *of Ballet Russe de Monte Carlo.*

as a virile force he negates his training and his artistry. The answer is not to develop a bold, coarse truculence in the male dancer but to give him socially, artistically, and psychologically a position of significance in America parallel to the paramount male position of the man dancer in all other countries, civilized or non-civilized.

When the Bolshoi Ballet and the other great companies appear onstage, their girls, whether dancing in ballets tragic or gay, by their soft and fragile grace or their astonishing aerial lightness emphasize the robust and splendid deportment of the men and boys. A great deal of ballet's enthrallment for the audience is the evocation of mysterious and almost mystic beauty. We allow this quality of beauty to the ballerina, and it must be complemented with a masculine elegance in her partner. The male dancer cannot possibly support a position authoritative and strong, far less one imperial, in the connotation of "elegance," when he approaches his role with a hangdog air. And the audience does well to despise this travesty of *le danseur,* who comes sulking or skulking out of the wings onstage. The American audience was amazed, in the early part of the century, to find men of the personal good looks and virile natures of Bolm, Mordkin and Kosloff in ballet. Recently the audience behaved like delighted children at the spectacle of the Russian dancers. Other audiences react in the same way, and the point of comparison was odiously pressed home for us when the New York City Ballet went to Japan, where a critic, comparing the American company with the Bolshoi—which had recently appeared in that theatre—criticized the American boys for loafing about onstage and being distinguishable from girls only because they were less competent as dancers. It is not my personal predilection to compare the American and the Russian *danseur,* but this contrast is emphasized in the international press which concedes that the gulf lies most widely between these types—a gulf, I may say, further marked by the fact that Russian and American ballet produce the most spectacular *danseuse* technicians.

What precludes overall excellence in the American *danseur,* when he is as well trained—and for as long a period and in the same fine schools where his feminine counterpart receives her American education? In what ways do the American boys and men differ from their contemporaries, especially in the Royal Danish Ballet and the Bolshoi? We have brains and brawn, a nucleus of academic pedagogues, and the most imperative need of producing a quality product if ballet is to survive in the American theatre. What more do we require? The *danseurs,* in the majority, believe that ballet needs state support, to establish an economy, and an academic responsibility.

Ted Shawn, who has done most, and did it first, to elevate the American man dancer to artistic and social prestige, says of the Moiseyev Ballet, "After watching twenty-four men, born in a country where there never was a prejudice against men dancing, but taken for granted as a thing in which men excel, I knew again that America will never have a truly great and enduring national ballet until we have licked the prejudice against male dancers. As I look back over my forty-eight years of dancing and see what a long way we have come, I feel sure that it will be licked. The first necessity is to reach boys in their formative years, for a physical and a mental attitude that is male in dance. And the economy will have to be drastically changed, so that a man dancer will not find living hazardous. Male dance students start with a disadvantage in age, compared to girls—fathers will pay for ballet lessons for their daughters but boys have to grow old enough to get jobs from which they earn enough money to take dancing lessons. And then the boy tries to command a physically onerous task after working hours, when his mind and his muscles are already fatigued! If in America we had the system of training that produces the men dancers we admire from Denmark and Russia, we would develop prodigies of men dancers also. But we also need to give the man dancer economic security after he makes the grade as a dancer, in a salary on which he can live and raise a family like a normal person—only then shall we get normal men in the majority going into dancing as a professional career. As it is, we are getting only a spoonful of talented male dancing out of an enormous reservoir of talent. And all the truly great male dancers in the Classic Dance have to be imported into American ballet, as in the case of Erik Bruhn, from the Royal Danish Ballet. When, again in the case of Bruhn, these male dancers withdraw from our theatre to other theatres, it is at once evident that they are an irreparable loss to American Ballet."

In the training of the man dancer, Shawn feels, part of the general education should be in the scientific knowledge of what is masculine movement, and what is feminine.

The man dancer should be informed of things anatomic, organic, functional, emotional and historical that combine to form the basic principles of masculine and feminine bodily movement in dancing. And the choreographer, Shawn emphasizes, must understand all these things before he begins to work for the dancer—what subject matter fits each sex, what kinds of music and rhythms are predominantly male, or predominantly female, in music's extension into dance.

There is almost no serious literature on ballet devoted entirely to boys, and a number of boys refrain from buying books on ballet because of the generally accepted view that these are meant for girls. This comes from the tradition among American and English audiences en masse that *ballet is beauty* and beauty, while suitable as an emotional and cultural avocation for girls, is very unsuitable to boys. Part of the visual beauty in ballet resides in the partnering of the *danseuse* by the *danseur,* and ballet in which only girls appeared, lifted by girls, held in pirouette turns by girls, and supported in the "fish dive" by girls might become physically possible in America, where girls are strong and athletic, but it would seriously affect the esthetic concept of American dance, to degrees bordering on narcissism, transvestitism, and the preoccupation with ballets of theme and style in negation of the accepted libidinal norm.

American ballet is clearly a matriarchy, and on the evidence of what befell French and Italian ballet, will suffer artistic attrition if the *danseur* is not given his rightful place in the national ballet theatre. He seems now to extol his best technique not in harmony with, but in contest with, the *danseuse.* A *maître* of fifty years experience in continental theatres who sometimes teaches the classic roles to American boys tells me wrily that very often his able students, when mastering the Variations for Prince Siegfried, will remark that it is "not much of a part" compared with that of the Swan Queen. The first time the good man was so informed he was thunderstruck to realize that the American *danseur* did not understand Siegfried to be dancing as the ardent, wilful lover of the tragic Swan Queen, but thought of him as a rival to the ballerina who was dancing the role of Odette. Outside of Eugene Slavin no *danseur* in our theatre now dances Hilarion in *Giselle* as a lover half-mad with jealousy. Hilarion is considered "a minor role" and "not the male lead," thereby throwing Albrecht out of focus.

The aged *maître's* recommendation was that potential American *danseurs* be put into clubs in schools, given an insignia, and a code or slogan, and treated as the male part of the ballet. Then, in special classes, they should be brought into classes with girls, and oriented so that they are dancing *with* girls, not against them —the opposite, in fact, of a co-sexual game of baseball or basketball, and as segregated as, for instance, a troupe of Cub or Boy Scouts.

And it seems necessary to emphasize for Americans the athletic and even the acrobatic qualities of dancing, in order to make it a permissible vocation for boys. The orientation will have to develop not the contesting part of sports, but the championship quality. Championship is sustained by being classic—the best of your kind. It makes the prize athlete and the *danseur*. And in sports as well as in the ballet there is the necessity for team work, for "good sportsmanship," in order for the individual and the team to produce "the best."

Many of the best dancers have received primary and advanced training from women teachers—Youskevitch is the pupil of Preobrajenska—but it is evident that an American ballet student, male, requires a masculine approach to dance that only a male teacher can give him. This "masculine approach" involves not only a muscularity in technique, but a thought, attitude, and projection that it is obviously impossible for a female to grant.

There have always been, and there remain, a number of homosexuals in ballet and the theatre in general but ballet alone cannot be held responsible for the pervert on the stage. Ballet should, however, accept the responsibility for the ugly perseverance of assumed homosexuality by normal males, who either submit or readily pretend, to homosexual tendencies. This is done out of bitter economic need or ambition, perhaps when an obscure dancer, usually at the beginning of his career, enters a company in which the authority is entrenched in a homosexual person. To achieve notice, to ingratiate himself, and out of the desperate need to "get on" in his profession, the boy accedes to an overt form of life to which he is not naturally inclined. This condition exists now, and not by any means only in the American theatre. There is another kind of apprentice who resolutely declares himself of homosexual tendencies, whether he inclines to them by nature or not, out of the assumption that to be "the artiste" it is necessary to be wholly different from his fellows in the bus, the subway and the street. This type appears more often in English and American ballet, where social prejudices still encourage what they are believed to condemn.

In all that I have observed in our theatre and audience nothing seems so urgent to me for the American ballet as the survival of the *danseur*. We have a habit of being resourceful and economical, of balancing the budget or inventing a means, when we are pushed hard enough against the wall. Our present precarious econ-omy in ballet will be solved by the famous American acumen in business if not by the lackadaisical American responsibility in the theatre. But for the immediate present nothing so lowers our prestige as the qualities lacking in our male dancers. The cadet arrangement, where a male class of youths receives instruction from a male authority, is the one advocated by other schools for the training of national dancers. It has worked with widely recognized results on the national ballets we most admire, or envy. It must be construed as necessary for ours.

Compared with other governments, our national government is well-nigh blind to the uses of a national ballet. A Washington congressman will, in this day and age, rise up and in public declare that a cultural center of theatre for Washington, D.C., is a waste of money for tap and toe-dancing. Officials persist in confusing the art of the dance with dancing as a form of infantile fun or wicked abandon, although there is hardly a religious sect that continues to forbid dance, either secular or sacred. The dance artist is largely ignored by officialdom, except to be shipped abroad, in choice lots, with the sponsoring of ANTA and such organizations. This does not apply only to the dancer but to all American artists. Van Cliburn was accorded little notice in Russia. The representatives of United States officialdom did not even plan to attend the concert at which the American pianist caused the international furore, and went only on last-minute urging by advisors, to save a red-faced U.S.A. Americans who live abroad regularly grow incensed at the embarrassing situation for American artists in foreign theatres, when American officialdom takes no notice of their presence. This has serious implications in some societies, such as the Japanese, where the dance is an integral part of the national culture. In Japan in 1958, the New York City Ballet seemed to Tokyo press and society to be publicly snubbed by Americans of distinguished positions in Japan. No advice or orientation is given to American dance companies at home before they journey abroad and the social errors that result are not so much funny as they are a disgrace to the national theatre and a reflection on the nation itself. To those who believe that the behavior of the stage personnel and the audience abroad is insignificant, some recognition of the American artist's influence abroad is to be gleaned from the report of Norman Cousins, in 1958, from Warsaw.

Writing in *The Saturday Review of Literature,* of which he is editor, Mr. Cousins tells of his attendance at American Ballet Theatre's gala performance in the Palace of Culture, a thirty-five story structure modeled after the Moscow University, and presented to Poland as a gift from the U.S.S.R. Here, in a series of eleven performances sponsored by the United States State Department and ANTA, American Ballet Theatre danced behind the Iron Curtain. The American company received stirring ovations, and inevitably, was compared by Polish critics with Russian companies, in which two hundred and more members are the norm. These critics thought that the American dancers had "a pronounced superiority" in spirit, precision, and artistry. But, more important to this discussion, Mr. Cousins reports that one of the Polish critics told him he had long been of the opinion that Americans were culturally barren—and that this was an opinion formed not by adverse political propaganda about the United States of America, but by the "art entertainment" exported out of the United States, in movies, through which the Polish critic had assumed the smoking gun and chewing gum to be the twin symbols of life in the United States. Now, after seeing the American Ballet Theatre dancers, and an American concert artist, Roman Totenberg, who had recently performed in a concert in Warsaw, the critic felt that America had to be considered an important cultural force.

We are now living in such times that our newspaper headlines every day compel us to examine our standing in the world. When that position is "an important cultural force" it seems no more than sensible and urgent to advocate the exploitation of our cultural merits. In the cold war skirmishes other nations are not blind to these advantages. It seems part of American ballet's artistic responsibility to convey these truths to our people, and to our government.

THE STAGE

Here, eventually, is the arresting responsibility. It is the theatre's ancient function to be *a place to view,* rather than to assume some of the prerequisites of the village green, the market place, the pulpit or the rostrum. The stage is where ballet lives, and never were creatures so dependent on an audience as are the dancers. A painter can stack his canvases; playwrights and authors can amass their written works; sculptors can mold and chisel in solid forms; scientists and mathematicians can compile formulae and graphs. The dancer ceases to exist unless he is discovered by the audience, here and now. The music of the ballet survives, and choreographers may now make use of dance notation to record their works. Designers leave sketches almost as lively as reality. Books and old programs yellow on the shelves but capture in the written word and the static photograph some memory of the illusive art. Only the dancer perishes unless he is beheld.

And he lives only according to what his company or choreographer decrees for him, if he lives recognizably, and in economic security. In the day of mass organization and with the present cost of theatre few dancers rise up like flaming meteors to track paths across the wastes in the romantic traditions of Duncan, St. Denis and Fuller. So it is to *the companies* that we must look for the animate dancer. and the theatre dance that is the ballet. What the companies produce onstage will largely determine the response of the audience and its support of the ballet.

Clearly, it is impossible to please all in any one audience, and the company that hopes to do so will be dismissed as paltry, because it will operate on the lowest level of mediocrity. A company that too shrewdly strives for an eclectic character will achieve a style as soothing but hardly as stimulating as cough syrup. It will be refuted in its claim of forming a national ballet. The ideal state lies in a compromise between a stubborn intent to give the audience what is artistically good for it, and a clear recognition of what the independent and sophisticated American audience will consent to pay for, as patrons.

American ballet will have to clean house, and discard some prides it cannot afford, and throw out some prejudices that now masquerade as "traditions." It must have a better economy, and a better balance between the men and women dancers, and it has to discover and support choreographers who will create the new repertoire. The repertoire we have produced in the first half of the century is full of striking examples of what an American ballet may become. It is a traveling salesman's sample case of American dance and dancers, but it is still only indicative—not a whole and significant theatre to rank with those accepted as national ballets. We have, so far, shown types of dancers, and styles of ballets, and because our choreographers and dancers are so widely admired we are now expected to reveal, in a growing repertoire, an American ballet. This, precisely, means the art of ballet in a distinctive, and a representative American spirit, and I use the word "art" in its plain definition: *skill as the result of knowledge and practice.*

American money finances musical and television theatres but is largely withheld from ballet, whose "angels" are few and far between. The blunt reason is that we produce no large-scale ballet, as we produce musicals, which are recognizable and evocative not only at home but in a world-wide theatre. One American millionaire puts it thus: philanthropy is directed toward organizations of scientific inquiry, such as Geriatrics; or the preservation of life, such as the state of crippled children. Ballet is not acceptable as a philanthropy—it must be treated as big business, if we are to invest money in it. This need not insinuate propaganda or puerility into the ballet theatre any more than it does into the "musical" theatre. Look at what has happened in *that* direction! At the turn of the century, only the intelligentsia and the most rabid avant-garde supported a writer like George Bernard Shaw. Now a "musical" called *My Fair Lady,* lifted from a Shaw play called *Pygmalion,* has set attendance records not only in the United States but in the world. In half a dozen countries, and as many languages, Shaw's Eliza is the triumph of her era. See what has been done with an American Eliza (the character in *Uncle Tom's Cabin*), although only in excerpt, by the American choreographer Robbins in the musical play and film, *The King and I.* But American ballet resists change, and will not wholeheartedly accept precedent, so it hangs on a ledge between daring invention and anonymity. There is a serious lack of libretti as literature, and a total ignoring of the related arts.

Again, to compare the national ballet closest to ours in age, ideals, and principles, observe what has formed the English ballet. Developed on the same Imperial Russian ballet foundation that is the basis of our ballet, the English have retained the national imprimatur of *ballet d'action.* Contrary to the statement, made in print in the United States, that the English have "only followed the old-fashioned Russian *ballet d'action* style" this is a style that *belongs* to the English. In 1717, John Weaver, an English dancing master, produced *The Loves of Mars and Venus* at the Theatre Royal, in Drury Lane. This was the first *ballet d'action.* When English ballet makes use of *ballet d'action* it does so with a vested authority, from a very old theatre which so developed the art of pantomime that it helped to form the art of Noverre, the first great ballet choreographer, and of Sallé, ballet's first great dance-actress.

On a graphic national taste, and a distinctive theatrical style, the English have created a national ballet theatre. It ranks with the best. It was formed during the depression between two wars, and depeloped during and in the aftermath of our most terrible war. Since 1930 the English ballet has produced a distinctive English repertoire, especially suited to the styles of its dancers and the tastes of its people. It may be said to represent the English, in the same way that architecture, literature, music and painting reflect a nation and a time.

The English draw from a reservoir of arts. They employ fairy tales on which to embroider fantasy, and show no compunction about employing profound themes, from the Bible to social indictments. The remarkable woman who organized the Royal Ballet is Ninette de Valois, direct from the Diaghilev Dynasty, a pupil of Cecchetti and Espinosa. Between 1931 and 1937 she created nineteen ballets, among the most notable *Job, The Haunted Ballroom, The Rake's Progress* and *Checkmate. Job* is based on William Blake's poem of that title, from a libretto written by Geoffrey Keynes, an authority on the poet. *The Haunted Ballroom* is the story of *The Master of Treginnis. The Rake's Progress* is inspired by Hogarth's pitiless painted documentary. *Checkmate* is, of course, a ballet with a relation to chess. All of these are immediately understood by audiences in England and, largely, by the audience of the world.

Frederick Ashton, who began his career with Rambert, was the protégé of de Valois and worked with Constant Lambert, the English composer and conductor, to create, under de Valois, an empathy of music and dance for the English ballet. Ashton's work has ranged from *Capriol Suite,* a group of Elizabethan dances, to *Rio Grande,* but his course has been closely set in the Classic genre— in style of dancing, form of ballet, and in principle, or ideal. He is not, as some American writers report, contriving a slavish imitation of Russian ballet, or, for that matter, the old ballets at the Paris Opéra. He is, more concisely, working in the métier described by the Abbé Michel de Pure in *Idée des Spectacles:* "Tragedy and ballet are two species of painting in which what is most illustrious in the world is placed on view." The statement was made quite some time ago; about 1658.

The English *idée des spectacles* (categorized by some American avant-garde balletomanes as English ballet-spectacle) satisfies the English audience—more, it is an authoritative art form for the English, and as national ballet produces an enthusiastic audience and a good box office. It is particularly worth while for us to observe what has formed it, because it still stands closest to our *idée,* if not our spectacle. Ashton's full-length ballets are essentially English dance, in style and spirit. These are, most notably, *Cinderella, Sylvia,* and *Ondine.* Ashton has also composed symphonic ballets. His *Symphonic Variations* for six dancers is his most successful abstract work.

Conscious of these things, and aware of the impression the great national companies make on the international theatre (and on the American one, especially) big business will interest itself in American ballet only when we are able to produce something large, lavish, and with the imprimatur MADE IN THE U.S.A. This type of investor is not concerned with Art, but with Theatre, and its interests in theatre other than ballet's has created an imagination and financial reservoir from which we have made new developments in "popular" theatre with musicals.

Foreign balletomanes visiting America invariably wonder why we have done nothing, in an American ballet, to rival the production in ballet of Fokine's *Prince Igor,* about the Polovtsian tribe. Balanchine declares that when this ballet was first produced in Western Europe it served to introduce "the unimagined color of Russian music and dancing combined in a striking single work." Foreign balletomanes, especially Russian ones, are immediately struck by the significance of the American Indian, whose dance was not only an art form, but a way of life, and who produced, incidentally, the best light cavalry of all time. Here are warriors galore, tribal fervency, historic ideology; and such a subject should compel American music and dancing. But except for Shawn's large American Continental repertoire, and an occasional "Indian number," the aboriginal Indian subject and dance is thoroughly ignored.

So is American literature, except by the animated cartoon characters of Walt Disney, who have danced through *The Legend of Sleepy Hollow* and parodied *Johnnie Appleseed.* Why, asks the mystified foreign balletomane, create an American ballet about Peter and the Wolf when you could create one about Tom Sawyer? And if your avant-garde factions dislike *Swan Lake* and *Giselle,* he adds, why not create a ballet to libretti by Dreiser or Faulkner?

The attempts to do so—as Loring's with Hemingway's *Capital of the World,* and Bettis' with Tennessee Williams' *A Streetcar Named Desire*—are few and far between. Loring created *Prairie* from the Sandburg epic, and de Mille, lacking a painter like Hogarth, was astute enough to seize from a newspaper the story of an American time and place for *Fall River Legend.*

In music, Bernstein, Copland and Gould have done exactly what Manuel de Falla did: they have written genuine musical expression of a people, without actually depending on folk song. This should be a point of interest to the American avant-garde faction, who despise anything "folk," as they barricade the ballet from the taint of "ethnic." When de Falla composed he breathed the spirit of Spain into the music—passionate Andalusia speaks with a different voice than that of the cold proud province of Castile. In one small country, Spain, he found enough contrasts to define its people. Think what ballet scores could do for a territory as vast as the American! In his ballet scores de Falla gives some of the most versatile and graphic descriptions of Spain—a passionate intensity in *El Amor Brujo,* and joyousness and malicious humor in *Le Tricorne.* They were not composed by accident. I have seen a letter written by de Falla to a friend when he was writing *Le Tricorne* for Diaghilev, and he says, "The Russians have danced (in *El Amor Brujo*) to Spanish love and ecstasy, and now I shall make them dance to the sounds of ringing laughter and the shouts of uncontrollable joy." A "freer" composer could hardly be found, if we are set on having freedom for American ballet. De Falla used all of Spain for his sources, from church modes in the Andalusian, to Oriental forms. His folk airs were not imitated; they were assimilated into the music.

It is this assimilation that we are expected to create—of dances, music, libretti and painting—when we produce an American National Ballet repertoire. The impresario, and the company, are the governing authorities who dictate what the repertoire shall be, in theme and production. Kirstein, under whose aegis *Filling Station* and *Billy the Kid* were produced, turned away from the national significances of ballet to devote his patronage to the Neoclassic métier of Balanchine. Amberg says that from Kirstein's beginnings to Loring's conclusions there was consistent evolution. Loring's Dance Players was "an all-American company offering dance plays on American themes." Kirstein's Ballet Caravan was created for the collaboration of predominantly American artists, who adapted the traditional technique of ballet to contemporary and national American subjects and functions. In those stirring times when American ballet was beginning the choreographers were young giants in an unexplored territory. All that they did was splendid, because it had never been done before. They were, actually, the only "free" exponents of our ballet theatre, and they seemed (as Amberg writes of Eugene Loring) to have had an enthusiasm for the expression of America in dancing. They had strong social consciences: Loring's indictment in *City Portrait,* de Mille's thesis in *Fall River Legend*—Hogarth never was more aware than these. The libretti were evocative and widely comprehensive. Loring's *Man from Midian* and his *Prairie* are drawn from the Bible and the American poet Carl Sandburg. Robbins knew perfectly well how to limn a contemporary portrait in *Fancy Free, Interplay* and *Facsimile*; he has given audiences food for thought with *Age of Anxiety,* and an education in music in *Fanfare*. These few examples are surely eclectic enough to prove the prodigious range, and the intelligent awareness, of the American choreographer.

On the other and equally important side of the ledger the great foreign influences have been at their most compelling and sustaining when they made use of broad canvases of human feeling or expression, as did Tudor in his great ballets, and Balanchine in his themes of exaltation, like *Le Baiser de la Fée, Apollo,* and *Orpheus*. At every performance that the audience was touched to the heart, and made to feel, or struck to the mind and made to think, the choreographers in America—native or naturalized—were employing the Abbé's *idée* of placing on view what is most illustrious in the world. But the views that other national ballets develop are in theatres with a sounder economy than ours, and ones where there is not an audience as large and independent as the American, at odds with a faction in authority which believes its responsibility is not to give the audience what it wants, but only what is good enough for it. American ballet fails to realize that its American audience, ignorant and agreeable to start with, is no longer the naïve and impressionable yokel in the European theatre that we inherited.

The ballet professional who despises the audience is an anachronism, but some persevere in the notion that the function of the theatre is to educate rather than to entertain. This may someday elevate the American audience, but it is an untenable idea that it will dictate to it. There are several kinds of chauvinistic attitudes. One derides all ballet that is not distinguished as American in theme and substantially of contemporary inflection. This makes a wholesale embargo against the "classics" which are then referred to as "old war-horses." Sometimes there is a condemnation of all other national ballet—the English for being slavish imitators of the

Russians, the French for being decadent, and the Russian for being too old-fashioned in repertoire and coarse or emotional in style. Paradoxically, the attitude also refutes, in some factions, the American locale, theme, or character as not being The Ballet, renders an adverse judgment against American folk music and dancing and disqualifies the Interpretive. Other insults, intentionally, are construed as "pantomime," "dance-spectacle," and "vaudeville."

These various coteries are often able to support or to participate in small expositions of their preferred theatres, but, unfortunately, they do not advance American ballet to the point of interest for the paying audience or the investing business financier. These two important parties seem intent on glamour in the ballet, and aspire to compete with American ballet in the international theatre, rather than to protect or relegate it to isolated métiers in the United States of America.

Ballet has continuously undergone the protection and relegation of dilettante societies. In the eighteenth century the Paris Opéra's *prima ballerina* Marie Guimard commanded a private and esoteric theatre, supported by lovers of a general amiability about Guimard and ballet. Her house was decorated by Fragonard, and her admirers and patrons included Jean de la Borde, *valet de chambre* to Louis XV, and the Prince de Soubise, and ballets described as "true to Nature" were presented for an esoteric-minded coterie of the rich, the noble and the politically important. They were of a genre too aesthetic for the *hoi polloi* of the Parisian theatre.

At another tangent is the attitude that Modern Dance must be construed as the pure and original American style of movement, and we must forsake the *pointe,* discard the *maillot,* and forswear the dance called Classic. The argument that is triumphantly offered by this thin group of thinkers is that America has never had princes and peasants in its society and these are therefore inadmissible as characters in American ballet.

While this artistic rankling is pursued, the theatre stands in direct need of an audience. It is competing with a way of life and a standard of economy that Louis XV, the Russian Czars and Serge Diaghilev never knew, and with an audience accustomed to take plane, boat and train in quest of business and pleasure. We in the audience no longer sit in one place, pacified by occasional glimpses of what our betters decree as good for us; we move about in a search for what we want to see or possess.

It is not my belief that the audience should dictate to the stage, but I believe that the stage cannot survive unless it remains aware of its audience. We go to the theatre not in search of national culture but like little children—longing to be made to feel, willing to be made to think. The theatre makes an indelible impression on its listening, looking audience; perceiving this, the Danes have inscribed over the Royal Theatre in Copenhagen EI BLOT TIL LYST—NOT FOR PLEASURE ALONE. In ballet the function is theatrical dancing but the prerogative is expression, or communication—the employment of a power to make an audience feel and think. American ballet addresses itself to a free and independent audience whose right it is to individually reject or accept what its members chose to regard as unsatisfactory or as fine. Political propaganda would not be admissible, and the audience has already proved impervious to ready-made opinions printed for its education in ballet. The humility that the audience feels in the theatre is before that kindled and animate thing that is the dance—an elemental instinct of rhythm. The knowledge that the audience needs to best satisfy itself and reward the ballet is the recognition older theatres have already made—that there is a wide variety in dancing; that there is a special motivation for every dance, and for every dancer.

There are dancers who dance seriously and very, very well, who are products of training and will power. These are the people who dance as a way of life, in the profession of the theatre.

Others are impelled to dance by an instinct that seizes and transforms them and, translating a state of mind into a physical act, takes them out of their normal environment and sets them to dancing on a stage.

Finally, there is dancing as a state of grace—the quintessence of the dance—in which the dancer attains a luminous quality, out of a spiritual beneficence. The hackneyed word "inspired" is usually applied to this condition. It is not often to be seen in the theatre, but when it is, it is universally recognized, as it was in the dancing of Anna Pavlova—not merely by a clique called *balletomane*, or by the paying customers who are idiotically described as "the average audience."

We do not often behold dancing as a state of grace, because our world seldom cares to support the spirit from its nourishing core in the dancer to the sustaining boards of the stage. People who know the ballerinas Markova and Ulanova declare that, in our time, they contain this spirit of the ballet—the kindling force, the mysterious effluvium, that makes a performance radiant. Arnold Haskell has written that Ulanova tries always to leave her audiences with an increased spiritual awareness. That she succeeds is attested to by another Haskell statement, quoting a Jesuit who said that Ulanova gives the impression of holiness. Beyond the orthodox recognitions of the spirit there is a universal understanding, from the evidence of human sight, and the thought and feeling communicated by sight, of dancing as a state of grace.

The fervor of primitive dancers is often to be understood, not as religious rite in a theatrical sense, but as the physical manifestation of the spirit. American choreographers are perfectly aware of this, and Agnes de Mille makes Biblical reference to it when she speaks of "the moving creature that hath life."

Dancing as a state of grace is the strongest and purest condition of dance, and, unconsciously, we go in search of it when we buy our way into the theatre. There we are likely to see only dancing as a state of mind, and dancing as a way of life, and we may as well make ourselves agreeable to them. We in the audience are often too devout in our attitude to the ballet, and, being cruelly disappointed, we behave as though we have been denied a religion, rather than granted an evening's entertainment. Others of us, too awed by the attitude *précieux* of the balletomane, believe ourselves too ignorant to judge and too crass to appreciate, whereas we are actually being presented with dancing which neither makes us feel nor causes us to think. When an audience is discomfited in the theatre it is time for it to go to church, or to be judged in court.

If the American ballet theatre fails it is not for lack of an audience, but for a lack of understanding, because it is too wilful and too stiffnecked with pride to accept the audience. That ballet existed at all in the last century was because it adapted itself from the *place de la opéra* to the Melodeon Beer Hall. It does better now.

We have come a long way since those times—longer, and faster, than any other national development of the ballet. We are well on our way to a better status, and a greater and more exciting development, but we must decide where and how we wish to proceed. When the theatre is bent on avoiding bathos it has to beware of sacrificing profundity, and while making efforts to appear wise and witty it must also sustain beauty and nobility. If the audience could address the theatre in its collective voice I believe it would ask nothing more of the creators and interpreters of the ballet than that they avoid platitudes, while taking care not to fall into stained-glass attitudes. In the theatre both the performers and the audience must accept "tradition" as a growing, living thing rather than a series of hard and fast rules about what was done then and what is done now—or what is "American" Ballet, as opposed to what we produce as a national ballet.

Whether we employ the old English contredanse of one American emigrant, or the polka of another American emigrant, we must so respect the dance as to retain the raw animal vigor of its original creation. When we dance with classic elegance and wit we need something beyond the spatial design: a recognition of noble thought; an understanding of purpose. The artistic responsibility begins with feeling and thinking, and only artists so inspired will arouse feeling and thought in their audiences.

The theme is valuable only for its scope. It matters only how we dance, whether to a *berceuse* or a symphony. We are said to be a musical people, and we have established in our dancing the conventional canons of the ballet—elevation; aerial grace and power; neat, clean Turnout and quick, light motion. Our nymphae, of the caliber of those in the American Ballet Theatre's *Les Sylphides*, are praised in Chopin's country. European audiences (which include Russians) speak with excitement of the freshness and vitality, the brilliance and clarity, of American classicism. They recognize, out of their very rich experience, the strong American characterization and the artistic significance of ballets like *Billy the Kid, Rodeo* and *Fancy Free*. It would seem, on the evidence of world-theatre judgment, that we can perform anything as ballet, and that what we do we do surpassingly well.

It must, then, be superfluous and ridiculous to limit what we shall dance—and cut back, for example, royal roles—when we have proved that we may dance sylphides as well as cowboys and sailors and their girls. Our physical flexibility and our enormous ethnic inheritance of dances enable us to choose the greatest repertoire in ballet history. Vanities alone will limit our range of style and repertory—or authorities who define too pedantically what we may or may not express when we dance. Beyond the Classic canon of performance there is a fathomless sphere of feeling which the stage must contain in good taste, while continuing to recognize it. Our dancers will have to develop an inner splendor if they are not to remain always the child prodigies imitating or astonishing the adult artists of the ballet.

Our theatre, stage and audience, has been reproved for gaucheries of taste, but we are by nature a people bent on creating something individual and identifiable. We have, indeed, a real need for producing a graphic national ballet. At heart, we want to command a secure and opulent theatre, although we have so cheerily made the best of our stark one. In popular theatres, we are fond of dynamic performers who evoke audience response. What would be our response if our ballet theatre were to conjoin great American authors, painters, musicians and architects with the dance artists, as other national ballet theatres have done? With such a confluence of arts we might create an inspired repertoire that would be worthy of us, artistically and spiritually, as Americans.

The best—and, by the way, the most successful—of the choreographers and dancers have accepted the whole range of contemporary theatre and not the "legitimate" one alone. In movies, once despised by the intelligentsia, Gene Kelly has produced such an evolutionary film as *Invitation to the Dance;* since *Oklahoma!* the musical stage occupies a new métier. Robbins, conceded to be the choreographer of his era, declares that he makes no differentiation in his work for the legitimate or the "popular" theatre, but lets the situation dictate the form and method of the choreography. He adds that what he has learned in the musical theatre has gone into his work for ballet, and vice versa. There is no longer a standard of quality for one kind of audience—there is only the need for the best quality, in the only true connotation of the term classic.

Free of isms, and with its schisms resolved, American ballet will still need a repertoire with which to claim a place in the international theatre. From the indigenous Amerind to our newest emigrant, we have accumulated the whole world's repertoire of dances. Fear of being called "folksy" has now and then driven choreographers into being so avant-garde as to be obtuse. While we persevere in a good-humored attempt to catch up with our geniuses we might do well to explore the local and contemporary materials.

Print flowed in a black ocean to describe and analyze the Moiseyev ballets. Statistics compiled by theatres and television indicate that this dance company reached a wider audience in the United States than any other—and elicited more interest than any other. Despite the near-hysterical adjurations from critics at home and in England and Europe, the American audience took no notice of the statement that Moiseyev's troupe was not dancing the ballet, but was simply dancing. Some experts denied that the dancing was ethnic or folk.

Igor Moiseyev was a *premier,* and ballet master of the Bolshoi Ballet in 1937 when he formed his Folk ensemble. For the repertoire he collected a symposium of Russian dances, as different as that performed by the Georgians (who dance on the toes) and the people from Tashkent, who are the half-Oriental Uzbeks. Moiseyev trained his company in a special repertoire, in which they performed leaps, jumps and turns, and some of the most wonderful gliding motions ever beheld. In precision, speed, and elevation we have seen nothing better. In bewitching theatrical glamour—a gamut of moods grave and gay, which includes the unclassified "Partisans"—the Moiseyev dancers give a performance of irreproachable style and quality. It has been estimated that the company's greatest attraction lies in its spirit —of exuberance and ease, as though the dancers are dancing for joy in the urgent and immediate moment. I am informed, and not by balletomanes or people commercially involved in the theatre, that nothing has had such an effect on Americans as the Moiseyev Ballet, which, between a live tour and two unprecedented hours of exposition on national television, convinced the average American that Russians were people, not a mysterious element behind an iron curtain.

In truth, the exuberance and ease are the signal accomplishments of these dancers, whose repertoire of nearly two hundred ballets—or "dance numbers"—is sustained by these things: a five year course of study, following three years of preliminary training, in the Moiseyev School, to which is added regular lessons in the traditional genre at the Bolshoi Ballet School. The two schools, although separate, are both state supported, and in physical distance stand some city blocks apart. The education for the Moiseyev dancer is the full-time one, in academic and dance subjects, of the foreign national theatres. Daily classes and daily rehearsals, hours in length, are conducted in segregated classes. There are classes for *pas de deux,* solos, and group dancing. Besides the full schedule of work for the entire *corps,* each dancer gets individual attention and is encouraged to retain a vital force. One of the dancers told me that a dancer may ask, and will receive, private tuition of an hour or more in some role for which he feels he requires special attention, and that if he is dancing a *pas de deux* and feels the necessity of practicing, in private supervision with the teacher, he can demand, and receive, the support of the partner—whether or not the partner feels a like necessity for rehearsal. I was also told by a Moiseyev dancer that if the ballet master felt the troupe to be slackening in style or form it was nothing to put in, between class, rehearsal, and performance, eighteen hours and more of the total day's twenty-four.

With such a regimen, the Moiseyev company achieves its personal fervor and élan. It is the quality of joyousness, and the absolute authority of perfection, that make the dancers the marvels they are. In moods of gaiety, and in ones so sombre —in themes so significant—as that of *Partisans,* the spirit animates different tempos, colors different atmospheres, but remains the sustaining and splendid fount of the dance.

Critical viewers of the theatre are still weighing the effects of the Moiseyev dancers on American ballet. One immediate reaction has been more dancing with feeling and pyrotechnical feats, as discussed in *The Ballet Russe de Monte Carlo.* Another is a new attention to folk dance in the popular theatre. Significantly, the Ballet Russe recruited for its 1959 company a dancer named Richard Tarczynski, from the Polka-Go-Round, a professional dance group directed by Felix Sadoski and seen in tour in the West and Midwest, and on local television. In the Ballet Russe, young Tarczynski thereafter leaped like a Tartar and skirmished with swords among his fellows in Edmund Novak's ballet suite *Slavonic Dances,* and was roundly cheered by audiences about the country. Yurek Lazowsky, following the success of the Moiseyev Ballet, has organized and trained a group of dancers which is already exciting interest among audiences and critics.

If we are averse to following the Russians, the Danes, or the English, in the typical national ballet repertoires of their greatly admired companies, we may with the use of a little imagination find a source for our own. The polka and the mazurka have come to America and stayed. These and other "native" dances are to be seen annually in great festivals held by whole cities and regions where the residents keep in mind their foreign ancestry. America has derived its vast and complex cultures from them.

If we were to look as far back as our view reaches, to the only indigenous American, we should find the Amerindian, to whom all life was ceremonial, and for whom one word means both *ceremony* and *dance*. Here, at the source of our nation's history, we find the fount of the dance in America. All American Indian arts are rooted in dance, although we may observe other forces working in other nations—the *sagen* of the Scandinavian, and song for the Celts. All that is indigenous we have inherited from the American Indian; all that we have otherwise acquired have come to us from immigrant influences. This is the theme on which our nation, and our dancing, is created.

After conquest, dancing was forbidden to the Indian—a law tantamount to destroying his religion, politics and society. Until 1934, when a law was passed to permit the Indian to dance as he chose, Indians danced in secret, to preserve their civilization. All would have been lost except for the Indians in the southwest, in areas so remote and worthless that the conqueror did not travel that far to establish the laws. Here the old ones taught, by stealth, the young ones; and to preserve not only the tribal tradition but all Indian dancing, the teachers taught all the dances they knew and remembered. The Plains Indian was a rampant individualist and danced in solo, and southwestern tribes danced in groups, or corps. Even in ancient times the Indian danced in something like ballet—as soloists and in corps, interpreting birds and insects, relating stories of hunts and heroic feats. The Hopi Butterfly Dance and the Apache Mountain Spirit Dance probably look now, in costume and gesture and step, as they were seen in America before Christopher Columbus was born.

Now, in the pueblo dances of the southwest the audience sees a merging of the tribal dances because a nation once divided into warring factions unified in order to preserve their dance arts. That nation, slowly vanishing, still dances, and with a pride and skill that makes the Indian dancer one of the finest in the contemporary world. Amid the confluent styles and the evolutions through which the Indian preserved his dance, no Indian dance has deteriorated, and no Indian dancer has become depraved. In the repertoire where some dances are held, step and gesture, to the original there are also dances evolved out of expediency and wit. After 1874, the Crows in Montana were forced to give up their Sun Dance and when they were allowed to resume it, it was found that it had been lost with the teachers who died in the interim. So the Crows borrowed the Sun Dance of the Wyoming Soshones, and this is what Crows dance, with piety. It satisfies its purposes, apparently, and the Crows say that with it they brought home their sons safely from World War II—in which no Crow was killed in combat, although Crows served in some of the most hazardous theatres of war. Wittily, the Indian has made up a brilliant *divertissement* called the War Dance, performed exclusively for tourists, having no connotation of sacred rite to the dancer, and called, in private, the white man's Happy Dance. This wonderful irony alters to a native joyousness, when they dance the Grass Dance and the Omaha Dance, which is, we may say, a regional ballet.

We may take some lessons from the Indian on how to evolve, in order to survive. He gives us abundant proof that the dance may be borrowed and used with artistic integrity—more, with piety, and he shows us how to adapt to a changing economy and a changing environment. A real eagle feather now costs one-and-a-half to two dollars at the trading post, and so the Indian dancer who cannot afford it uses another kind of feather when dancing the Eagle Dance. His roaches and bustles that used to be made of eagle feathers and beads, balsa and rawhide, have given way to cheaper facsimiles made of more easily obtained materials. But when we stand at the powwows in Anadarko and Pawnee, or at Gallop and Flagstaff, we see an Eagle dancer literally soar in flight and the heart of the audience leaps with him, with a shock that brings tears to the back of the eyelids. Here the force lies in the dancer's passion and his skill. The force is the dance, not the costume. A glance at the impassive Indian audience informs us that here are not balletomanes and reviewers, but people drawing to themselves a spirit, or a feeling, as old as the land and its rhythms. The Indian dancer calls his costume regalia, and it is artistically wrought—but only for its purpose in the dance. He is a craftsman of awesome technique and prodigious repertoire, whose complicated dances are extremely difficult to perform. Every Indian dancer is a virtuoso. There is a duplicate and substitute for every basic step, and a further versatility to be obtained by the dancer in shifts in weight and stance, while dancing. Moreover, his dancing is exposed to the view of an informed audience, which sets, fundamentally, the standard for the dance.

And here the dance is the distinguished priority of the man, who permits women to dance only by special favor, or in certain dances. Dancing was once the exclusive right of the warriors and the chiefs, and women were permitted to dance only as a reward for a heroic act.

Into the new decade, the Indian dances. A continuous evolution in costume and dance design, an inspired use of heritage and influence transformed into living environments from traditional ones, and a primal urge to dance—these are the endowments offered to American ballet, and the extraordinary example set by the first Americans. For the Indian, the dance is much more than moving in a pattern, in order to set records for feats of activity or intrigue the reviewers for the next day's newspapers. The dance here remains supreme, and the dancer is recognized as its instrument, as inseparable from it as the singer from the song. Dancing out of the impulse as well as by the skill, the Indian dancer gives his audience the clear interpretation of force which thrusts him out and up and down. He is animate, impelled by a heart and mind, or by thought and feeling. We who have broken all the barriers between styles—as in Loring's Technic that admits no separation in dance between contortion, distortion and naturalness—have a boundless stage and a limitless theatre. We need only to know—the dancer and the audience, and all the persons that link these two communicating entities— why we dance. It is because we are human beings, so shaped and so motivated as to have created the art that is dance. The great ballet and the great dancer

The epitome of American ballet classicism: prima ballerina Maria Tallchief, with Nicholas Magallanes in Balanchine's Symphony in C (Palais de Cristal).

derive from this understanding, or are worthless without it. The audience is also committed to the knowledge, because there must be no permanent isolation of the stage from life. In this response we are all equally involved, and the responsibility is not to an art form alone, but to a national culture. Our responsibility goes beyond contention as to where to set boundaries for the ballet, and how to make the nice distinction between ethnic and folk dancing, or how to claim an influence and make use of it as an inheritance. The audience responsibility stretches beyond the theatre to official recognition and civic undertaking. The theatre does not consist entirely of the stage and the wings, but of all the arts and artifacts by which it is sustained. A living wage is due not only to the artisans but also to the artists, and these two, instead of living in armed truce, need each other to found a national theatre.

The graphic repertoire of a national ballet does not so much represent scene and character as it incorporates the spirit of its people. In the end, the responsibility cannot be divided and allocated, and is not so much an artistic responsibility as it is a national one. Ballet and its related arts is still what the dance was in other times—that same thing of which an ancient Oriental wrote, *One may judge a king by the state of dancing during his reign.* For the audience and the dancers there is no more salutary thought, no greater inspiration, when looking at American ballet.

Our audience stretches far beyond national boundaries, and into those of the international theatre. There we both delight and amaze. In the words of the critic and dancer Witaly Osins: ". . . when we first heard about American Ballet (we said) Now, that for sure could not be true! Classical Ballet in America! Academic traditions in a country which seemed to produce only jazz and cowboy movies! No! . . . With all due respect to the Russian dancers from the Bolshoi . . . I must admit that the New York City Ballet may at the moment be the best ballet company in the world. I confess that I make this admission grudgingly. . . . It is with a note of perhaps pardonable regret that I find the New World eclipsing what was once the exclusive domain of the Old. There are many people in Europe who still wonder how it did happen. The answer to that, I am sure, is hard work, enthusiasm, faith and recognition of the fact that Ballet, like any other art, is not the property of one country, nor the characteristic feaure of one nation."

We inherited a tradition, and we received an influence. In our artistic maturity we must not rest content with the ability to astound and amaze. We must achieve such a tradition as will, in return, influence and inspire others. In Shawn's philosophy and Loring's formula the spirit and the science of American dance have established complete freedom for us to dance not with feet alone, but with the whole body. In a society which now recognizes him as a cultural part of the nation, the dancer must develop a mind and heart. He must be as integral a part of the nation as all the other creators of its sciences and arts, and he will become integral only when he is worthy, and his society is fully aware, of the art of dance.

The impulses to dance that move the American dancer down, or thrust him out and up, the feeling heart and the thinking mind—both must combine in the motivation that is dance. Dancing in the ways we must, out of our prides and prejudices, we give the audience a view not only of our stage but of American life itself, and the American audience finds itself reflected there. Brought together as American Dance, it represents us to others and is a part of our history—past, present and future.

THE BEGINNING

1. In *The Ballet Companion* the Romantic Era and the ballerinas Taglioni, Cerito, Grisi and Grahn are discussed in the sections of *La Sylphide* and *Le Pas de Quatre*.

2. Elssler, whose permanent escort was John van Buren, son of the President in office, was the subject of lithographs and whiskey advertisements, and appeared in miniature on gentlemen's shirt studs and cuff links. A pair of such studs is in the Dance Archives of the Museum of Modern Art in New York.

3. Danilova was the matchless interpreter of flesh-and-blood characters in *Coppelia, Gaîté Parisienne,* and *Le Beau Danube,* and danced the cancan in *Boutique Fantasque*—all with Classic technique and a bewitching femininity.

4. Céleste then had her own company at the London Adelphi. Her remark about Turnbull is amusing, in view of the fact that Céleste danced Taglioni's *La Bayadère* and *La Sylphide* in America.

5. The message was directed less at the management than at the Paris Opéra audience, which treated Elssler badly when she unsuccessfully danced Taglioni's roles. The Opéra had, in the first place, employed Elssler as a way of disciplining the temperamental Taglioni, who went to St. Petersburg.

6. Montez was an Irish adventuress named Eliza Gilbert, whose only dance training was a five-month study in London under a Spanish dancer. She was a poor dancer but a successful femme fatale, and had notorious love affairs, one of which cost Ludwig I of Bavaria his throne. She had little success in the ballet theatre in America but ladies flocked to her lectures in New York on "The Care of the Bust," and she published *The Art of Beauty* in America.

7. *Sylvia* was a distinguished ballet, with music by Delibes. It has been reconstructed by Ashton for Fonteyn at the Royal Ballet.

8. AGMA—American Guild of Musical Artists—has jurisdiction over dancers in ballet companies, Modern Dance groups, and opera-ballet. AGVA—American Guild of Variety Artists—has jurisdiction over dancers in variety revues, circuses and night clubs. Into the nineteen forties there were episodes involving American dancers not unlike that of the Chicago "Dramatic Agency" from which dancers too gullibly accepted mysterious engagements in the Caribbean and South America.

9. The Bournonville System is described in *The Ballet Companion*.

10. Despreaux in *L'Art de la Danse,* 1806: ... *se dit lorsque la tête et les reins sont en ligne perpendiculaire audessus de la partie du pied sur laquelle tout le corps est porté. On peut être en équilibre sans être d'aplomb; mais il n'y a pas d'aplomb sans équilibre.* (When the head and the small of the back are in a straight line and held directly above the supporting foot. One can be in equilibrium without aplomb— but not in aplomb without equilibrium.)

11. Eurhythmics was one of the new sciences of movement that affected twentieth-century dance. The first was the analysis of gesture and expression by the French François Delsarte (1811–1871), which divided all movements into eccentric, concentric and normal characters, and codified the laws that control the movements of the body. His influence on Modern Dance has been especially notable in Shawn's work. (Quod vide *Every Little Movement* by Shawn—published in 1954—for a comprehensive study of Delsarte's philosophy, science of applied aesthetics, and its influence on American dance.) Eurhythmics was developed by a music teacher, Emile Jacques Dalcroze. Its value was soon recognized in other arts and it is now integrated into the dancer's basic training. Dalcroze's celebrated pupils are Uday Shankar, Marie Rambert and Mary Wigman. Diaghilev was impressed with the science of eurhythmics and Rambert assisted Nijinsky when he was creating *Le Sacre du Printemps*. Labanotation, the best-known system of dance notation, was invented by a Hungarian, Rudolf von Laban, whose students were Wigman and Kurt Jooss. Laban founded Central European Dance in 1911, at Munich. These scientific savants influenced the movement, and the composers created the spirit of the new dance. Diaghilev's Ballets Russes at first danced to lyrical compositions by Rimsky-Korsakov and Glazunov, and later to the music of Poulenc, Auric, Satie and Stravinsky. The contemporary styles in painting were also featured in Diaghilev's ballets, where the opulent colors and forms of Bakst and Benois were replaced by cubism and constructivism in the paintings of Picasso, Matisse, Derain and Marie Laurençin.

12. Fokine's Five Principles for the New Ballet:

(1) Not to form combinations of ready-made and established dance steps, but to create in each case a new form corresponding to the subject, the most expressive form possible for the representation of the period and the character of the nation represented.

(2) Dancing and mimetic gestures have no meaning in a ballet unless they serve as an expression of its dramatic action, and they must not be used as a mere *divertissement* or entertainment having no connection with the scheme of the whole ballet.

(3) The New Ballet admits the use of conventional gesture only where it is required by the style of the ballet and in all other cases endeavors to replace hand gestures with mimetic ones of the whole body. Man can and should be expressive from head to foot.

(4) The New Ballet advances from the expressiveness of the face to the expressiveness of the whole body, and from the expressiveness of the individual body to the expressiveness of a group of bodies and the expressiveness of the combined dancing of a crowd.

(5) The New Ballet, refusing to be the slave either of music or of scenic decoration, and recognizing the alliances of the arts only on conditions of complete equality allows perfect freedom to the scenic artist and to the musician. In contradistinction to the older ballet, it does not demand of the composer "ballet" music as an accompaniment to dancing, but accepts music of every kind provided only that it is good and expressive. It does not demand of the scenic artist that he should array the ballerinas in short skirts and pink slippers. It does not impose specific "ballet" conditions on the composer or the decorative artist, but gives complete liberty to their creative powers.

13. Diaghilev's company came to America without many of its dancers, Karsavina among others. It made two appearances, the first without Nijinsky, and in New York danced at the Century Theatre and the Metropolitan. On tour, *Schéhérazade* was feared to be corrupting to the proper Bostonians; and the *Faune* was condemned as disgusting in Chicago. *Petrouchka* was the only acceptable ballet but its music offended Americans, who were outraged by Stravinsky's compositions. Modern music and the Neoclassic dance had to become acquired tastes. As late as 1924 the *Boston Herald* cried, "Who wrote this fiendish *Rite of Spring?*—What right had he to write this thing?—Against our helpless ears to fling—Its crash, clash, cling, clang, bing, bang, bing." The imperturbable composer is said to have pointed out that there was one *bing* too many; *Le Sacre du Printemps* begins with six, not seven notes on the bassoon.

14. Diaghilev employed the composers Stravinsky, Debussy, Ravel, Richard Strauss, Fauré, Satie, Respighi, De Falla, Prokofiev, Poulenc, Auric, Milhaud, Dukelsky, Rieti, Berners, Sauguet, and the painters Bakst, Benois, Saudekine, Picasso, Derain, Matisse, Braque, Gris, Utrillo, Miro, Di Chirico, and Rouault, among others.

15. The dance-actress Marie Sallé, contemporary of Noverre and Comargo, appeared in her ballet, *Pygmallon,* in London, in 1734, with unbound hair and nothing except a corset and one petticoat under a gown of muslin, draped in the fashion of Greek statuary. Sallé was the inspiration of Noverre's "simple and touching graces," which he advocated in place of the "leaps and frolics" of ballet. Noverre wanted ballet to be "a living picture of passions, manners, habits, ceremonies and customs of all nations." In ideals, Noverre and Sallé were forerunners of twentieth-century ballet. When Sallé's *Pygmalion* was produced in 1745 in Berlin with the ballerina Barberina Campanini, it had the first ballet score, by C. H. Graun. Before that, ballet was danced to miscellaneous airs unrelated to the theme and action of the dance.

16. Quod vide statements by John Martin.

17. Humphrey died at 63 on December 29, 1958, after forty years of vital influence on the national theatre. In her later years, bedridden with arthritis, she wrote *The Art of Making Dances* on a Guggenheim fellowship, and the book was published posthumously in 1959. It records her years to 1927. Humphrey declared that she wished her dance to be based on reality illuminated by imagination; to be organic rather than synthetic; to call forth definite reactions from her audience; and to make its contribution to the drama of life. She wrote, "My entire technique consists of the development of the process of falling away from and returning to equilibrium. Exciting danger of the fall, and the repose and peace of the recovery." Her celebrated pupils are Weidman, José Limon, Sybil Shearer and Pauline Koner.

18. *With My Red Fires* derives from William Blake's *Jerusalem II:* "For the Divine Appearance is Brotherhood, but I am Love Elevate into the Region of Brotherhood with my red fires." Humphrey created the work on three characters, YoungWoman, Young Man and Matriarch. Blake's words construe the Humphrey feeling and intent. A consensus of European and English opinion ranks Humphrey as the most mature and compassionate of American choreographers in her view of human nature. Her technique was, in its spirit, the struggle of her society to bal-

ance between a desire for progress and a longing for stability—an equilibrium of mind and soul, as well as of the physical body, which Blake called one.

19. Quod vide *The Ballet Companion,* page 163—*Basic Technique.*

20. Lois Fuller was one of the most famous American Interpretive dancers of the era. Born in 1862, she became a child temperance lecturer and then a singer-actress, turning to Interpretive dance by accident. Idly playing with a scarf she invented her *Serpentine Dance,* which made her famous, within weeks, in the United States. She went to Europe, where her *Danse de Feu* was soon the rage, although it was less Fuller dancing than Fuller manipulating a few hundred yards of silk. The new electric light abetted her style, and with inventive lighting and quantities of diaphanous material Fuller established herself as a great American performer. She died in 1928 and her biography, *Quinze Ans de ma Vie,* has a preface by Anatole France.

21. So did Tamara Geva, in a company called "Chauve Souris." She was at once popular in the United States, as a Ziegfeld star, dancer-choreographer for Broadway and Hollywood productions, and dramatic actress. She briefly rejoined Balanchine, as his guest ballerina, when he formed The American Ballet, and was the "ballerina" in the first musical for which Balanchine choreographed a ballet— *Slaughter on Tenth Avenue,* in the Rodgers and Hart *On Your Toes,* in 1936.

22. William Dollar formed a group of sixteen dancers, including Shea and Bolender, called American Concert Ballet. It lasted from spring to autumn in 1943, and performed *Concerto Barocco, Five Gifts,* Bolender's *Mother Goose Suite,* and a work of Shea's called *Sailor's Bar.*

23. Quod vide *Stravinsky in the Theatre,* published by Pellegrini and Cudahy.

24. A balletomane is a serious ballet enthusiast. The word, according to *Dance Encyclopedia,* was coined in Russia. To an English-speaking public it is apt to convey a connotation of lunatic enthusiasm over ballet. It is an untranslatable definition of the kind of audience that has an intelligent and informed interest and a discriminating taste in the art of ballet.

THE COMPANIES

1. Quod vide *The Ballet Companion.*

2. *Le Tricorne* was created by de Falla and Massine for Diaghilev, and had a London première in 1919. It was first seen in New York in 1934. La Argentinita choreographed a version; José Greco another, which is featured in his 1959 world tour.

3. Not to be confused with Balanchine's *Divertimento* to music by Alexei Haieff, in which a girl is shown going from one party to another. *Divertimento* has been mistaken for a contemporary American ballet, because the *danseurs* wear polo shirts and black tights, and the *danseuses* short white tunics. Balanchine corrects the erroneous assumption and states that the ballet is Neoclassic, not at all "American" in its movement or intent.

4. The great companies are not only great by reason of age, although the French, Danish and Russian have existed for centuries. More remarkably, they have an

endurance that has weathered two world wars and, in the French and Russian theatre, the most violent civil revolutions. The great companies are state-supported or endowed with government subsidies, and the mass audience in America has no concept like that of the older countries where ballet is not considered merely entertainment but an integral part of national culture. The Paris Opéra is administered by the French government as part of its National Lyric Theatre. The Royal Danish Ballet is state-supported and royally patronized. The Bolshoi Ballet, as may be perceived by news reports rather than ballet reviews, is the pride and cultural ambassador of the Soviet theatre. These theatres survived the losses by death and resignation of their founders and great stars, and they continue to be great companies long past the eras of Noverre, the Vestrises and Taglioni; Valeotti, the Bournonvilles, and Grahn; and Landé, Perrot, Dauberval, Petipa and the Imperial Russian ballet.

5. *Accent* is the gift of knowing the precise instant at which to emphasize a step, to give it maximum effect.

6. *Épaulement* is literally shouldering, and in ballet terminology a placement of the shoulders. In *épaulé,* the dancer's shoulders and hips face downstage, the leg nearer the audience is extended in a back *arabesque,* with the corresponding arm in front *arabesque,* the opposite arm in back; and the dancer's head is turned to look over her shoulder at the audience. *Épaulement* is a characteristic of modern classicism, but not of the old *danse d'école.*

7. Quod vide *The Ballet Companion, Le Pas de Quatre.*

8. *Waltz Academy* was created by Balanchine for Ballet Theatre, with a première at the Metropolitan October 11, 1944. Gollner and Petroff, and Nora Kaye, danced alternately with Rosella Hightower and Dimitri Romanoff. The ballet is an academic ballet classic in the nineteenth-century style, set in the Paris Opéra.

THE CHOREOGRAPHERS

1. Camp Tamiment may in time become known as the swaddling clothes for American dancers and choreographers. In 1952 the name of its choreographer was Herb Ross.

2. Quod vide the program notes of the Philharmonic Symphony Society of New York, 1949–1950.

3. Comte de Salvandy: *We are dancing on the edge of a volcano,* is quoted by Ravel in his notes to *La Valse,* which Balanchine has taken for his theme in his ballet of the same name. Balanchine describes *Age of Anxiety* and *La Valse* as ballet comment on our times, and on all times of insecurity and change.

4. *Opus Jazz* has a city locale, bristling with television antennae; the dancers appear to be prototypes of the "beat generation," and the romance is as abrupt and violent as that of alley cats.

THE SCHOOLS

1. Where other and complimentary influences have come from Balanchine, Robbins and Tudor in America, from Ashton and Bruhn in English ballet, and from

the individual contributions offered by the Danes' own Harald Lander, the first native choreographer of merit to emerge in his time. Lander joined the Paris Opéra in the 'fifties and assumed French citizenship. He became the subject of the greatest schism ever to rend the Danish ballet, and almost terminated its centuries-old history in 1959 when he and his wife Toni returned to Copenhagen's Royal Theatre.

2. For the student of ballet, or the reader of this book, who wishes to identify a dancer or teacher by name and "school," and in professional métier, I recommend a study of that indispensable *Who's Who* for American ballet, Anatole Chujoy's *Dance Encyclopedia,* published in Canada and the United States in 1949.

3. *Petit rat* is the affectionate and traditional name for a student of the school at the Paris Opéra. It is said to have started as a nickname for the children who swarmed in their skinny packs about the sacred precincts of *l'Opéra* with their childish predilection for always nibbling, like mice, at edibles.

4. Anthropologists have seen the great apes dancing, and there is also reason to believe that elephants and bears, in their natural wild states, perform dances. Shawn has told me that the brolga, a bird of northern Australia, performs a dance in which ballet's three principles are evident: rhythm, pattern and purpose.

5. The thesis has been explored often. "Dancing is no mere translation or abstraction from life, it is life itself." *Havelock Ellis.* "A dancer's world is the heart of Man. . . . The History of the dance is the social history of the world." *Martha Graham.* To the opinions of a psychologist and a modern dancer is added a very old Gallic proverb: "What cannot be spoken can be sung; and what cannot be sung can be danced."

6. Beyond the two examples of schooling for the theatre dance here given, I refer the reader to the monograph, *European Dance Teachers in the United States,* by Ann Barzell, in the Dance Index volume for May-June, 1944.

LOOKING AT AMERICAN BALLET

1. *Opus 34* is danced in a revolutionary style for Balanchine. The dancers do not employ the Turnout. The score is played twice, and accompanies two different dance pieces, composed on Threat, Danger, Fear and Catastrophe. One scene is laid in a contemporary ward, where surgery is performed (by dancers costumed as doctors and nurses) to skin the "patients" alive. The patients then arise, dance as skeletons, and are swallowed by primeval ooze. The second dance piece is about (apparently) persons in a concentration camp. The evocation is of abyssmal nothingness and the negation of everything, and it is colloquially described as Balanchine's "nightmare ballet."

2. Among these were the Royal Danish Ballet dancers introduced by Shawn to America, who later had a brilliant debut at the Metropolitan in New York and a hugely successful tour of the United States and Canada. Others brought to the Pillow by Shawn for debuts are the National Ballet of Canada, the San Francisco Ballet, and Ballet Rambert.

INDEX

343

ABOUT THE AUTHOR

Olga Maynard was born in Brazil at the end of World War I, of French and Anglo-American parentage, and lived and was educated abroad until the nineteen forties. When she came home to the United States she knew of nothing called American ballet, although she had seen the American dancer Agnes de Mille. Excited by the burgeoning of American ballet during World War II, she began to collect impressions and criticisms, and to write to and talk with all the Americans closely associated and most concerned with the development of American dance. These included everyone she could find, from Ted Shawn to retired dancers and obscure wardrobe women, as well as balletomanes who had followed the course of the developing theatre. She amassed data from documents in print and from private collections in the United States and, through connections in the press and theatre in Europe and England, collected firsthand impressions of American ballet when it toured abroad. In 1956 Miss Maynard began to compile the story of American ballet and its lively existence from the start of the century.

"My greatest task," she writes, "was to discipline my native pride in the American ballet, lest enthusiasm run away with the book. So much had been achieved in such a short time that the story had a fairy-tale quality, but an over-all view of ballet kept check on the book. If we dare to claim that we have a ballet theatre, then we must be prepared to have it scrutinized within the history of the international theatre that is ballet.

"The credit for the book must go to the people from whom I drew it: this is actually the story of their lives and times. The credit that I claim is that I have written without prejudice, and this is possible for me only because I have no affiliation with the personal or commercial aspects of ballet. I have written of what I have seen, of how it has seemed to me, and of the effects noticed on the public and the artists of the theatre. At the end of my task, I find that my pride and enthusiasm for American ballet are undiminished. The book itself does not have an ending—it is simply a record of the unalterable beginning of the bright, brave story of our national ballet."